Rethinking
social history

Rethinking social history

English society 1570–1920 and its interpretation

edited by
Adrian Wilson

Manchester University Press
Manchester and New York
Distributed exclusively in the USA and Canada by St. Martin's Press

Copyright © Manchester University Press 1993

While copyright in the volume as a whole is vested in Manchester University
Press, copyright in individual chapters belongs to their respective authors, and
no chapter may be reproduced wholly or in part without the express
permission in writing of both author and publisher.

Published by Manchester University Press
Oxford Road, Manchester M13 9PL, UK
and Room 400, 175 Fifth Avenue,
New York, NY 10010, USA

Distributed exclusively in the USA and Canada
by St. Martin's Press, Inc.,
175 Fifth Avenue, New York, NY 10010, USA

British Library Cataloguing-in-Publication Data
A catalogue record for this book is available from the British Library

Library of Congress Cataloging-in-Publication Data
  Rethinking social history : English society 1570–1920 and its
  interpretation / edited by Adrian Wilson.
      p. cm.
    ISBN 0–7190–3525–2
    1. England—Social conditions. 2. Social history. I. Wilson,
  Adrian, 1947– .
  HN398.E5R44 1993
  306′.0942—dc20   93–18697

ISBN 0 7190 4650 5 *paperback*

Typeset in Hong Kong
by Graphicraft Typesetters Ltd., Hong Kong

Printed in Great Britain
by Biddles Ltd., Guildford and King's Lynn

Contents

Editor's acknowledgements

For their encouragement I wish to thank Derek Aldcroft and Tony Sutcliffe; for their tolerance of my own delays, the contributors to this volume; and for unstinting measures of both these qualities, Jane Thorniley-Walker of Manchester University Press.

Notes on contributors

Patrick Curry was born in Canada but lives in London. After completing his University of London Ph.D. in History and Philosophy of Science, he held a post-doctoral research fellowship from the Social Sciences and Humanities Research Council of Canada (1987–9). He is editor of *Astrology, Science and Society: historical essays* (Boydell and Brewer, 1987), and author of *Prophecy and Power: astrology in early modern England* (1989), and *A Confusion of Prophets: Victorian and Edwardian Astrology* (1992). He has also published papers in *History Today, History of Science* and the *Times Literary Supplement*, and has lectured in Oxford, Cambridge, and in America. He is now working on a study of J.R.R. Tolkien.

Joanna Innes is a Fellow of Somerville College, Oxford. Born in London in 1954, she was educated in England and the United States. She has written numerous articles on the social history of eighteenth-century England, the most recent of which is 'The domestic face of the military-fiscal state', in *An Imperial State at War: Britain 1688–1815*, edited by Lawrence Stone (1993). She is currently at work on a book to be published by Oxford University Press: *Inferior Politics: Social Problems and Social Policies in Eighteenth-Century Britain*. She is co-editor of *Past and Present*.

John Landers is University Lecturer in Historical Demography and Fellow of All Souls College, Oxford, having previously been Lecturer in Biological Anthropology at University College London. He read Human Sciences at Oxford University, and was then a research student at the Cambridge Group for the History of

Population and Social Structure, where he completed a Ph.D. on the demography of eighteenth-century London. He is the author of a number of articles in this field, and of *Death and the Metropolis: studies in the demographic history of London 1670–1830* (1993).

Philippa Levine   was born in London and educated at the Universities of Cambridge and Oxford. She is currently an associate professor of history at the University of Southern California. Her publications include *The Amateur and the Professional: antiquarians, historians and archaeologists in Victorian England 1838–1886* (Cambridge, 1986); *Victorian Feminism 1850–1900* (London, 1987); and *Feminist Lives in Victorian England: private role and public commitment* (Oxford, 1990). She also works in the public policy arena, with a particular interest in prostitution and women at risk. She is now working on the relationship between the state, legal ideology and the construction of gender in the British Empire.

Linda Pollock   is Professor of History at Tulane University and a former Research Fellow of both Churchill College and the Wellcome Unit for the History of Medicine, Cambridge. Having taken a joint honours degree in Psychology and History at St Andrews, she researched the history of parent-child relationships in England for a doctorate, which led to her highly acclaimed *Forgotten Children* (Cambridge, 1983), of which several translations have since been published. This has been followed by *A Lasting Relationship* (1987), and *With Faith and Physic: the life of a Tudor gentlewoman, Lady Grace Mildmay 1552–1620* (1993). She has also published a number of essays on the history of the family in learned journals and edited collections, and is now working on a study of the élite family, to be published by Cambridge University Press.

Simon Schaffer   is Reader in History and Philosophy of Science at Cambridge University. He has published widely on the history of astronomy and of experimental philosophy in early-modern Britain. He is co-author of *Leviathan and the Air Pump* (Princeton, 1985); and co-editor of *The Uses of Experiment* (Cambridge, 1989) and of *Robert Hooke: New Studies* (Boydell, 1989).

John Styles is Head of the V&A/RCA M.A. course in the History of Design at the Victoria and Albert Museum, and has taught at the Universities of Bradford, Bath and Bristol before assuming his current post. He was co-editor of *An Ungovernable People: the English and their law in the seventeenth and eighteenth centuries* (Hutchinson, 1980) and has published numerous articles. He is currently working on a study of clothes and consumption in eighteenth-century England.

Adrian Wilson is Lecturer in History of Medicine (Wellcome Award) in the History and Philosophy of Science Division of the Philosophy Department, University of Leeds. He is author of *The Making of Man-Midwifery: childbirth in England, 1660–1770* (UCL press, 1995) and is now working on a study of the provincial voluntary hospitals of eighteenth-century England.

Keith Wrightson is Reader in English Social History at Cambridge University and a Fellow of Jesus College. He is the author of *English Society 1580–1680* (1982) and the co-author (with David Levine) of *Poverty and Piety in an English Village: Terling 1525–1700* (1979) and *The Making of an Industrial Society: Whickham 1560–1765* (1991). In addition he has published many articles on aspects of the social and cultural history of early modern England and is the co-editor of *The World we have Gained* (1986). Dr Wrightson is a member of the editorial boards of *Social History and Rural History*, and an editorial adviser for *The Seventeenth Century*.

Introduction   *Adrian Wilson*

English social history has now been established as a major division of the historical discipline for about a quarter of a century. The essays in this book seek both to reflect its achievements and to reflect upon them: that is, to capture both the strengths and the weaknesses of what is now a very large field. The contributors were encouraged to write in both substantive and historiographic vein, to convey a sense of both the subject-matter and the conceptual orientation of their own specialist areas. Most of the essays are published here for the first time; the two contributions which have been reprinted (those by Wrightson and by Innes and Styles) have both been rewritten for this volume.

In so wide a field as social history, representative coverage could scarcely be achieved in a single volume. Some of its restrictions should be mentioned at the outset. In the first place, the present essays are deliberately confined to English society – since different national cultures not only present different substantive issues but also have developed different cultures of social-history writing, and since the English case presents variety enough on its own.[1] Second, the work presented here is illustrative rather than representative of English social history itself. Some major fields such as economic history and anthropological historiography are not included; chronologically the contributions are restricted to the period from about 1550 to 1900, and moreover there is a strong bias in favour of the eighteenth century. Nevertheless it is hoped that this collection reflects several of the main areas of traditional interest in English social history, conveys the rich variety of the subject, and indicates some of the new directions it is now taking.

The very diversity of the themes treated in this book reflects the contemporary paradox of English social history. On the one hand, the subject displays an enormous vitality and a very wide range of active concerns – and this despite the recession in academic funding of recent years. Yet on the other hand, its breadth of interests is achieved at a price, for it lacks a clear sense of direction or unifying perspective: thus very different eighteenth-century Englands emerge here in the contributions of Landers, Schaffer, Curry, and Innes and Styles. This paradox is the starting-point for Keith Wrightson's contribution. Focusing upon the historiography of the important early-modern period, Wrightson counterposes the high hopes aroused by English social history in the 1960s against the sense of fragmentation which besets the subject today. Academic specialisation, both of subject-matter and of period, has made for 'enclosure' into different fields 'farmed in severalty'; and interpretative models, originally imported from other disciplines, have tended to fossilise once implanted within social history. As a result, social history has tended to lose both its integrative potential and its ability to grapple with historical change. Amongst the solutions Wrightson suggests are a reintegration of different themes, and a greater awareness of relevant theoretical developments; and he urges social historians to be bolder and more imaginative both in theorising and in representing past society.

The historiography of the family has often searched for the presence or absence in the early-modern past of putatively essential features of 'the modern family'. The theme of 'privacy' typifies this treatment; Linda Pollock's essay argues for a more nuanced approach to this subject, focusing on the specific concept of privacy deployed by the English elite from the late sixteenth to the late seventeenth century. Her revision of the standard picture deploys both a conceptual redefinition – distinguishing between different aspects both of the 'private' and of the 'public' – and the use of family letters to explore the specific ways and contexts in which privacy was invoked. While Dr Pollock stresses that this area requires further research, her findings suggest two interim conclusions. First, despite many appearances (such as the design of houses and the ubiquity of servants), members of the elite in fact enjoyed a lively sense of the private, and showed a consistent concern to protect this privacy by a range of devices such as speaking French to conceal conversations from the ears of servants. Second, this concept of privacy was specific to the social order of the period, and in particular was formed by the ubiquitous system of patronage. Thus secrecy, honour and reputation were among its watchwords, and the private realm was a resource for efforts in the public world: for instance, greater trust was reposed in family members than in others. Dr Pollock concludes by suggesting that private and public in this period should be interpreted not as mutually-exclusive alternatives but as connected aspects of familial and political relationships; and that the same applies to other interpretative 'couplets' such as interest and affection, emotional and material.

In 1966 Le Roy Ladurie both proposed and celebrated a shift of historiographic focus 'from Waterloo to Colyton', which embodied not only a move from the unique grand event to the counting of many small events but also the replacement of events of State by events in the lives of the people. John Landers inverts Le Roy Ladurie's title in order to highlight his aim of integrating these two historiographies. Recent studies in historical demography, particularly the work of Wrigley and Schofield, have already established that one side of demographic patterns – the fertility side – was closely connected with wider social phenomena. Landers argues that the same is true of mortality, and indeed that in the test case he explores – eighteenth-century London – the explanation of changes in mortality traverses a range of phenomena from migration, through housing, land tenure and the politics of credit, to the pattern of peace and warfare and thus to the very nature of the State. He thus takes issue with Chambers's earlier postulate of the 'autonomous death rate' – the assumption that mortality in the past was entirely determined by biological, extra-social causes, itself linked to the further assumption that social causes were to be restricted to 'the single dimension of the wage–price ratio'. Dr Landers combines spatial and seasonal analysis to show the complexity of eighteenth-century metropolitan mortality, and thereby opens the subject to the wider explanatory possibilities which had been precluded by assumptions such as those of Chambers. This opens the way to an integration of themes which have customarily been parcelled out between different historical specialists, making it possible to connect the history of events such as Waterloo with that of communities such as Colyton.

Historians have always been fascinated by the distant figure of natural science, seeing it variously as an object of envy, contrast, comparison, or – as for much of social history – emulation. The history of science should therefore hold a special significance for the wider historical discipline, not least for social history. Moreover historians of science have in recent years increasingly situated science, and its predecessor natural philosophy, in such historical contexts as social interest, political conflict, religious allegiance – the very stuff of social and political history.[2] Yet very few 'historians' even seem to realise that 'historians of science' have been seeking to traverse the gulf between these sub-disciplines. Simon Schaffer's chapter, which reflects and illustrates this remarkable shift of focus on the part of historians of science, can be read as a plea to social historians to concern themselves with the history of science. Focused upon a 'social history of plausibility', this essay situates the eighteenth-century mathematisation of knowledge as a contingent social process, tied to specific existing interests – such as those of 'improving' landlords – and creating new ones – notably those of the self-proclaimed detached intellectual characteristic of the Enlightenment. Disinterest, Schaffer argues, was itself constructed through the play of interests; moreover all aspects of the process were contested, as for instance in the dispute between Adam Smith and his contemporary Ferguson over the relationship between elite knowledge and artisanal production. This study also indicates the pervasiveness of issues in natural philosophy: for instance, the fertility of the earth, which was divine for traditional 'moral economy', became man-made in Jethro Tull's analysis, with the effect that Tull contested sacred histories of the earth and their affiliated chemistries. Thus, just as the conceptual landscape of history of science embraces Tull, so too the horizons of social historians can and should extend to natural philosophy.

Patrick Curry reminds us – in fittingly passionate tones – that social history is inevitably political, elaborating this with particular reference to the recent and future historiography of eighteenth-century England. He proposes a 'post-Marxist' social history, which would correspond to the radical democratic politics of Ernesto Laclau and Chantal Mouffe precisely as E.P. Thompson's historical writing of the 1960s and 1970s corresponded to Thompson's particular Marxism. The need for such a 'post-Marxist' historiography is indicated by the link between the recent rise of right-wing histories, particularly exemplified by the work of J.C.D. Clark, and the present political conjuncture of an apparent Tory hegemony. The possibility of the proposed new historiography Curry demonstrates by suggesting some of its substantive themes (in particular, the historical construction of cultural identity) and conceptual resources. Those resources include not only the Gramscian concept of hegemony, but also the central methodological underpinnings developed by Clark himself – specifically, his cogent critique of teleology, reductionism and anachronism; for that critique, Curry argues, can in fact be detached from Clark's own, explicitly right-wing synthesis. Indeed, in these respects Clark's work actually converges both with the neo-Gramscian argument of Laclau and Mouffe and with the historiography of Thompson: each has been pitched, both intellectually and politically, against a determinist Marxism, as is Curry's own argument. However, it is specifically with Thompson's work that Curry's proposed radical democratic historiography would be filiated. Though by no means uncritical of Thompson, Curry makes it clear that the new historiography he is proposing would have a complex resonance with Thompson's earlier work: in substantive interests, in democratic aspirations, and in a concern to engage with social theory. Moreover, it would offer to Thompson's own, Marxist historiographical tradition the very renewal which (so he argues) that tradition now needs.

One of the stimulating effects of E.P. Thompson's work has been the new impetus, and the redirection, which his *Whigs and Hunters* and associated writing gave to the study of eighteenth-century crime and law. The subsequent 'crime wave' is critically reviewed in Chapter 7 by Joanna Innes and John Styles, who not only bring out the strength of the field – its wide range of perspectives, substantive interests, historiographic implications and technical expertise – but also offer a rich fabric of new interpretative and methodological suggestions. Three particular points may illustrate the range of their study. First, it emerges that 'there can be no history of criminality separate from the history of law enforcement': the most fruitful line of further research in this field will be a closer focus on institutions and their actual workings. I suspect that this lesson is of much wider application in social history. Second, taking up this very line of attack, Innes and Styles shed new light on Parliament itself, showing through a consideration of its legislative procedures that its significance has been misunderstood by both social and political historians. A third implication of the chapter arises from the chronology of legal reform. It used to be thought that the flowering of legal and penal reform in the late eighteenth century was a novel development, specific to that period. But it has recently emerged, thanks chiefly to the work of John Beattie, that major changes in the functioning of the criminal law had taken place much earlier, in the late seventeenth and early eighteenth centuries. Beattie has been able to disinter these hitherto unsuspected developments through an integrated approach, studying crime, trial and punishment together. What had obscured these changes for previous historians was the fact that the reforms of the late eighteenth century involved a much greater element of public debate, thus generating a wealth of printed sources whose very accessibility led to an optical illusion of novelty. The consequent historiographic 'reform perspective' entrapped not only the whiggish Radzinowicz but also many subsequent authors who made use of manuscript records, but only from the period pre-defined by the *printed* sources as one of change. This issue is of substantive as well as historiographic importance. It adds a further strand to the problem of the public sphere which recurs in several essays in the present volume. And it poses an explanatory problem – since, as Schaffer's essay reminds us, early eighteenth-century England was not short of public 'projectors', yet the reform of the law was at that period conducted without recourse to public campaigns. Thus our attention is drawn towards explaining what might be called the profile of public debate: in any given period, which projects were pushed into the public domain and which were not?

Philippa Levine's study of the meanings of prostitution, focused on the period from the 1860s to the end of the Great War, touches on several themes of earlier chapters: the public/private relationship, the study of crime, the political engagement of the historian. Three central themes run through her essay. First, late-Victorian and Edwardian prostitution was located precisely at the boundary between the private and public realms, and this perspective illuminates many aspects of prostitution in the period. Just as the perceived dangers of prostitution arose in large measure from its being public, so too the legal treatment of prostitutes manipulated them across the public/private boundary: the publication of their names could fix their status, whereas domestic confinement could reclaim them. Second, the two central forms of public policy towards prostitution – criminalisation and sanitary legislation – were linked by an underlying continuity, converging not only in shared punitive practices but also in their common fountainhead of a coercive State. Third, this subject confronts the historian with particular responsibilities. A century ago, the elaboration of motives for prostitution defined it as work that is not work, 'pathologised' prostitutes – for such questions were not asked of other female occupations – and fixed them in a paradoxical role of culpable victims. Modern attempts to elucidate past motives are in danger of replicating in discursive form the same 'rough usage' which was meted out to the women whose history they are seeking to recount.

Several of the essays express dissatisfaction with social history's external and internal conceptual boundaries. Just as Wrightson criticises the tendency towards specialist 'enclosure', so Landers argues against the division of past societies into distinct 'levels', Innes and Styles propose a shift of focus from crime to the law, and a number of contributors (Pollock, Schaffer, Innes and Styles, Levine) challenge prevailing conceptions of the relationship between private and public spheres. Such discontent within social history is far from new: as long ago as 1971 Eric Hobsbawm wrote that 'its best practitioners have always felt uncomfortable about the term itself'.[3]

My own two contributions seek to shed light on this malaise by exploring social history's origins, disciplinary setting, and methodological basis. Chapter 1 suggests that social history's sub-disciplinary character is defined by its particular academic and political relationships: relationships of closure towards State historiography, openness to progressive politics, and asymmetrical openness towards the social sciences. I enter a plea – supported by some recent developments in the social sciences themselves – for the transformation of the elements of closure and asymmetry in these relationships, that is, for the creation of a more unified and self-confident historical discipline. An approach to this end is developed in Chapter 9, which explores the nature of what E.P. Thompson has called 'historical logic', that is, the methodological foundations of the discipline of history.[4] I argue that the central issue for that 'logic' is not, as is usually supposed, the historian's conscious category-frame, but rather what I describe as the hermeneutic stance which the historian adopts towards the relics of the past. It is suggested that this foundation is inherent in the very enterprise of the historian, and that the traditional method of source-criticism is superseded by a different hermeneutic stance which treats past documents not as evidence but as effects. On this basis, I conclude, the discipline of history can indeed be unified and can also 'speak outwards' to the social sciences on equal terms.

Notes

1 On the distinct national cultures of social history, see Charles Tilly, 'Retrieving European Lives', in Olivier Zunz, ed., *Reliving the Past: the worlds of social history* (Chapel Hill and London: University of North Carolina Press, 1985), pp. 11–15, at pp. 13–14.
2 This development is discussed briefly in Chapter 1.
3 Eric Hobsbawm, 'From social history to the history of society', *Daedalus* **100** (1971), p. 24.
4 E.P. Thompson, *The Poverty of Theory* (London: Merlin, 1978), p. 231.

1 *Adrian Wilson*

A critical portrait of social history

What is social history?

The term 'social history', as used in English historiography, covers
three different yet overlapping approaches: first, the history of the
people; second, what I call the 'social-history paradigm', consisting in the historical application of concepts derived from the social
sciences; and third, the aspiration to a totalising or integrating
history, which has been called 'total history' or 'the history of
society'.[1] I shall outline these historically, beginning with the origins of 'history of the people' about a century and a quarter ago.[2]

History of the people
'Social' history first arose in England as a by-product of the
professionalisation of history from the 1860s onward. Previously
English history had been written about the English nation in the
past, and for that nation in the present – a structure of concerns
which made for literary form and wide-ranging content. But
professionalisation radically narrowed both subject-matter and
audience. The new professionals focused not on the nation but
instead on the State and its activities: hence their concentration
upon constitutional, political, administrative, legal and ecclesiastical history. They increasingly wrote for an audience of fellow-
professionals, therefore pursuing the technical at the expense of
the popular. This approach gained ascendancy in the professoriate
and in the professional organs of the discipline: its first manifestations were the constitutional and political histories of Stubbs
(Oxford) and Gardiner (London), and the cognate vision of Seeley
(Cambridge) that 'History is not concerned with individuals
except in their capacity as members of a state.' English 'social

history', conceived as *history of the people*, arose precisely in
rebellion against these novel tendencies. Whereas State historiography concentrated on a small elite and chiefly on its political
activities, 'social' history would reconstruct the lives of all the
people in all their aspects, including their economic activities and
relationships. Moreover, it would seek to reach out to that wider
audience which the professionals were abandoning, and it duly
flourished on the margins of the academy, notably in extra-mural
teaching. In this genre were the pioneering studies of social and
economic history produced by the Oxford-connected men J.R.
Green, Arnold Toynbee and J.E. Thorold Rogers. (Their Cambridge
counterpart Archdeacon William Cunningham was an ambiguous
figure, linking economic history to the State but regarding the
State as the reflection of the people.)[3]

The former historiographic unity of the nation had now been
divided into State historiography on the one hand and history-of-
the-people on the other. Both schools produced their founding
texts between the mid-1860s and the late 1880s. A further
historiographic classic produced in this same period was Marx's
Das Kapital, vol. I – published in 1867 and translated into English
in 1887 – but although this book was written in England and to
no small extent about English history, it was effectively ignored by
English historians for several decades.

It seems clear that the division between State historiography and
history-of-the-people arose initially from the concentration of the
professionals upon the State; but the underlying reasons for that
concentration await systematic exploration. The politics of ap-
pointments to chairs played a major part: thus the Tory bishop
Stubbs was a safer appointment as Oxford Regius Professor in
1866 than the liberal political economist Thorold Rogers would
have been. Ranke's example was also important, for his critical
method had been honed on State archives (just as his salary derived from the Prussian State). State archives were newly available
for British historians, thanks to the creation of the Public Record
Office and the publication of its Calendars from the 1850s. Yet
these pressures hardly seem adequate to explain the seemingly
inexorable force pulling the first generation of professional historians towards the State as their object of study. That force was
well illustrated by James Bryce's 'Prefatory Note' to the first issue
of the new professional organ, the *English Historical Review* (1886):

Two views prevail concerning the scope of history. One regards it ... as being concerned solely with states ... The other ... conceives it to be a picture of the whole past, including everything that man has either thought or wrought. Of these views the former appears to us narrow, and therefore misleading; the latter so wide as to become vague ... It seems better to regard history as the record of human action ... *States and politics will therefore be the chief parts of its subject*, because the acts of nations ... have usually been more important than the acts of private citizens.

In almost the same breath Bryce moved from depicting the State as too narrow a focus to describing it as the central core of history.[4]

From the 1890s academic history developed a broader base. New institutions of higher education were founded (notably the London School of Economics (LSE) in 1895) or upgraded (Manchester's acquisition of University status in 1903 was particularly important). Partly as a result of this expansion, economic history gradually gained institutional status in various settings. And meanwhile, the slow-moving admission of women to higher education since 1870 was now beginning to produce a cadre of trained women historians – of whom many were interested in history-of-the-people, and a few were able to secure academic employment. From this point onwards, English history-writing comprised four streams: State historiography on the right; social history on the left; economic history occupying an uneasy middle ground of contest and compromise; and a continuing tradition of literary history.

The academic mainstream remained *State historiography*, expanded after the Boer War and the Great War to include imperial and diplomatic history respectively, and pursued by men such as Firth and Powicke in Oxford, Pollard and Neale in London, Acton and Temperley in Cambridge, Tout in Manchester. Although its concerns remained tightly focused on the activities of the State, a few of its leading practitioners (Maitland, Bury) hoped to widen its scope. The activity of teaching was giving it a further audience – undergraduate pupils and readers – intermediate in character between fellow-professionals and the general public, prompting some State historians (such as Neale) to write more accessible books. Against this background, the intervention of the outsider Namier not only shifted political history sideways in substance, but also narrowed it back towards a professional audience. *Social*

history acquired a particular set of social and institutional moor-
ings: it was always progressivist, it was often Fabian (though
sometimes Christian Socialist and/or Independent Labour), and it
was strongly connected to the LSE (though a tradition of Oxford
training persisted, notably in the cases of the Hammonds and
Tawney). *Economic history* had complex associations. On the one
hand, it retained its earlier connection with progressivist social
history – most notably in the figure of Tawney, who was involved
with the Economic History Society (founded in 1926) and its
Review. On the other hand, in a form more detached from social
history, economic history acquired a foothold in the universities;
and while some of its teachers (notably Unwin at Manchester)
retained a populist conception, others (Clapham in Cambridge,
Ashley at Birmingham) duly gave the subject a more conservative
cast. *Literary history*, continuing the Macaulay tradition, was the
polished Whig counterpart of social history; its leading exponent
was Trevelyan, who wanted to restore 'the tie between history and
the reading public', but on a literary terrain rather than through
the political commitment of the social historians. Fittingly, Trevelyan
pursued this vision and practice for over twenty years outside the
academy; his appointment as Cambridge Regius Professor in 1927
was a remarkable moment, for it brought literary history into the
academic heartland, where he passed on the torch to his one and
only doctoral student, J.H. Plumb.[5]

English 'social history' was 'history of the people' down to the
end of the Second World War; its concerns remained as stable as
did the wider pattern of which it was a part. To no small extent
it was still practised outside the academy or on its margins: J.L.
Hammond's position as a journalist on the *Manchester Guardian*
was emblematic. In keeping with its lineage and concerns, it sought
a popular audience at least as much as an academic one, and this
was true even of those, such as Eileen Power at the LSE, who
wrote social history from the security of academic posts. Its political loyalties were firmly on the left: it was often socialist, usually
populist, and chiefly interested in the past antecedents of current
social problems. Its main concerns were social and economic relations (Tawney); the labour movement and its institutions (the
Hammonds, the Webbs); the history of the 'common people' (Cole,
Postgate, Power); and the history of everyday life (George). One
of its striking features was the prominent part played by women

scholars, some in famous marital partnerships (Margaret Cole, Alice Stopford Green, Barbara Hammond, Beatrice Webb), others working more or less alone (Alice Clark, Dorothy George, Georgiana Hill, Margaret James, M.G. Jones, E.M. Leonard, Dorothy Marshall, Ivy Pinchbeck, Eileen Power, Gladys Scott Thomson, Kathleen Wood-Legh). Many of these women historians wrote on similar topics to those treated by their male colleagues, but some of them investigated the changing position of women in English society: Hill, Clark, Pinchbeck. Several of the works produced by the women historians retain an authoritative standing today: Alice Clark's *Working Life of Women in the Seventeenth Century*, Dorothy George's *London Life in the Eighteenth Century*, Beatrice and Sidney Webb's voluminous *English Local Government*.[6]

The structural limitation of this social history was that its research seldom included the activities or development of the national State. This was a direct result of its origins: political, constitutional, administrative and diplomatic history were left to the mainstream professionals who had claimed these spheres since the 1870s. The exclusion of the State was aptly summed up by Trevelyan in his now notorious dictum that 'Social history might be defined negatively as the history of a people with the politics left out.' Both the omission of politics and the focus on 'the history of a people' accurately reflected the tradition on which Trevelyan was drawing in his *English Social History* – published in America in 1942 but in Britain not until 1944 on account of paper shortage. That book was itself a complex product: as his contribution to the war effort, the Whig Trevelyan here moved a long way towards the populist school, just as the Tory Butterfield made his rapprochement with the Whig approach in *The Englishman and his History*, which also appeared in 1944.[7]

Yet meanwhile – in 1938 – there had appeared a very different work of synthesis: A.L. Morton's *A People's History of England*, a Marxist interpretation extending from prehistoric times to its own present, which drew upon the three traditions of State, economic and social historiography.[8] After the Second World War Morton's lead was taken up by a new generation who pursued original historical research within a Marxist framework: Dobb, Hill, Hilton, Hobsbawm, Rudé, Saville, Thompson. At long last Marx's history-writing had been taken up in his country of exile.

The new tradition of British Marxist historiography effectively succeeded the earlier history-of-the-people tradition, and transformed the subject by infusing a new tough-mindedness: history was to be informed by theory. Although they retained some of the populist leanings of the social-history tradition (for instance, in the Society for the Study of Labour History and in the aspiration for 'history from below'), the Marxists were much more oriented towards the academy: some of them took doctorates, most of them managed to get academic jobs, they played a major role in establishing the journal *Past and Present* in 1952, and many of their books had a pronounced technical bent. The academic interests of the group were diverse, showing both connections with, and differences from, those of the populist tradition. Sometimes the State now came into focus (notably in Christopher Hill's studies of the English Revolution), though in ways tightly constrained by the Marxist problematic. In particular, high politics was still mostly ignored or was seen as an epiphenomen of social change: the politics of popular protest, in contrast, became one of the central themes of this new tradition.[9]

Marxism has remained a central focus of British history-writing ever since. Seventeenth-century historiography, though now painting very different pictures from those of Christopher Hill, still pays indirect obeisance to Hill by calling itself 'revisionist'. Eighteenth-century England has indeed, as Eric Hobsbawm predicted, never been the same since the publication of E.P. Thompson's *Whigs and Hunters* in 1975. Similarly the historiography of nineteenth-century Britain was earlier transformed by Thompson's *Making of the English Working Class* (1963), along with other subsequent Marxist works such as Hobsbawm and Rudé's *Captain Swing*. Moreover a new generation of Marxist historians, recruited in the late 1960s and stimulated by *New Left Review*, has produced a substantial body of work on the nineteenth-century working class: its work, culture, struggles, beliefs, divisions, organisations, achievements. Meanwhile, there has developed a parallel Marxist reworking of the earlier populist tradition, in the form of the 'History Workshop' movement (founded in 1967) and journal (1975) – organised by Raphael Samuel from the fitting base of Oxford's Ruskin College.

Yet the Marxist historians have in the main pursued an implicit policy of separate development: while devoting a major effort to the reconstruction of popular protest and the history of the working class, they have seldom challenged mainstream State historiography on its own chosen high ground of political narrative, State formation and development, foreign policy and diplomacy. Christopher Hill is at one with the revisionist John Morrill in accepting Gardiner's narrative of the events of *The History of the Great Civil War*. The theme of the eighteenth-century British State has now become a battleground between Whig and Tory historians, in which Marxist historians have taken little interest. Similarly it has been observed of nineteenth-century history that Marxists 'oddly shy away from the history of parliamentary politics'.[10] To this self-limitation of British Marxist historiography there have been two major exceptions. The first is the work of E.P. Thompson. Thompson's *Making of the English Working Class* and *Whigs and Hunters*, while centrally concerned to reconstruct history 'from below', were both framed around particular actions of the State. Moreover, his 1965 essay on 'The peculiarities of the English' has more recently provided the inspiration (and the very title) for the first systematic Marxist study of English State formation – Corrigan and Sayer's *The Great Arch* (1985). The second such exception has arisen in the historiography of the Chartist movement. In 1983 Gareth Stedman Jones put forward a reinterpretation of Chartism in terms of political language – initiating a 'linguistic turn' which will be mentioned again below, and situating the content and fortunes of Chartism in a political rather than a social frame. Partly in response to this revisionism, John Saville subsequently produced a book on *1848* which focuses directly on the actions of the State and places these in a dual context of domestic class relations and the international setting.[11]

Nevertheless, as has recently been noted by both Geoff Eley and Harvey Kaye, these remain exceptions to the overall trajectory of the tradition. The continuing division between (in Eley's words) 'the fractured labours of political and social historians' attests to the inheritance by the British Marxist tradition of the mantle of history-of-the-people. The historiographic division between the State and the people, which first arose in the late 1860s, has been perpetuated not only by what Eley describes as 'the pedantries of administrative history' but also by its Marxist opponents.[12]

The social-history paradigm
What I call the 'social-history paradigm' consists of the application to history of concepts, methods or inspiration taken from one

[handwritten annotation: paradigm = a pattern or approach or example, espec. one underlying a theory or methodology.]

or another of the social sciences. In principle this approach can draw upon any of the social sciences. In practice, the most fertile or favoured disciplines have been economics, sociology, demography and anthropology, though others are also important: geography, political science, psychology and very recently linguistics. Such an approach was prefigured by economic history – the extension of economic studies into the past – beginning a century ago; but the social-history paradigm proper began when the history discipline expanded its range of borrowing from economics to other social sciences. This took place at very different rates in different national academic cultures: in France it began in 1929 (when Marc Bloch and Lucien Febvre founded the journal *Annales d'histoire économique et sociale*, renamed *Annales: Economies, Societies, Civilisations* in 1946), in the USA it developed from the late 1940s, and in Britain it only emerged in the 1960s. Similarly, the balance of influence between the different social sciences has varied considerably from one country to another. Much of this national variation is attributable to the different national histories of the social sciences themselves. For instance, the early establishment of geography and sociology in France was partly responsible both for the precociousness of the *Annales* school and for some of its concerns: Durkheim's *représentations collectives* and the ideas of Lucien Levy-Bruhl gave it the concept of *mentalité*, and French geography stimulated both Marc Bloch's concern with landscape and Fernand Braudel's later *Méditerranée* (1949).[13]

In England the classic statement of this approach was made by Keith Thomas, in a widely-quoted essay entitled 'The tools and the job' which was published in the *Times Literary Supplement* in 1966. This was nothing less than a manifesto for the transformation of history. The social sciences would bring about a 'refinement of the historian's social vocabulary', statistical methods would confer precision upon historians' statements, and the disciplines of social anthropology and social psychology would provide the historian with new and incisive questions. This new conceptual apparatus – described as the successor to Marxism – would permit historians at long last to explain, as political and constitutional history had not, 'the workings of human society and the fluctuations in human affairs'.[14]

Thomas's essay accurately captured the mood of the time; the approach he described was already being seen as a new and exciting departure. With the enthusiasm of late converts, the pro-gressively-inclined amongst British historians embraced the new paradigm in droves, admiring and emulating the French *Annales* school. Some erstwhile political historians (Laslett, later Holmes) abandoned their former pursuits to take up quantification, demo-graphy, historical sociology. Other, younger, scholars came into history from other disciplines (economics, geography, sociology) or deliberately acquired a social-science training (Alan Macfarlane took doctorates in both history and anthropology). As Keith Wrightson attests, the hopes of these new historians were high. History would at last be scientific and objective: often this meant quantification, but it might also mean the exhaustive scrutiny of qualitative evidence. In either case, impressionism would be re-placed by a rigorous concern for representativeness, naivety by sophistication, the art of interpretation by explicit conceptual frameworks, narrative writing by what was celebrated as analysis. New sources were tapped and mapped, new techniques devised for interpreting them. The very language of history changed: his-torians spoke of laboratories, collective teamwork, quantification; instead of 'sources' the talk was now of 'data'.

Yet the new paradigm called itself by an old name, for it was soon known as 'social history'. This was indeed appropriate, for there were several continuities linking the social-history paradigm with history-of-the-people. Thus Tawney's *Religion and the Rise of Capitalism* (1926) had been influenced by the work of Max Weber, and both he and Power suggested in the 1930s that social history should make use of the social sciences; the social-history paradigm treated many of the same substantive themes as had 'history of the people'; most of its practitioners were politically progressive; and there was personal continuity in such figures as Lawrence Stone, who began as an Oxford devotee of Tawney and became one of the pioneers of the new paradigm. But the new social history was sharply differentiated from the old in two linked respects: it was technically more rigorous (or at least arduous), and it was firmly situated inside the academy. A few pioneers of the new genre (notably Laslett and Thomas) succeeded in reaching a wider audience, but even these scholars wrote from an academic base and firmly anchored their books in professional practice; and subsequently the social-history paradigm became as technical as State historiography, albeit in a very different way. Thus from the late 1960s onwards the social-history paradigm rapidly gained ground in British universities, swiftly making up for its late arrival. Four material circumstances assisted its progress: the academic expansion of the 1960s (providing jobs for the new historians); the creation of County Record offices (making accessible the local sources which were particularly suited to the new approach); the advent of the computer (which served both as a real tool and as an icon); and, in a more modest way, the photocopier (which materially assisted some of the new techniques such as record-linkage). The movement was soon institutionalised in departments of Economic *and Social* History, offering undergraduate courses; in new journals and textbook series; and in postgraduate training and research projects large and small (chiefly funded by the Social Sciences Research Council (SSRC), which had a separate Economic and Social History Committee from its foundation in 1965 until its 1983 reconstitution as the Economic and Social Research Council (ESRC)). Monographs and scholarly articles poured from the presses, testifying to the productivity of the new approach and furthering its momentum.[15]

The application of an old name to a new practice made it notoriously difficult to define 'social history', for the term embraced different yet overlapping usages. To compound this problem, the social-history paradigm was itself diverse: it meant very different things according to whether, say, demography, anthropology or sociology was being used (or invoked) as the model or tool-kit. The new paradigm, most of whose practitioners were loosely aligned with the Labour Party, had a complex and ambiguous relationship with Marxist history. On the one hand, there were many signs of harmony and points of overlap. Proponents of both approaches sat side by side on the board of *Past and Present*, and the new journal *Social History* (founded in 1976) leaned strongly to Marxism. The new genre of 'oral history' was inspired both by the social sciences and by the ideal of 'history from below'; the reconstruction of popular attitudes was a common quest between the social-history paradigm, the new populism of *History Workshop*, and Marxist history informed by the concept of ideology. Moreover, the work of the British Marxist historians might be seen in retrospect as the first embodiment of the social-history paradigm; for that school, too, had applied to the study of the past a conceptual framework derived from outside the history discipline, with scientific aspirations (*Past and Present* was initially subtitled 'A journal of scientific history'), in admiration of the *Annales* school, and in more or less open hostility to traditional British State historiography. On the other hand, there were also important tensions. The social-history paradigm proper was actually formulated and practised in explicit opposition to Marxism: this was true, for instance, of Laslett's *The World We Have Lost* (1965), of Thomas's 1966 manifesto, of Lawrence Stone's *Causes of the English Revolution* (1972). Conversely, the most important early piece of Marxist 'social history' – Thompson's *Making of the English Working Class* – was written against the grain of the social-history paradigm, for it opposed the mechanical importing into history of frameworks from the social sciences or indeed from Marxism itself.

In one important respect the social-history paradigm harmonised both with the Marxist school and with the earlier populist tradition: once again, the State was marginal. This took many different forms, corresponding to the several varieties of the new paradigm. In the picture of early-modern England painted by Peter Laslett, William III and his wars appeared by accident as the customer for Ambrose Crowley's pioneering iron factory of the 1690s; to Alan Macfarlane the clergyman Ralph Josselin was an anthropological informant on daily life rather than a witness to troubled times; for Keith Thomas, the Royal Touch was a reflection of popular beliefs rather than an instrument of monarchy, an aspect not of kingship but of credulity; in the eyes of Lawrence Stone, the outbreak of the English Revolution posed an interesting challenge of explanation, its course and outcome did not. But in all cases, politics and the State now loomed small. Change was to be explained not by political narrative but by social forces and economic developments. Stability was to be found not in administrative structures but in popular attitudes (the English formulation of *mentalités*). In place of constitutional development, historians now traced the rise of social classes and professional groups. This tendency to marginalise the State was reinforced by the increasing use of local studies: as Le Roy Ladurie put it, the historiographic focus had shifted 'from Waterloo to Colyton'.[16]

The relegation of the State to the margins of historical enquiry was no accident, for the proponents of the social-history paradigm were actively hostile to traditional State historiography. The peaceful-coexistence policy put forward by Trevelyan in the 1940s,

although restated in more sophisticated form by Harold Perkin in
1962, was soon replaced by an agonistic conception – of which
E.H. Carr and Keith Thomas put forward two distinct versions. In
Carr's view, political and constitutional history would automatically be superseded by social and economic history, since the latter
reflected the concerns of 'a broader and more advanced stage in
human development'. But for Thomas this same change – seen as
the 'dethronement of politics' from the writing of history – had to
be advocated and would require an active struggle. Here Thomas
was of course reiterating a view long familiar from the *Annales*
founders Marc Bloch and especially Lucien Febvre.[17]

Social history as a totalising historiography

Social history has repeatedly sought to play an integrating or
totalising role, reuniting the various 'sub-histories', 'adjectival histories' or 'tunnels' into which the study of the past has *de facto*
been divided. Expressed in different ways, such an aspiration runs
through the 120 years and different varieties of 'social history'. It
seems to have been at work in Green's *Short History of the English
People* of 1874, one of the founding works of 'history of the
people'. Trevelyan, too, saw social history in such a light – as
providing 'the required link between economic and political history', since 'without social history, economic history is barren and
political history is unintelligible'. Within the *Annales* school this
integrating aim was expressed in the idea of 'total history'; amongst
Marxist historians – whose inspiration has precisely been a totalising
theory – it was voiced in Eric Hobsbawm's early call for a 'history
of society'. A similar need has been expressed from time to time
within the social-history paradigm; thus in 1976, on the funding
of the Social History Society, its president Asa Briggs suggested
that 'future social history can transform the relationship between
the existing "sub-histories", not least the relationship between political history and the rest'.[18]

Social history as totalising history has always been an aspiration, an unfulfilled dream; the aspiration's repeated re-emergence
serves to underline its remoteness from realisation. Part of the
reason for its present elusiveness lies, as Keith Wrightson observes,
in increasing academic specialisation. Yet the problem, like the aspiration, long predates modern specialisation, and its original source
persists today independently of the internal divisions of social

history. That source was the nineteenth-century separation between State historiography and 'social' history; as we have seen, this separation remains in force today, over a century after it was first implanted.

From this outline we see that the domain of social history has been defined by three structural relationships, one of closure and two of openness. A relationship of mutual closure separates it from State historiography (and to a lesser but significant degree from economic history). By contrast, it is open – in a way which State historiography and economic history are not – to progressive political influences and to the social sciences. As a result of its openness, new historiographic specialisms (such as history of medicine) routinely look to social history for an academic shelter and rationale. Both its openness and its closure are accurately captured by social history's self-image as 'the new history' in opposition to 'traditional' history. That image is itself a tradition, going back – according to one recent account – to at least 1912. It has led to a certain amnesia, as David Cannadine has rightly pointed out with respect to Trevelyan's wartime synthesis of the history-of-the-people tradition: 'Although most social historians today implicitly or explicitly reject Trevelyan's definition, and believe themselves to belong to a more professional, more rigorous, more recent tradition, those who read a little further in his book would be surprised by both the catholicity and contemporaneity of his conception of the subject.'[19]

If the image of novelty has a certain mythical character, it also has a real content in social history's openness to political movements and to developments in the social sciences. Recent years have seen significant developments in each of the latter two spheres. In progressive politics the major change of the past twenty years has been the rise of the feminist movement; in the social sciences, there has been a parallel move towards linguistic analysis in place of more traditional sociological and anthropological frameworks. These two shifts – which are linked together in the academic sphere within feminist theory, and in the political sphere by the decline of Marxism – are duly being absorbed by social history. A fitting emblem of the impact of feminism was that *History Workshop Journal* in 1982 changed its subtitle from 'A journal of socialist historians' to 'A journal of socialist and feminist historians'. Symptoms of a 'linguistic turn' in social history (seen by

some as the implementation of the lessons of postmodernism)
include a developing debate over language, class and politics in the
recent historiography of the nineteenth-century working class.[20]
The rise of modern feminism has had a dual impact on the
writing of history, calling both for a redefinition of its subject-
matter – history should be *about* women – and for a shift in
perspective – history should be written *from* the viewpoint of
women, that is to say by women, for women, and from a feminist
perspective. '*History about women*' has expanded the scope of
history in two ways. The first, which could be called 'women *in*
history', comprises a recognition and reconstruction of the part
women played in history as traditionally defined – in already-
recognised themes such as economic activity, popular protest,
political movements. The second – the history *of* women – has been
more radical, entailing new priorities and an extension of subject-
matter. In the 'public sphere' this has meant raising the profile
both of well-known episodes (for instance suffragette history), and
of some which were not so familiar to historians (such as the
struggles against the Contagious Diseases Acts). In the 'private
sphere' it has opened up to historical scholarship whole areas
of activity which had previously escaped notice: women's own
particular activities such as childrearing are now recognised as
legitimate themes for historical enquiry. (The predominantly
male-written genre of history-of-the-family arose partly as a response
to feminism, though also from historical demography). In both
public and private realms the 'history of women' has broken its
own boundaries by leading outwards to the very broad theme of
relations *between* the sexes, that is, to the dialectic of resistance
and power in women's experience.

The call for '*history from the viewpoint of women*' is associated
with three major reorientations which are still at an early stage of
development. First, it requires an integration between the new
themes revealed by the history of women and more traditional
historiographic concerns. Such integration makes for changes in
the very content of 'history', particularly by connecting the public
and private spheres. Second, it has led to a re-examination of the
canonical subject-matter itself. This approach is illuminating even
– or especially – with respect to historical activities in which women
seem to have played no part (such as wars), or discursive traditions which apparently wrote women out of existence (such as

early-modern political thought). For in such cases it is possible to explore the strategies of exclusion and marginalisation by which such domains were constituted as specifically masculine. Third, 'history from the viewpoint of women' has opened the discipline of history to the conceptual distinction between biologically-given sex and socially-constructed gender; and the implications of this distinction are particularly widespread and profound. Since the very categories 'women' and 'men' are historically specific, the process of their construction can be reconstructed – leading to explorations not only of female identities in the past, but also of the history of masculinity. Because those categories were at work in all human activities in the past, and in every document surviving from the past, the perspective of gender is relevant throughout the entire domain of historical enquiry.

The 'linguistic turn' in social history comprises three aspects. First, a new focus on the historical efficacy of linguistic categories (vocabularies), grids (relations of difference between signifiers) and systems (discourses). Second, the apprehension of past language as an object of historical research in its own right. Third, an increasing awareness of the rhetorical structures deployed by historians themselves, entailing a gradual engagement with the work of Hayden White.[21] Of these the first is the most important and problematical, carrying as it does an ambiguous significance in relation to the social-history paradigm. On the one hand, it simply extends that paradigm into a new theoretical domain, using resources drawn from linguistic theory just as a previous generation deployed the tools of sociology and anthropology. Yet, on the other hand, its effect has been to undermine some of the categories and explanations which have traditionally characterised social history. This revisionism centres especially on the concept of social class – particularly with reference to British working-class history, where it has put into question both class *identity* as a socio-economic reality, and class *interest* as an explanation for political allegiance or 'ideology'.[22]

At present these issues remain highly contested: although its influence has grown in the past decade, the linguistic turn has proceeded much more slowly than did the social-history paradigm itself in the late 1960s. It is not yet possible to appraise its long-term significance, but two observations may be offered here. First, the linguistic turn is connected with a wider set of developments which can be characterised as the critique of the concept of 'society'. I discuss the implications of this critique below. Second, it seems likely that the lessons of the linguistic turn itself will in due course be absorbed within more traditional forms of historical enquiry. One way of indicating this is by means of Wittgenstein's conception of what he called 'language-games' and 'forms of life'. A 'language-game' – that is, a real-life set of linguistic transactions – is not 'played' (performed) within language, still less by language, but rather *with* language, that is to say by means of language. It takes place *within* a specific 'form of life', that is, within an interlocking pattern of human actions of which language-use is merely a part. Language-games only work within the particular forms of life in which they are embedded. In effect Wittgenstein thus extended the well-known dependency of meaning on context to the concrete setting of action in which language-use takes place. On this view, it is misleading to abstract language from the historical context of its use, positing it either as an independent governor (of action or of belief) or as a separate object of enquiry. Hence even if, for the sake of argument, we set out to study the history of some aspect of language (for example, vocabularies of class), we would have to attend to the action-contexts of utterances – asking, in every instance of usage, who was addressing whom through what medium in what context and to what ends. Seen in this light, the study of language simply dissolves into social history – enriching it in the process, but by no means displacing its traditional concerns.[23]

The structural setting of social history

Social history's recurrent malaise arises from its inability either to fulfil its totalising aspirations, or to give them up. This suggests the need to appraise its place in the wider disciplinary structure of the modern human sciences. Here I sketch a critical map of social history's disciplinary relationships, beginning with brief observations on its internal structure, and proceeding outwards in two directions: first to the historical disciplines and then to the social sciences. This 'map' will admittedly be incomplete and provisional. A balanced discussion of social history's significant neighbours would have to consider many fields which I have not explored here – for example, amongst the historical disciplines the history of art, of education and religion; of the social sciences anthropology, geography and economics. Such a wider exploration would be very welcome: perhaps the present limited sketch will stimulate others to attempt it.

The internal divisions of social history

One of the characteristics of the social-history paradigm is its implicit catholicity and permissiveness: it can draw its tools or inspiration from any of the social sciences. Clearly this has vastly enriched the scope of historical research; yet it has also had the damaging side-effect of working against the 'integrative' or totalising aspirations of social history. This is particularly regrettable because the discipline of history, alone amongst the human sciences, has the potential to achieve such an integration – precisely because it is potentially free of ontological presuppositions as to the primacy of any particular sphere of human life. Whereas (for instance) sociology must privilege the social realm, economics the economic sphere, and so on, history can in principle explore the whole terrain of human life. To the extent that the discipline has lost its integrating potential, it has lost its way.[24]

The most telling commentaries on this phenomenon have been produced by Keith Wrightson and Joan Scott. Wrightson aptly describes the problem as a form of 'enclosure': the separate 'fields' of social history are 'farmed in severalty' and know little of each other's existence. Scott formulates the issue as 'the contradictory logic of the supplement': social history adds to itself new fields and themes without incorporating such new fields into its self-conception. This latter problem is of particular relevance to women's history, the theme for which Scott has developed this concept; but it also applies to the entire structure of social history. Scott's argument, as I understand it, can be briefly summarised as follows. Social historians have now accepted that first the history of women, and then more radically the construction of gender, must be included in any adequate understanding of the past. From this it follows that the previous exclusion of these themes was not merely a politico-moral wrong (though it was certainly that), but also effected substantive distortions in our conceptions of history. Logically, therefore, everything must be revised in this light: we must rethink politics, economics, war, society in the light of the sexual division of roles and the social construction of gender. But this rethinking is exactly what does not happen. Instead, women's history and the theme of gender are permitted to enter academic discourse and institutions in the role of 'supplements', a role which on the one hand acknowledges their importance and on the other hand denies it. Scott argues that this 'logic of the supplement' is in its different way a political instrument, accepting such issues in such a way as to exclude their implications. What we must notice is that this 'contradictory logic' is built into the very structure of the social-history paradigm.[25]

Social history and the historical disciplines

As we have seen, social history has developed in separation from, and to a large extent against, that State historiography which continues to function as the core of the historical discipline. The most obvious effect has been a closure against political history, a problem which has attracted a long tradition of comment. Another and rather different closure – perhaps associated more with the social-history paradigm than with the earlier history-of-the-people approach – is against the history of 'high' culture, for instance literature and science. If the totalising aspirations of social history are ever to be realised, such disciplinary barriers will have to be broken down; and the first step in such a process is to identify their existence.

Political versus social history   The relationship between political and social history has consistently troubled social historians ever since the emergence of the social-history paradigm in the late 1960s. The dominant worry has been the exclusion of the political from social history; and it has also been observed from time to time that where social history does consider politics, it tends to approach this theme in a reductionist manner. We have now heard these laments for two decades, and there is no sign of their abating. As early as 1971 Lawrence Stone was concerned that 'political history and social history . . . are all too often treated in largely watertight compartments', and expressed the hope that prosopography could 'form the missing connection' between them. In 1976 the Genoveses wrote of a 'political crisis of social history'; in 1979 Tony Judt launched a devastating attack on what he saw as an apolitical social history; in 1980 Eley and Nield asked 'Why does social history ignore politics?'; and the same disquiet animated

Gareth Stedman Jones's essay on 'Rethinking Chartism' of 1983. In 1986 the issue was still troubling Pat Thane and Tony Sutcliffe, who endorsed Judt's earlier argument; and in recent years the same concern has been voiced again from State, Marxist and social historiographies (in 1989 Patrick Collinson called for 'history with the politics put back'; in 1990 Geoff Eley hoped as we have seen to 'reunite the fractured labours of political and social historians'; in 1993 David Cressy is advocating the 'recombination of social and traditional history'). Nor are these complaints merely rhetorical, for the problem remains a very real one today, despite some areas of intersection such as the historiography of twentieth-century welfare legislation. Thus we find almost no point of overlap or contact between the political and social historiography of eighteenth-century Britain, as surveyed in two very able reviews published side by side in the *Journal of British Studies* for 1986. Again, two recent studies of the English middle class, each dealing with a 70-year period spanning a major political watershed (1688 and 1832), have both effectively excluded national politics from consideration. Politics and the State are not included in the remit of either of the new social-history journals *Continuity and Change* (founded in 1986) and *Rural History* (1990).[26]

From the other side of this divide, the political historians seem to have adopted a range of different attitudes towards social history. Some continue the venerable tradition of ignoring it; others define their subject in such a way as to include the social (to varying degrees) within the political. One such commentator – Gertrude Himmelfarb – has attacked social history in the name of Reason: 'the social historian . . . denies or belittles . . . reason itself: the reason embodied in the polity, in the constitutions and laws that permit men to order their affairs in a rational manner – or, on occasion, in an irrational manner, which other men perceive as such and rationally, often heroically, strive against'. Now what Himmelfarb was trying to defend – that is, the historical study of 'the polity, the constitutions and laws' – seems eminently worth defending, and these themes have indeed been neglected by social historians. But the terms of this defence were surely ill-chosen, for at least two reasons. First, although Himmelfarb was careful to say that the 'reason' which is to be 'restored' to history 'is not Hegel's Reason', nevertheless it partakes rather largely of the latter's transcendental quality: the study of history as Himmelfarb conceives it seems to comprise a sort of communication of Reason with itself across the ages. If this were to be made a governing condition of historical research, historians would either cease to write about the vast majority of people in the past, or they would have to substitute assumptions about those people for the effort at research. Second, Himmelfarb's picture of institutions as embodiments of reason forecloses the scope of interpretation by imposing *a priori* categories upon even its chosen objects of research.[27]

Himmelfarb's hostility is unusual; more commonly, political historians have sought something of a rapprochement with social history. Thus for the early-modern period, some of the most notable works of intersection between the two traditions have been produced by historians of a primarily political stamp – often pupils of J.H. Plumb and thus standing in the Trevelyan lineage – such as Speck, Hirst and Kishlansky on Parliamentary electoral processes, Brewer on the eighteenth-century British State. Those political historians who have addressed the issue most squarely at a conceptual level are Geoffrey Elton and J.C.D. Clark. Elton sees political history as central, social history as ancillary, and argues that political history 'must . . . absorb as well as criticise the findings of other forms of historical study' – which refers to social and economic history – 'not reject them'. Clark goes further, arguing for a redefinition of the social in terms of the political, yet it is remarkable how many familiar themes of social history are retained in the framework he proposes: 'the historical sociology of power, ideology and belief, of structure, cohesion, allegiance, faith and identity as well as of innovation and dissent'. From a very different angle, then, Elton and Clark endorse the concern expressed by social historians themselves: neither political history nor social history can ignore each other. Moreover, both their formulations fundamentally accept the existence and concerns of social history, however they might want to appropriate or reshape those concerns.[28]

The troubled relationship between political and social history results from the longstanding division between State historiography in general – of which political history is simply the most prominent aspect – and social history. It is a mark of social history's success that political historians are increasingly looking for some form of rapprochement across that division. At the same time, it is clear that the gulf between the two will have to be bridged from both sides, and that this will entail a fundamental rethinking of categories on the part of social historians.

Literature and history   Students of English literature long ago 'discovered' history: in what is called the 'new historicism' they have increasingly located their classic texts – and, to an increasing extent, not-so-classic ones – in a historical setting. But historians have yet to repay the compliment; despite the existence of a journal *Literature and History*, imaginative literature looms small indeed amongst the concerns of the great majority of historians. Perhaps the central reason for this neglect is the tendency of historians to look in works of literature for 'evidence' about the past, and then to interrogate those works for the adequacy of this 'evidence'. The three conclusions typically yielded by the latter approach are indeed unsurprising: that this evidence is untrustworthy as to matters of fact; that nevertheless it can reveal something of ideology or attitudes; and that it may also be useful for decorative or illustrative purposes.[29]

In the case of the eighteenth-century novel, there is a striking contrast between the narrowness of these historiographic concerns and the rich fabric of historical argument and inference woven around this theme by literary scholars. Beginning as early as 1957 with Ian Watt's *Rise of the Novel*, and revitalised by feminist scholarship in the 1980s, this latter tradition has increasingly seen the new genre of the novel as a social phenomenon, a historical product, a reflection of and an influence upon its age. In a substantial series of important monographs and scholarly articles, literary scholars have connected the emergence of the novel with literacy, with the politics of both class and party, with relations of gender, and with the family. Yet when historians (both social and political) discuss any of the latter themes they usually ignore this very substantial body of work, and indeed pay little or no attention to the novel itself.[30]

No doubt historians will want to revise some of the inferences and connections made by the literary scholars; and certainly this is a field which historians will find it difficult to enter, faced as they will be with very different disciplinary conventions of inference and of writing. But there can surely be no justification for the continued neglect of this theme by social historians. For it can scarcely be disputed that the novel was a central cultural product of eighteenth-century England, with a twofold significance: first, in its importance for the women and men (in that order) of the period; second, in the longer term as an enduring literary form, a major feature of modern life. What the literary scholars have taught us is that the novel was a social phenomenon. Yet it has remained almost off the map of the 'social history' of the period.

Social history and the social history of science   As we see below, the historiography of science has undergone a conceptual revolution in the 1980s. This has entailed a widening of focus from products (say: Boyle's Law) to their genesis (for instance, in contests); from thought (metaphysics, conceptual methodology) to action (experimental practices, social technologies for securing assent); and from what is taken as science (a lineage through time) to its context (linkages in social space). The central effect of this transformation is that science – or in the early-modern period, natural philosophy – is now seen as a social activity, with implications for our very conception of the 'social'. One of its by-products has been that historians of science are becoming increasingly literate in 'general' history.[31]

Yet, just as with literature, this development has very largely been ignored by social historians: the compliment of cross-disciplinary literacy has yet to be returned. As Roy Porter has recently lamented, the history of society has long been written and continues to be written almost without reference to the history of science. Porter's clarion call for social historians to break down this conceptual barrier is both timely and welcome. But in order to heed that call, we must understand how the barrier came to be erected in the first place; and here there are two issues specific to the history of science. First, both science and its early-modern predecessor natural philosophy pose real technical problems for the student of the humanities, and this difficulty is particularly acute in England with its rigid pedagogic separation of the 'two cultures'. Yet it must be observed that in other respects historians routinely educate themselves in recondite technical matters, simply in order to read and understand the documents of the past. If we can master (say) Restoration Hearth Tax records, then surely we can come to grips with (say) the writings of Boyle and Newton in the same period. Second, social historians partake in a particular way of that awe of science which until recently has been so general in modern culture. For the social-history paradigm draws its concepts from the 'social sciences', whose aspiration is precisely to emulate science, or rather, a certain image of what science is taken to be. To the extent that science is taken as a model, even an indirect and implicit one, it tends to be placed outside the sphere of historical objects: admiration precludes interrogation.[32]

Unlike the marginalisation of the State, the exclusion of literature and science from the concerns of social historians has attracted relatively little comment. Yet its effects are surely no less damaging: once again, such closure limits the domain of social history and works against its totalising ambitions.

Social history and the social sciences

An asymmetrical interchange Under the social-history paradigm, the relationship between social history and the social sciences is seen as *asymmetrical*: as a pupil–teacher relationship, with the history discipline as pupil and the social sciences as teacher. Sometimes it is recognised that the pupil-discipline can and will adapt the lessons to its own requirements; occasionally it is suggested that the social sciences might have a little to learn from history; but the dominant imagery clearly places history in an inferior role. This is explicit in the classic manifesto statement of Keith Thomas (1966): the 'job' was to understand 'the workings of human society and the fluctuations in human affairs', and all the 'tools' for this enterprise existed ready-made in the social sciences. The asymmetry continued through the substantive implementation of that paradigm: thus one looks in vain in, say, Thomas's *Religion and the Decline of Magic* (1971) or Stone's *The Causes of the English Revolution* (1972) for the possibility that the social sciences might learn from history, or want to do so, or that historians might try to teach them. With minor changes, this emphasis has continued ever since. The call of Peter Stearns in 1976 – that 'social history must be directly entered into the spectrum of the social sciences', and that it 'may serve as a lever to reinvigorate the social sciences generally' – has seldom been either heeded or echoed. Thus when Lawrence Stone began in the late 1970s to voice doubts about some implementations of the social-history paradigm, he did not suggest that this had any implications for the social sciences themselves, not indeed for the social-history paradigm itself;

historians simply had to be more selective in their appropriation of theoretical resources. Again, when Philip Abrams wrote in 1982 of an 'interchange of techniques', adding that 'we are rapidly reaching a point where the disciplines [of history and sociology] will quite obviously share a common armoury of technique', all the concrete examples he gave were cases of new techniques being imported into history from sociology; there were no instances of the reverse process. Despite the achievements of social history, the same conception continues today at the programmatic level, in the recent 'linguistic turn'. Thus we are told that historians, in need of 'a methodology for reading' the 'sources', can derive this from 'other philosophies and approaches', such as 'modern linguistic analysis . . . literary criticism and . . . critical theory', which encourage 'a close internal reading of texts'. Or again, that 'social historians of language have much to learn from the ethnographers of communication, sociologists of language and others who entered the field before we did. We would do well to begin by learning *their* language. We will doubtless discover the need to make alterations in order to adapt it to our own purposes.' Here there is no hint that historians could speak *to* the 'ethnographers of communication, sociologists of language and others', nor that the latter group might learn *our* language. This has aptly been called the 'producer–consumer relationship' between the social sciences and history: social sciences produce theories and techniques, history consumes them.[33]

In fact, social historians have by no means been as supine as these conceptualisations suggest. Not only have they adapted the methods of the social sciences, translating these through their own 'historical metaphysics' as we shall see in a moment, but also they have produced findings which put in question some of the premises of the social sciences themselves. Yet the assumed relationship of tutelage has shown a remarkable tendency to survive.[34]

The corollary of this is that social historians have made little attempt to *speak outwards*, to address the social sciences. Without doubt this is part of a wider problem, discussed in a recent essay by Alan Megill. Megill's main concern was the response of historians to the work of Michel Foucault, but in the course of this discussion he made some striking observations on the response of other humanities disciplines to works by historians. This was on the basis of citations in the arts and humanities in 1977–8 as reconstructed by Eugene Garfield from the *Arts and Humanities Citation Index* (*A&HCI*). From Garfield's 100 most heavily-cited authors Megill extracted a list of sixty 'twentieth-century' authors. His observations on that list should give all historians food for thought:

the list includes not a single social or political historian, though it is precisely these fields that constitute the core of the discipline [by which Megill meant the arts and humanities in general]. An important reason for this absence, I suggest, is that the discipline [here Megill was referring to history] is hostile to the intellectual vigor and originality that would make historians' work of interest to scholars in other disciplines. Historians in our century are rarely original thinkers. Twenty years ago, Hayden White characterized history as 'perhaps the conservative discipline par excellence,' suggesting that it combines 'late nineteenth-century social science' (Freud, Weber, *et al.*) with 'mid-nineteenth-century art' (Scott, Thackeray, *et al.*) There has been some movement since White wrote these words: such historians as Carlo Ginzberg, Le Roy Ladurie, and Natalie Davis have profited from mid-twentieth-century anthropology and even from mid-twentieth-century literary criticism. On the quantitative side, there is now some use of mid-twentieth-century statistics. But for the most part, the discipline does not produce the insights and innovations that would make it interesting to those outside it.

Here we may notice in passing that Megill conceived progress in history as updating the process of borrowing, much along the lines of the social-history paradigm. Megill continued:

To be sure, it is possible and perhaps likely that historians' publication patterns and citation conventions, which differ in various ways from those in other fields, may have some effect on how frequently citations to their work appear in the *A&HCI*. This is a problem worthy of investigation within the larger context of the reception of ideas generally . . . In any case, whatever the results of such an investigation, it remains true that some historians *are* highly cited. Six appear on the list: Erwin Panofsky, Ernst Gombrich, Frances Yates, Thomas S. Kuhn, Mircea Eliade, and Foucault. These writers all happen to be on the margins, even outside, the 'generic' discipline of history . . . None is close to the socio-political mainstream. None made his (her) home in a standard department or institute of history; perhaps none could have . . . A striking feature of the six writers in question is the extent to which they are not parochial . . . In short, if a historian is to do work that will be widely seen as interesting and important, he or she must become something *more* than a historian.

Megill's value-judgments aside, his findings indicate that the reluctance of social history to 'speak outwards' is true of political history as well. It would be interesting to have a comparable – and more recent – analysis of the *Social Sciences Citation Index*, in order to assess the reception of social history by such disciplines as sociology and anthropology. I know of no such study, but casual observation suggests that the pattern detected by Megill in the late 1970s persists today and applies in the social sciences as well as in the humanities. What must be stressed is that such a fate is inscribed within the social-history paradigm, for that paradigm has conceived the relationship between history and the social sciences as a one-way theoretical traffic.[35]

The historical metaphysic of the social historian   The historian who adopts the social-history paradigm faces two issues which the social sciences themselves cannot in principle resolve. First, the social sciences are deeply divided from one another, and each of them is internally differentiated as well: just as there exists no unified social science, so there is no one 'economics', 'sociology, 'anthropology' or 'linguistics'. (This is another reason why a totalising 'history of society' has proved so elusive; no single social science discipline can provide its necessary tools.) Hence the social historian must make a *choice*, both between the different social sciences, and within each of these. Second, the social sciences are ahistorical, in the specific sense that their conceptual frameworks have on the whole been conceived with an eye to universals, detached from specific contexts and largely framed without reference to the dimension of time. Thus some *translation* is needed in order for those frameworks to be applied to the study of the past. How should social historians make the requisite choice, and how should they effect the necessary translation? These questions seem to have received very little attention. Choice has been exercised by the discipline as a whole in waves of fashion, and by individual historians on the basis of accident and personal taste. Translation cannot be guided by the traditional procedures of either the social sciences or the history discipline.[36]

In practice these decisions are governed by what I shall call a *historical metaphysic*, that is, an underlying conception of the relationship between past and present. This can be illustrated in the individual case of Lawrence Stone – himself a notable, if ambivalent, exponent of the social-history paradigm. Stone's particular 'metaphysic' is relatively accessible to reconstruction because he has recently written autobiographically about his own 'restless quest for theories, concepts, approaches and models'. From his account a certain pattern emerges, the key to which is Stone's self-description as 'the last of the Whigs, and in many ways still a child of the Enlightenment'. The latter cast of thought seems to have entailed three consistent beliefs: in progress; in a voluntarist account of that progress; and that knowledge of the past must be continuously updated and attuned to the shifting categories of the present. It was precisely this third conviction which propelled his 'restless quest' amongst the social sciences: thus Stone's very receptiveness to those disciplines was itself rooted in what I am calling his 'historical metaphysic'. Further, that metaphysic dictated that some social-science approaches were acceptable while others were not. Thus on the one hand, Stone embraced a series of approaches which either depicted the emergence of the modern world as an essentially progressive development (at first Marx, then Weber, later modernisation theory), or at least licensed sharp contrasts between past and present (symbolic anthropology). On the other hand, he explicitly rejected a series of other approaches, each of which seems to have conflicted with his Enlightenment Whig metaphysic: Parsonian functionalism and French structuralism (which perhaps seemed in his eyes to posit history as unchanging), Freudian psychology (history as tragic), linguistic deconstruction (history as unknowable). And he adopted an intermediate position of ambivalence towards the historiography of the *Annales* school – welcoming its use of modern methods, but distrusting both its tendency to depict history as 'immobile' and its leanings towards determinism.[37]

Every historian's appropriation of theoretical resources and methodological tools from the social sciences will be governed by some such historical metaphysic; and the particular metaphysic will differ from historian to historian. Thus in the social-history paradigm, the categories of the social sciences are never simply applied 'to the past'; rather, those categories are brought to bear upon the past *as apprehended through a specific historical metaphysic.* To put this another way, the apparent detachment and objectivity associated with the application of social-science categories is illusory. This by no means vitiates the social-history paradigm; but it suggests that we need a greater degree of collective self-awareness if we are to understand the nature of our own enterprise. Attention to this issue might help to clarify the relationship between social and State historiographies.[38]

Some recent developments in the social sciences
The issue of the historian's metaphysic concerns *how* the social-history paradigm is put into effect. But a more fundamental question has often been raised, as to *whether* it can be implemented at all. As we shall shortly see, this problem is now arising in an unfamiliar way; first let us briefly examine the issue in its original form.

Traditionally, history and the social sciences have been separated by fundamental differences of outlook. To paint a stylised picture: the social sciences are 'nomothetic', seeking universals rather than particulars, and taking pride in conceptual rigour; they tend to posit the dominance of structure over human agency; and, as a corresponding research technique, they often deal in abstractions constructed by amalgamating individual events. (A classical example of the latter procedure is Durkheim's use of the suicide rate to turn a seemingly individual action, self-murder, into a 'social fact' – the statistical rate of suicide.[39]) By contrast, history is 'idiographic', concerned with the particular and the concrete, and priding itself upon rigour in the use of empirical evidence; thus historians have typically paid more attention to agency than to structure, and this tendency survives even amongst social historians. Historians see these characteristics of their discipline as reflecting the reality it studies: according to them, agency and particularity are aspects of human life itself. In contrast, social scientists see historians' stress on agency and particularity as a more or less arbitrary choice made by the historians themselves. In part, both tendencies are 'professional deformations', idols of these particular academic tribes, arising from their complementary affiliations with the natural sciences on the one hand and the humanities on the other. But whatever the origin of this rift, it has deeply divided history from the social sciences. Hence the unease of many traditionally-minded historians with the social-history paradigm.

But in recent years the scientific aspirations of the social sciences have come under an unprecedented series of challenges: from the hermeneutic tradition, from feminist studies and from linguistic philosophy. The effect of these challenges is to displace the positivistic conception of 'social sciences' with a hermeneutically-informed and relativistic notion of 'human sciences'. For social history the implications are ambiguous. On the one hand, the new rubric is much more accommodating to the historical; indeed a new openness towards history is already apparent, as we will see below in the particular case of historical sociology. On the other hand, the reorientation of the social sciences creates a new problem for the social-history paradigm. For the new outlook has put in question the very concept of 'society'.[40]

The critique of 'society' What I call the 'critique of "society" ' has arisen from several different angles. First, the *autonomy* of the concept has been challenged by critiques of its implicit and explicit conceptual boundaries. Thus Bruno Latour disputes the conceptual division between 'society' and 'nature'; Anthony Giddens criticises the disciplinary boundary which separates the study of 'society' (sociology) from its extension in space (geography) and time (history); and the work of several scholars has put into doubt the post-Enlightenment division between 'society' (originally 'civil society') and the State. As Geoffrey Hawthorn pithily expresses this latter point: 'The world has turned out to be very different from the one the social theorists expected. It is not, if it ever was, governed by social forces. It is governed by governments.'[41] Second, and intersecting with Hawthorn's argument, Michel Foucault long ago observed that the concept of 'society' had specific historical *origins*: that it was a discursive creation of the early nineteenth century, an aspect of a wider process which Foucault characterised as the construction of the object 'man' and of the human (including social) sciences which aspired to knowledge of this object. Third, in what could be seen as a postmodernist development of Foucault's insight, Laclau and Mouffe have argued that this discursive invention performs *work*: that the concept of 'society' actually constitutes society, incessantly 'suturing' a body politic which is inherently broken. This view precisely inverts the objectivist postulates of classical sociology, claiming instead that society is not the premise but the product of sociology – a point also made by Latour as part of his critique of the 'nature'/'society' conceptual dichotomy.[42]

Finally, Derek Sayer has argued that this work of 'suturing' can be *undone* by historical critique, exactly as Marx sought to do for political economy. This immensely stimulating proposal puts the critique of 'society' on a different plane. For whereas the other arguments we have been examining have tended to 'deconstruct' the concept of society, Sayer's approach offers the promise of reinstating that concept, though in an entirely novel way – namely, by situating it historically. Sayer's wider argument is that the supposedly founding 'concepts' of 'Marxism' are in fact reifying distortions – fetishisations – and that what truly characterised the work of Marx was not a fixed set of concepts but rather a method, a method which consisted precisely in historicising *all* concepts. In developing the implications of this view, Sayer makes it explicit that the concept of society itself requires just this historical criticism: 'We need, then, to carry out the same sort of critique for the "simple abstractions" of sociology (or political science, or jurisprudence) as Marx himself did in *Capital* of the elementary categories of political economy.'[43]

The effect of the critique of 'society' is to undermine the resort to 'social' categories (social structure, interests, roles) as unproblematic 'causes' (of action, belief, ideology, politics), and indeed to put in question the very notion of causality in human affairs. Seen from this standpoint, traditional sociology had hypostatised 'society' into an external entity with the characteristics of an organism or machine rather than those of a human product. This move entailed the assumption that the sociologist was a detached observer; both aspects were well adapted to the sociologist's actual position, of seeking to construct disciplinary autonomy from a position of State service.[44]

Yet there has developed in parallel with this critique at least one remarkable counterpoint, which we must also notice here. In the field of social studies of science, and especially in the history of science, there has emerged what is known as the 'strong programme' in the sociology of scientific knowledge – an approach which applies social interests to the explanation of science itself. In the traditional sociology of knowledge, associated particularly with Mannheim, scientific knowledge had been seen as residing outside the domain of social explanation – perhaps chiefly because sociologists modelled themselves upon natural scientists. Even the relativistic framework of Thomas Kuhn's *Structure of Scientific*

Revolutions (1962) explained changes in scientific knowledge as taking place within science, through such mechanisms as the accumulation of anomalies within a paradigm. In sharp contrast, the 'strong programme' – first enunciated by David Bloor in 1976 – has set itself the novel and highly ambitious aim of explaining the content of scientific knowledge in social terms; and meanwhile Charles Webster (independently of Bloor) began to demonstrate the rich possibilities in his pioneering *The Great Instauration*. In the 1980s this approach has proved extraordinarily fertile, generating a large and distinguished body of highly original work and transforming the very shape of the historiography of science. Though the claims of the strong programme have been and remain in dispute, it has effected a decisive shift in the grounds of argument and explanation throughout the various science-studies disciplines. It also represents a remarkable innovation in the study of history at large: by breaking down the wall surrounding science, it has dramatically enlarged the frontiers of historical explanation and now presents a major challenge of historiographic integration.[45]

If we juxtapose the aims and achievements of the 'strong programme' against the parallel 'critique of "society" ', we arrive at some complex results. In the first place, these two recent traditions have in large measure been talking past each other: few of those contributing to the critique of 'society' seem aware of developments in the science-studies field, and vice versa. As if in confirmation of this disciplinary barrier, the most notable exception – Bruno Latour – is perhaps the least historically-minded of the participants concerned. Second, the two developments appear to be in radical conflict: the one retreats from social explanations in their traditional domain, the other extends such explanations into a radically novel domain. But third, there is an interesting point of potential convergence. For the historiography of science developed under the influence of the strong programme has increasingly demonstrated the web of social 'interests' and their mode of operation to be far more complex, subtle and fine-grained than was supposed in traditional, reductionist sociology of knowledge. Thus, by implying a much subtler picture of 'society', such historiography implicitly supports the parallel critique of the traditional picture of society as an organism or machine. Finally, these two traditions attain agreement over the strong programme's demand for *reflexivity*. One of the four tenets of that 'programme' was (in the

words of David Bloor) that it 'would be reflexive. In principle its
patterns of explanation would have to be applicable to sociology
itself.' Strikingly, this requirement of reflexivity removes at a stroke
the assumption of the detached observer and therefore – in principle,
at least – its obverse, the hypostatisation of 'society'. In this respect,
therefore, the implications of the strong programme harmonise
with the critique of 'society', particularly in Sayer's formulation.[46]
   Standing back from these developments, we can suggest three
implications for social history. First, the requirement of reflexivity
opens the possibility of a new and more symmetrical relationship
between social history and the social sciences. For reflexivity entails seeing the social sciences themselves as historical products:
they thus become objects of historical scrutiny, rather than
unproblematic sources of neutral tool-kits. Second, history itself
should also cultivate such a reflexive self-understanding. This means
that the various themes which this chapter has merely broached –
internal development, disciplinary setting, historical metaphysics
– need a systematic interrogation and merit the collective attention of the historical discipline. Third, the critical reappraisal of
the conceptual division between the State and 'society' corresponds
precisely to the need to integrate the two traditions of State and
social historiographies.

Historical sociology and the discipline of history   We saw earlier
that historians in general, and social historians in particular, have
made little attempt to 'speak outwards' to other disciplines. But if
historians started to 'speak outwards', would anyone listen? Does
history (whether social or otherwise) have any constituency outside itself? There is indeed such a constituency: the new 'historical
sociology', or what is perhaps better described as the recent historical turn within sociology. As we shall now see, this new disciplinary development turns out to need a rapprochement with
history not only for substantive findings but also at the level of
method.[47]
   A decade ago, in his posthumously published *Historical Sociology*, the late Philip Abrams effectively demolished the traditional
conceptual barriers between history and sociology – showing, for
instance, that the alleged distinction between narrative and analysis was unfounded. Whether they admitted it or not, historians
were doing sociology and sociologists were writing histories. Writing

in the mid-1980s, Anthony Giddens reached very similar conclusions from a more theoretical angle: 'Structure, or structural properties, or "structural parameters", exist only in so far as there is continuity in social reproduction across time and space. And such continuity in turn exists only in and through the reflexively monitored activities of situated actors, having a range of intended and unintended consequences.' As a result, 'every research investigation in the social sciences or history is involved in relating action to structure ... No amount of juggling with abstract concepts could substitute for the direct study of such problems in the actual contexts of interaction.' Hence 'historical research is social research and vice versa', and 'sociologists have a great deal more to learn from the work of historians than most would currently admit'. In similar vein, Charles Tilly has recently argued that 'social processes are path-dependent. That is why history matters.' Tilly portrays historical sociology as having grown 'out of a sustained critique of the ideas of "development" and "modernization" that dominated sociological analyses of large-scale social change for two decades after World War II'. In short, in their different ways Abrams, Giddens and Tilly are agreed that *sociology entails history*.[48]

But the extended arguments of Abrams and Giddens remain programmatic, for they offer no guidance on the use of historical evidence. Giddens has not addressed the exigencies of empirical research; Abrams argued for the integration of theoretical and empirical work, but concluded that the relationship between the two in historical sociology posed 'a difficult problem' which he was unable to resolve. This reproduces, from a different angle, the same disciplinary asymmetry which underlies the social-history paradigm. The discipline of sociology has classically been oriented towards theory; that of history, towards an engagement with evidence. What Giddens and Abrams have achieved is to remove the *conceptual* barriers between the two disciplines, that is, the obstacles which loom largest in sociology's frame of reference. But they have not bridged the *practical* gulf between history and sociology, which is the issue of concern to historians. As a result, historical sociology as they have formulated it is bereft of any method for testing theories about the past against the surviving materials from that past.[49]

This same asymmetry was given a philosophical rationale by

Christopher Lloyd in his study of *Explanation in Social History*, published in 1986. At an early stage in this work, Lloyd constructed a discursive space for his own exploration by juxtaposing against each other the traditional mutual criticisms of historians and sociologists. Subdivided into numbered propositions, his argument in this passage has the following structure:

1.1 'Social historians are . . . sceptical about the models and theories of many sociologists.'
1.2 They 'are right to be sceptical' about these.
1.3 'But theory and models are indispensable, whether historians like it or not, and there are some very useful theories and models available.'
2.1 Sociologists 'see the common-sense empiricism of some historians as philosophically and theoretically naive and inadequate.'
2.2 They 'are right' to see this 'empiricism . . . as inadequate'.
3.   'And attention to the philosophical foundations of socio-historical explanation can greatly aid the construction of better empirical explanations.'

Here there was symmetry between 1.1 and 2.1 (the mutual criticisms of sociologists and historians), and between 1.2 and 2.2 (the judgment that each of these criticisms is justified). But at this point the symmetry ended, for there was no 2.3 to match 1.3. What 1.3 asserted was that historians' criticisms of sociologists are only justified *up to a point*; beyond that point, the historians are wrong, for 'theory and models are indispensable'. By contrast, sociologists' criticisms of historians were justified *without limit*: historians were given no counter-claim corresponding to that which 1.3 assigned to sociologists. What stood instead of the missing proposition 2.3 was proposition 3, that is, the need for 'attention to the philosophical foundations of socio-historical explanation'. This installed Lloyd's own discipline of philosophy as the master-discourse; indeed a clear hierarchy was established, with philosophy at the top, sociology in the middle and history at the bottom. With respect to the relations between sociology and history, this ratified the asymmetrical picture emanating from historical sociology itself.[50]

But meanwhile, a significant approach towards disciplinary symmetry was made in a 1984 collection of essays on *Vision and Method in Historical Sociology* – comprising nine studies of the work of leading individual scholars, together with an introduction and a methodological concluding chapter by the editor, Theda Skocpol. This book indicated that historical sociology entails three levels of method: (a) the interpretation of primary sources; (b) as an alternative, the appropriation of secondary works; and (c) the use of conceptual frameworks to order the evidence acquired through (a) or (b). Many of the essays concentrated on (c), implicitly reproducing the same asymmetry we have seen in Giddens, Abrams and Lloyd. However, Daniel Chirot's chapter on Marc Bloch attended to level (a), mentioning Bloch's enthusiastic claims for the 'critical method', and observing that 'those of us who teach sociology and history might ask ourselves if Bloch's program is being followed today'. All three levels were considered in Skocpol's concluding essay, which left no doubt that Chirot's question was well posed. Skocpol depicted three alternative approaches to historical sociology: first, 'applying a general model to history'; second, 'interpretive historical sociology' (a style concerned to reconstruct contrasting meanings rather than causal relationships); and third, her own preferred strategy of 'analytic' or 'comparative' historical sociology (the elucidation of historical causes through the application of Mill's inductive logic to contrasting historical case-studies). The first approach turned out to raise an intractable problem at level (a) of method: as Skocpol rightly asked, 'Could some arbitrarily selected facts perhaps always be found to illustrate any conceivable general model?' With respect to the second approach, Skocpol's account concentrated upon level (c). The third approach was dependent for its evidence upon secondary sources, that is, methodological level (b); and here Skocpol observed that 'comparative historical sociologists have not so far worked out clear, consensual rules and procedures for the valid use of secondary sources as evidence'. Thus wherever the issue of empirical methods was addressed it turned out that this was problematic for historical sociology.[51]

A more recent methodological discussion of historical sociology, by Roger Penn, is the first to devote systematic attention to problems of evidence and inference. Penn demonstrates convincingly that historical sociologists have not found it easy to implement their programmatic aims in empirical practice, and argues that sociologists still have much to learn from historians about the fundamentals of method: 'The great strength of historical science

is its experience in the use of evidence.' By contrast, 'within contemporary sociology . . . there is an endemic failure to develop
theoretical arguments within rigorous empirical analysis.' He
supports these critical conclusions with two lines of argument,
each based on recent case-studies in sociological historiography.
First, sociologists are ill-equipped to evaluate the competing claims
of different historians (level (b) as I have described this above).
Penn illustrates this from recent 'sociological images of the British
working class': when sociologists 'trawl . . . for data' in the historical
literature, they fail to appreciate 'the contested nature of historical
interpretation'. This is fatal, for if sociologists persist in this
naivety they 'will select the evidence that they want to fit their
preconceived "theoretical" abstractions and their accounts will be
still-born'. Second, where sociologists have carried out historical
research for themselves (level (a)) they have only succeeded in
producing 'clear examples of how not to integrate sociology and
history'. Here Penn's example is the 'new economic sociology' of
the 1970s and 1980s: for instance, Braverman's *Labour and
Monopoly Capital* – by no means the worst such case, according
to Penn's account – 'demonstrates clearly how *not* to conduct
research.' Specifically, Braverman produced 'a complex conceptual
architecture . . . supported by . . . examples that fit the argument',
with '*no* attempt to look for counter-examples'. As a result, 'his
evidence is weak in the extreme'. Penn then observes: 'The question that must be raised is why so many sociologists have been
impressed by these arguments and why many still fail to admit
that their emperor really had no clothes.' His answer to this question
is 'the general lack of historical training [and] historical skills
. . . endemic within . . . contemporary sociology'. The import of
Penn's argument is that historical sociology *has to learn from* the
discipline of history.[52]

In short, the empirical dimension of method raises problems
which historical sociology has so far not resolved. Giddens's observation, that 'sociologists have a great deal more to learn from
the work of historians than most would currently admit', is truer
than he seems to have suspected. The implications are twofold.
First, historians would be justified in having a greater belief in the
integrity of their own discipline than the social-history paradigm
implies. This should encourage historians to to 'speak outwards'
with greater self-confidence. Second, historical sociology stands in

asymmetry: lack of harmony or balance
closure possibly closeness

urgent need of historical method – of an understanding of how it is that historians actually construct their accounts of the past. Although there are already available many accounts of historical methods written by historians for historians, historically-minded sociologists have evidently either not consulted these or have not found them satisfactory. It would seem that such sociologists require a study of historical methods addressed to their own concerns. Indeed, a call for such assistance was made over a decade ago; but to the best of my knowledge, the need has yet to be supplied.[53]

Conclusion

This survey suggests that the most fruitful way to realise social history's totalising ambitions will be to redress its relationships of closure and asymmetry with the historical disciplines on the one hand, and the social sciences on the other. With respect to the historical disciplines, social history must actively seek to integrate itself both with State historiography and with the historical study of 'high' culture: it is now high time to create a unified historical discipline. As regards the social sciences, historians at large can and should begin to 'speak outwards', taking up the new opportunities opened by recent developments in the social sciences themselves, especially the rise of historical sociology. To this end, historians should develop a more sophisticated methodological understanding of their own discipline. This will entail an attention to 'historical metaphysics'; the cultivation of conceptual reflexivity; and a greater interest in those practical procedures by which they reconstruct their accounts of the past. I take up the latter issue in the final chapter of this book.

metaphysics: the theoretical philosophy of being & knowing

Acknowledgments

For their help in the writing of this essay I wish to thank Alessandra d'Acconti, John Forrester, Mark Goldie, Felicity Hunt, Patrick Joyce, Maria Kiely, Philippa Levine, Paul Nixon, Brian Outhwaite, Andrew Pickering, Simon Schaffer, Keith Snell and Tony Sutcliffe. I am also grateful to Colin Brooks and Peter Hennock, who first encouraged me to reflect critically upon social history. Special thanks go to Timothy Ashplant, both for present help and for his sustained

reflexivity: of mental operations — turned or directed back on the mind itself
concept

historiographic advice and encouragement; and to Mike Woodhouse
for reading part of the text, discussing it with me, and offering many
valuable corrections. Those who have helped so generously are of
course not responsible for the errors that remain.

Notes

1 For different classifications see John Tosh, *The Pursuit of History:
   aims, methods and new directions in the study of modern history*,
   (London: Longman, 1984), pp. 82–5 (1992 edn, pp. 96–7); Pat Thane
   and Tony Sutcliffe, 'Introduction', in Thane and Sutcliffe eds., *Essays
   in Social History*, vol. 2 (for the Economic History Society, Oxford:
   Clarendon Press, 1986), pp. vii–xxxiv, at pp. ix–xvi. The term
   'social-history paradigm' has also been used by Patrick Joyce, though
   with a somewhat different meaning, in his contribution to the debate
   in *Past and Present* cited in note 20 below.

2 The account sketched below is indebted to Fritz Stern ed., *The
   Varieties of History From Voltaire to the Present* (London: Macmillan,
   1956); Arthur Marwick, *The Nature of History* (London: Macmillan,
   1970); John Kenyon, *The History Men: the historical profession in
   England since the Renaissance* (London: Weidenfeld, 1983); D.C.
   Coleman, *History and the Economic Past: an account of the rise and
   decline of economic history in Britain* (Oxford: Clarendon Press,
   1987); Alon Kadish, *Historians, Economists, and Economic History*
   (London: Routledge, 1989); G.M. Trevelyan, *English Social History*
   (first published 1942; cited below from 1973 edition, London:
   Longman); Miranda Chaytor and Jane Lewis, 'Introduction' to Alice
   Clark, *Working Life of Women in the Seventeenth Century* (London:
   Routledge, 1982 reprint; first published 1919; see also the 1992
   reprint with a new introduction by Amy Louise Erickson).

3 William Stubbs, *Constitutional History of England* (3 vols., 1874–8);
   Samuel Rawson Gardiner, *A History of England . . . 1603–16* (2 vols.,
   1863) and subsequent works; John Seeley, *The Expansion of Eng-
   land* (1883), quoted from Kenyon, *The History Men*, p. 170; J.R.
   Green, *A Short History of the English People* (1874); Arnold Toynbee,
   *Lectures on the Industrial Revolution of the Eighteenth Century in
   England* (posthumously published, 1884); J.E. Thorold Rogers,
   History of Agriculture and Prices in England (8 vols., 1866–1902);
   William Cunningham, *The Growth of English Industry and Com-
   merce* (1882). Ecclesiastical history can be regarded as a marginal
   case of State historiography; see Owen Chadwick, 'Dr Samuel Johnson
   and the Dixie Professorship of Ecclesiastical History', *Journal of
   Ecclesiastical History* 35 (4), October 1984, pp. 583–96. On

Cunningham see Kadish, *Historians, Economists, and Economic History*, pp. 141–6.

4 For the possibility that Thorold Rogers might have been appointed to the Oxford Regius chair in 1866, see Christopher Harvie, *The Lights of Liberalism: university liberals and the challenge of democracy 1860–86* (London: Allen Lane, 1976), p. 127. Bryce is quoted, with emphasis added, from Stern ed, *Varieties of History*, p. 175; for his authorship of the 'Prefatory Note' to the *Economic History Review* see Kenyon, *The History Men*, p. 192.

5 For Trevelyan's vision of a continuing literary tradition, deployed against Bury's version of scientific history, see his essay 'Clio Rediscovered' of 1903 and 1913, abridged in Stern ed., *Varieties of History*, pp. 227–45. I quote from p. 242, where Trevelyan counterposed against scientific history such writers as 'Motley, Froude, Lecky, Green, Symonds, Spencer Walpole, Leslie Stephen, John Morley'. Despite including Green, Trevelyan made no explicit mention here of social or economic history. On Trevelyan see the recent biography by David Cannadine, *G.M. Trevelyan: a life in history* (London: Harper Collins, 1992). Note that the theme of religion was pursued, though of course in very different ways, both in State historiography (see Chadwick, 'Dixie Professorship') and in social history (especially by Tawney). On imperial history see Frederick Madden and D.K. Fieldhouse eds., *Oxford and the Idea of Commonwealth* (London: Croom Helm, 1982). On the shifting concerns of State historiography, see P.B.M. Blaas, *Continuity and Anachronism: Parliamentary and constitutional development in Whig historiography and in the anti-Whig reaction between 1890 and 1930* (The Hague: Nijhoff, 1978); Christopher Parker, *The English Historical Tradition Since 1850* (Edinburgh: John Donald, 1990).

6 Eileen Power's attitude to the question of audience is nicely suggested by the following discussion of Neale's popular success with his 1934 biography of Queen Elizabeth: 'Someone said to . . . Power: "He has sold the pass". Power . . . replied: "He has also sold 20,000 copies"' (Kenyon, *The History Men*, p. 207). The studies of Hill, Clark and Pinchbeck were supplemented by the interesting work of an American scholar: Wanda Neff, *Victorian Women Workers: an historical and literary study of women in British industries and professions 1832–1850* (London: Allen and Unwin, 1929; reprinted by Cass, 1966).

7 Trevelyan, *English Social History*, p. vii. Trevelyan dedicated this book 'to the memory of Eileen Power, economic and social historian', and his citations were strongly inclined towards the populist tradition. Thus he quietly footnoted the Hammonds and delicately criticised Clapham (without hinting at the battle that had raged between them), mentioned Tawney and Cunningham, and used the

work of many of the women historians (George, James, Jones, Leonard, Pinchbeck, Power, Green, Taylor, Wood-Legh) – though not, so far as I have found, Alice Clark, Wanda Neff or the Webbs (see pp. 24, 35, 55, 91, 96, 171, 205, 229, 251, 287, 342–3, 362, 364, 370, 381, 485, 486, 543, 545). Herbert Butterfield, *The Englishman and his History* (Cambridge University Press, 1944), to be contrasted of course with his earlier *The Whig Interpretation of History* (London: Bell, 1931).

8 A.L. Morton, *A People's History of England* (London: Gollancz and Left Book Club, 1938).

9 Others of this generation were V. Gordon Childe, Victor Kiernan, and George Thomson. See Raphael Samuel, 'British Marxist Historians, 1880–1980', *New Left Review* **120** (1980), pp. 42–55; Bill Schwartz, 'The People in History: the Communist Party Historians' Group 1946–56', in S. Hall *et al.* eds., *Making Histories* (London: Hutchinson, 1982), pp. 44–95; Harvey J. Kaye, *The British Marxist Historians* (Oxford: Polity, 1984); Harvey J. Kaye, 'E.P. Thompson, the British Marxist Historical Tradition and the Contemporary Crisis', in Harvey J. Kaye and Keith McClelland eds., *E.P. Thompson: critical perspectives* (Cambridge: Polity, 1990), pp. 252–75.

10 J.S.A. Adamson, 'Eminent Victorians: S.R. Gardiner and the Liberal as Hero', *The Historical Journal* **33** (1990), pp. 641–57, at p. 641; Linda Colley, 'The politics of eighteenth-century British historiography', *Journal British Studies* **25** (1986), pp. 359–79, at pp. 361, 373 (for some blows in the battle see J.C.D. Clark, *English Society 1688–1832: ideology, social structure and political practice during the ancien regime* (Cambridge University Press, 1985); and John Brewer, *The Sinews of Power: war, money and the English state, 1688–1783* (London: Unwin Hyman, 1989)); Roy Foster, 'What is political history?', in Juliet Gardiner ed., *What is History Today?* (London: Macmillan, 1988; essays published in *History Today* 1984–5), pp. 23–5, at p. 24.

11 E.P. Thompson, 'The peculiarities of the English', in Ralph Miliband and John Saville eds., *The Socialist Register* No. 2 (1965), reprinted in *The Poverty of Theory and Other Essays* (London: Merlin, 1978), pp. 35–91, at p. 47; Philip Corrigan and Derek Sayer, *The Great Arch: English state formation as cultural revolution* (Oxford: Blackwell, 1985); John Saville, *1848: the British State and the Chartist movement* (Cambridge University Press, 1987). Another exception was Royden Harrison's *Before the Socialists: studies in labour and politics 1861–1881* (London: Routledge, 1965).

12 Geoff Eley, 'Edward Thompson, social history and political culture: the making of a working-class public, 1780–1850', in Kaye and McClelland eds., *E.P. Thompson: critical perspectives*, pp. 12–49, at

pp. 36–9; Harvey Kaye, 'E.P. Thompson, the British Marxist historical tradition, and the contemporary crisis', in *ibid.*, p. 259.

13 The most illuminating discussion of the *Annales* school is Stuart Clark, 'The *Annales* historians', in Quentin Skinner ed., *The Return of Grand Theory in the Human Sciences* (Cambridge University Press, 1985), pp. 177–98. See also Traian Stoianovich, *French Historical Method: the Annales Paradigm* (Cornell, University Press, 1976); Peter Burke, *The French Historical Revolution: the Annales school, 1929–89* (Cambridge: Polity, 1990). On *mentalité* see especially Geoffrey Lloyd, *Demystifying Mentalities* (Cambridge University Press, 1990); also Rodney Needham, *Belief, Language, and Experience* (Oxford: Blackwell 1972); and Michael A. Gismondi, ' "The gift of theory": a critique of the *histoire des mentalités*', *Social History* 10 (1985), pp. 211–30.

14 Keith Thomas, 'The tools and the job', *Times Literary Supplement*, 1966, pp. 275–6 (the leading article in a special issue entitled 'New Ways in History').

15 On the institutional developments, see Harold Perkin, 'Social History in Britain', *Journal of Social History* 10 (1976), pp. 129–43, and Coleman, *History and the Economic Past*, Chapter 6. For Power and Tawney on the social sciences, see *ibid.*, pp. 89–90; on Stone, see 'Epilogue: Lawrence Stone – as seen by himself', in A.L. Beier, D. Cannadine and J.M. Rosenheim eds., *The First Modern Society: essays in English history in honour of Lawrence Stone* (Cambridge, 1989), pp. 575–95.

16 Peter Laslett, *The World We Have Lost* (London: Methuen, 1971 edn), p. 164; Alan Macfarlane, *The Family Life of Ralph Josselin, a Seventeenth-century Clergyman: an essay in historical anthropology* (Cambridge University Press 1970); Keith Thomas, *Religion and the Decline of Magic: studies in popular beliefs in sixteenth- and seventeenth-century England* (London: Weidenfeld and Nicolson, 1971; Penguin edition, 1973, pp. 227–42); Lawrence Stone, *The Causes of the English Revolution 1529–1642* (London: Routledge, 1972); Emmanuel Le Roy Ladurie, 'From Waterloo to Colyton' (1966 and 1979), cited by Landers, this volume, Chapter 4.

17 H.J. Perkin, 'Social history', in H.P.R. Finberg ed., *Approaches to History: a symposium* (London: Routledge, 1962), pp. 51–82, *passim*, particularly pp. 68, 74, 80f (for some links with history-of-the-people see pp. 74, 81); E.H. Carr, *What Is History?* (London: Macmillan, 1961), p. 118; Thomas, 'The tools and the job', p. 276; Jacques Le Goff, 'Is politics still the backbone of history?', *Daedalus* (1971), pp. 1–19, at p. 1.

18 Trevelyan, *English Social History*, p. vii; Eric Hobsbawm, 'From social history to the history of society', *Daedalus* C (1971), pp. 20–45; Asa

Briggs, 'A message from the president', *Social History Society Newsletter* **1** (1) (Spring 1976), p. 1. Thane and Sutcliffe (*Essays in Social History*) distinguish 'total history' (pp. x–xi) from social history as an 'integrating praxis' (pp. xv–xvi), but as they describe them these seem to amount to the same ambition.

19 Peter Burke, 'Overture: the new history, its past and its future', in Burke ed., *New Perspectives on Historical Writing* (Cambridge: Polity 1991), pp. 1–23, at p. 7; David Cannadine, 'What is social history?', in Gardiner ed., *What is History Today?*, pp. 54–6, at p. 55.

20 The most accessible introduction to the now burgeoning literature on women's history and the perspective of gender is Joan Wallach Scott, *Gender and the Politics of History* (New York: Columbia University Press, 1988). Various viewpoints are collected in the essays on 'What Is Women's History?', in Gardiner ed., *What is History Today?*, pp. 82–95. On the link between the linguistic turn and postmodernism, see the debate in *Past and Present* on 'History and post-modernism': *Past and Present*, nos. **131** (1991), pp. 217–18 (Lawrence Stone); **133** (1991), pp. 204–13 (Patrick Joyce, Catriona Kelly); and **135** (1992), pp. 189–208 (Stone again, Gabrielle M. Spiegel).

21 An overview can be gained from two recent collections with helpful introductory essays: Peter Burke and Roy Porter eds., *The Social History of Language* (Cambridge University Press, 1987) and Penelope J. Corfield ed., *Language, History and Class* (Oxford: Blackwell, 1991). Other relevant discussions include Peter Schottler, 'Historians and discourse analysis', *History Workshop Journal* **27** (1989), pp. 37–65; Raphael Samuel, 'Reading the Signs', *ibid.*, **32** (1991), pp. 88–109; Tosh, *The Pursuit of History* (1992 edn), pp. 86–90; Jean-Jacques Lecercle, 'Postmodernism and language', in Roy Boyne and Ali Rattansi eds., *Postmodernism and Society* (London: Macmillan 1990), pp. 76–96.

22 The pioneering essay in labour history's linguistic turn was Gareth Stedman Jones, 'Rethinking Chartism', in his *Languages of Class: studies in English working class history 1832–1982* (Cambridge University Press, 1983), pp. 90–178. Illuminating responses and critiques include Joan Wallach Scott, 'On language, gender and working-class history', in her *Gender and the Politics of History*, pp. 53–67; David Mayfield and Susan Thorne, 'Social history and its discontents: Gareth Stedman Jones and the politics of language', *Social History* **17** (1992), pp. 165–88; and Saville, *1848*. Bryan D. Palmer, *Descent into Discourse: the reification of language and the writing of social history* (Philadelphia: Temple University Press, 1990) is notable for its sustained hostility. Another strand of the linguistic turn is represented in the recent work of Patrick Joyce: see his *Visions of the People:*

Industrial England and the question of class 1848–1914 (Cambridge University Press, 1991) and his (ed.) *The Historical Meanings of Work* (Cambridge University Press, 1987). See also the debate in *Past and Present*, cited in note 20 above, and the separate debate between John Smail and Adrian Randall in the pages of *Social History*: Smail, 'New languages for labour and capital: the transformation of discourse in the early years of the Industrial Revolution', 12 (1987), pp. 49–71; Randall, 'New languages or old? Labour, capital and discourse in the Industrial Revolution', 15 (1990), pp. 195–216; Smail, 'New languages? Yes indeed: a reply to Adrian Randall', 16 (1991), pp. 217–22.

23 Ludwig Wittgenstein, *Philosophical Investigations* (trans. G.E.M. Anscombe; Oxford University Press, 1953).

24 An oblique yet eloquent testimony to the in-principle openness of history is Foucault's critique of the transcendental subject. On the one hand, Foucault argued that this hypostatised subject was an illusion manufactured by historians. On the other hand, the means he adopted to destroy this illusion was precisely the study of history. See Mark Poster, *Foucault, Marxism and History: mode of production versus mode of information* (Cambridge: Polity Press, 1984), Chapter 1; Gary Wickham, 'The currency of history for sociology', in Stephen Kendrick, Pat Straw and David McCrone eds., *Interpreting the Past, Understanding the Present* (London: Macmillan, 1990; British Sociological Association conference volume series 'Explorations in Sociology', vol. 30), pp. 38–58, at p. 43.

25 Wrightson, 'The enclosure of social history', this volume, Chapter 2; Joan Wallach Scott, 'Women's history', in Peter Burke ed., *New Perspectives on Historical Writing* (Cambridge: Polity, 1991), Chapter 3.

26 Lawrence Stone, 'Prosopography', reprinted in *The Past and the Present* (London: Routledge, 1981), p. 73; Elizabeth Fox-Genovese and Eugene Genovese, 'The political crisis of social history', *Journal of Social History* 10 (1976), pp. 205–20, reprinted in their *Fruits of Merchant Capital* (1983); Tony Judt, 'A clown in regal purple: social history and the historian', *History Workshop* 7 (1979), pp. 66–94; Geoff Eley and Keith Nield, 'Why does social history ignore politics?', *Social History* 5 (1980), pp. 249–71; Gareth Stedman Jones, 'Rethinking Chartism'; Thane and Sutcliffe, *Essays in Social History* p. xv; Patrick Collinson, *De Republica Anglorum: or, history with the politics put back* (Inaugural Lecture delivered 9 November 1989 as Regius Professor of Modern History at Cambridge (Cambridge University Press, 1990); Eley, 'Edward Thompson, social history and political culture', p. 39; David Cressy, 'Purification, thanksgiving, and the churching of women in post-Reformation England', *Past and*

Present. See also Le Goff, 'Is politics still the backbone of history?';
Glenn Burgess, 'On revisionism: An analysis of early Stuart
historiography in the 1970s and 1980s', *The Historical Journal* 33
(1990), pp. 609–27, at p. 612; Dror Wahrmann, 'National society,
communal culture: an argument about the recent historiography of
eighteenth-century Britain', Social *History* 17 (1) (1992), pp. 43–72,
at p. 69. The two reviews in the *Journal of British Studies* 25 (1986)
were Linda Colley, 'The politics of eighteenth-century British historiography', pp. 359–79 (who expressed concern over the political-
social history relationship at pp. 361, 373); and R.A. Houston, 'British
society in the eighteenth century', pp. 436–66. Studies of the middle
class: Peter Earle, *The Making of the English Middle Class: business,
society and family life in London, 1660–1730* (London: Methuen
1989); Leonore Davidoff and Catherine Hall, *Family Fortunes:
men and women of the English middle class, 1780–1850* (London:
Hutchinson, 1987). *Continuity and Change* deals with law, social
structure and demography (potentially making contact with State
historiography through the theme of law); *Rural History*, in explicit
homage to *Annales ESC*, with economy, society and culture.

27 Gertrude Himmelfarb, *The New History and the Old* (Cambridge,
Mass: Harvard, and London: Belknap, 1987), p. 21.

28 W.A. Speck, *Tory and Whig: the struggle in the constituencies, 1701–
15* (London: Macmillan, 1970); Derek Hirst, *The Representative of
the People?* (Cambridge University Press, 1975); Mark A. Kishlansky,
*Parliamentary Selection: social and political choice in early modern
England* (Cambridge University Press, 1986); John Brewer, *The
Sinews of Power: war and the English state, 1688–1783* (London:
Unwin Hyman, 1989); Geoffrey Elton, 'What is political history?'
and J.C.D. Clark, 'What is social history?' in Juliet Gardiner ed.,
What is History Today? (London: Macmillan, 1988), pp. 19–21, 51–
2, quoted from pp. 21, 52; see also the further essays on these themes
in *ibid.*, pp. 18–30, 42–57 (originally published in *History Today*,
1984–5).

29 Peter Laslett, *The World We Have Lost* (London: Methuen, 1965;
1971 edn, pp. 84–91); Marwick, *The Nature of History*, pp. 138–41;
Michael Anderson, *Family Structure in Nineteenth-Century Lancashire* (Cambridge University Press, 1971); Laslett, 'The wrong way
through the telescope: a note on the use of literary evidence in sociology and historical sociology', *British Journal of Sociology* 27 (1976),
pp. 319–42; W.A. Speck, *Society and Literature in England 1700–
60* (Dublin: Gill and Macmillan, 1983). On the 'new historicism',
see J.R. de J. Jackson, *Historical Criticism and the Meaning of
Texts* (London: Routledge, 1989); and H.A. Veeser ed., *The New
Historicism* (London: Routledge, 1989). For a recent response by a

historian, see David Cressy, 'Foucault, Stone, Shakespeare and social history', *English Literary Renaissance* **21** (1991), pp. 121–33.

30 Ian Watt, *The Rise of the Novel: studies in Defoe, Richardson and Fielding* (London: Chatto and Windus, 1957; reprinted Hogarth Press, 1987); Terry Eagleton, *The Rape of Clarissa* (Minneapolis: University of Minnesota Press, 1982); John Barrell, *English Literature in History 1730–80: an equal, wide survey* (London: Hutchinson, 1983); Rosemary Bechler, ' "Triall by what is Contrary": Samuel Richardson and Christian dialectic', in Valerie Grosvenor Myer ed., *Samuel Richardson: passion and prudence* (London: Vision, 1986), pp. 93–113; Jane Spencer, *The Rise of the Woman Novelist: from Aphra Behn to Jane Austen* (Oxford: Blackwell, 1986); Dale Spender, *Mothers of the Novel: 100 good women writers before Jane Austen* (London: Routledge, 1986); Nancy Armstrong, *Desire and Domestic Fiction: a political history of the novel* (Oxford University Press, 1987); M. McKeon, *The Origins of the English Novel 1600–1740* (Baltimore: Johns Hopkins University Press, 1987); Lincoln B. Faller, *Turned to Account: the forms and functions of criminal biography in late seventeenth- and early eighteenth-century England* (Cambridge University Press, 1987); A.D. Harvey, *Literature into History* (Macmillan, 1988); J. Paul Hunter, *Before Novels: the cultural context of eighteenth century fiction* (New York and London: W.W. Norton, 1990); Richard Kroll, *The Material Word: literate culture in the Restoration and early eighteenth century* (Baltimore and London: Johns Hopkins University Press, 1991); Ros Ballaster, *Women's Amatory Fiction 1684–1740* (Oxford: Clarendon Press, 1993).

31 In addition to the works cited in note 45 below, an accessible introduction to the new historiography of science is provided by recent biographies of perhaps the three most important individual figures of nineteenth-century British science: Geoffrey Cantor, *Michael Faraday, Sandemanian and scientist: a study in nineteenth-century religion and science* (London: Macmillan, 1991); Adrian Desmond and James Moore, *Darwin* (London: Michael Joseph, 1991); Crosbie Smith and Norton Wise, *Energy and Empire: a biographical study of Lord Kelvin* (Cambridge University Press, 1989).

32 Roy Porter, 'The history of science and the history of society', in R.C. Olby, G.N. Cantor, J.R.R. Christie and M.J.S. Hodge eds., *Companion to the History of Modern Science* (London: Routledge, 1990), Chapter 3.

33 Thomas, 'The tools and the job'; Thomas, *Religion and the Decline of Magic* (1971); Lawrence Stone, *The Causes of the English Revolution 1529–1642* (London: Routledge, 1972); Peter N. Stearns, 'Coming of Age', *Journal of Social History* 1976 **10** (2), pp. 246–55, at p. 255 (Stearns was arguing that social history should attain

'recognition as a separate discipline with its own identity', independent
both from 'conventional' history and from the social sciences: p.
254); Stone, *The Past and the Present* Chapters 1, 3 (essays first
published in 1976 and 1979); Philip Abrams, *Historical Sociology*
(Shepton Mallet: Open Books, 1982), p. 318; Corfield, 'Introduction'
to Corfield ed., *Language and Class*, p. 20; Burke, 'Introduction' in
Burke and Porter eds., *The social history of language* (Cambridge
University Press, 1987), p. 17; Cynthia Hay, 'What is sociological
history?', in Stephen Kendrick, Pat Straw and David McCrone eds.,
Interpreting the Past, Understanding the Present (London: Macmillan,
1990; British Sociological Association conference volume series *Explorations in Sociology*, vol. 30), pp. 20–37, at pp. 22–3, 29.

34   For some claims by historians that history can in fact shed light on
the concerns of the social sciences, see E.P. Thompson, *The Making
of the English Working Class*, (first published by Gollancz, 1963;
cited here from Pelican edition, 1968) pp. 9–12, esp. pp. 11–12;
Hexter, *Doing History*, pp. 127–34; Elton, *The Practice of History*,
p. 55; E.P. Thompson, 'Anthropology and the discipline of historical
context', *Midland History* 1 (1972), pp. 41–55, at p. 46; Robert
Gray, 'History, Marxism and theory', in Harvey J. Kaye and Keith
McClelland eds., *E.P. Thompson: critical perspectives* (Cambridge:
Polity, 1990), pp. 153–182, at p. 177; Tosh, *The Pursuit of History*,
1984 edn, p. 136; 1992 edn, p. 163.

35   See Allan Megill, 'The reception of Foucault by historians', *Journal
of the History of Ideas* 48 (1987), pp. 117–41, at pp. 119f.

36   On the issue of choice, it has been argued that the historian should
specifically get to know the social sciences by unsystematic, random
access: J.H. Hexter, *Doing History*, pp. 113–16. The translation
problem is addressed, though indirectly and in largely implicit fashion, by Peter Burke, *Sociology and History* (London: Allen and Unwin,
1980), and by Abrams, *Historical Sociology*.

37   See 'Epilogue: Lawrence Stone – as seen by himself', in Beier *et al.*
eds., *The First Modern Society*, pp. 575–95, at pp. 592–3 (restless
quest), 580 (last of the Whigs), 584–5 (Marxism), 585, 588 (Weber),
588–9 (modernisation theory), 590 (Freud), 593 (Parsonian functionalism, French structuralism and linguistic deconstruction), 584,
591 (*Annales*). Stone's rejection of his youthful Marxism may perhaps be connected with his voluntarism, though he himself attributes
this shift in his thinking to 'close contact with the empirical evidence'
(p. 585). For his objections to functionalism and to the 'immobile
history' of the *Annales* school, see also *The Past and the Present*, pp.
9–11, 79 (essays first published in 1976 and 1979 respectively). On
the link between Whig interpretation and social-science categories in

the particular case of Stone's *The Causes of the English Revolution*
see Burgess, 'On revisionism', p. 612.

38 There are some similarities between Stone's outlook and that of Keith
Thomas, who also writes from a progressivist standpoint and deploys
Weber in lieu of Marx; but there are also differences, for Thomas
inclines to functionalism whereas Stone is hostile to this. See Alan
Macfarlane, *The Culture of Capitalism* (Oxford: Blackwell, 1987),
pp. 77–97, 102–3; Stone, *The Past and the Present*, pp. 9–11. A
different case again, though once more hostile to Marxism, is Peter
Laslett: see *The World We Have Lost* (London: Methuen, 1965). E.H.
Carr's distinctive metaphysic had affinities with both Whig and
Marxist approaches; his famous 'dialogue between past and present'
turned out to entail 'a dialogue between the events of the past and
progressively emerging future ends': see Carr, *What Is History?*, p.
118. On Gertrude Himmelfarb's metaphysic see above (pp. 27–8).

39 Emile Durkheim, *Le suicide: étude de sociologie* (Paris: Alcan, 1897);
translated by J.A. Spaulding and G. Simpson as *Suicide: a study in
sociology* (Glencoe, Ill.: Free Press of Glencoe, 1951; London:
Routledge, 1952).

40 In addition to the works cited below, see Peter Winch, *The Idea
of a Social Science and its Relation to Philosophy* (London: Routledge, 1958); Donna Haraway, *Simians, Cyborgs and Women:
the reinvention of nature* (London: Free Association, 1991). On
hermeneutics, see Josef Bleicher, *Contemporary Hermeneutics:
hermeneutics as method, philosophy and critique* (Routledge, 1980);
Paul Ricoeur, *Hermeneutics and the human sciences: essays on language, action and interpretation* (trans. and ed. John Thompson;
Cambridge University Press, 1981); John B. Thompson, *Critical
Hermeneutics: a study in the thought of Paul Ricoeur and Jurgen
Habermas* (Cambridge University Press, 1981); Susan J. Hekman,
Hermeneutics and the Sociology of Knowledge (Cambridge: Polity,
1986); Jurgen Habermas, *The Philosophical Discourse of Modernity:
Twelve lectures* (trans. Frederick Lawrence; Cambridge: Polity, 1987);
Agnes Heller, 'From hermeneutics in social science toward a
hermeneutics of social science', *Theory and Society* 18 (1989), pp.
291–322.

41 Bruno Latour, *Science in Action* (Milton Keynes: Open University
Press, 1987), p. 257; Latour, 'Postmodern? No, simply amodern.
Steps towards an anthropology of science', *Studies in the History and
Philosophy of Science* 21 (1990), pp. 145–71; Anthony Giddens, *The
Constitution of Society: outline of the theory of structuration*
(Cambridge: Polity, 1984) *passim*, e.g. p. 355; John A. Hall, 'They
do things differently there, or, the contribution of British historical

sociology', *British Journal of Sociology* **40** (1989), pp. 544–64, at
pp. 553–7; Geoffrey Hawthorn, *Enlightenment and Despair* (Cambridge University Press, 1987), p. 269.

42 Michel Foucault, *The Order of Things: an archaeology of the human
    sciences* (London: Tavistock, 1970; French original 1966), pp. 357–
    8; Ernesto Laclau and Chantal Mouffe, *Hegemony and Socialist
    Strategy: towards a radical democratic politics* (trans. Winston Moore
    and Paul Cammack; London: Verso, 1985), *passim*. On the argument
    of Laclau and Mouffe, see Patrick Curry's essay in the present vol-
    ume (Chapter 6), and Michelle Barrett, *The Politics of Truth: From
    Marx to Foucault* (Cambridge: Polity, 1991), Chapter 3. Barrett also
    cites other relevant literature: see for instance pp. 64ff, 75.

43 Derek Sayer, *The Violence of Abstraction: the analytic foundations
    of historical materialism* (Oxford: Blackwell, 1978), p. 139. Starting-
    points for such a historical critique would include Hawthorn, *En-
    lightenment and Despair*; Wolf Lepenies, *Between Literature and
    Science: the rise of sociology* (1985, trans. 1988); Bruce Mazlish, *A
    New Science: the breakdown of connections and the birth of sociol-
    ogy* (Oxford University Press, 1989). For some criticisms of Sayer's
    study see David Parker, 'French absolutism, the English state and the
    utility of the base-superstructure model', *Social History* **15** (1990),
    pp. 287–301, at pp. 291, 294, 297.

44 An early intimation of the impossibility of the sociologist's detached
    position was Alvin W. Gouldner, *The Coming Crisis of Western
    Sociology* (London: Heinemann, 1971).

45 Thomas Kuhn, *The Structure of Scientific Revolutions* (University of
    Chicago Press, 1962); David Bloor, *Knowledge and Social Imagery*
    (London: Routledge 1976; 2nd ed. University of Chicago Press, 1991);
    Charles Webster, *The Great Instauration* (London: Duckworth, 1975).
    An outstanding example of the new historiography is Steven Shapin
    and Simon Schaffer, *Leviathan and the Air-Pump: Hobbes, Boyle
    and the experimental life* (Princeton University Press, 1985). The strong
    programme has spawned a vast literature and has stimulated a still-
    widening debate. The 'interest theory' which it deploys has been
    subjected to critique, particularly from the perspectives of ethno-
    methodology and discourse analysis, and is now contested by the
    more recent 'actor network theory' of Bruno Latour, Michel Callon
    and John Law. For some recent surveys see Olby *et al.* eds., *Com-
    panion to the History of Modern Science* (London: Routledge),
    Chapters 1, 5, 6, 7, 8 and 9. The current state of the art is conveyed
    by Andrew Pickering ed., *Science as Practice and Culture* (University
    of Chicago Press, 1992), which includes some intense polemical ex-
    changes; Simon Schaffer, 'The Eighteenth Brumaire of Bruno Latour',
    Studies in the History and Philosophy of Science **22** (1991), pp. 174–

92; and Nicholas Jardine, *The Scenes of Inquiry* (Oxford: Clarendon Press, 1991).

46 Bloor did not explicitly specify any source for his concept of reflexivity: a possible source was Gouldner, *The Coming Crisis of Western Sociology*, Chapter 13. See also Hekman, *Hermeneutics and the Sociology of Knowledge*, pp. 56–75, who derives from Mannheim an analogous concept of 'relational knowledge', seen at one point (p. 60) as 'reflexivity', but does not cite Gouldner, Bloor or the strong-programme tradition.

47 There seems to be no consensus as to what constitutes historical sociology; different commentators emphasise different traditions and groupings. If Giddens and Abrams may be bracketed together as representing one strand (which itself can be disputed), at least three other such strands need to be distinguished: the Leicester tradition from Norbert Elias to Eric Dunning; such historical synthesisers and comparativists as Barrington Moore, Perry Anderson, Theda Skocpol and Michael Mann; and the 'new economic sociology', exemplified by Braverman. In addition to the references cited below, see J.A. Banks, 'From universal history to historical sociology', *British Journal of Sociology* 40 (1989), pp. 521–543; Hall, 'They do things differently there'; Dennis Smith, *The Rise of Historical Sociology* (Cambridge: Polity, 1991); and R.C. Helmes-Hayes, ' "From universal history to historical sociology": by J.A. Banks – a critical comment', *British Journal of Sociology* 43 (3) 1992, pp. 333–44.

48 Philip Abrams, *Historical Sociology*; Giddens, *The Constitution of Society*, pp. 212, 219, 358, 362; Charles Tilly, 'Future History', in Kendrick, Straw and McCrone eds., *Interpreting the Past, Understanding the Present*, Chapter 2, pp. 9–19, at pp. 16, 12.

49 Abrams, *Historical Sociology*, p. 333.

50 Christopher Lloyd, *Explanation in Social History*, (Oxford: Basil Blackwell, 1986), p. 15. See also his 'The methodologies of social history: a critical survey and defence of structurism', *History and Theory* 30 (1991), pp. 180–219, and 'Realism, structurism, and history', *Theory and Society* 18 (1989), pp. 451–94. For some interesting critical reflections on the wider tendency for philosophy to be privileged over sociology, see Richard Kilminster, 'Sociology and the professional culture of philosophers', in Hans Haferkamp ed., *Social Structure and Culture* (Berlin/New York: Walter de Gruyter, 1989), pp. 289–312.

51 Theda Skocpol ed., *Vision and Method in Historical Sociology* (Cambridge University Press, 1984), essays by Daniel Chirot, 'The social and historical landscape of Marc Bloch', pp. 22–46, at pp. 43–4; and Theda Skocpol, 'Emerging agendas and recurrent strategies in historical sociology', pp. 356–91, at pp. 366, 368–74, 378–83. For

some criticisms of the applicability of Mill's inductive logic in comparative historical analyses see Michael Burawoy, 'Two methods in search of science: Skocpol versus Trotsky', *Theory and Society* 18 (1989), pp. 759–806.

52 Roger Penn, 'History and sociology in the new economic sociology: a discourse in search of a method', in Kendrick *et al.* eds., *Interpreting the Past, Understanding the Present*, pp. 165–76, pp. 174, 166–7, 170–1 (his emphasis). For a more sympathetic but still critical reading of Braverman's study, see John Foster, 'Conflict at work', *Social History* 14 (1989), pp. 233–41, at p. 240. For some confirmation of Penn's views on historical evidence see Banks, 'From universal history to historical sociology', at p. 540; this issue is not discussed in Hall, 'They do things differently there'.

53 Christopher Vanderpool, reviewing Peter Burke, *Sociology and History* (1980), observed that the book 'introduces to historians the contribution that sociological methods and concepts can make to the development of a viable social history', and concluded: 'Burke should next turn his attention to writing the first methods book in historical sociology, a sociological historiography': *Contemporary Sociology* 10 (1981), pp. 666–7. Historians' accounts of historical method are considered in Chapter 9; very few of these were discussed by Abrams, *Historical Sociology*, and none (so far as I have been able to find) is discussed by Giddens in any of his works. Of the 91 items in the annotated bibliography appended to Skocpol ed., *Vision and Method in Historical Sociology*, about a third were concerned with empirical historical methods; very few of the latter were cited in the body of the book.

The enclosure of English social history* *1990*

It is now roughly a quarter of a century since the proponents of a new social history of early modern England offered students of the period a novel agenda and an unprecedented opportunity.[1] Prior to the 1960s social history had been variously understood as the history of everyday life, of the lower classes and popular movements, or as a junior partner in the relatively recently-established firm of economic and social history (occupied in the main with the study of social institutions and social policy). As such, it had produced more than a few pioneering works of out-standing quality and lasting value (some of them about to enjoy a revived recognition after decades of relative neglect). But it was not a field close to the centre of historical preoccupation. It was at best contextual, at worst residual.

From the early 1960s, however, came a call for a social history of a new type, one conceived as the history of social relationships and of the culture which informs them and gives them meaning. The new agenda was deeply influenced by the social sciences and envisaged an ever closer relationship with sociology, social anthro-pology and demography. Peter Laslett wrote of 'sociological his-tory' or 'historical sociology' and Keith Thomas of the need for a 'more systematic indoctrination' in the concepts and methodolo-gies of the social sciences.[2] As applied to history, all this was both radical and liberating. In the face of an established curriculum which appeared in many respects restrictive and in some desiccated, it proposed a massive and necessary broadening and deepening of historical concern: the creation of a range of historical enquiry appropriate to the preoccupations and understandings of the late twentieth century. Alongside the established and continuing historiographies of politics and government, religion, thought and economic growth, were to be placed histories of family structure, marriage and childhood, adolescence, old age and death; of social stratification and class relations; of popular attitudes and values, literacy, crime and social control; of gender relations and sexuality; of kinship and neighbourhood, deference and resistance, work and leisure, geographical and social mobility, living standards and consumption and the social basis of participation in religious and political movements. The past teemed with questions which had scarcely been asked let alone answered and with untested assumptions which now appeared to demand attention. For these were matters relating to central, though neglected, areas of human experience. If they were considered of little significance in the traditional hierarchy of historical concerns, then that hierarchy needed to be demolished and the subject restructured.

By simply pointing out the existence of a vast array of new subjects for historical investigation, the advocates of a new social history immediately drew attention to an enormous historical opportunity. Former states of being were to be reconstructed and apprehended. Forgotten histories were to be recovered. All this would enable us the better, in Peter Laslett's phrase, to 'understand ourselves in time', to appreciate the actualities of the distant past and the processes of development which shaped our own attitudes and practices, the ancestry of our every act.[3]

But there was also a further area of opportunity: an opportunity to rethink the familiar past as well as to rediscover the unfamiliar. The proposed transformation of the historical landscape would enable us to view conventional landmarks from new perspectives, to perceive unexpected dimensions of established problems, to discern unsuspected interconnections and to draw together accumulating knowledge of the social world of our ancestors into a more meaningful whole. For the new social history was not envisaged as a discrete area of study, another specialisation in a subject already replete with 'hyphenated histories'.[4] On the contrary, it would resist such isolation and compartmentalisation. It would be a meeting point; an intersection linking diverse routes to the past. It would thrive upon the interconnectedness of the historical process and it would transform understanding of the whole. In Thomas' words 'The social history of the future will . . . not be a residual

no longer residual but central

subject but a central one, around which all other branches of history are likely to be organized.'[5]

This, then, was the agenda and the opportunity as they were envisaged a generation ago. Both were exhilarating. 'Bliss was it in that dawn to be alive.' But what has been achieved? Where do we stand now?

First, and most obviously, there has been a vast expansion of historical knowledge. The enthusiasm generated by the clarion calls of the 1960s has remained undimmed even by the contraction of research awards and career opportunities which has overcome the historical profession as a whole. Energetic and imaginative researchers from throughout and beyond the English-speaking world have addressed all the issues listed above as part of the agenda of the new social history, and many more besides. There has been an 'outpouring of historical writing' and an 'enormous elaboration' of the subject matter of modern historiography. If academic history could be defined in the late nineteenth century as 'past politics', it is now, as Professor Collinson has recently observed, 'not so much past politics as past everything'.[6] All this constitutes a massive assault upon the 'structural amnesia' which for centuries expunged fundamental aspects of the structures and dynamics of early modern English society from historical consciousness.[7] The achievement in terms of sheer historical recovery has been such as to exceed the boldest imaginings of those who first proposed a radical restructuring of the territory of the historian. The new history of early modern England, as of other periods, is alive and kicking and the vitality of many of its practitioners is marvellous to behold.

This is not, however, intended to be simply an essay of celebration. For if the achievement has indeed been remarkable, there are also reasons for disquiet as to the extent to which historians have risen to the broader opportunities presented by the new social history. Of these, the most disturbing in my view is a tendency towards what, to adopt a metaphor from the agrarian history of early modern England, I think of as the *enclosure* of English social history: the gradual emergence of an excessive professional specialisation and compartmentalisation.

One aspect of this is a compartmentalisation in time. The historiographical new wave of the 1960s and 1970s affected all

(enclosure ?
periodisation)

periods of recorded history from the ancient world to the twentieth century and the new agenda was vigorously addressed across the whole. More than one voice has been raised to assert that the problems now being explored by historians demand chronological perspectives of their own: an awareness of what Laslett has called 'social structural time'.[8] Examples certainly exist of historians who have recognised the force of such arguments and chosen to write their history across spans of years appropriate to their concerns.[9] Yet in the main the practitioners of the new social history have remained content to operate within the constraints of an inherited, and for many purposes inappropriate, periodisation. The most obvious manifestation of this is that the social history of modern England tends to be written from a variety of points in the mid to late sixteenth century up to around 1660, and then from around 1760 into the nineteenth century. These two sub-periods have become the focus of activity while the intervening, linking, period has been relatively neglected.

There are certain problems of source survival and continuity which encourage such a chronological concentration and unevenness of development. In the main, however, it remains more a matter of habit and inclination than of necessity. Historians schooled in the literature of sub-periods which originated because of their supposed appropriateness to the discussion of major developments in political and constitutional history have tended to devote their energies to widening the range of enquiry within these familiar units of time. As a result we have two largely distinct historiographies. This might not matter too much if these were indeed successive historiographies and if determined efforts were made to establish interpretative dialogues across the whole. But with notable exceptions, it can hardly be said that either is the case. Cumulative endeavour and expanding bibliographies (or in the case of the late seventeenth and early eighteenth centuries a relative neglect which has only recently begun to be reduced) have served rather to reinforce and elaborate an artificial separateness. The result is a historiography which is at best uneven and at worst broken-backed.

Much the same, of course, can be said of the distanced relationship of the historiographies of medieval and early modern England, and once again reciprocal influence and interpretative coherence are inhibited by a relatively neglected 'linking' period – in this case the later fifteenth and early sixteenth centuries.[10] But

compartmentalisation by period
1) by subject

there is no need to labour the point. The broader task of 'understanding ourselves in time' is hampered by a chronological specialisation which in the extreme amounts to confinement. This persists not only because of the increasing difficulty of keeping abreast of a rapidly expanding literature within particular subperiods, but also because many historians appear to find it professionally congenial. We live with the consequences in the form of an arbitrary chronological fragmentation which threatens to frustrate the apprehension of long-term processes of continuity and change which was formerly regarded as a primary objective.

Compartmentalisation by period is compounded by compartmentalisation by subject, a problem which has attracted much more critical comment. Whereas we aspired to a history of society, we have produced in effect a cluster of loosely related topics and subject areas. If it can be said of historians in general that nowadays they are commonly 'labelled by one or another set of qualifiers' denoting particular specialisations,[11] social history has proved outstandingly energetic in begetting new sub-disciplines each with its own distinctive identity as a separable area of research. To be sure these do overlap to a greater or lesser extent, but they can also, to a sometimes disturbing degree, be pursued in virtual independence, acquiring in the process what has been called a certain 'hermetic quality'.[12] An historical division of labour which was already fairly advanced has become markedly more complex, creating in the process constellations of activity, worlds within worlds, each with its own degree of introversion, many with journals of their own.

Perhaps all this was simply to be expected. The very success of the new social history and the energy and determination of its practitioners, it might be argued, was bound to lead to a high degree of specialisation, of technical accomplishment and methodological precision. In an expanding historical universe, focused activity is essential if new knowledge is to be assimilated and the quality of analysis and debate are to be advanced. True. And in Durkheimian terms, an elaborating division of labour might be expected ultimately to produce new and more complex forms of integration, of 'organic solidarity'. Perhaps. But the proof of the pudding is in the eating and as yet the signs are not encouraging that such coherence will be achieved, or even that it is being seriously attempted. The problem is that the 'tunnels' of

sub-disciplinary specialisation, once constructed, 'take on an identity, a life of their own. At the same time as focusing historical
enquiry they also narrow it, eliminating great tracts of the past from
the historian's field of vision'.[13] Symptomatic of the consequences
is the fact that a recent reviewer of *The Cambridge Social History
of Britain, 1750–1950*, while praising the excellence of individual
thematic chapters, felt bound to complain that 'the broader contours and implications of social development somehow get lost
sight of', and that the three substantial volumes of this major
collective work provide *prima facie* evidence that 'social history is
in real danger of imminent and unrestrainable fragmentation'.[14]
This seems the more disturbing when one considers two further
tendencies observable within at least some of the currently flourish-
ing areas of specialisation.

One of these is a gradual process of conceptual and interpretative closure. It has been pointed out more than once, and with
some justice, that in the early years of the new social history too
much reliance was placed upon received ideas and interpretative
models borrowed uncritically from the social sciences or from the
more developed historiography of other countries (notably France)
and applied with insufficient sensitivity to particular historical
situations. 'Theoretical work in history', warned Gareth Stedman
Jones, 'is too important to be subcontracted to others'.[15] Yet if
mistakes of this kind now seem less apparent in the social history
of early modern England, this is in part because some newly-
established subject areas have already become complacently bogged-
down within their own particularist agendas of conventional
questions and familiar answers. While a certain amount of internal redecoration and rearrangement of the furniture takes place
within the many mansions of the new historical heaven, their
inhabitants seem to be less prone not only to borrowing the neighbours' labour-saving gadgetry, but also to benefiting from the
stimulation of their conversation. The introduction of fresh perspectives from outside the little boxes of particularism and anglo-
centricity has become rarer and it has not been compensated for
to a significant degree by a conceptual and interpretative crea-
tivity of our own. Historians faced with the difficulties of how to
approach new sets of problems once sought help in the formulation of questions and on occasion made the mistake of accepting
model answers ready made. The current problem is more that

historians working within a fairly developed literature of their own seem insufficiently aware of its limitations, or of the extent to which it sometimes perpetuates sociological archaisms.[16] This can lead to a neglect of larger questions of conceptualisation while focusing attention upon technical problem-solving within particular sub-disciplines.[17] It can produce sterile internal controversies which sputter on unresolved, rather than reinvigorating reconceptualisations of the problems at issue. This threatens a closing of the social-historical mind, a confinement of historical imagination.

Another, and related, tendency is a disinclination to engage with problems of medium and long-term historical change. In part this might be attributable to the influence, either directly or at second-hand, of the synchronic perspectives formerly characteristic of the social sciences. More than a decade ago E.P. Thompson cautioned against the potential dangers of approaches to social analysis more concerned with states of *being* than with processes of *becoming* for history as 'a discipline of context and of process'. Tony Judt similarly argued that social history must not become a form of 'retrospective cultural anthropology', and both warnings retain their relevance.[18]

More significant influences, however, are two developments internal to English social history. One of these is something of a nervous reaction to excessively schematic and empirically ill-supported theories of change which have proved wanting in explanatory conviction and have attracted barrages of hostile criticism sufficient to deter more cautious spirits from interpretative boldness. The other is the cumulative influence of the fragmentation by period and by subject area which has already been described. The former discourages and the latter inhibits attempts at integrated accounts of social change. Where both are operative together constructive historical imagination can be doubly confined, failing as a result to confront the problem of change, or whiling away lost years of opportunity with fantasies of seamless continuity.[19]

Taken together, these various tendencies constitute a gradual process of enclosure. Increasingly, the social history of early modern England is being farmed in chronological, thematic and conceptual severalty. This process proceeds piecemeal and largely, it appears, by agreement. In the short term it might be said to have enhanced productivity and certainly it has not prevented some impressive husbandry within particular fields. The cost, however, may prove to be the disintegration of social history as a community of scholarship expressing its collective identity in the exercise of common grazing rights.

Problems of this kind are not unique to social history, or to the historiography of early modern England.[20] Nevertheless they pose a particular threat to the continued vitality of an approach to the past which was expected to promote a more holistic conception of the historical process, and to the study of a period which witnessed long-term transitions of exceptional significance. For the enclosure of social history serves also to contain the subject's interpretative power. And such containment renders it vulnerable in two ways: first to a form of selective appropriation and secondly to a new kind of marginalisation.

We are perhaps too prone to celebrate the achievements of the new social history and to ignore the very limited nature of its impact on the traditional historical curriculum. Despite their conventionally-assumed affinity, the influence of social history upon the economic history of early modern England has been negligible, with the single exception of historical demography.[21] For the rest, economic historians of the purist school seem content to remain within the confines of their ghetto, albeit somewhat resentful of their reduced circumstances. Political and ecclesiastical history have proved more responsive, but again in rather limited ways. Historians of the 'high' politics of church or state seem for the most part happy to confine their attention to decision making and the pursuit of power at the centre of affairs. They remain secure enough in their conviction of the supreme significance of their own preoccupations and in the central place which these retain in the history of the period as it is taught in most sixth-forms and many universities. Social history has proved influential only where it has proved of value in the explanation of major political and ecclesiastical events, or where it has posed a direct challenge to their interpretation – above all in discussing the origins and significance of the English Civil Wars or the nature of the English Reformation.

That such dialogues have been established at all is of course to the good, and no mean achievement given the inertia of academic curricula. But it must also be recognised that they represent at best a kind of selective cooption and assimilation to the dominant historical tradition. Much of the best and most original work in social history remains outside the historical mainstream. Most students of the period can confidently be expected, for example, to complete their historical education without more than fleeting contact with such outstanding contributions to the historiography of early modern England as Keith Thomas' *Man and the Natural World*, Paul Slack's *The Impact of Plague*, and Michael Macdonald's *Mystical Bedlam*.[22] Such works cannot easily be incorporated into the old agenda. As for the new agenda, its existence is principally to be detected only in the form of a broadened range of specialist options. This situation of partial incorporation is both unsatisfactory in itself and potentially disastrous. It is unsatisfactory because it leaves the old hierarchy of what matters in history essentially intact. Social history is in effect tolerated but subject to a Test Act of significance. It is potentially disastrous because it leaves social history vulnerable to changes in intellectual fashion or political climate which might favour a narrower, more traditional, approach to the past.

Such a prospect might seem unduly alarmist in these still relatively latitudinarian times, but it is not beyond the bounds of possibility. In the United States, Gertrude Himmelfarb has accused social history of rendering historical study incoherent by 'devaluing the political realm' and thereby devaluing 'history itself' and 'reason itself'. Her solution is a restoration of the primacy of politics and government as the core of the historical curriculum.[23] If we have witnessed no such impassioned attacks on social history in Britain in recent years this is scarcely because such views are not held. Rather it is because social history has had a less significant impact upon the basic academic curriculum. Any future decline in English social history would be less likely to be the outcome of open debate over historical priorities than of a contraction of the historical profession and of the range of courses taught in institutions of higher education. The decline of economic history, a process rendered the more possible by that subject's manifest preference for a segregated existence, is instructive. And social history, partly because it has for the most part neither sought nor acquired departmental entrenchment, might be the more easily reduced to its former contextual and residual status.

If so it would be a tragic outcome indeed. For the essential aim of the new *social* history was not that of obtaining a small place in the sun for a novel range of historical enthusiasms. It was a step towards a new *history*, a richer, inclusive, non-hyphenated, non-hierarchical, approach to the past and to the complexity of the causation, costs and benefits of historical change. In projecting such a new history Keith Thomas observed that 'it remains to be seen whether the prevailing system of historical training can generate the flexibility necessary for the new history to sustain itself'.[24] As yet it has not done so. Social historians have tended instead to follow the classic patterns of professional specialisation set by traditional historiography. By doing so they have exacerbated a situation in which 'most knowledge of the past is now fragmented into segments exclusive to small clusters of specialists, so that even members of the historical profession know no more than a tiny fraction of known historical knowledge and the consensually shared past has shrunk to a thin media-dominated veneer'.[25] Means have too often become ends in themselves. The larger purpose of the enterprise remains unfulfilled.

All this may well appear an inappropriately carping and pessimistic assessment. But if this essay appears so far to be a sermon on the theme of 'Social History in Danger', replete with doom-laden rhetoric, it is not intended to disparage or discourage social-historical research. On the contrary, it is, to pursue the enclosure analogy, an incitement to riot.

Personally, I remain optimistic (though not naively so) about both the future of social history and the larger historiographical endeavour of which it is part. If the historiography of the last generation is lacking in overall coordination and coherence, the solution to that problem does not lie in a retreat towards the secure defensive lines of traditional priorities. A far more positive and creative alternative lies in Bernard Bailyn's call for a more determined attempt to integrate the 'latent' and the 'manifest' events of history; to examine 'the active and continuous relationship between the underlying conditions that set the boundaries of human existence and the everyday problems with which people constantly struggle'; to illuminate the landscape surrounding major public events and to reassess them accordingly; to establish 'systems of filiation and derivation among phenomena that once were discussed in isolation from each other'; to relate the public and the private; to 'put the story together again, now with a complexity and an analytical dimension never envisioned before'. The opportunity remains open, as Eric Wolf has argued, not only to produce a new history, but also to overcome the impoverishing fragmentation of the social sciences by reintegrating their perspectives in historical study. I believe, with Peter Laslett, that historians have a duty both to the people of the past and to our own generation to attempt to do so.[26]

In fact the opportunities to reinvigorate the ideal of a new history and to move towards its realisation have never been better. We have a formidable and still expanding historical literature on which to draw if we can bring ourselves to pull down some of our hedges, or at least take the time to pause in our labours and peer over them. We have the collaboration and stimulation of a sociology in which temporality has been restored as a dimension of social analysis and in which theorists like Anthony Giddens and the late Philip Abrams have asserted that history and sociology are now 'methodologically indistinguishable', and engaged in 'a common explanatory project': the reciprocal 'shaping of action by structure and transforming of structure by action . . . as processes in time'.[27] In England, with the expected evolution of Advanced Level History in secondary schools and the rethinking of university and polytechnic courses which this will entail, we also have a chance to provide historical training of a new kind. It is surely not beyond our wit to devise courses which can successfully reintegrate English historiography, and if this is achieved the teaching and the writing of the new history will proceed together.

If all this is so, then the immediate practical issue becomes that of what kind of historical research, writing and teaching we should endeavour to practice and promote. The simple answer is work that attempts to reverse the trends towards chronological, thematic and conceptual enclosure within social history specifically and to advance more generally a reintegrated, interpretatively revitalised, approach to the English past. More specifically, this requires fresh thinking on the questions of periodisation, contextualisation, conceptualisation and representation, coupled with a willingness to undertake more ambitious interpretative synthesis.

To begin with the problem of periodisation, there is an urgent need to break through, or at least loosen, the constraints of a received periodisation. For some this might mean a rejection of conventional terminal dates in order to pursue particular problems over spans of time appropriate to the tracing of significant social change.[28] For others it might mean a determined assault upon those relatively neglected periods which disrupt and distort our sense of the flow of social development.[29] For those whose concerns can properly be pursued within the boundaries of conventionally established periods, it might mean at least a more sensitive awareness of what came before and afterwards and a willingness to develop a broader chronological perspective. Social historians, like their colleagues in more traditional fields, are more prone to emphasise the significance of developments within their own periods of interest than to assess the implications for their arguments of the findings of colleagues working on others. Yet there are enormous potential benefits to be gained by removing the blinkers of chronological specialisation and fostering interpretative dialogues between the largely introverted literatures of different periods.[30]

Secondly, there is an equal need to reintegrate what have become disturbingly discrete subject areas by addressing particular issues in a more thoroughly contextualised manner. This involves not so much the rejection of a necessary division of labour among historians as a willingness to explore the potential interrelationships in time between aspects of social development which are all too often depicted in relative isolation, and recognition of the fact that 'it is precisely in their interconnectedness that the events and phenomena of [a] period can be understood and explained'.[31] Too much otherwise valuable work in social history lacks analytical and explanatory power, or remains essentially descriptive, because of a lack of awareness of the range of variables which might be active in the structuring and restructuring of particular social situations. The current inability, for example, of historians of the family in early modern England to cope with the problems of continuity and change appears to derive ultimately from a failure to reconsider systematically the contextual influences – ideological; legal; economic; demographic; material; sociological and cultural – which might act to sustain or to erode and modify traditional familial practices and values. Yet there are also counter examples of what can be achieved – in Paul Slack's complex and subtle approaches to the social impact of plague, for example, or in the multi-faceted *tour de force* of C.W. Brooks' exploration of the increase of litigation in Tudor and Stuart England[32] – and each successful venture of this kind provides a signal demonstration of the centrality of a social historical perspective to the production of a more inclusive, reintegrated historiography.

A third requirement for a reinvigorated social history is that the subject becomes more explicitly conceptual, more theoretically deliberative. If some areas of English social history have become diminished in interpretative vitality, more imaginatively sluggish, trapped in a series of tired and predictable debates, this is in large part a consequence of its under-theorisation. The answer to this problem lies most obviously in the development of a greater awareness of relevant social theory. This might be achieved by the regular inclusion of appropriate readings in student bibliographies, or by the mounting of special training courses for postgraduates which lay emphasis upon approaches to the shared interpretative problems of history and the social sciences. It is most likely to be successful, however, if social historians themselves take the trouble to set their own work in its appropriate theoretical context; introduce, evaluate and apply relevant concepts in the course of their analysis and go on to develop their own vigorously conceptualised interpretations of the nature of social structures and social processes in past societies. Some, of course, already do this – one thinks immediately of Lawrence Stone, Peter Laslett, or E.P. Thompson – and their influence is correspondingly enormous, not only as instigators of historical debate but in their reciprocal impact upon kindred disciplines. Only if such practice is generalised will social history cease to be either imaginatively dependent upon the social sciences or (worse) a repository for outmoded sociological discourse, and participate fully in the 'common explanatory project' to which I have already alluded.

Finally, and briefly, a concern with more explicit conceptualisation leads naturally to the need to consider more innovative approaches to historical representation. Recent critical theory, mediated through the expanding sub-discipline of cultural history, has led to a new sensitivity to the 'mechanics of representation'. It demands that historians think harder not only about their textual sources, but also about their own analytical and explanatory strategies, about what they actually do when they create texts representing historical processes. Getting the conceptual apparatus by which the 'facts' are ordered up onto the surface of historical texts might well encourage a more critical, self-conscious and ultimately more creative historiography. There is more than enough room for experiments in modes of historical representation, for imaginative forms of sequential analysis, more theoretically deliberative narrative, multiple perspective narratives or still more radical departures in the demonstration and explanation of processes of continuity and change.[33]

All this may well appear to be a counsel of perfection. It threatens to raise immediately the classical scholarly and pedagogical dilemma of whether it is better to do a little well or a lot superficially. What I am suggesting, however, is merely a purposeful consolidation, a redefinition of what we could do well by a relatively modest redeployment of time and energy and what we should do well if social history is to maintain its vitality as an approach to the past. The alternative is to settle for the goal of achieving comprehensive bibliographical mastery of a few dimensions of a relatively narrow period of history and to accept the consequences. But as should be clear from the references cited above, more than a few English social historians are already practising most, if not all, of what is recommended here. All that is truly required is the fostering of such best practice to the degree that it will counteract the rigidities observable in the structures of the discipline.

That accomplished, we might build upon the formidable positive achievements of English social history by attempting those more ambitious interpretative syntheses which might restore a sense of 'the broader contours of social change'. What I have in mind is not the production of textbook compendia of a blandly comprehensive nature, or critical catalogues of recent publications (though both have their value) but works which attempt to characterise and explain the most significant social developments of particular periods and still more works which go beyond this to address the problems of long-term historical change.

It is here above all that a revitalised social history can make its contribution. Conservative critics of the 'new history' appear to have been animated for the most part by a form of intellectual agoraphobia, by anxiety that the diversification of historical activity occasioned by the eruption of social history threatens to destroy both their sense of the flow of history and the values enshrined in the formerly dominant historiographical tradition. ''Tis all in pieces, all coherence gone.' What they lament is the loss of the comforting cadences of a litany of established reference points in time, the canonical hours of historical development. As should be clear, I am not for one moment advocating a return to a narrow and austere, if consensual, canon of what matters in history. Nor, for that matter, do I anticipate what Lynn Hunt has wryly characterised as a classical 'comic ending': one 'that promises reconciliation of all contradictions and tensions'.[34] What I do envisage, however, is a variety of fresh approaches to what David Cannadine has called 'the evolving social landscape' of England's history.[35] These might be structured around any one or more of a number of central themes: class, power, gender, religion, personal identity, political culture, the family, for example. What they should have in common is the attempt to produce, from a variety of perspectives, properly contextualised explanatory accounts of the manner in which social, cultural, economic and institutional structures have been created, maintained and transformed over time.

Without the development of social history in the last quarter century none of this could be envisaged. Yet it can hardly be denied that as an approach to the past social history is at the crossroads. To some the subject appears 'a hard hat area which sometimes seems to threaten us with the kind of intolerant hegemony once exercised by political and constitutional history'.[36] To others it seems 'decidedly soft centred', 'a mindless extension of Trevelyan's original laundry list, an inchoate amalgam of fashionable fads, trivial inanities and prurient sensationalism'.[37] Both characterisations can be hotly disputed. But if forced to choose, I am for hard hats, not in the hope of participating in the exercise of an intolerant hegemony, but in the belief that hard hats are usually worn on busy construction sites. If some of the site workers are busy digging themselves into holes, then at least those holes can be utilised in due course for the laying of foundations by more constructively minded colleagues. Despite its manifest deficiencies, all of which are remediable, social history, broadly defined, remains our best hope of 'understanding ourselves in time'. In its English form it has proved an extraordinary melting pot of influences. The result is a somewhat unstable compound in which can be traced elements of local history, folklore, agrarian and industrial history, the history of ideas, historical geography, demography, political science, sociology and social anthropology, criminology, linguistics, development economics, literary criticism, Marxism, populist radicalism and romantic conservatism, to name but a few. All this constitutes an extraordinarily rich inheritance of empirical expertise and interpretative potential which can be put to work in new and unpredictable ways, if we so choose, to illuminate England's many histories. Looking back to Keith Thomas' rallying call of 1966, it can be said that we have the tools now. If we retain the will to use them well, the job remains as exciting a prospect as ever.

Notes   *written*   *1990*

* This essay is a modified and expanded version of an article originally published in *Rural History* I, 1, 1990. I am grateful to the editors for permission to reproduce much of that article here. In what follows I have chosen not to illustrate negative criticisms with reference to the work of individual historians, since to do so would be unnecessarily invidious. Besides, several of them could be illustrated from my own work. I am primarily concerned with the constraints imposed by certain general characteristics of the social history of early modern England, and in describing them, I by no means exempt myself from criticism.

1 Among the most influential of such calls for a new social history were, in chronological order: K.V. Thomas, 'History and anthropology', *Past and Present*, XXIV, 1963; P. Laslett, *The World We have Lost*, London, 1965; K. Thomas, 'The tools and the job', *Times Literary Supplement*, 7 April 1966; E.J. Hobsbawm, 'From social history to the history of society', *Daedalus*, C, 1971. There was also, of course, the powerful influence of those who taught by example rather than precept, notably Christopher Hill and Lawrence Stone.

2 Laslett, *World We Have Lost*, chapter 10 and *passim*, and his later 'Introduction: the necessity of a historical sociology', in *Family Life and Illicit Love in Earlier Generations*, Cambridge, 1977; Thomas, 'The tools and the job', p. 275.

3 Alluding to the striking chapter heading of Laslett, *World We Have Lost*, chapter 10.

4 Quoting the phrase used by Hobsbawn in 'From social history', pp. 24–5.

5 Thomas, 'The tools and the job', p. 276.

6 Quoting B. Bailyn, 'The challenge of modern historiography', *American Historical Review*, LXXXVII, 1982, pp. 2–3, and P. Collinson, *De Republica Anglorum. Or, History with the Politics Put Back*, Cambridge, 1990, p. 10.

7 Alluding to J.A. Barnes' concept of 'structural amnesia' as discussed in J. Goody and I. Watt, 'The consequences of literacy', in J. Goody ed., *Literacy in Traditional Societies*, Cambridge, 1968, pp. 32–3.

8 P. Laslett, 'The character of familial history, its limitations and the conditions for its proper pursuit', *Journal of Family History*, XII, 1987,

p. 273, and 'Social structural time: an attempt at classifying types of social change by their characteristic paces', in M. Young and T. Schuller eds., *The Rhythms of Society*, London, 1988. See also the discussion of periodisation in J. Kelly Gadol, 'The social relationship of the sexes: methodological implications of women's history', *Signs*, IV, 1976, pp. 810–12.

9 For example, the works of Keith Thomas, Lawrence Stone, Peter Laslett, Alan Macfarlane and John Bossy.

10 Again, some notable exceptions demonstrate the value of bridging the medieval/early modern divide. See, for example, the works of Christopher Dyer, R.M. Smith, Charles Phythian-Adams, Marjorie McIntosh, Ian Blanchard, Paul Glennie and Judith Bennett.

11 Quoting T.G. Ashplant and A. Wilson, 'Present-centred history and the problem of historical knowledge', *Historical Journal*, XXXI, 1988, pp. 261–2.

12 A. Wilson, 'The politics of medical improvement in early Hanoverian London', in R. French and A. Cunningham eds., *The Medical Enlightenment of the Eighteenth Century*, Cambridge, 1990, p. 4. Wilson is particularly trenchant in his criticism of the separatism of sub-disciplines, which he describes as having 'the non-relationship of parallel stories, linked only by the fact that they inhabit the dimension of time'. Cf. the comments of Lynn Hunt in the introduction to L. Hunt ed., *The New Cultural History*, Berkeley, Los Angeles and London, 1989, p. 9.

13 Ashplant and Wilson, 'Present-centred History', p. 262.

14 D. Cannadine, 'The way we lived then', *Times Literary Supplement*, 7–13 September 1990, p. 936. (Reviewing F.M.L. Thompson ed., *The Cambridge Social History of Britain 1750–1950*, 3 vols., Cambridge, 1990.)

15 G. Stedman Jones, 'From historical sociology to theoretical history', *British Journal of Sociology*, XXVII, 1976, pp. 296, 300. Cf. T. Judt, 'A clown in regal purple: social history and the historians', *History Workshop Journal*, VII, 1979, p. 67.

16 A good recent example is provided by Diana O'Hara's criticism of the way the continuing discussion of kinship and kinship relations in early modern England has failed to take account of shifts of emphasis in the social-anthropological understanding of kinship: ' "Ruled by my friends": aspects of marriage in the diocese of Canterbury *c*. 1540–1570', *Continuity and Change*, VI, 1991, pp. 10–11.

17 A point made forcibly in Bailyn, 'Challenge', p. 6.

18 E.P. Thompson, 'Folklore, anthropology and social history', *Indian Historical Review*, III, 1978, pp. 251, 256, 260; Judt, 'A clown in regal purple', p. 71.

19 Both influences are very evident in the history of the family. Fierce critical response to Lawrence Stone's interpretatively ambitious *The Family, Sex and Marriage in England, 1500–1800*, London, 1977, has now given way to a general failure to confront the problem of change, a task rendered ever more difficult by the sub-disciplinary introversion of family history and further compartmentalisation by period and specialisation even within that field.

20 See, for example, David Cannadine's general discussion of the 'cult of professionalism' and its consequences in 'British history: past, present – and future?', *Past and Present*, CXVI, 1987, pp. 176–9.

21 See, for example, the contents of the two most frequently used textbooks: D.C. Coleman, *The Economy of England 1450–1750*, Oxford, 1977, and C.G.A. Clay, *Economic Expansion and Social Change: England 1500–1700*, 2 vols., Cambridge, 1984.

22 K. Thomas, *Man and the Natural World: Changing Attitudes in England 1500–1800*, London, 1983; P. Slack, *The Impact of Plague in Tudor and Stuart England*, London, 1985; M. MacDonald, *Mystical Bedlam: Madness, Anxiety and Healing in Seventeenth-century England*, Cambridge, 1981.

23 G. Himmelfarb, 'Denigrating the rule of reason: the "new history" goes bottom-up', *Harper's Magazine*, April 1984, pp. 84–90.

24 Thomas, 'The tools and the job', p. 276.

25 T. Arkell, 'History's role in the school curriculum', *Journal of Education Policy*, III, 1988, p. 34.

26 Bailyn, 'Challenge', pp. 5, 10–11, 18–19, 22, 24; E.R. Wolf, *Europe and the People Without History*, Berkeley, Los Angeles and London, 1982, pp. 7ff.; Laslett, 'Character of familial history', pp. 263–4.

27 A. Giddens, *Central Problems in Social Theory: Action, Structure and Contradiction in Social Analysis*, London, 1979, pp. 3, 8; P. Abrams, *Historical Sociology*, Shepton Mallet, 1982, pp. x–xi, xv, 3. Cf. for developments in social anthropology, A. Biersack, 'Local knowledge, local history: Geertz and Beyond', in Hunt ed. *The New Cultural History*, p. 74 and *passim*.

28 Good examples can be found in C. Dyer, *Lords and Peasants in a Changing Society: The Estates of the Bishopric of Worcester, 680–1540*, Cambridge, 1980 or J.M. Beattie, *Crime and the Courts in England, 1660–1800*, Oxford, 1986. In their recent study of changing attitudes towards the crime of self-murder, MacDonald and Murphy have also stressed the importance of adopting a very long perspective by means of which 'both large-scale changes and per-durable continuities are more easily identified than they would be in a briefer period': M. MacDonald and T.R. Murphy, *Sleepless Souls: Suicide in Early Modern England*, Oxford, 1990, p. 7.

29 A currently prominent example is the marked revival of interest in the social history of the late seventeenth and early eighteenth centuries which has already produced work which not only reassesses the character of that period but also has potentially profound implications for the interpretation of the immediately preceding and succeeding centuries. For valuable discussions of some of the most significant recent publications, see the two review articles by Jonathan Barry, 'Consumers' Passions: the middle class in eighteenth-century England', *Historical Journal*, XXXIV, 1991, pp. 207–16 and 'The state and the middle classes in eighteenth-century England', *Journal of Historical Sociology*, IV, 1991, pp. 75–86.

30 Maurice Keen's recent synthesis of the work of late medieval historians on the problem of aristocratic violence, for example, has more than a little to offer historians wrestling somewhat inconclusively with the problem of the apparent decline of homicide in early modern England: M. Keen, *English Society in the Later Middle Ages, 1348–1500*, London, 1990, chapter 8. Similarly Marjorie McIntosh's examination of responses to poverty 1388–1600 does much to help explain the local implementation of the poor laws thereafter: M.K. McIntosh, 'Local responses to the poor in late medieval and Tudor England', *Continuity and Change*, III, 1988, pp. 209–45.

31 Wilson, 'Politics of medical improvement', p. 38.

32 Slack, *Impact of Plague, passim*; C.W. Brooks, *Pettyfoggers and Vipers of the Commonwealth: The 'Lower Branch' of the Legal Profession in Early Modern England*, Cambridge, 1986, chapters 4–6.

33 These issues are very helpfully discussed in L. Hunt, 'Introduction: history, culture and text', and L.S. Kramer, 'Literature, criticism and historical imagination: the literary challenge of Hayden White and Dominick La Capra', both in Hunt ed., *The New Cultural History*, and in P.J. Corfield, 'Introduction: historians and language' in Confield ed., *Language, History and Class*, Oxford, 1991, esp. pp. 25–6. See also L. Stone, 'The Revival of Narrative', *Past and Present*, LXXXV, 1979, and E.J. Hobsbawm, 'The revival of narrative: some comments', *Past and Present*, LXXXVI, 1980.

34 Hunt, 'Introduction: history, culture and text', p. 22.

35 Cannadine, 'The way we lived then', p. 936.

36 Collinson, *De Republica Anglorum*, p. 14. This striking passage has been much quoted, usually without reference to its context in an inaugural lecture which called for a 'new political history' which would have social depth.

37 Cannadine, 'The way we lived then', p. 936. The second quotation was not an expression of Cannadine's own views so much as a characterisation of the views of hostile critics.

3 *Linda A. Pollock*

Living on the stage of the world: the concept of privacy among the elite of early modern England

Introduction

The history of the family was a minor element in the 'new' social history until the 1970s when it developed rapidly into a fertile and highly contentious field. Notwithstanding the fervour and multiplicity of the scholarly debates, there does seem to be general agreement on one issue: the private family is a modern development.[1] At the beginning of the sixteenth century, it is claimed, privacy was virtually non-existent whereas two hundred years later it was actively sought and cultivated. Support for the argument has been culled from a wide array of evidence. Weddings, funerals, and more surprisingly, births and deaths were social gatherings. Houses were professional as well as domestic centres, constantly open to the influx of clients and neighbours. Rooms in houses were large and communal, allowing of no distinction between domestic and public affairs, family and servant activities. Bedchambers were used as reception rooms and facilities for basic personal needs were limited; in fact there was little sense of modesty associated with the performance of bodily functions. Within the family itself there was scant opportunity for marital privacy. Hordes of servants abounded and these not only infringed upon privacy by their physical presence and pronounced tendency to gossip but also through their aggressive manipulation of family relationships, especially quarrels, to their own advantage. Authorities, friends, kin and neighbours frequently intervened in the domestic and personal affairs of individuals. Any reading of the records of the church courts demonstrates the familiarity of some villagers with the illicit acts of their less conforming peers. As

Professor Amussen has clearly stated: 'The family was a social, public institution, not a private one that could be left to its own devices.'[2]

However, dating particularly from the late seventeenth century, matters changed. According to the late Philippe Ariès, the concept of privacy was transformed because of the increased role of the state, increased literacy and the development of new forms of religion. The new concept of privacy can be gauged using several measures: the growth of manners and modesty indicating a different attitude to the body; the development of self-knowledge as witnessed by private diaries, memoirs and correspondence; an increased taste for solitude and the emergence of intimate friendships; a new conception of daily life so that living became a matter of externalising one's inner values and finally the alteration in housing as seen in the construction of smaller and more specialised rooms as well as the introduction of stairways and corridors. The number of servants also declined since these freshly domesticated families wanted above all to escape the prying eyes. There may be quibbles over when exactly a concept of privacy emerged (the late eighteenth century being the preferred choice) but little dissension with the overall picture.

At the heart of the evolution of a concept of privacy lay the family, most historians postulating a positive correlation between the rise of privacy and the rise of affectionate domesticity.

Ultimately the family became the focus of private life . . . It became something it had never been: a refuge, to which people fled in order to escape the scrutiny of outsiders; an emotional center; and a place where, for better or for worse, children were the focus of attention.[3]

Gradually disassociating itself from the mass sociability of the middle ages, the family by the late eighteenth century had turned in on itself, shunning the outside world, nurturing a heightened sense of intimacy among its members and culminating in the nineteenth-century ideal of the home as a sanctuary and haven from the material world.[4]

There have been a few critics of this thesis. A concept of privacy certainly existed before the eighteenth century, argue Ralph Houlbrooke and Martin Ingram, although it was not well established. The latter in particular demonstrates that the incidents of spying only too familiar to the scholar of ecclesiastical records did not represent normal spontaneous behaviour; rather these constituted a 'carefully planned, legally purposeful activity' deliberately designed to incriminate targeted offenders in court.[5] The penchant of ordinary people for regarding their marriages as 'private affairs', to the despair of church and secular authorities, has been noted.[6] Other scholars have disagreed with the concept of a private family even for the twentieth century.[7] The assumption that privacy is an unqualified good has also been challenged through the examination of the conflict and violence which can occur behind closed doors.[8] Nevertheless, the general idea of a lack of distinction between the public and the private in early modern England has proved persuasive and has been recently reinforced by a powerful wave of new scholarship on the court, patronage and the role of women in politics, a scholarship which seeks to challenge the traditional approach to political history.

The political theorist Sir Robert Filmer, writing in the late seventeenth century, envisaged no split between the public and private realm – that is no private sphere in the sense of an arena demarcated from politics nor a political sphere in the sense of an arena diverging from the private.[9] Later historians concur in viewing the early modern state as a realm in which the public domain was not clearly distinguished from private interests.[10] Norbert Elias in particular has supplied a memorable portrayal of court society in France, a society which performed a double function both as an arena for relaxation and as a direct instrument of career. Elias highlights the way in which courtiers developed an acute sensitivity to the status which should be accorded people on the basis of their bearing, speech, manner and appearance: 'as an individual's stock was identical to his social existence, the nuances of behaviour by which people reciprocally expressed their opinion on it took on extraordinary importance'. In a court society, the ordering of rank fluctuated, there was no security and keeping abreast of upheavals was important. Who took precedence over whom, the seating order, the amiability of reception by others and so forth were not mere externals: 'They were literal documentation of social existence.'[11] Even the most intimate acts could be used to achieve political ends, politics was not distinct from living.[12]

In England the court was only one of the centres of good society and thus English society was not as saturated with the ways of courtiers as France. Nevertheless, many of Elias' insights hold true. England was a patronage society and patronage 'may be understood as a routine way of exercising power and authority at a time when the public and the private were not yet clearly separated'.[13] As in France, the competition for favour was intense and clients were quick to change patrons.[14] Insecurity was rampant and well-founded since courtiers had real power. As J.E. Neale has pointed out, court rivalry was not merely concerned with prestige, a leader's own solvency and that of his servants was at stake.[15] Courtiers could control the financial futures of those dependent on the court.[16] Those who refused to play the game incurred substantial penalties.[17] Moreover, the boundary between private and public interests was obligingly fluid. In Norfolk, quarrels between the local gentry families arose essentially from personal issues and participants endeavoured to subvert offices of local government to their particular ends. The justices of the peace in particular were prone to using their office to 'harass an enemy or help a friend'.[18]

The earlier conceptual division of public from private life, it is argued, has especially impoverished our understanding of women's relationship to political life.[19] Revisionist historians have risen to the challenge, finding much new evidence on the active role women played in politics. Not only could domestic patronage develop into political, but women also themselves acted as patrons, brokers and clients and the courts of the Stuart queen consorts offered rich opportunities to talented women.[20]

In the realm of politics as well as sentiments, the family is perceived to be at the core of the public/private fusion. In fact, orthodox political historians have been taken to task for adhering too long to the principle that politics belonged to the public sphere and had no influence on life within the home. The two spheres, it is now claimed, were interdependent.[21] Domestic life was resoundingly public, due to the use of domestic occasions such as meals and the morning toilette for purposes of display and political manoeuvring. In addition, the household aided a lord's political life through the provision of services and messengers – and was a place to organise political strategies.[22]

Moreover, since politics in the Tudor–Stuart era was a dangerous game, who better to trust than those who were personally loyal, especially members of your family whose fame rose and fell with your own. The elite family characteristically offered its members help, protection and opportunities for advancement and these relationships were highly valued.[23] As Professor Aylmer has pointed out, all established families would find it prudent to have one of their members at the hub of national politics, either at court or in the crown's service.[24] It has been convincingly demonstrated that in Norfolk, at least, gentry families such as the Gawdys, Knyvetts, Woodhouses and the Pastons certainly relied on family members at court to consolidate their power and improve their status.[25]

The stress on personal relationships in politics and the part played by women seems to strengthen the belief that there was no clear boundary between the private and public in early modern England. The family, far from being a sanctuary from the public world, is viewed as the place 'where the private and public spheres of life intersected and affected each other'.[26] Since, too, the family was seen as the basis of the social order and behaviour within the family was regulated, 'it is inappropriate to dismiss what happened in the family as "private"; the dichotomy so familiar to us today between private and public is necessarily false when applied to the experience of early modern England'.[27] The new scholarship does go a long way to rectify what has been seen to have been one of the major flaws of family history: that the family had been analysed in isolation from the rest of society.[28] However, it brings further problems in its wake for our understanding of the concept of privacy in early modern England.

There are notable deficiencies in our approach to the history of privacy so far. We seem to have been too reliant on architectural evidence, for instance. This has often been misinterpreted: although rooms were often communal and bedchambers were indeed reception rooms, there were also rooms intentionally designed to allow solitude and privacy. Closets were the private rooms and usually placed beyond the bedchamber with which they were associated so that they formed the innermost and most secluded room of the apartment concerned.[29] Furthermore small rooms and corridors certainly made privacy *easier*, but not necessarily *obtainable* for the first time. We have also placed too much credence on the behavioural evidence of people snooping on their neighbours, in effect using breaches in a system to prove the lack of one. We seem also to have embarked on research relying on an anchronistic concept of privacy: that the family was and should be the place of refuge from external pressures[30] and that the separation of society into public and private spheres was linked to the development of a concept of privacy in the individual.[31]

It may be more fruitful to explore how the concept of privacy was understood and applied in the early modern era. We should be investigating what people themselves wanted to keep private as opposed to what historians think they should have been keeping private. Furthermore, we should bear in mind that the terms public and private have two meanings: public refers both to the sense of public space and to the state and private both to domestic life and to everything outside of the state's purview.[32] We should reconsider our assumption that the two facets are linked and that the organisational categories of the Tudor–Stuart era will mirror our own, albeit at an earlier stage of development. Our understanding and usage of the concepts public and private arise from the conditions and context of a modern Western society. Similarly, the specific nature of early modern society will affect how it perceives and makes sense of the world. As Linda Levy Peck has inadvertently demonstrated in her recent work, there is a distinction made between the public and the private in seventeenth-century England. It is a distinction, however, arrayed along a different continuum from the one we deploy. In describing the activities of female brokers, Peck comments: 'Their political role belies the separation between public and private spheres.' Later in the same work, however, when discussing corruption trials in the star chamber she challenges the idea that a sense of public and private existed only sketchily in the early modern period. In these trials, corruption was defined as the use of 'monies designed for the public service for private ends' and as 'monies taken corruptly for rewards and gratuities and private gain from public service'.[33]

The remainder of this essay examines the concept of privacy mainly between 1570 to 1670 in an attempt to discover if it existed, and what it entailed. It may well be the case that whereas a concept of privacy was absent in some areas, it was firmly entrenched in others. The focus is on the family and the evidence is derived from the personal papers of the landed elite.

Concepts of private and public

The landed elite of early modern England were public people, inhabiting a world in which their activities were the object of intense scrutiny by their peers. In his 'Certaine directions for my sonne Ferdinando', Henry Hastings, fifth Earl of Huntingdon reminded his son that 'As by thy birth thou art a publique person, soe it is likely thou shalt be called to a publique place and imployment.'[34] Appearances mattered and a certain standard should be maintained in public. Lettice Gawdy bewailed to her husband Framlingham that 'my satten is so voyded in the couller that it is not fit to wear when I goo forth'. Years later Framlingham's son was to make a similar appeal to his father, that the clothes of himself and brother William, both students, were so old 'as we are ashamed to passe in the streets'.[35] The competition for political prominence was severe, reputations were jealously guarded – as Richard, Earl of Carberry advised his son Frank 'Endeavour after a good reputation. He that cares not to be well spoken of may shrewdly be suspected to have scarce done anything to deserve it'[36] – and all eyes and ears were alive to any indication of scandal which could be used to demote a competitor. Lady Mary Jollife reminded her brother Theophilus, seventh Earl of Huntington, 'consider yt the eyes of ye world, (amongst which are many very severe and envyous) are now upon you'.[37]

It is also undeniable that family members, male and female, furthered the private interests of the family in the public world of politics.[38] Younger sons proved remarkably valuable assets in such an undertaking.[39] Any connection in a patronage society was useful and capitalised on. Even such a basic domestic bond as wetnursing a child could lead to a public benefit. Anne, Lady Chandos, was a suitor to her father, Lord Chancellor Ellesmere, for an office for a Mr Timothy Gates, 'one whom I am much beholdinge to in respecte that my chylde is nursed in his house'.[40] Furthermore, it is certainly true that the reigning monarch would intervene in marital affairs, not only in the arranging of matches, but also in an attempt to reconcile antagonistic spouses.[41] The willingness to merge the public and private spheres in the area of politics as well as the realisation that the 'eyes of the world' were upon them did not, however, mean that the elite had no concept of a private realm.

The advice tracts so beloved of the landed ranks contain many instances of the precise usage of the terms public and private and of the distinction made between them. Sir Walter Raleigh's popular advice to his son urged him to avoid public disputations; to shun private fight; never to defame a woman in public and not to endure public disgrace if he had committed no fault.[42] Lord Burghley's prescriptions on bringing up children advised 'praise them openly; reprehend them secretly'.[43] Richard, Earl of Carberry, recommended to his son Frank that every night he should 'withdrawe yourselfe into your closett or some private parte of your chamber'.[44] The Earl of Huntingdon concluded his tract with a section on 'the disposing and due orderinge of thyne owne private affaires' and suggested that his son should 'live alone with thy wife, let her not keep private company or unseasonable hours'.[45] Sir Henry Slingsby, composing advice for his sons 'During my late privacy occasioned by my captivity' and awaiting execution for treason, urged 'In private and retired hours consult with the *dead*' (i.e. past authors), the best way, he thought, to acquire wisdom. He also recommended that 'In the carriage of publick affairs my advice is that you appear cautious.'[46] Sir Francis Osborne warned his son not to be too intimate with a prince in 'public' since this caused both suspicion in enemies and envy in friends.[47]

The family was regarded as a private institution. 'As every man's house is his Castle, so is his family a private Commonwealth' wrote Richard Braithwaite.[48] Robert Cleaver's domestic conduct book was expressly conceived for 'the ordering of private families'.[49] Lady Grace Mildmay referred to 'a private household of family (which may resemble a whole commonwealth), consisting of the master and mistress, the husband and the wife, children and servants'.[50] Anthony Gawdy, while studying at Cambridge University in 1627 resided in 'an honest private house'.[51]

There are also many instances of events or pieces of information which are specifically described as being kept private.[52] Sir Thomas Barrington informed his mother that with reference to his cousin's wedding 'My wife and myselfe are solemnly invited to-morrow to be there when is the festivall, this day not allowing it, and the joyning of hands being altogether private.'[53] John Finch enjoyed expanding on intellectual matters to his sister Lady Anne Conway but had no desire for others, apart from her husband, to peruse his letters: 'I would not have my private thoughts made publique to any one else.' Sir Edward Conway confided his excitement about the possibility of his wife being pregnant to a friend, ending his letter with the caution: 'We keep this as private as it is possible till we have more assurance that we may not be made a town-talk, and I hope you will do so too.'[54] The scriptural notations of Elizabeth, Countess of Huntingdon, are inscribed 'for her owne private use'.[55] Philip Gawdy, courtier, eagerly relayed to his father how 'it pleased her Majesty to use me more graciously then I deserved . . . It may be you may heare of it by some other, for it was not private.'[56] George, sixth Earl of Shrewsbury, informed the tutor of his sons, Thomas Baldwin, that with reference to the discord between himself and his wife, he would like his sons Edmund and Harry to enquire how people were disposed towards him as he suspected 'private designs' against him.[57]

Thus the elite did differentiate between the private and the public. Their problem lay not in the arena of conceptualisation but in that of attainment. Privacy in this period was only precariously achieved and the elite were acutely aware of the potential for their personal business to be made public. Sir Philip Gawdy has given us a graphic description of the rapid and extensive dissemination of good news. He had heard of reports 'of an extraordinary marriage' his elder brother Bassingbourne had managed to achieve for his man: 'I heard of it at courte, in good places, in London at the best, ordinaryes and other places ther besydes in Essex at noble houses and other places wher I was.'[58] Titillating gossip could spread even faster, damaging reputations. Gilbert, Lord Talbot, urged his father, George, Earl of Shrewsbury, to try and resolve his dispute with the tenants on the Countess of Shrewsbury's land as quickly as he can. If news of the discord spread, the earl's standing with Queen Elizabeth would be harmed.[59]

Servants were a perennial hindrance in the quest for privacy and recognised as such.[60] Richard, Earl of Carberry, reminded his son that 'the truest discovery of any man is to be gathered from his servant, most men's formality being layd by wth his cloake'.[61] Lady Grace Mildmay in her memoirs, composed about 1618, was caustic on the subject. Servants:

will seek to know all that their master knoweth and observe all that he doth and will harken diligently unto every word he speaketh, of whom or whatsoever it doth concern. They will ponder thereupon and make what use they can, as is best pleaseth them, being furnished thereby to take what part they will with or against their master as may make most fit for their own advantage.[62]

Sabine Johnson employed her niece as a maid in her home and while yet unmarried the girl became pregnant. The family would have preferred to have kept the event hidden but a servant noticed the girl's morning sickness and spread the news in the village.[63] In the dispute with the Talbot tenants mentioned above, Robert Dudley, Earl of Leicester hoped 'that my Lord and Lady have none but faithful and true servants about them' who would not spread tales.[64]

As well as being aware of the extent to which servants could be privy to intimate details, the elite also took steps to minimise the intrusion of servants. Lady Elizabeth Hatton spoke to her husband in French when she considered some matters too personal for the servants to overhear. During a strife-ridden period of their marriage, for example, when she desired a reconciliation, Lady Hatton wanted to know whether 'I should lye in his chamber again.'[65] Unable to find her spouse alone and forced to converse with him in the presence of his man-servant, Lady Hatton asked the question in French. The greater the sensitivity of the business, the greater the reluctance to employ servants in it. The Earl of Shrewsbury proposed a marriage between his son and Lord Burghley's daughter. Burghley rejected the offer: his daughter was too young but more importantly, since he too had been accused of favouring the Queen of Scots, an alliance with the Talbots would not be politic. Burghley wrote the letter himself because he would 'not use my man's hand in such a matter as this is'.[66]

The elite clearly endeavoured at times to keep personal matters, many of which appear to us as relatively trivial things, as secret as possible. Lady Brilliana Harley warned her son Edward 'Your father does not knowe I send [letters]. Thearefore take no notis of it, to him, nor to any . . . Nobody in the howes knowes I send to you.'[67] Philip Gawdy beseeched his elder brother Bassingbourne 'to delyver this letter to Jertrard, and as ever thow lovest me let not any lyving know therof'.[68] Elizabeth, Countess of Huntingdon, in discussing a financial disagreement with her husband over her jointure arrangements, asked the recipient of her letter to 'take noe notice that you know anything concerning this business because he [her husband] may suspect you put it into my head to aske this security'.[69] Lady Anne Clifford, in a letter to her mother concerning a proposed marriage her father was arranging for her entreated, 'let nobody know of these matters, though they be but trifling'.[70] Individuals would reprimand others if concealed activities were uncovered. Dorothy Denne blamed the discovery of a

secret courtship on her suitor and castigated him for not being
more careful: 'If you had borne any true and reall affection to me
and vallewed my reputacion you would never have runne that
hazerd.'[71]

Members of the landed ranks were above all else concerned to
keep family discord from becoming public knowledge. Simonds
D'Ewes was involved in a dispute with his brother-in-law and
although they had not yet resolved the issue 'wee shall continue
together for soe shorte a time howsoever least the worlde should
imagine wee weare fallen out.'[72] Judith Culpeper beseeched her
brother not to make their quarrel over her annuity public. She
wished for neither pity from people nor 'that they shall have any
reason to rejoice at my misfortune of your unkind dealing by
me . . . If you have noe kindnese for me yet for your own sake doe
not let my concerns come upon the stage of the world.'[73] Lady
Phelips was embroiled in a heated squabble with her son over the
payment of her jointure and her late husband's debts. She begged
Edward to carry out his obligations before her plight and the
unpaid debts became a source of gossip: 'Ned doe not for yor
owne credit sufer yor father's slips, to be brought upon the stage,
to his dishonor, by yor undutyfullness towards me.'[74]

Those involved in matrimonial discord particularly tried to keep
the matter quiet and hidden from public view. Samuel Pepys was
horrified when he discovered that his wife Elizabeth kept a copy
of a letter she had written describing 'the retirednesse of her life
and howe unpleasant it is, that being writ in English and so in
danger of being met with and read by others, I was vexed at . . . a
paper of so much disgrace to me and dishonour if it should have
been found by anybody.'[75] Margaret Verney and Thomas Elmes
after years of enduring a troubled marriage, did agree to part.
Thomas wished to separate amiably and the whole affair 'donn in
a way that nobody may know, certainly guess they will, but *know*
they need not.'[76] Sir John Reresby was asked to intervene in a
dispute between the Duke and Duchess of Welbeck over whom
their daughters should marry. As the friction between them increased, one of the suitors decided he would rather remain single
than marry into this family. Reresby observed:

soe fatall to families are those differences occasioned by the folie of husband or wife, or both, and if of the latter, though the man hath sperit
(if hath sence with it), he will suffer in some degree the insolencie of a

woeman rather then make it publique to the prejudice of his children, especially daughters, who are seldome desired out of such families.[77]

One of the reasons it was desirable to keep family discord private was, as James Montagu, Bishop of Bath and Wells, reminded his elder brother Sir Edward Montagu, that any breach in family unity 'would be a reproach to ourselves and a rejoycinge to oure enimies.'[78] Those born to the landed ranks were required to demonstrate by their behaviour that they were entitled to their exalted status.[79] Protecting their honour and keeping their reputations publicly unsullied were material concerns to them. Charles Hatton suggested to his elder brother Christopher, Viscount Hatton that they should be reconciled and hence 'put a stop to the scandal and disquiet which from an open variance, whersoever the offence be, must yet equally encrease upon them both.'[80] Elizabeth Bourne pressed Anthony to reform his lifestyle so that they could mend their marriage, commenting, 'peace would better become us, [and] profit both then dissention.'[81] Foes chuckled, of course, because public dissensions would incur royal disfavour. The Earl of Essex relayed to Gilbert, seventh Earl of Shrewsbury, that the queen had been informed of the enmity between him and his brother Edward Talbot: 'I discover a great jollity in some of your enemies upon this occasion. They think . . . that this day will make the Queen alienated from you.'[82] And in the era of personal monarchy, royal favour was all.

Conclusion

The landed elite of early modern England indisputably resided in a world in which people were only too eager to discover and gossip about the personal affairs of others. Servants spied on and the state intruded in domestic matters. Regular use was made of family members for business purposes. Yet, notwithstanding, the elite also had a well developed sense of privacy. It was undoubtedly a concept of privacy shaped by the mechanisms of a patronage society. It did not involve a perception that an arena existed which was totally beyond the range of and separate from the state. The concept of privacy possessed by the landed ranks was based on a desire for concealment, a predisposition towards secrecy. Their concern for their honour and anxiety about their reputation, their knowledge of gossip networks and awareness of the public costs incurred by private slips, ensured that they were unwilling to make public anything which may reflect badly on them. Thus the fluidity of the boundary between public and private in one area intensified the search for it in another.

In examining the concept of privacy in the past, historians have been too willing to evaluate the existence of a concept by using evidence of the failure to obtain it. We should keep in mind, however, that we are unlikely to discover information about events which were successfully kept private. Philip Gawdy reported to his brother Bassingbourne on an undertaking probably involving their rivalry with Sir Arthur Heveningham, 'I will not tell you how I speeded in my concealed business till I come myself but I will be seacrat.'[83] If Philip wrote no letters about the business and if no-one eavesdropped on his conversation with his brother, the affair will forever remain 'seacrat'. We may be fair in concluding that privacy was harder to obtain in the past – although this, in the midst of a tabloid blitz on the British royal family and the press coverage of the US presidential campaign highlighting how little privacy we accord public officials, is by no means certain – but we would be wrong to assume it was not sought after.

This essay has merely skimmed the surface of the historical concept of privacy. Much remains to be done. We need to know more precisely what the elite wanted to keep hidden and why. The concept of privacy suggested here is a negative one – keeping information from becoming public – and we should investigate if a more positive understanding of the concept existed. We should also examine the gendered construction of a concept of privacy. It may well be that the keeping of disreputable family affairs quiet was of greater importance to men than to women. The latter were assuredly willing to solicit aid from relatives, friends and the state if they required it.[84] Finally, as we investigate concepts and emotions of the past, we may well have to jettison some familiar, comfortable but unnecessary baggage. The family could be a refuge from an unfeeling world, but it was not only that. It was also a potent source of much of the conflict experienced by men and women. Furthermore, the analytical categories we intuitively deploy as dichotomies grotesquely distort the past. Polarised couplets like loyalty/disloyalty; interest/affection; emotional/material and public/private carve up society and culture in a way which would be baffling to our ancestors and the problem is compounded by our assumption that as one member of the pair increases the other must decrease.[85] If we could curtail our enthusiasm for binary section, much of what is yet incomprehensible to us about the past may become clearer.

Acknowledgements

This essay forms part of a larger project on the early modern elite family. The research was financed by grants from the ESRC (award number G00232047), the British Academy and a summer fellowship from Tulane University.

Notes

1 The argument of this section is derived from: Susan Dwyer Amussen, *An Ordered Society. Gender and Class in Early Modern England*, Oxford, 1988, pp. 2, 36, 129, 188; Philippe Ariès, *Centuries of Childhood*, London, 1962, pp. 380–91; Philippe Ariès and G. Duby eds., *A History of Private Life*, vol. 3, Roger Chartier ed., *Passions of the Renaissance*, Cambridge, MA, 1989, pp. 2, 4–7; Stephanie Coontz, *The Social Origins of Private Life. A History of American Families 1600–1900*, London, 1988, pp. 85–7, 97; Alice Friedman, *House and Household in Elizabethan England. Wollaton Hall and the Willoughby Family*, Chicago, 1989, pp. 48, 65, 149; Jean-Louis Flandrin, *Families in Former Times. Kinship, Household and Sexuality*, Cambridge, 1979, pp. 109–10, 169–73; Tamara Hareven, 'Modernisation and family history: perspectives on social change', *Signs: Journal of Women in Culture and Society*, 2, 1976, pp. 190–206; Mervyn James, *Family, Lineage and Civil Society. A Study of Society, Politics, and Mentality in the Durham Region 1500–1640*, Oxford, 1974, pp. 11–15; B. Laslett, 'The family as a public and private institution: an historical perspective', *Journal of Marriage and the Family*, 35, 1973, pp. 480–92; Kate Mertes, *The English Noble Household 1250–1600. Good Governance and Political Rule*, Oxford, 1988, p. 269; Edward Shorter, *The Making of the Modern Family*, London, 1976, pp. 3, 227; Lawrence Stone, *The Family, Sex and Marriage in England 1500–1800*, London, 1979, pp. 6–8, 253–7; Keith Thomas, *Religion and the Decline of Magic*, London, 1971, p. 629.

2 Amussen, *An Ordered Society*, p. 36.

3 Ariès, *History of Private Life*, vol. 3, p. 8.

4 Leonore Davidoff and Catherine Hall, *Family Fortunes. Men and Women of the English Middle Class 1780–1850*, London, 1987,

chapter 8; Mary Ryan, *Cradle of the Middle Class. The Family in Oneida County, New York, 1780–1865*, Cambridge, 1981, chapter 4.

5   Ralph Houlbrooke, *The English Family 1450–1700*, London, 1984, p. 23; Martin Ingram, *Church Courts, Sex and Marriage in England 1570–1640*, Cambridge, 1987, p. 245

6   Roger Lee Brown, 'The rise and fall of the Fleet marriages' in R.B. Outhwaite ed., *Marriage and Society. Studies in the Social History of Marriage*, London, 1981, pp. 117–36; John Gillis, *For Better, For Worse. British Marriages, 1600 to the Present*, Oxford, 1985, pp. 90–100; Martin Ingram, 'Spousals litigation in the English ecclesiastical courts' in Outhwaite ed., *Marriage and Society*, pp. 35–57; Ingram, *Church Courts, Sex and Marriage*, pp. 195–7.

7   Coontz, *Social Origins of Private Life*, p. 74; Christopher Lasch, *Haven in a Heartless World. The Family Beseiged*, New York, 1977; Rayna Rapp, Ellen Ross and Renate Bridenthal, 'Examining family history', *Feminist Studies*, 5, 1979, pp. 174–200.

8   Heidi I. Hartmann, 'The family as the locus of gender, class, and political struggle. The example of housework', *Signs: Journal of Women in Culture and Society*, 6, 1981, pp. 366–94; Rapp *et al.*, 'Examining family history', pp. 175, 183; Judith E. Smith, 'Family history and feminist history', *Feminist Studies*, 17, 1991, pp. 349–64.

9   Jean Bethke Elshtain, *Public Man, Private Woman. Women in Social and Political Thought*, Princeton, 1981, p. 103.

10 Robert Harding, 'Corruption and the moral boundaries of patronage in the renaissance' in Guy Fitch Lytle and Stephen Orgel eds., *Patronage in the Renaissance*, Princeton, 1981, pp. 47–64; Linda Levy Peck, *Northampton. Patronage and Policy at the Court of James I*, London, 1982, p. 5.

11 Norbert Elias, *The Court Society*, Oxford, 1983, first published in German 1969, pp. 53, 55, 84, 91, 94.

12 Kristen B. Neuschel, *Word of Honor. Interpreting Noble Culture in Sixteenth-Century France*, Ithaca and London, 1989, is a fascinating account of the mentality of noble culture in France, emphasising that the political life of the elite cannot be separated from their material culture and cognitive world.

13 Antoni Mączak, 'From aristocratic household to princely court. Restructuring patronage in the sixteenth and seventeenth centuries' in Ronald G. Asch and Adolf M. Birke, *Princes, Patronage and the Nobility. The Court at the Beginning of the Modern Age c.1450–1650*, London, 1991, pp. 315–27.

14 Linda Levy Peck, 'Court patronage and government policy. The Jacobean dilemma' in Lytle and Orgel eds., *Patronage in the Renaissance*, pp. 27–46; Linda Levy Peck, *Court Patronage and Corruption in Early Stuart England*, London, 1990, p. 56.

15 J.E. Neale, *Essays in Elizabethan History*, London, 1958, p. 83.
16 Peck, *Northampton*, p. 70.
17 For example, the Duke of Norfolk's ability to attract clients was weakened by his shunning of the court: A. Hassell Smith, *County and Court: Government and Politics in Norfolk, 1558–1603*, Oxford, 1974, p. 22; Gilbert, seventh Earl of Shrewsbury, was never called to public office under Elizabeth as she believed he was disaffectionate to her: Edmund Lodge, *Illustrations of British History, Biography, and Manners, in the Reigns of Henry VIII, Edward VI, Elizabeth, and James I*, London, 1838, 2nd edn, vol. 1, p. xxx.
18 Hassell Smith, *County and Court*, pp. 60, 183.
19 Shanley, 'History of the family', p. 741.
20 Leeds Barroll, 'The court of the first Stuart Queen' in Linda Levy Peck ed., *The Mental World of the Jacobean Court*, Cambridge, 1991, pp. 191–208; Barbara J. Harris, 'Women and politics in early Tudor England', *Historical Journal*, 33, 1990, pp. 259–81; Caroline M. Hibbard, 'The role of a queen consort. The household and court of Henrietta Maria, 1625–1642', in Asch and Birke eds., *Princes, Patronage and the Nobility*, pp. 393–414; Sharon Kettering, 'The patronage power of early modern French noblewoman', *Historical Journal*, 32, 1989, pp. 817–41; Linda Levy Peck, *Court Patronage and Corruption*, pp. 47–8, 68–74.
21 Neuschel, *Word of Honor*, pp. 173, 195; Mary Lyndon Shanley, 'The history of the family in modern England', *Signs: Journal of Women in Culture and Society*, 4, 1979, pp. 740–50.
22 Mertes, *The English Noble Household*, pp. 121–2, 169.
23 Christopher Durston, *The Family in the English Revolution*, Oxford, 1989, chapter 3; Werner L. Gundersheimer, 'Patronage in the renaissance. An exploratory approach' in Lytel and Orgel eds., *Patronage in the Renaissance*, pp. 3–23; Jonathan Powis, *Aristocracy*, Oxford, 1984, p. 53.
24 G.E. Aylmer, *The King's Servants. The Civil Service of Charles I 1625–42*, London and New York, 1961, p. 82.
25 Hassell Smith, *County and Court*, p. 66.
26 Coontz, *Social Origins of Private Life*, p. 1.
27 Amussen, *An Ordered Society*, p. 2.
28 James Casey, *The History of the Family*, Oxford, 1989, p. 3; Rapp *et al.*, 'Examining family history', pp. 175, 183; Louise A. Tilly and Miriam Cohen, 'Does the family have a history? A review of theory and practice in family history', *Social Science History*, 6, 1982, pp. 131–79.
29 Peter Thornton, *Seventeenth-Century Interior Decoration in England, France and Holland*, New Haven and London, 1978, p. 296.
30 See the statement of purpose in vol. 1 of Philippe Ariès and Georges

Duby eds., *A History of Private Life. From Pagan Rome to Byzantium*, p. viii, and the critique of this by Linda Colley in *London Review of Books*, vol. 12, no. 15, 1990, pp. 11–12.

31 Joan Kelly, 'The social relation of the sexes: methodological implications of women's history', *Signs: Journal of Women in Culture and Society*, 1, 1976, pp. 809–23; Neuschel, *Word of Honor*, p. 195.

32 Ariès, *History of Private Life*, vol. 3, p. 9.

33 Peck, *Court Patronage and Corruption*, pp. 68, 161.

34 Huntington Library, Hastings papers, HA 15/8, f. 13, c.1613.

35 British Library, Gawdy papers, Additional mss 27395, ff. 139, 222, early seventeenth century and 1631 respectively.

36 Huntington Library, Ellesmere papers, EL 34/B/2, f. 24v, 1651.

37 Huntington Library, Hastings papers, HA 7903, 1672.

38 For a few examples of this behaviour, see Lambeth Palace Library, Shrewsbury and Talbot papers, vol. G, ff. 172, 294; vol. O, ff. 32, 100; Warwick Record Office, Fielding papers, CR 2017, vol. C1, ff. 7, 10, 12, 16, 126, 137.

39 Linda Pollock, 'Younger sons in Tudor and Stuart England', *History Today*, 39, June 1989, pp. 23–29.

40 Huntington Library, Ellesmere papers, EL 416, 1615–18.

41 Barbara J. Harris, 'Marital conflict and breakdown. The politics of the early Tudor elite family', paper presented at the American Historical Association Conference, San Francisco, 1989; Richard L. Greaves, *Society and Religion in Elizabethan England*, Minneapolis, 1981, pp. 264–7. For specific examples see the case of Sir Anthony and Lady Elizabeth Bourne in the 1570s, British Library, Conway papers, Additional mss 23212 and that of Lady and Sir John Ferrers in 1609, Huntington Library, Hastings papers, HA 14/24.

42 Louis B. Wright, *Advice to a Son. Precepts of Lord Burghley, Sir Walter Raleigh and Francis Osborne*, New York, 1962, pp. 23, 25. Copies of Sir Walter's precepts, written in 1570, can be found in many family archives, see for example Somerset Record Office, Phelips papers, DD/PH, vol. 227/6.

43 Wright, *Advice to a Son*, p. 10. Copies of Lord Burghley's precepts, composed c.1584, can be found in Hertford Record Office, Cowper papers, D/EP/F37, ff. 49–53, and Kent Archive Office, Honywood commonplace book, U1522/F1, end of book.

44 Huntington Library, Ellesmere papers, EL 34/B/2, f. 16, 1651.

45 Huntington Library, Hastings papers, HA 15/8, c.1613, ff. 7, 19.

46 Daniel Parsons ed., *The Diary of Sir Henry Slingsby of Scriven, Bart.*, London, 1836, pp. 199, 214, 215, 1658.

47 Francis Osborne, *Advice to a Son or Directions for your Better Conduct*, Oxford, 1658, 6th edn, first published 1656, pp. 31, 110.

48 Richard Braithwaite, *The English Gentleman. Containing Sundry Excellent Rules, or Exquisite Observations*, London, 1630, p. 155.

49 Robert Cleaver, *A Godly Forme of Household Government, for the Ordering of Private Families, According to the Direction of God's Word*, London, 1630, first published 1612.

50 Linda Pollock, *With Faith and Physic. The Life of a Tudor Gentlewoman, Lady Grace Mildmay 1552–1620*, London, 1993, p. 47.

51 Historical Manuscripts Commission Reports, *Tenth Report, Appendix. Report on the Manuscripts of the Family of Gawdy*, part 2, 1885, p. 124.

52 See also an intriguing example quoted in Peck, *Court Patronage and Corruption*, p. 93. In 1620 George Villiers, Duke of Buckingham as Lord Lieutenant of Buckinghamshire had asked for a voluntary contribution for the Palatinate and advised his deputies 'not to call any publique assembley of the countrey for that purpose but to deale privatly with your friends and such as are well affected to contribute'.

53 Arthur Searle ed., 'Barrington family letters 1628–1632', *Camden Society*, 4th series, 28, 1983, p. 124, 1630.

54 Marjorie H. Nicolson ed., *Conway Letters. The Correspondence of Anne, Viscountess Conway, Henry More and their Friends, 1642–86*, London, 1930, pp. 78–9, 153, 1652.

55 Huntington Library, Hastings papers, HM 15369, c.1633.

56 Isaac Herbert Jeayes, *Letters of Philip Gawdy of West Harling, Norfolk, and of London to Various Members of his Family 1579–1616*, London, 1906, p. 25, 1587.

57 Lambeth Palace Library, Shrewsbury and Talbot papers, vol. G, f. 221, 1583.

58 Jeayes, *Letters of Philip Gawdy*, p. 117, c.1602.

59 Lodge, *Illustrations of British History*, vol. 2, p. 155, 1579.

60 Servants were as much a problem in fomenting dissent and encouraging rivalries between family members as they were for spying and reporting on their employer's affairs. See for example the activities of the servants of the Countess of Shrewsbury and her son William Cavendish, Lambeth Palace Library, Shrewsbury and Talbot papers, vol. P, f. 957, 1579 and those of Lord Willoughby described in Friedman, *House and Household in Elizabethan England*, pp. 58, 65.

61 Huntington Library, Ellesmere papers, EL 34/B/2, f. 27, 1651.

62 Pollock, *With Faith and Physic*, p. 45.

63 Barbara Winchester, *Tudor Family Portrait*, London, 1955, p. 86, 1546.

64 Lodge, *Illustrations of British History*, vol. 2, pp. 156–7, 1579.

65 British Library, Hatton-Finch papers, Additional mss 29571, ff. 60–1, c.1668.
66 Lodge, *Illustrations of British History*, vol. 2, pp. 56, 1575.
67 Thomas Taylor Lewis ed., 'Letters of the Lady Brilliana Harley', *Camden Society*, 1854, p. 17, 1638.
68 Jeayes, *Letters of Philip Gawdy*, p. 55, 1591.
69 Huntington Library, Hastings papers, HA 8/4827, 1620.
70 V. Sackville-West ed., *The Diary of Lady Anne Clifford*, London, 1923, p. xxviii, c.1605.
71 Dorothy Gardiner, *The Oxinden Letters 1607–42. Being the Correspondence of Henry Oxinden of Barham and his Circle*, London, 1933, p. xxvii.
72 British Library, D'Ewes papers, Harleian mss 379, f. 39, c.1630.
73 Kent Archive Office, Wykeham-Martin papers, letters of Culpeper family, C1/16, c.1675.
74 Somerset Record Office, Phelips papers, DD/PH vol. 29, f. 16a, 1638.
75 R.C. Latham and W. Matthews eds., *Diary of Samuel Pepys*, London, 10 vols., 1970–83, vol. 4, pp. 9–10, 1663.
76 Frances P. Verney, *Memoirs of the Verney Family*, London, 1892, vol. 2, p. 135, 1657.
77 Andrew Browning ed., *Memoirs of Sir John Reresby*, Glasgow, 1936, pp. 438–9, 1686.
78 Northampton Record Office, Montagu of Boughton papers, vol. 3, f. 138, 1616.
79 Mervyn James, 'English politics and the concept of honour 1485–1642' in Mervyn James, *Society, Politics and Culture. Studies in Early Modern England*, Cambridge, 1986, pp. 308–415.
80 British Library, Hatton-Finch papers, Additional mss 29571, f. 158, c.1670.
81 British Library, Conway papers, Additional mss 23212, f. 13, c.1578.
82 Lodge, *Illustrations of British History*, vol. 2, p. 469, 1594.
83 Jeayes, *Letters of Philip Gawdy*, p. 76, c.1593. For the rivalry between Bassingbourne Gawdy and Arthur Heveningham see Hassell Smith, *County and Court*, pp. 192–8.
84 Harris, 'Marital conflict and breakdown'.
85 For a critique of these categories see Hans Medick and David Warren Sabean, *Interest and Emotion. Essays on the Study of Family and Kinship*, Cambridge, 1984, p. 10; Neuschel, *Word of Honor*, pp. 15, 31.

From Colyton to Waterloo: mortality, politics and economics in historical demography

The rise of empirical 'parish register' historical demography in the 1960s and 1970s was part of a broader movement of historiographic interest from the elite to the population at large; from qualitative accounts of great 'Events', considered in their uniqueness, to the quantitative analysis of event frequencies; and from the national and international plane to the 'micro' study of local communities: a movement caught by Le Roy Ladurie in a juxtaposition of place names.

From Rocroi to Crulai; from Waterloo to Colyton, these four place names could be said to sum up the course taken over the past hundred and fifty years by a certain school of history, from the resounding, action-packed historiography of the nineteenth century, battle-history to the silent mathematical resurrection of a total past represented today in *historical demography*. (Ladurie 1979, p. 223)

Crulai and Colyton saw the first application of family reconstitution – then historical demography's 'leading edge' methodology – to the parish registers of France and England, but the significance of these names rested on more than such accidental celebrity. Their very 'parochial' character, their apparent remoteness from the traditional preoccupations of historians, from great events, above all from the tides of war and high politics, rendered them into emblems of the new historiography.

Crulai and Colyton: Waterloo and Rocroi. Differences in the academic politics of the two countries were such that explicit statements of this opposition – of the quantitative analysis of demographic structure, to narrative accounts of politico-military events – were heard more often in France than in England. Thus Goubert for instance, listing the traditional shibboleths whose destruction would be 'indispensable' for future progress in population history gave pride of place to the primacy of politics and the domination of structure by event.

We read that the good administration of a Sully or a Colbert led the population to increase, whilst maladministration reduced it. More widely held still is the belief that the minor wars of the *Ancien Régime* had an adverse effect from a demographic point of view. A few years ago a geographer, who shall be nameless, attributed the exceptionally high mortality in a village in the centre of France between 1693 and 1694 to the War of the League of Augsburg. Wars, however, made use of little manpower as soldiers could only kill on the battlefield itself, and the wars fought by France after 1660 were almost always pursued outside her own territory. (Goubert 1965, p. 457)

English historical demography adopted a less polemical tone, but its relationship to political history was no closer than that prevailing in France. If anything the reverse was true. However, the established tradition of economic history in England furnished the new discipline with a pre-existing historiographic 'space' outside the domain of high politics. Its practitioners were thus spared the necessity of establishing a new intellectual terrain but, on the other hand, found their research agenda dominated by an inherited set of questions concerning the relationship between the industrial revolution and population growth in eighteenth century England.

It is as an answer to the latter that the work of Wrigley and Schofield is best known to the wider world, but these authors' achievement in *The Population History of England 1541–1871* goes much further than this. The book's chronological spread is, of course, much broader, but the central question is one of theory. Fifteen years after Le Roy Ladurie's pronouncements Wrigley and Schofield could claim to have validated his assertion that 'demographic history . . . has attained the enviable position of having matured into a science . . . we have moved on from the descriptive *picture* to the logical *system*' (Ladurie 1979, p. 233).

The reality, however, differed in two respects from the vision offered by Ladurie. In terms of method, the road to 'system' in English population history did not in fact lead to Colyton. The logistical and heuristic limitations of family reconstitution proved such that it was necessary to develop an alternative technique – 'aggregative back projection' – based on a sample of 404 English parishes. The new technique was, to a degree, based on earlier family reconstitution findings, but unlike reconstitution it provided information on population size and age-structure, together with crude vital rates.

Wrigley and Schofield's work dominated English historical demography in the 1980s. The 'neoclassical' framework to which it gave rise manifested the characteristics of a 'logical system' in full measure. For all this, however, it failed to deliver the promised 'resurrection of a total past' – if this totality is understood to require the conceptual incorporation of demography as a whole within the domain of economy and society. The logical integration of the new system was accomplished by the exclusion of mortality and its determinants, not merely from the sphere of high politics and the event, but from the world of human affairs in its entirety. In this respect the neoclassical system differed markedly from the two alternatives which had preceded it.

Theories of population change

For economic historians the problem of eighteenth century population growth had been the relative contribution of birth and death rates, and the order of causality between these and the economic changes of the period. Historical demographers, however, situated England's experience within the broader framework of European population history, and the global process of secular change termed 'demographic transition'. From this point of view the key theoretical task was less to quantify fertility or mortality's empirical significance than to delineate sets of relationships between each of them and their socio-economic environment – and between the variables themselves – and to map the transformation of such sets (or 'demographic regimes') over time. In such a context both the traditional 'birth rate' and 'death rate' explanations fell within the scope of an overarching conceptual framework which I call 'classical theory'. This had long constituted the orthodox interpretation of pre-transitional population dynamics but in the course of the 1970s it was challenged by an alternative frame of reference which can be termed 'crisis theory'.

Classical theory

'Classical' population theory developed first in Britain during the later eighteenth century, and rose to prominence in the nineteenth.

It was implicated in the rise of Darwinian evolutionary theory, among other things, and remains an important element in the 'folk demography' of the industrial west (Ardener 1974). The classical arguments are, of course, best known through the writings of Malthus, and the system itself is often simply termed 'Malthusian'.[1] This is, however, unfortunate for it 'over identifies' with Malthus assumptions common to his intellectual peers, and which he advanced in a more flexible and pragmatic form than did some others (Wrigley 1987, 1989). Furthermore, the label has now become confusing since Wrigley and Schofield's (1981) neoclassical model is equally 'Malthusian', in some respects, but diverges significantly from the classical assumptions in others.

Classical theory can encompass a wide range of interpretations, united however by two underlying assumptions which differentiate the theory from earlier, and from more recent, views of population dynamics. These assumptions are:

(i) That fertility and mortality levels are determined 'naturalistically' by discoverable causes and are not the immediate consequences of divine judgement.

(ii) The determinants of fertility and mortality are to be sought in the underlying characteristics of economy and society, and particularly in the level of subsistence resources – chiefly food.

The first of these – the 'naturalistic' principle – underlies all subsequent theorising on population, but this is not true of the second one which can be termed the principal of 'structural explanation'.[2] This principal establishes the study of past populations as a discipline cognate with economic and social history, but there are two pathways through which social and economic structures might affect population growth. Classical theory generally gave priority to the first of these, which involved mortality, and assumed that variations in the latter would be determined by changing living standards.

This mechanism is familiar – following Malthus – as the 'positive check' to population. For Malthus, 'positive check' regimes constituted a kind of 'general case' for population analysis, and they dominated his early writings. Coupled with the postulate of diminishing returns, it was this which earned him the aura of 'gloom and doom' pessimism that still surrounds his name, but Malthus also recognised that if nuptiality too were sensitive to changing living standards the positive check might be ameliorated, and in his later work he dwelt increasingly on the workings of such a 'preventive check' cycle in western Europe and particularly his native England (Wrigley 1983, 1986).

Classical theory, in linking mortality change to changing living standards, assumed what economists would term an 'endogenous' role for mortality as a demographic variable. But the classical assumptions could also be interpreted more broadly, and early twentieth century writers such as Talbot Griffith (1926), Margaret Buer (1926) and, in the case of London, Dorothy George (1966), explained England's eighteenth century mortality decline in terms of a range of social changes which included the growth in medical knowledge and practice, improvements in social administration, and a growing 'spirit of humanity'. Such arguments contributed to the traditional 'death rate' interpretation of population growth during the industrial revolution, but exponents of the birth rate argument also invoked classical theory – via the preventive check – when they pointed to the relationship between nuptiality and labour demand as the mainspring of demographic expansion.

Thomas McKeown – who became the best known post-war exponent of the classical position – rejected both the birth rate explanation and the wider range of influences on mortality invoked by Griffith and his contemporaries. McKeown expounded a particularly 'strong' variant of classical theory, which he eventually extended to cover world population growth from the paleolithic to the present, but which remained grounded in an interpretation of the English case.[3] In essence, McKeown advanced three propositions:

(i) World population growth from the later eighteenth century should be treated as a unitary phenomenon – the so-called 'modern rise of population' – subject to a single explanation.

(ii) The modern rise of population itself resulted from a decline in mortality and was not due to any change in birth rates.

(iii) The decline of mortality was principally due to an improvement in nutritional levels, with nutrition being, in practice, the sole determinant of mortality decline before the later nineteenth century.

Paying relatively little attention to any historical evidence on the question of living standards, he concentrated on cause-specific mortality from the Civil Registration period and applied a series of arguments by exclusion (the celebrated 'Sherlock Holmes' procedure). Consistently rejecting the birth rate argument as impossible *a priori*, his initial contribution subjected the case for eighteenth century medical improvement to a devastating empirical scrutiny from which it has never recovered. Subsequently he eliminated both a reduction in exposure to infection and spontaneous decline in pathogenic virulence as equally 'impossible' thus arriving at nutrition as the 'only possible' explanation of the decline in mortality.

The nutritional explanation has been given an important part in nineteenth and twentieth century studies, but where earlier periods are concerned McKeown's direct influence was largely confined to the debate on eighteenth century medicine.[4] There are a number of reasons for this – not least his consistent rejection of parish registers as a useful source of demographic information – but his indirect influence has been considerable, if somewhat ironic in its effect. Through McKeown's writings the classical 'structural' approach to mortality became identified with a very narrow 'standard of living' – indeed nutritional – determinism. This in turn was widely adopted as the 'null hypothesis' in studies of mortality decline, and its widespread falsification came to be seen as an indictment of structural explanations as a whole.

Crisis theory
An alternative approach to historical population change developed from the 1950s onwards and was centred around the violent 'short-run' disturbances termed 'mortality crises'.[5] As against classical theory, crisis theory was unequivocally 'mortality driven', and allowed mortality to respond – at least in the short to medium term – to factors outside economy and society. In the long term, however, the fact that crises occurred at all was attributed to the underlying backwardness – whether economic, social or administrative – of pre-transitional populations. The decline of mortality could thus be explained in terms of structural modernisation, and in this way historical and present day concerns were related to each other and the 'crisis' framework incorporated within the broader manifold of demographic transition theory (DTT).[6]

Crisis theory, as it developed from the 1950s to the 1970s, embodied three general assumptions, whether implicitly or explicitly:

(i) That a qualitative distinction can be made between crisis mortality levels and the so called 'background' levels of mortality characterising 'normal' years.

(ii) Secular variations in the mortality levels of pre-industrial populations resulted primarily from changes in the incidence and severity of mortality crises, with background levels of mortality varying relatively little in time or space.

(iii) The mortality transition, at least in its initial stages, was caused by a reduction in the incidence and severity of crises, background levels of mortality being little affected.

The first of these points concerns the definition of crises themselves and is fundamental to the theory as a whole. For assumptions (ii) and (iii) oppose 'background' and 'crisis' mortality in a way which requires them to be fundamentally different from each other, and implies that the latter had an essential character of their own qualitatively distinct from that of 'normal' years. This in turn reflected the breakdown of normal conditions in the face of some external 'shock', from which it followed that crises could best be understood in terms of the shock, or 'trigger', which had been the proximate cause.

This fostered a typological approach which set out to correlate external triggers with demographic outcomes, paying relatively little attention to the intervening causal pathways through which the latter were realised. Early studies blamed mortality crises primarily on harvest failures, and Goubert famously termed grain prices the 'demographic barometer' of early modern Europe (Goubert 1952). In Ladurie's words, however, 'man does not die by lack of bread alone', and subsequent research led to a threefold typology featuring 'epidemic' and 'military' crises alongside 'subsistence crises' of the Beauvais variety. As Flinn pointed out, 'whatever the basic cause of a crisis, epidemic disease generally took over, so that mortality crises of all kinds very commonly appear as great increases in the number of deaths from infectious diseases' (Flinn 1981, p. 53).

The work of J.D. Post goes beyond the typological analysis of external 'triggers' to investigate the networks of intervening variables between these and their demographic outcome. Episodes of extreme mortality are now treated in the context of, rather than in opposition to, 'normal' conditions, since infections such as dysentery, typhus, typhoid and relapsing fever had become endemic among Europe's working population. These smouldering infections could become epidemic under a variety of environmental and social conditions. The stress and wretchedness created by dearth and war were the most common of such circumstances. The pre-existing endemic foci of infection could extend their range and become epidemic under both sets of social conditions. (Post 1984 p. 24)

The countries of north west Europe responded differentially to the exceptional weather conditions of the early 1740s, but this was not due to differences in the severity either of the weather or of the ensuing price rises, but to underlying variations in social structure and administration. Whereas Goubert and Meuvret emphasised the role of malnutrition in reducing resistance to infection, Post's model is based on mechanisms through which climatic extremes promote exposure to infection. Thus shortage of money for fuel and accommodation – and its redirection towards the purchase of food – leads to an increase in effective population densities and a decline in hygiene.

These developments increase the density of the matrix of pathways through which pathogens can move within the population – a variable I have elsewhere termed the degree of 'conduction' of the vital regime (Landers 1990). At the same time, the regime's spatial 'bounding' may collapse through stress-induced migration, fostering the diffusion of pathogens and exacerbating the problems of housing, population density and hygiene. For Post, 'the relationship between climatic variability and the higher incidence of infection was social rather than physiological' (Post 1984, p. 5), and differences in mortality reflected differences in societies' ability to cope. Such arguments underlay Flinn's concept of the 'stabilisation of mortality', by which new administrative, economic and political structures reduced mortality by eliminating crises. This restored the vision of a 'total past' – integrating demography with economy and society – but its empirical premises were seriously undermined by the work of Wrigley and Schofield.

Neoclassical theory

Wrigley and Schofield vindicated the 'birth rate' explanation of eighteenth century population growth, demonstrating the inadequacy of a population theory cast wholly in terms of mortality.

But the resulting treatment of mortality itself diverged significantly from both classical and crisis theory. The main lines of the 'neo-classical' framework established by Wrigley and Schofield can be summarised in three propositions:

(i) Demographic regimes fall into two categories according to nuptiality's responsiveness to changes in living standards. 'Low pressure' regimes are relatively responsive, whereas 'high pressure regimes' are not.

(ii) The secular level of mortality is independent of its short-run stability. There is no necessary relationship between the incidence and severity of mortality fluctuations and the level of cohort life expectancy.

(iii) Mortality is sensitive to a variety of factors other than changes in living standards. In 'low pressure' regimes it is factors of this kind which dominate secular movements.

If fertility's role in regulating English population compromised crisis theory's status as a general account of population change, proposition (ii) questioned its adequacy even as a treatment of mortality. The latter proposition was, however, abundantly supported both by the English data, where life expectancy declined as mortality 'stabilised' in the later seventeenth century and in Scandinavia, where substantial fluctuations in mortality persisted throughout the early phases of secular mortality decline into the latter part of the nineteenth century.

Neoclassical theory also departed from the classical framework with proposition (iii). At this point it is important to be clear exactly what Wrigley and Schofield's arguments do – and do not – imply concerning secular mortality change, for they can be interpreted in two quite different ways. The *Population History of England* revealed two long cycles in life expectation, which could not be attributed to real wages. This finding supported Lee's earlier claim that secular mortality should be seen as an 'exogenous' variable within the English demographic-economic system, but the term 'exogenous' in this context bears a narrowly technical, econometric, meaning. It implies simply that mortality levels could not be defined within a set of simultaneous equations linking vital rates to population size, wages and prices.

Wrigley and Schofield's findings have, however, been used to support the more far reaching claim developed by Helleiner in the 1950s and associated particularly with the work of J.D. Chambers. Chambers wrote of

the irrevocable fact which historians have been loath to recognize, the fact of the autonomous death rate, the death rate which could override countervailing influences, such as low prices, an abundance of free land, a shortage of labour, and rising real wages. (Chambers 1972, p. 82)

The concept of 'exogenous' mortality recognises that mortality might be determined by social or economic variables other than real wages, but the 'autonomous death rate' relegates these determinants to the realms of climate or microbiology. From this point of view:

it is arguable that random biological causes operating in successive onslaughts on an already high death rate were so powerful through to the middle of the eighteenth century that they could initiate long waves of demographic depression independently of available *per capita* resources; and that conversely the absence of such biological factors could result in lowering the death rate and in inducing a population rise.[7]

The notion that eighteenth century mortality declines were 'autonomous' – in this absolute sense – has found wide acceptance,[8] but its implications are strongly counter-heuristic. By moving the determinants of secular mortality into the domain of viruses and bacteria, it effectively prevents their being examined any further, since these are matters on which our data can tell us nothing. In view of this, acceptance of the 'autonomy' argument can only stem from a variant of McKeown's 'Sherlock Holmes' procedure and follows the failure of attempts to demonstrate an improvement in real wages.

This exercise is only valid if we equate 'exogenous mortality', in the econometric sense, with the broader notion of the 'autonomous death rate', but to do this is to conflate the world of human affairs in its totality with the single dimension of the wage–price ratio. Such 'real-wage reductionism' has nonetheless proved attractive. The indirect influence of McKeown has been partly responsible for this, but more important has been the privileged role accorded the real wage variable as a general indicator of material well-being in neoclassical theory. This has allowed the construction of empirically testable quantitative models, but the implied substitution of real wages for economy and society as a whole has placed mortality studies in an anomalous position within historical demography.

Neoclassical theory has restored the discipline to a much closer relationship with economic and social history, but this has come about through their shared interest in nuptiality and its associated institutions. By contrast secular mortality changes are seen as random, unprogrammed, disturbances to the smooth running of the demographic-economic system. Events which in Wrigley's words

may have momentous effects, but, like an earthquake, a typhoon, or a great flood [are] external to the normal functioning of society. Consequences flow from such events but the links all run in one direction. Societies may fall victim to such events but they cannot influence them. (Wrigley 1981)

The causes of mortality change are thus removed from observation and from structural explanation. At the same time, however, as Lee has pointed out, the inescapable conclusion of Wrigley and Schofield's account of the demographic/economic interactions, is that 'exogenous changes in *mortality* drive the long run changes in fertility, population and wages . . . because mortality is the only variable with substantial exogenous variation' (Lee 1986, p. 100). In terms of its substantive importance mortality has thus been put through the door only to come back through the window, but it has become now – to change the metaphor – a 'ghost in the machine', a mysterious entity which drives the system but whose behaviour cannot be accounted for in its terms.[9]

The lack of a structural framework for mortality analysis is a serious handicap and contrasts sharply with the state of nuptiality theory where a rich and controversial literature has developed around the relationships between marriage ages and proportions marrying on the one hand, and systems of inheritance, kinship and household formation on the other. Indeed the lack of such a framework has meant that mortality analysis – which until recently commanded both analytical and substantive priority in historical demography – remains excluded from the promised reintegration of the discipline into the broader manifold of historical enquiry.

Mortality and spatial structure

A number of attempts have been made to develop a framework of this kind by exploring dimensions of economic, social and political life beyond the real wage – particularly the influence of spatial structure on levels of exposure to infection through such variables as population density, migration flows, and patterns of short-range mobility. The most ambitious is that of W.H. McNeill whose *Plagues and Peoples* (1977) commanded a readership rarely enjoyed by works of academic population history. McNeill developed a theory of mortality change based heavily on population distributions and geographical movement. Stressing the minimum population size and density required to maintain many pathogens in a host population, McNeill traced the origin of the majority of killing infectious diseases, first to that of agriculture, and then to those of large urban concentrations.

The emergence of dense population masses in certain regions was accompanied by that of correspondingly specific pools of infectious diseases to which the human population became adapted, both immunologically and culturally. The growth of inter-regional contacts, through trade, migration or conquest, then allowed the movement of pathogens into 'virgin soil' populations producing a substantial 'die-off' in the regions concerned, followed by a period of adaptation and a consequent secular reduction in the level of mortality.

McNeill was particularly interested in the relationships between large metropolitan centres and their more thinly settled rural hinterlands. These zones developed very different sets of relationships between the level and stability of both mortality and morbidity by age and cause – sets of relationships that we shall refer to as *epidemiological regimes* (McNeill 1980). Metropolitan populations, he argued, were large enough to act as perennial reservoirs of infection, and people born there suffered high mortality in childhood, but acquired powerful immunological resistance if they survived to adult life.

The pool of susceptibles to a given infection was thus largely restricted to children and recent immigrants, and so death rates were high – especially at the younger ages – but also fairly stable because of the restricted scope for epidemics. 'Hinterland' populations, however, were too thinly distributed for serious endemic infections to persist. They thus had lower secular mortality levels, but their reduced immunological resistance made them vulnerable to recurrent epidemics of 'metropolitan' infections.

These arguments point the way to a structural explanation of 'exogenous' mortality by showing how human agency promotes or retards the spread of pathogens, but their ambitious scope is not matched by detailed empirical analysis, and their treatment of mortality decline is less developed than that of mortality increase. Kunitz' account of eighteenth and nineteenth centuries mortality trends in Europe incorporates a more detailed consideration of the problem of decline and invokes changes in both exposure and resistance to infection (Kunitz 1983). In Kunitz' view, the growing density of trading and communication networks from the later seventeenth century promoted the spread of pathogens, with a corresponding increase in mortality from epidemics. Beyond a certain threshold, however, the effects of this process changed both qualitatively and quantitatively as epidemic manifestations gave way to endemic diseases of childhood with, Kunitz claims, lower levels of case fatality and overall mortality.

In a development of this argument, with reference to English mortality from Roman times to the nineteenth century, the author has suggested that secular levels were long dominated by the degree of exposure to infections – such as smallpox or bubonic plague – which were little affected by nutritional status (Kunitz 1987). It was diseases of this kind which were most implicated in the eighteenth century decline of mortality, and 'nutritionally sensitive' conditions, such as tuberculosis, pneumonias and diarrhoeas, thus began to predominate in the following century. Diet-based variations in resistance thus emerged as important determinants of mortality variations, leading to corresponding socio-economic differentials.

Regional studies
The influence of spatial structure on mortality has been examined in a number of regional studies using empirical 'parish register' techniques. Thus Wrigley and Schofield found an evolving spatial pattern to local mortality fluctuations in their 404 parish sample. To begin with, upswings in mortality due to price rises occurred chiefly in the north west of England, whilst the south east, East Anglia and the southern midlands were most affected by epidemics of plague and airborne infections. This pattern of 'two Englands', distinguished by differential access to grain and communication networks, subsequently weakened and disappeared as the growing integration of market networks reduced the bounding of epidemiological regimes in the north-western hinterland.

This contrast is pursued further in Mary Dobson's comparative analyses of mortality patterns in the North American colonies and in south east England (1989a, 1989b). In these studies the author shows how differences in population distribution and mobility, the density of trading networks, and the characteristics of the physical environment, produced variations in both the absolute level of mortality and its short-run instability. In the New England colonies dispersed settlement and low population density produced a moderate level of secular mortality and a 'background : crisis' pattern of instability reflecting the irregular arrival of pathogens across the Atlantic sea lanes.

In the southern colonies, by contrast, low lying coastal conditions allowed old world tropical diseases to become established with a high level of mortality and a pattern of violent instability which prevented the recognition of a 'background' level of mortality in any useful sense. A third pattern was found in the south east of England in the late seventeenth century. Here an increase in the density of trading contacts produced frequent local epidemics and an intermediate level of mortality – with a secular increase from the early part of the century – but because they were generally 'out of phase' the regional burial series was deceptively flat in the short term, producing a misleading impression of stabilisation.

The case of London

Dobson's study presents three forms of regional epidemiological regime, distinguished by different combinations of secular mortality level and short-run instability. McNeill's arguments add a fourth – the 'metropolitan' regime with severe secular mortality and moderate short-run instability. Eighteenth century London provides an important opportunity to test the latter's predictions and – more broadly – the adequacy of the structural framework we have been considering. Numbering around half a million inhabitants in 1700, and nearly twice this number at the 1801 Census, it combined substantial long term growth with a recorded burial surplus every year until the 1790s. Elsewhere we have shown that the available mortality data fit the predictions of the 'metropolitan' epidemiological model to a remarkable extent.[10] For most of the century mortality levels were much higher than those prevailing

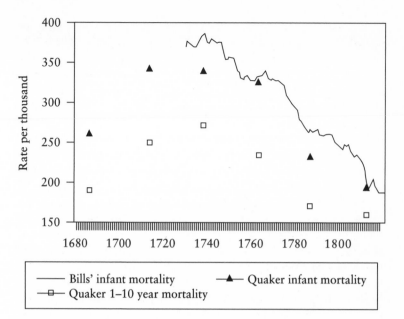

Figure 4.1 Infant and child mortality in London 1680–1800

elsewhere in England, whilst the annual burial totals taken from the London Bills of Mortality show relatively little short-run volatility.

A substantial decline in mortality set in from the 1780s (see Figure 4.1), but the pattern of the preceding century, with which we shall be concerned here, was anything but static. Absolute mortality levels are hard to measure before the 1730s as the Bills do not classify burials by age until 1728, but the vital registers of London's Quaker meetings reveal a rise in mortality from the last quarter of the seventeenth century to the first quarter of the eighteenth,[11] and the Bills evidence is sufficient to rule out a substantial decline over this period. Nationally, however, life expectation was improving at this time,[12] and there seems to have been a particular improvement in conditions in the south east of England (Dobson 1989a).

London's peculiarity emerges more strongly in relation to mortality by cause of death. This cannot be examined directly in the Bills – except in certain special cases such as smallpox – but it can be approached indirectly through variations in the seasonality of burials.[13] The weekly Bills reveal substantial changes in seasonality from the late seventeenth century to the mid eighteenth – particularly a reduction in the relative numbers of summer burials in the decades around 1700 with a corresponding increase in the cold weather months – and it seems reasonable to link these to shifts in the main cause of death categories.

The reduction in summer burials seems to have been linked to a substantial decline in mortality from an old-established gastroenteretic condition – probably that known to contemporaries as 'griping in the guts'. This also happened in London's rural hinterland (Greatorex n.d.), and its origins are likely to have been 'autonomous'. The rise in the 'cold weather diseases' – amongst which typhus and the bronchitis/influenza/pneumonia groups seem to have predominated – is more difficult to explain in such terms and was more specific to London itself.

London also diverges from the national pattern in the second quarter of the century when England suffered a set back in life expectancy. Nationally this took the form of a series of violent fluctuations linked to epidemic crises in the late 1720s and 1730s, but these abated after 1742, and the remainder of the decade saw a recovery. In London, however, the 1730s saw a rise in mortality which persisted as a 'high plateau' with only a modest recovery in the third quarter of the century. The seasonality data suggest that much of the additional mortality was associated with a cause, or causes, of death with a marked autumn seasonality.

Typhus and the respiratory diseases are both thought of as diseases of poverty, but the available real-wage data present a familiar paradox for these were relatively high throughout the period of elevated mortality – reflecting low food prices – but declined as mortality fell in the latter part of the century. If we accept the real-wage data as indicators of real incomes[14] then the trend of eighteenth century mortality was, econometrically speaking, 'exogenous'. But was it also 'autonomous' in the absolute sense defined above?

We can pursue this question by looking at short-run relationships. There are many possible ways of doing this, and we have adopted two complementary techniques. In Figures 4.2 and 4.3 I have plotted the relationship between extreme values in the series – using the Bills' cause of death labels – and corresponding values for prices, whilst Table 4.1 gives values for Goodman's Z coefficient

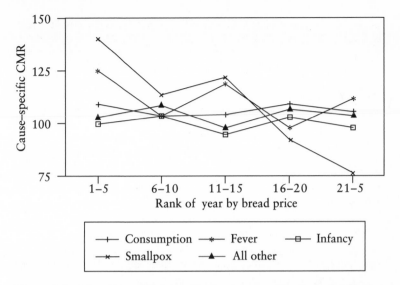

Figure 4.2 The effect of high bread prices on mortality in the London Bills, 1675–1824. For the derivation of the crisis mortality ratio (CMR), see note 15.

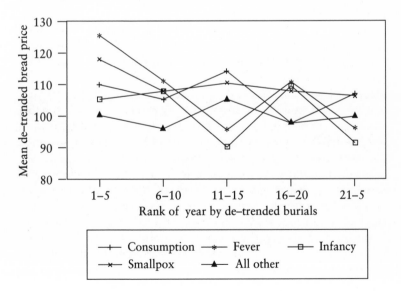

Figure 4.3 Level of bread prices in years with exceptionally severe mortality, 1675–1824

Table 4.1 'Co-movements' between bread prices and burials by cause in London Bills of Mortality: Goodman's Z (1675–1824)

Cause of death	Z Score
Consumption	1.62
Fevers	.68
Infancy	.62
Smallpox	3.11[a]
All other	1.88[b]
All burials	1.54

Significance levels
[a] 0.1%
[b] + 10%

which measures the statistical significance of 'co-movements' between the two series as a whole.[15]

The results show relatively strong relationships between prices and deaths from smallpox and 'fevers',[16] with weak or non-existent effects of prices on deaths in the other categories. This is inconsistent with a 'resistance side' mechanism based simply on food intake as nutrition was not a factor in resistance to smallpox and apparently of secondary importance in resistance to typhus. It is, however, consistent with a set of 'exposure side' relationships of the kind discussed by Post. These have yet to be fully disentangled, but two factors seem to have been of particular importance.

The first is migration. Smallpox was endemic – and probably universal – as a childhood infection in eighteenth century London, but the Quaker data reveal some 20 to 25 per cent of smallpox casualties to have been adolescents and young adults, most, if not all of them immigrants to London from elsewhere (Landers 1986, 1990). If, as seems to have been the case, migration to the capital was one response to economic stress elsewhere in the country, these conditions would have increased the proportion of London's population at risk to the disease. Migration also figured in the relationship between prices and fever, although here the mechanisms were rather different and it is likely that a proportion of the immigrants were already infected on arrival.

These relationships can be seen at work in the post-war waves of smallpox mortality at intervals throughout our period (see

Table 4.2 'Post-war' burial totals in London Bills of Mortality
1697–1817 (as % of trend)

Year	Burials				Armed forces (thousands)
	Fever	Smallpox	Female	Males	
1697	94	60	102	104	87
1698	102	209	92	105	36
1699	113	90	98	105	13
1712	90	108	95	92	153
1713	87	85	91	90	46
1714	135	145	115	113	29
1748	116	96	103	104	105
1749	135	145	112	113	75
1750	128	62	103	104	39
1762	122	115	121	120	151
1763	106	157	118	119	136
1764	121	97	103	101	48
1783	94	89	96	98	234
1784	80	99	88	92	57
1785	95	119	99	96	48
1802	120	115	103	105	274
1803	130	82	108	102	194
1815	126	85	104	101	326
1816	125	83	110	105	257
1817	123	143	106	104	203

Table 4.2). The wartime armed forces provided a temporary 'home'
for tens, and later hundreds, of thousands of under- and unemployed young men many of whom would otherwise have been
migrants. With demobilisation they were again on the road, and
many ended up in London. The underlying mechanisms were not
purely immunological, however, but were mediated by economic
and social structures specific to their time and place. And migration was not the whole story. Childhood mortality also displayed
a sensitivity to prices (see Landers 1993, Chapter 7) – and it seems
certain that smallpox preponderated among the excess deaths –
whilst post-war increases in burials affected females as well as males.

The key intervening variable was probably housing. The pressure that waves of immigration, with their accompanying socio-
economic dislocation, placed on the supply of cheap accommodation

can readily be appreciated, whilst for many 'native' Londoners living space was probably among the first areas where economies were sought in times of economic stress. Under these circumstances housing densities would have risen and 'conduction' increased in the way described by Post. This can be seen in the behaviour of the parish burial totals where statistically significant price-associations are mostly found in the belt running around the old City walls to the north and west – the zone particularly associated with artisanal production and the crowded and insanitary 'lodging houses' where many immigrants found their first shelter.[17]

Such problems were, of course, experienced very widely, but the supply of accommodation in London was afflicted by particular difficulties that seem to have been at their most acute in the central decades of the eighteenth century. Political interference with the supply of credit, small scale organisation and – above all – the peculiarities of land tenure fostered a building industry which was chronically undercapitalised, highly speculative and catered directly for a very restricted section of the population.[18] This was largely due to the system of 'building leases' under which aristocratic proprietors released land in parcels of varying size to speculative middle men who assumed responsibility for the actual construction.

Such leases afforded landowners the avenue to a substantial cash income from their property without putting up any capital in advance. They could thus maintain their estates – and consequently their passport to the arena of high politics – intact whilst at the same time passing the burden of speculative risk to their social inferiors. The speculative system had its strengths – under the right conditions it could generate large numbers of houses in a very short space of time. That it failed to do so for much of the eighteenth century can plausibly be linked to two factors.

The first of these was the alternation of war and peace which was such a feature of the period.[19] War brought economic benefits to London, but they were unequally distributed and restricted to certain war-related industries. Others experienced depression and this was above all true of construction. Governments borrowed heavily to finance war-making and offered both a return and a degree of security with which private borrowers could not compete.[20] Starved of capital in wartime the industry also found its supplies of raw materials – particularly imported timber – seriously disrupted, and levels of activity were generally very low.

The coming of peace usually brought an economic boom, but the immediate post-war period was generally one of economic recession with a rapid decline of war-related industry and a consequent reduction in the demand for labour. Housing was still affected by the wartime depression, and the stream of ex-soldiers and sailors arrived at the very time when the capital was least able to accommodate them. 'Shocks' of this kind generated vagrancy and overcrowding – transforming endemic pools into epidemic currents of infection – and both trade recessions and financial crises of a kind familiar to eighteenth century London could have similar effects even when prices remained steady.[21] But can mechanisms of this kind explain the secular persistence of high mortality for so much of the century?

The question is complex, but the answer seems to be yes, and in order to see how this came about we should return to the problem of housing and the second of the two factors referred to above. New housing in this period was constructed almost entirely for people in the middle and upper ranks of society, and the housing stock expanded 'from the top down'. Incremental popular accommodation appeared through involutionary processes of 'internal colonisation' – properties being divided and sub-divided as they were abandoned in the westward migration of the elite and the 'middling sort'.[22] The standard of building was often very poor, and uncertainties of tenure combined with the volatility of markets to hold investment below the level required for adequate maintenance. Many buildings deteriorated until they were fit only 'for such as pay no rent'.

The situation was tolerable as long as the stock was 'topped up' with new tranches of housing generated by London's physical growth, but the central decades of the eighteenth century were a period of secular stagnation, broken only by fitful and short-lived recoveries. The expansion of the metropolis virtually ceased, and the result seems to have been a general deterioration of the housing stock, manifested in the proliferation of decaying lodging-houses, 'night shelters' and ruinous shells inhabited by discharged soldiers and other vagrants.

War-related 'supply side' problems no doubt played an important part in this stagnation, but there seems also to have been a secular failure of housing demand in the upper reaches of society, as well as a general recession in the economic life of the capital.

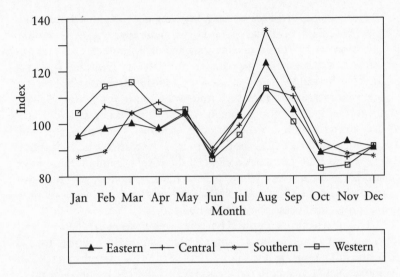

Figure 4.4   Parish register child burial seasonality 1695–1704

The reasons for this are not entirely clear, but the most plausible explanation is the heavy dependence of so much of London's economy on luxury consumption, funded by incomes from land, at a time when such incomes were badly hit by low agricultural prices. In any case, the process of decay seems to have gone furthest in the extra-mural parishes ringing the City itself, and some of its results are visible in the seasonality of burials from the relevant parish registers.

Figures 4.4 and 4.5 plot the seasonality of burials for four groups of parishes in the two decades 1695–1704 and 1750–9. Seasonality differences exist in both cases, but in 1695–1704 they are a matter of degree with each of the three groups manifesting the same underlying pattern. The situation has, however, changed dramatically by the second decade. The western parishes now show a qualitatively different pattern from the remainder. The autumn peak is confined to the latter, and comparison of the ratio of child burials to baptisms suggests substantially higher mortality in the 'autumn peak' parishes.

The late 1730s had witnessed the arrival of a 'new disease', probably a form of streptococcal infection, from the American colonies.[23] At first this caused epidemic mortality throughout

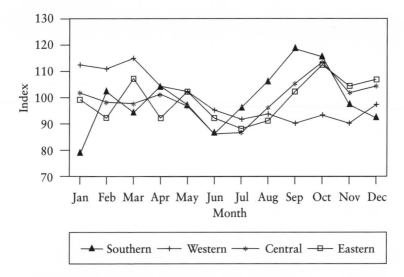

Figure 4.5 Parish register child burial seasonality 1750–59

London, but – judging by the seasonality data – its persistence was much more selective. It was able to establish itself in an endemic form in an area roughly corresponding to that in which burial totals were sensitive to price movements but apparently disappeared from the higher status – and increasingly self-contained – districts of the west.

For much of our period London thus acted as an endemic focus of infection in a manner close to that predicted by McNeill's model, but the nature of the infections involved, their relationship to the national epidemiological regime, and the absolute scale of London's 'mortality penalty' all varied in response to developments specific to their place and time. At the end of the seventeenth century, mortality from an old established food-borne cause of death apparently declined – probably as a result of an 'autonomous' microbiological change[24] – at a time when national mortality was also improving.

London, however, gained little benefit from this – and mortality may actually have increased – due to the rise of cold weather mortality associated with typhus and the respiratory infections. The latter, in turn, seems to have reflected increases in exposure to infection stemming from a deterioration in housing conditions.

Things were at their worst in the 1730s and 1740s when mortality was aggravated by the new 'autumn disease'. Although this is likely to have caused only a relatively small proportion of deaths in the capital at this time, its differential persistence can serve as a useful indicator of spatial variations in the level of exposure to airborne infections in general, and it appears to have become endemic in those areas worst affected by the contemporary cessation in London's growth.

Conclusion: mortality and political economy

The phenomenon of 'exogenous' mortality change – so prominent in the demographic history of early modern Europe – can be restored to the domain of economy and society by adding the dimension of space to that of time in our analyses. This is more than just a 'concession to geography', for it involves processes such as warfare,[25] colonisation and the integration of trading networks, which were part and parcel of the phenomena of state formation and consolidation that marked the course of early modern European history (Kennedy 1989, Tilly 1990).

To recognise this is, of course, to return to our starting point – the historiographic opposition of demography to high politics – and find that our road has run by both Waterloo and Colyton, Rocroi as well as Crulai. Yet historical demographers should not renounce the legacy proclaimed by Ladurie, for we are still in a terrain dominated by structure and process, as much as by events, and mapped by a 'demographic political economy' that traces such phenomena to the 'intersection of global and local histories' (Greenhalgh 1990).

In the case of London, the underlying demographic structure may have been imposed by environmental factors common to contemporary cities, but its dynamics can be only be comprehended with reference to the social distribution of resources in eighteenth century England, and the uses to which these were put by the governing elite. The latter converted their property into both financial and socio-political assets by manipulating a form of land-tenure which made building in London speculative and chronically undercapitalised.

The resulting system had strengths, but serious potential

weaknesses, and the latter were realised partly because of low agricultural prices – and thus in part the weather – and partly because of the war-making and war-financing policies of successive ministries. An overcrowded and decaying housing stock combined with London's position in the national migration system to produce a distinctive and deadly epidemiological regime. The diseases of Whig London did not spring from Whig politics alone, but their course cannot be understood if the latter are excluded from the analysis.

Notes

1 Varying assessments of Malthus' place in the development of population studies are provided by the contributions to Dûpaquier, *et al.*, (1983) and Coleman and Schofield (1986). See James (1979) for a biography and Winch (1987) for a brief survey of his intellectual development.

2 In this context, and throughout, we use the term 'structure' in the very general sense employed by Braudel – 'a coherent and fairly fixed set of relationships between realities and social masses', whether of a biological, social, economic or other order (Braudel 1980, p. 31).

3 See McKeown and Brown (1955), McKeown and Record (1962) and McKeown (1976).

4 See Szreter (1988) for a discussion of McKeown's influence on interpretations of mortality decline in the later period, together with a critique.

5 The schema set out here is a distillation of the views of a number of writers, and, though it approximates most closely to the view of Flinn (1974, 1981), it's not entirely attributable to any single author. The substantive and methodological literature on European mortality crises is very large, but see Charbonneau and Lerose (1979) for a representative sample.

6 See for instance Cipolla (1962), Omran (1971), Woods (1982).

7 Chambers (1972) p. 87. Given the influence of Chambers' argument for the 'autonomous death rate' it is worth nothing that he did not himself view the mortality decline of the later eighteenth century in these terms, preferring to attribute it, primarily, to changing living standards and medical advances (*ibid.*, pp. 99–104).

8 See, for instance Perrenoud (1984), and the contributions to Lee (1979).

9 Flinn has also pointed out, in his initial review of the *Population History*, that the substantive contribution of mortality change to

population growth was rather larger than some of the authors' statements seem to imply; see Flinn (1982).

10 See Landers (1987) and, for a more detailed analysis, Landers (1993), chapters 3 and 5.

11 The high level recorded in the Quaker registers is strong evidence against Dorothy George's attribution of London's severe mortality at this time to excessive gin-drinking. Clark (1988) has recently argued that the scale of the latter has, in any case, been greatly exaggerated.

12 The estimated decadal period life expectancies for the period 1680–1719 are 30.1, 34.5, 36.7 and 36.5 years respectively (Wrigley and Schofield 1981, p. 230).

13 For a discussion of the methods and assumptions involved see Landers and Mouzas (1988). A more detailed analysis is provided in Landers (1993), chapter 7.

14 See Schwartz (1985) for a review of the available data and a discussion of the problems involved in relating these to real incomes.

15 The effects of trends in burial totals and prices were removed by dividing each observation by a ten point de-centred moving average. See Goodman (1963) for details of the Z coefficient and its calculation.

16 The consequence of high prices for fever burials is more apparent when the effect on the following year's burials is taken into account. The relationship also seems to have more of a 'threshold' character than does that with smallpox; for details see Landers (1986) and (1993), chapter 7.

17 For details see Landers (1993) chapter 8. An outline of London's social geography at this time can be found in Spate (1936). Clark (1987) provides a discussion of immigrants and their accommodation in the City.

18 The comments in this and the following paragraphs are based primarily on Ashton (1959), George (1966), Summerson (1978) and Sheppard *et al.* (1979).

19 The following account is based primarily on the arguments set out in Ashton (1959). John (1954–5) has painted a more optimistic picture of war's effects on the national economy in this period, but implicitly accepts its deleterious consequences for the capital. For some related arguments see Hoppitt (1987), chapter 8; and Jones (1988), pp. 309–17.

20 Strictly speaking this can only be demonstrated for the period before 1713 and after 1760, when the yield on Funds moved above the level permitted to private borrowers by the Usury Laws (Ashton 1959, pp. 104–5). In the intervening period, however, levels of building activity seem to have declined in step with increases in the yield (see Landers 1993, chapter 2).

21 In this connection it is interesting to note that, of the thirteen years generally acknowledged to have witnessed financial crises (see Hoppitt 1986), three were among 'top ten' years of the eighteenth century for de-trended smallpox burials whilst another four fell in years adjacent to one of the ten.

22 This phenomenon is particularly visible in the decline of the Soho and Covent Garden districts (Phillips 1964, pp. 119–42, 231–9; George 1966, pp. 92–3, 338–9). See Sheppard (1971), p. 94 for an account of the process as it operated in the early years of the following century.

23 This was associated with a series of outbreaks occurring from 1739, which seem to have been part of a series of epidemics affecting the Atlantic world as a whole: for some supporting evidence see Landers (1993), appendix 2.

24 This is, perhaps, a 'Sherlock Holmes' conclusion, but the reduction in the summer peak seen outside London at this time seems to rule out a 'metropolis-specific' explanation. A similar change has occurred in developed countries this century where older forms of *Shigellosis* (bacillary dysentery) have been replaced by the *Sonnei* strain which is milder in its effects but apparently has a lower infectious dose (Rowland and Barrell 1980).

25 The demographic significance of warfare has not been discussed here, but, *pace* Goubert, its regional effect could be considerable (see Flinn 1981, chapter 4). Much of this occurred through the spread of infection. As Ladurie noted, in 1627–8 Richelieu dispatched an army of 8,000 men from La Rochelle to Montferat resulting in a series of plague epidemics which claimed over a million casualties (Ladurie 1981, p. 14).

References

Ardener, E. (1974), 'Social anthropology and population', in H.B. Parry ed., *Population and its Problems: a plain man's guide*, Oxford: Clarendon Press, pp. 25–50.

Ashton, T.S. (1959), *Economic Fluctuations in England 1700–1800*, Oxford: Clarendon Press.

Bengtsson, T., Fridlizius, G. and Ohlsson, R. (1984), *Pre-Industrial Population Change*, Stockholm: Almqvist and Wiksell.

Braudel, F. (1980), 'History and the social sciences: the *longue dureé*, in *On History*, London: Weidenfeld and Nicholson, pp. 25–54.

Buer, M.C. (1926), *Health, Wealth and Population in Eighteenth-Century England*, London: Routledge.

Chambers, J.D. (1972), *Population, Economy and Society in Pre-Industrial England*, Oxford University Press.

124   *Mortality, politics and economics in historical demography*

Charbonneau, H. and Larose, A. eds. (1979), *The Great Mortalities: methodological studies of demographic crises in the past*, Liège: Ordina.

Cipolla, C.M. (1962), *The Economic History of World Population*, Harmondsworth: Penguin.

Clark, P. (1988), 'The "Mother Gin" controversy in the early eighteenth century', *Transactions of the Royal Historical Society (5 ser.)* 38: 63–84.

(1987), 'Migrants in the city: the process of social adaptation in English towns, 1500–1800', in P. Clark and D. Souden, eds; *Migration and Society*, London: Hutchinson, pp. 267–91.

Coleman, D. and Schofield, R.S. eds. (1986), *The State of Population Theory: forward from Malthus*, Oxford: Basil Blackwell.

Davis, K. (1950), *The Population of India and Pakistan*, Princeton University Press.

Dobson, M. (1989a), 'The last hiccup of the old demographic regime: population stagnation and decline in late seventeenth and early eighteenth-century south-east England', *Continuity and Change* 4 (3): 395–428.

(1989b), 'Mortality gradients and disease exchanges: comparisons from old England and colonial America, *Social History of Medicine* 2 (3): 259–98.

Dûpaquier, J., Fauve-Chamoux, A. and Grebenik, E. eds. (1983), *Malthus Past and Present*, London: Academic Press.

Durand, J. (1967), 'The modern expansion of world population', *Proceedings of the American Philosophical Society* 111 (3): 136–59.

Flinn, M.W. (1982), 'The population history of England, 1541–1871', *Economic History Review (2nd ser.)* 35: 433–57.

(1981), *The European Demographic System, 1500–1820*, Brighton, Harvester.

(1979), 'Plague in Europe and the Mediterranean countries', *Journal of European Economic History* 8: 139–46.

(1974), 'The stabilisation of mortality in pre-industrial western Europe', *Journal of European Economic History* 3: 285–318.

(1970), *British Population Growth, 1700–1850*, London: Methuen.

George, D. (1966), *London Life in the Eighteenth Century*, Harmondsworth: Penguin.

Glass, D.V. and Eversley, D.E.C. (1965), *Population in History*, London: Edward Arnold.

Goodman, L.A. (1963), 'Tests based on the movements in and the comovements between M-dependent time series', in C.F. Christ *et al.*, *Measurement in Economics: studies in mathematical economics and econometrics in memory of Yehuda Grunfeld*, California: Stanford University Press, pp. 235–69.

Goubert, P. (1952), 'En Bouvaisis: problèmes démographiques du XVII siècle', *Annales, ESC* 7: 453–68.

(1965), 'Recent theories and research in French population between 1500 and 1700', in Glass and Eversley, *Population in History*, pp. 457–73.

Greatorex, I. (n.d.), 'Burial seasonality in early-modern England', unpublished MS in library of ESRC Cambridge Group.

Greenhalgh, S.G. (1990), 'Toward a political economy of fertility', *Population and Development Review* 16: 85–106.

Griffith, T. (1926), *Population Problems of the Age of Malthus*, Cambridge University Press

Harrison, G.A., Weiner, J.S., Tanner, J.M. and Barnicot, N.A. (1977), *Human Biology: an introduction to human evolution, variation, growth, and ecology* (2nd edn), Oxford University Press.

Hoppitt, J. (1987), *Risk and Failure in English Business 1700–1800*, Cambridge University Press.

(1986), 'Financial crises in eighteenth century England', *Economic History Review (2nd ser.)* 39: 39–58.

James, P. (1979), *Population Malthus: his life and times*, London: Routledge and Kegan Paul.

Johansson, S.R. and Mosk, C. (1987), 'Exposure, resistance and life expectancy: disease and death during the economic development of Japan, 1900–1960', *Population Studies* 2: 207–36.

John, A.H. (1954–5), 'War and the English economy, 1700–63', *Economic History Review (2nd ser.)* 7: 329–44.

Jones, D.W. (1988), *War and Economy: in the age of William III and Marlborough*. Oxford: Basil Blackwell.

Kennedy, P. (1989) *The Rise and Fall of the Great Powers*, New York: Vintage Books.

Kunitz, S.J. (1987), 'Making a long story short: a note on men's heights and mortality in England from the first through the nineteenth centuries', *Medical History* 31: 269–80.

(1983), 'Speculations on the European mortality decline', *Economic History Review (2nd ser.)* 36: 349–64.

Ladurie, E. Le Roy (1981), 'History that stands still', in *The Mind and Method of the Historian*, Brighton: Harvester, pp. 1–27.

(1979), 'From Waterloo to Colyton', in *The Territory of the Historian*, Brighton: Harvester, pp. 223–34 (first published *Times Literary Supplement*, 1966).

Landers, J. (1993), *Death and the Metropolis: studies in the demographic history of London 1670–1830*, Cambridge University Press.

(1990), 'Age patterns of mortality in London during the "long eighteenth century": a test of the "high potential" model of metropolitan mortality', *Social History of Medicine* 3: 27–60.

(1987), 'Mortality and metropolis: the case of London 1675–1825', *Population Studies* 41: 59–76.

126   *Mortality, politics and economics in historical demography*

(1986), 'Mortality, weather and prices in London 1675–1825: a study of short-term fluctuations', *Journal of Historical Geography* 12: 347–64.

Landers, J. and Mouzas, A.J. (1988), 'Burial seasonality and causes of death in London 1670–1819', *Population Studies* 42: 59–83.

Lee, R.D. (1986), 'Population homeostasis and English demographic history', in R.I. Rotberg and T.K. Rabb eds., *Population and History: from the traditional to the modern world*, Cambridge University Press, pp. 75–100.

(1973), 'Population in pre-industrial England: an econometric analysis', *Quarterly Journal of Economics* 87: 581–607.

Lee, W.R. ed. (1979), *European Demography and Economic Growth*, London: Croom Helm.

Lewontin, R. (1974), *The Genetic Basis of Evolutionary Change*, New York: Columbia University Press.

Lunn, P.G. (1991), 'Nutrition, immunity and infection', in R. Schofield, D. Reber and H. Bideau eds., *The Decline of Mortality in Europe*, Oxford: Clarendon Press, pp. 131–45.

McAlpin, M.B. (1985), 'Famines, epidemics and population growth: the case of India', in R.T. Rotberg and T.K. Rabb eds., *Hunger in History: the impact of changing food production and consumption patterns on society*, Cambridge University Press, pp. 153–68.

McKeown, T.R. (1976), *The Modern Rise of Population*, London: Edward Arnold.

McKeown, T.R. and Brown, R.G. (1955), 'Medical evidence relating to English population changes in the eighteenth century', *Population Studies* 9: 115–41.

McKeown, T.R. and Record, R.G. (1962), 'Reasons for the decline of mortality in England and Wales during the nineteenth century', *Population Studies* 16: 94–122.

McNeill, W.H. (1980), 'Migration patterns and infections in traditional societies', in N.F. Stanley and R.A. Joske eds., *Changing Disease Patterns and Human Infections*, London: Academic Press, pp. 27–36.

(1977), *Plagues and Peoples*, Oxford: Basil Blackwell.

Meuvret, J. (1946), 'Les Crises de subsistances et la démographie de la France de l'Ancien Régime', *Population* 1: 643–50.

(1965), 'Demographic crisis in France from the sixteenth to eighteenth century', in Glass and Eversley eds., *Population in History*, pp. 507–22.

Omran, O.R. (1971), 'The epidemiologic transition', *Millbank Memorial Fund Quarterly* 49: 509–38.

Perrenoud, A. (1984), 'Mortality decline in its secular setting', in Bengtsson et al., *Pre-Industrial Population Change*, pp. 41–69.

Phillips, H. (1964), *Mid-Georgian London: a topographic and social survey of central and west London around 1750*, London: Collins.

Post, J.D. (1984), 'Climatic variability and the European mortality wave of the early 1740s', *Journal of Interdisciplinary History 15*: 1–50.

Rowland, M.G.M. and Barrell, R.A.E. (1980), 'Ecological factors in gastroenteritis', in E.J. Clegg and J.P. Garlick eds., *Disease and Urbanization*, London: Taylor and Francis, pp. 21–36.

Schwarz, L.D. (1985) 'The standard of living in the long run: London, 1700–1860, *Economic History Review (2nd ser.)* 38: 24–41.

Sheppard, F. (1971), *London 1801–1870: the infernal wen*, London: Secker and Warburg.

Sheppard, F., Belcher, V. and Cottrell, P. (1979), 'The Middlesex and Yorkshire deed registries and the study of building fluctuations', *London Journal 5*: 176–217.

Spate, O.H.K. (1936), 'The growth of London A.D. 1660–1800', in H.C. Darby ed., *An Historical Geography of England Before 1800*, Cambridge University Press, pp. 529–48.

Srikantia, S.G. (1985), 'Better nutrition and India: a comment', in Rotberg and Rabb, eds., *Hunger and History*, pp. 169–172.

Summerson, J. (1978), *Georgian London*, London: Peregrine.

Szreter, S. (1988), 'The importance of social intervention in Britain's mortality decline *c.*1850–1914: a re-interpretation of the role of public health', *Social History of Medicine 1*: 1–38.

Tilly, C. (1990) *Coercion, Capital and European States, AD 990–1990*, Oxford: Basil Blackwell

Winch, D. (1987), *Malthus*, Oxford University Press.

Woods, R.I. (1982), *Theoretical Population Geography*, London: Longman.

Wrigley, E.A. (1989), 'Some reflections on corn yields and prices in pre-industrial economies', in J. Walter and R. Schofield eds., *Famine, Disease and the Social Order in early modern society*, Cambridge University Press, pp. 235–78.

(1987), 'The classical economists and the industrial revolution', in *People, Cities and Wealth*, Oxford: Basil Blackwell, pp. 21–45.

(1986), 'Elegance and experience: Malthus at the bar of history', in Coleman and Schofield eds., *The State of Population Theory*, pp. 46–64.

(1983), 'Malthus's model of a pre-industrial economy', in Dûpaquier, *Malthus Past and Present*, pp. 111–24.

(1981), 'The prospects for population history', *Journal of Interdisciplinary History 12*: 207–26.

Wrigley, E.A. and Schofield, R.S. (1981), *The Population History of England 1541-1871: a reconstruction*, London: Edward Arnold.

A social history of plausibility: country, city and calculation in Augustan Britain

These noble Houyhnhnms are endowed by Nature with a general disposition to all Virtues . . . Neither is Reason among them a Point problematical as with us, where Men can argue with Plausibility on both Sides of
a Question . . . I remember it was with extreme Difficulty that I could
bring my Master to understand the Meaning of the Word Opinion, or
how a Point could be disputable . . . When I used to explain to him our
several systems of Natural Philosophy, he would laugh that a Creature
pretending to Reason, should value itself upon the Knowledge of other
Peoples Conjectures and in Things where that Knowledge, if it were certain, could be of no Use (Jonathan Swift, *Travels into Several Remote
Nations of the World by Lemuel Gulliver*, 1726)

In early eighteenth century Britain, a Kentish woman could apparently return after her death and an Oxford astronomer could
apparently foretell the return of comets. A Surrey woman had
given birth to rabbits and ordure from the nation's privies was to
be recycled to make the ground fertile. The Royal Society heard
that great wheels could be moved perpetually by hidden springs
and that the permanently fixed stars had motions of their own.
One Lincolnshire virtuoso, William Stukeley, stated that the Druids built Stonehenge; another, Isaac Newton, said that the
Pythagoreans knew that the inverse square law of gravity drove
the solar system.[1] The social history of such stories has typically
been described in terms of the 'decline of magic' and the 'dis-
enchantment of the world'. Somehow or other, it is claimed, early
modern culture managed to tease apart the rational, scientific,
veridical wheat from the superstitious, traditional, eccentric chaff.
This is to take the equipoise of intellectual authority for granted.
In his canonical study of English social history, published in

wartime Britain, G.M. Trevelyan recalled 'that perfectly beautiful equilibrium between man and nature' established in the early eighteenth century and the development of 'a society with a mental outlook of its own, self-poised, self-judged, and self-approved, freed from the disturbing passions of the past and not yet troubled with anxieties about a very different future'.[2] So property and propriety went hand-in-hand. But such self-assurance can be exaggerated. Bubbles, projects, new philosophies and new systems of credit urgently raised the problem of the judgment of matters of fact. Rival criteria of assessment of the possible contents and capacities of the world were hotly disputed. Relations of knowledge hinged on social relations. To know what might happen in the world it was important to know who to trust.

Thus instead of the secular advance of rational enlightenment, we can propose a social history of plausibility. In the country and the city, at the Exchange and at the Royal Society, before early eighteenth century Britons came to accept or reject a claim, they judged whether it deserved investigation or investment.[3] These judgments relied on explicit and on tacit conventions drawn from socially sanctioned repertoires of credit and trust provided by public culture. Changes in credit had major political effects. Rendering stories about the origin of fertility or the effect of marvellous engines plausible or implausible helped bankrupt dupes or enrich scoundrels, enforce use rights or empower rentiers, subvert the state or restore the commonwealth. The study of plausibility does not imply a social history of what is known, rather a study of the boundaries of what might ever be knowable. There has been a great deal of recent interest, both from philosophers of science and from historians of society, in the exploration of the limits of the conceivable, the arguable or the questionable for a given culture. Epistemologists using the work of Kuhn or Foucault have sought to describe 'scenes of inquiry' or 'positivities', the set of questions judged urgent and proper by a well-defined community of investigators. Here communities are defined by shared questions rather than common answers. We may ask sociohistorical questions about the genealogy of such apparently secure communities.[4] In suggestively similar terms, social historians have often been concerned with the history of sensibilities which might subsequently define the realm of knowledge. At exactly the same moment as Trevelyan's celebratory *English Social History* (1942), Lucien Febvre produced from Nazi-occupied France his analysis of sixteenth century unbelief. In Rabelais' world 'no one then had a sense of what was impossible'. Indeed, 'a concept of the impossible' was not among the 'mental tools' of the epoch. Febvre defended the project to historicise such mental tools by pointing to the threat of 'the exaltation of primitive feelings [and] animal behaviour at the expense of culture'. A social history of feelings and of mental tools would show the specifically cultural origins of apparently sempiternal categories and would prevent 'our universe' becoming 'a stinking pit of corpses' in the name of an antihistorical 'nature'.[5]

A social history of plausibility is inevitably bound up with political critique and contested authority. In response to Febvre's programme, Jacques Revel has recently pointed out a significant change in the meaning of accusations of superstition or vulgar error at the start of the eighteenth century. Superstition switched from threatening nonconformity to inferior and antique mistakes. The wardens of such beliefs, such as the clergy, could be damned by the savants as no better than their flock. Scholasticism was conflated with vulgarity. 'What had been denounced in the name of accepted reason or of scientific knowledge was now invalidated by being labeled the product of an inferior social group.' In this genealogy of the 'intellectual', Revel gives the examples of early modern debates about diabolical possession and about comets to show the move to new conditions of plausibility through new institutions of authority.[6] Such transformations happened at levels of presumptive, tacit behaviour. As Mary Fissell points out, when eighteenth century hospital physicians increasingly deployed Latinate diagnoses of the poor's ailments, they implicitly disqualified dialect descriptions of illness, and thus rendered a range of received terms implausible and incredible. When an eighteenth century agricultural writer explained the rate of plant growth by appealing to 'the growth of an annual rent of one pound continually put out at interest after the rate of five per cent', he implicitly made capital investment more natural than the life of seeds, heretofore the chief exemplar of the process of growth. Changes of language, of technique and of imagery could all subtly shift the bounds of the plausible.[7]

In what follows, historiographies of the eighteenth century public sphere and of the credit crises of Augustan Britain are discussed in order to highlight these ways in which social relations set up varying accounts of plausibility. These accounts are grounded in the emergence of a new public sphere in the market and the city, from which the 'vulgar' were supposedly excluded. It has proved difficult to write a social history of savants' accounts of the boundaries of their world because it has seemed that this world was so insulated from social pressure. But eighteenth century philosophers did a great deal of work in defining the preconditions of their position, and this work can itself be a resource which historians can use. Calculation and measurement are shown to be especially important for this process. The strife surrounding the capitalisation of agricultural markets and the measurement of surplus is used as an example of the change in stories about nature's capacities which accompanied changes in authority and economy.[8]

The new public sphere

A social history of plausibility directs our attention towards the relationship between authorship and authority. In the sixteenth century the term 'plausible' solely referred to the approval, the applause, with which a public claim might be greeted. Only from the eighteenth century does it include the sense of superficiality and deceptive veracity. The suspicion of what passes as general and the restriction on the properly trustworthy forms the burden of this history. In the sciences, we are told, the facts speak for themselves. Here communal authority and individual dogmatism allegedly have no place. Early modern natural philosophers' slogans set the pace. Francis Bacon's 'knowledge is power' was taken to refer to the benefits which disinterested natural knowledge might bring to the social order. The Royal Society's *nullius in verba* was used to urge the independence of the realm of knowledge from the conventions of that order. Messianic and millenarian mottoes, such as 'To the greater light', were considered and apparently rejected by the Society's early fellows. The exercise of force might pervert, but could never warrant, the production of natural knowledge.[9] For this reason, the development of a social history of scientific knowledge has always seemed rather difficult. At best, it might be supposed, such a history could tell stories about the emergence of those rather special institutions in which value-free knowledge and disinterested debate might safely proceed. The function of such institutions would be to insulate the making of natural knowledge from extraneous social pressure. Indeed, early modern Europe saw the appearance of a number of social formations which boasted their autonomy and their mutually collaborative relationships. A series of important studies documents the emergence of such societies. In the Republic of Letters, the scientific clubs, academies and salons, an intelligentsia proclaimed as free from dependency and linked by new systems of information exchange and peaceable debate pursued inquiries in natural philosophy and mathematical sciences.[10]

No doubt this social haven helped define the role of the intellectual in the early modern period and thence provided the resources with which the plausible might be recognised. In this genealogy of the literary critic's self-conscious disengagement from high politics, Terry Eagleton tells us of the 'distinctive discursive space' of the early modern bourgeois public sphere, 'a realm of social institutions – clubs, journals, coffeehouses, periodicals – in which private individuals assemble for the free, equal exchange of reasonable discourse'. However, as Peter Stallybrass and Allon White point out, such references to the public sphere are insufficient unless accompanied by attention to the processes of social exclusion, boundary maintenance and satirical ribaldry which helped intellectuals fashion themselves as uniquely privileged bearers of culture and knowledge. The 'cultured' and the 'rational' worked very hard to control their world against plebeian or vulgar life.[11] The purity of public knowledge was fragile and contested, a social accomplishment which cannot be taken for granted. Roy Porter's account of the social structure of eighteenth century geology explains that the insulation of the intelligentsia prevented earth theorists being soiled. In this contribution to a *Festschrift* for Joseph Needham, Porter counsels against a hasty reduction of high science to the material demands of the economic base.

A mere glance will show that because men of science in East and West have always comprised some sort of mandarinate or clerisy, whether as an elite set apart by wealth, talent, privilege, or by state patronage, they have often been cushioned from some of the more obvious and potent social movements of their day, often isolated from economic and technical pressures from below, by systems of cultural mediations.[12]

However, too many historians of science have found these cushions comfortingly seductive. The clerisy's fragile isolation is used as an excuse for intellectual laziness. Links between scientific problems and economic purposes are dismissed as vulgar Marxism. Connections between natural knowledge and social interests are damned as sociological relativism. Despite this facetious blackguarding, social historians have begun to see how practitioners stipulated the proper and improper contents of their carefully-defined social spaces. Such studies examine how the historically contingent boundaries between different social sites were made, maintained, challenged and breached. A stiff, if carefully measured, dose of reflexivity usefully highlights the accounts of science's institutions which members produced for themselves. These accounts provided resources which practitioners used to define the plausible content of their world and to exclude what they judged illicit and extraneous.[13]

Philosophers and artisans: an enlightened interpretation

In a survey of recent arguments about the character of the eighteenth century public sphere, Roy Porter understandably describes the Enlightenment on this side of the Channel as an 'historiographical Loch Ness Monster' and then claims a sighting of the wondrous beast. Porter finds signs of 'the Enlightenment in action' in new experiences of birth, now managed by Edinburgh trained accoucheurs in well-lit, airy and socially mixed spaces, and of death, increasingly secular and undramatic.[14] The search for enlightened forms of life (and death) has not been easy. Historical studies of the institutions of enlightened philosophy have all too often assumed, or insisted on, the insulation of the *lumières* from their own society. As David Miller has pointed out in his recent study of the Royal Society of the period, 'tackling the eighteenth century problem ... involves understanding how and why these programmes emerged as the heartland of "science" from the cultural morass that was the eighteenth century learned world.' Monsters and morasses – the intellectual landscape looks quite unpromising.[15] Significantly, some historians have assumed that eighteenth century savants are peculiarly in need of defence against the charge of interest in mundane issues. In an important study of such concerns, Eric Hobsbawm argued that the political economy of Smith, Hume and their colleagues was developed in response to the problems of Highland development after the '45. He claimed that they set out the virtues of capitalist agricultural management in contrast to the evils of the gothic system of northern communal peasantry. But this reading of the 'high theorists' of the Scottish Enlightenment was unacceptable to Michael Ignatieff. He countered that 'the political economists of Scotland . . . had the institutional prestige of Scottish universities behind them and were treated as leaders of polite society, indeed as the source of their society's civic identity'. This elevated status was enough to remove them from 'the parochial antinomies of British political debate . . . From this position of relative social autonomy and political detachment, their theorising . . . could develop with a degree of speculative autonomy from the prejudices, commonplaces and ideological exigencies of their immediate social milieu.'[16]

In a more extended analysis of Smith's 'crucial context', Ignatieff and Istvan Hont sought to place his attack on the corn laws in 'its full European setting', specifically French debates about physiocracy in the 1760s. Their internationalisation of the civic humanism of Scottish political economy was designed to answer E.P. Thompson's celebrated discussion of the 'moral economy' of early modern English grain rioters. Thompson treated Smith's 'model of a natural and self-adjusting economy working providentially for the best good of all' as a key moment in the imposition of political economic management over a grain market heretofore widely understood in terms of a divinely-sustained surplus generated from the land. Ignatieff and Hont answered that 'the encounter with the English or Scottish crowd' was not an important context for Smith's work.[17] But what is to be explained here is the construction of a civil society from whose workings the interests of clansmen and plebs were self-evidently absent. Categories such as 'prejudice' and 'ideology', which Ignatieff uses to describe 'parochial' Lowland conversation, were the very stuff of eighteenth century discourse, and their sense cannot be taken for granted. Models of the speculative autonomy and international communality of philosophers were themselves the result, rather than the unproblematic cause, of enlightened philosophical projects and their social formation. Many Scottish philosophers set out a programme for the history of the intellectual, described the cultural origin of their own status, and explicitly linked their social position with the history of the sciences.

Adam Smith, for example, sternly condemned the 'vanity of the philosopher' who was 'scarce willing to acknowledge any resemblance' between himself and the plebeian artisan. Smith insisted on a rather egalitarian picture of the philosopher's status and role. As society progressed, 'philosophy, or speculation ... naturally becomes, like every other employment, the sole occupation of a particular class of citizens'. Were any citizen to review the knowledge he possessed, he would find that most of it 'has been purchased, in the same manner as his shoes or stockings, from those whose business it is to make up and prepare for the market that particular species of goods'. Philosophers were as commercially implicated as other tradesmen. Their superior role, however, was not denied but reinterpreted. Smith insisted that the most significant improvements in machinery, especially 'the application of new powers', demanded philosophers with 'a greater range of thought and more extensive views of things than naturally falls to the share of a meer artist'. Division of labour produced a special profession distinguished by their leisure, by their liberal capacity to oversee those forces of society and nature invisible to those enmeshed in everyday concerns.[18]

The capacities of machines played a central role in the world of projects and schemes which dominated commercial culture. Thomas Reid, theorist of Newton's philosophy of powers and moral philosophy professor at Glasgow, wrote with some approval of the effect of this machine philosophy upon public culture in an age of credit scandals and visionary projects. Half a century after the South Sea Bubble, he recalled the

Phrenzy in the Nation about mechanical Projects. Many were ruined and many more were in danger of being drawn into Ruin by such Projectors. This Disease seems to have been cured in a great degree by shewing men clearly upon principles of Science the utmost Effects that the Mechanical Powers can produce.

Significantly, Reid named John Theophilus Desaguliers, doyen of Augustan philosophical engineers and public lecturers, as the hero of this therapeutic success.[19] The implications of the cure of the public mind for the status of philosophical demonstration were not missed. In the Scottish academies the link between the artisan construction of machines and the philosophical construction of world-systems was often stressed. In his youthful essay on the history of astronomy, composed in the 1750s, Smith urged that

systems in many respects resemble machines. A machine is a little system, created to perform, as well as to connect together, in reality, those different movements and effects which the artist has occasion for. A system is an imaginary machine invented to connect together in the fancy those different movements and effects which are already in reality performed.[20]

The implication of this constructivist version of natural philosophy was that philosophical work should be interpreted as machine-building, and that the design and improvement of machinery was a legitimate philosophical concern. At the end of his tenure of the Glasgow chair of moral philosophy in the early 1760s, just before Reid's appointment, Smith set down his thoughts on the role of the division of labour in the invention and improvement of machinery:

He who first thought of substituting, in the room of the crank or handle, an outer wheel which was to be turned round by a stream of water . . . was probably no work man of any kind, but a philosopher or meer man of speculation; one of those people whose trade it is not to do anything but to observe every thing, and who are upon that account capable of combining together the powers of the most opposite and distant objects.[21]

Smith's opposite number at Edinburgh, the natural and moral philosopher Adam Ferguson, was altogether less sanguine about the claims of philosophy over mechanics. In his 1767 *Essay on the History of Civil Society* he stated that 'ignorance is the mother of industry as well as superstition . . . Manufactures, accordingly, prosper most where the mind is least consulted, and where the workshop may . . . be considered as an engine, the parts of which are men'. Ferguson agreed with Smith that 'thinking itself, in this age of separations, may become a peculiar craft.' But the principal function of this craft was just to overcome the ill effect of such separations by generating liberal contemplation. Philosophy was the cure for that social division which gave the leisure to philosophise. Liberal and mechanic professions were utterly sundered. Ferguson judged it 'certainly reasonable to form our opinion of the rank that is due to men of certain professions and stations, from the influence of their manner of life in cultivating the powers of the mind'.[22] Problems of rank and of profession dominated the ways in which enlightened philosophers placed themselves in a rapidly commercialising society. Smith understood the importance of mechanisation in this process, and so displayed philosophy as an enterprise which could master the machine. But mastery should never be confused with veracity. Smith emphasised that philosophical systems were best understood as machines so as to display the ingenuity and the conventionality which went into their construction. Ingenious conventions, he reckoned, would assuage the superstitious wonder and vulgar gawping after marvels which infected public belief. This was what made Newtonian astronomy plausible. While accepting that the Newtonian 'system now prevails over all opposition, and has advanced to the acquisition of the most universal empire that was ever established in philosophy', he insisted that this system remained an invention. So Smith rightly treated the systems of natural philosophy and of the mathematical sciences as institutions whose worth must be assessed in terms of their effect on the social order of the public sphere.[23]

Crises of public credit

On this account, scientific institutions mediated social relations. They did not insulate science from these relations. Since the construction of plausible knowledge demanded the construction of stable communities, such institutions embodied and developed new forms of social relations rather than existing as passive reflections of them. The characteristic social formation of enlightened sciences, the public sphere, can therefore be treated as in part a product of organised natural philosophical action. For this reason, the appearance of Jan Golinski's *Science as Public Culture* and Larry Stewart's *The Rise of Public Science* is very welcome.[24] Both studies, as their homophonous titles suggest, draw our attention towards public conduct in the social spaces of eighteenth century Britain. Coffeehouses and city streets, the Stock Exchange and the bleach works, play as much a role as the heavenly city of familiar histories of enlightenment. These works enable us to see the way in which the status of that enlightenment has much more general implications, especially in the light of canonical interpretations of the origins of modern society. Jürgen Habermas, for example, has offered a celebration of the Augustan public sphere as a prefiguration of modern civility. Reinhart Koselleck has argued that this public sphere was explicitly distinguished from that of the state,

which enlightened philosophers judged hostile to the free pursuit
of truth. Hence, Koselleck argues, arose the masonic clubs and
conspiratorial associations of eighteenth century savants. Larry
Stewart's work responds with a nuanced interpretation of the
scandalous and productive projects of scheming jobbers and self-
styled philosophical engineers which characterised this public sphere
and its technologies, a milieu scarcely devoid of self-interest and
of capitalist rationality, dominated by economic plots and public
projects. In similar terms, Norbert Elias argued that processes
characteristic of the Scientific Revolution and the Enlightenment,
specifically the emergence of the absolutist state and of rational
knowledge, both involved the construction of a new persona, the
homo clausus, a self-contained individual capable of knowing the
world as an external system from which the human was absent.
The 'self-poise' celebrated by Trevelyan is treated here as a sociological precondition of plausible knowledge. But Elias complained
that the emergence of this basic figure of enlightened epistemology
was not accompanied by an equivalent contemporary analysis of
the specifically social processes through which the *homo clausus*
was constructed. Jan Golinski answers with a detailed analysis of
the cultural resources through which such figures as the philosophical chemist, a proper member of civil society and a self-
contained expert in the workings of material nature, were
constructed in the public sphere of the Enlightenment. He shows
that contemporaries in enlightened Scotland, such as Smith's
colleagues William Cullen and Joseph Black, and in radical England,
such as Joseph Priestley and Black's student Thomas Beddoes,
were centrally concerned with the sociogenesis of the bearer of
reliable public knowledge and with participation in the workings
of public politics.[25]

So this fresh attention to the cosmopolitan public sphere
addresses issues of central concern both for the Enlightenment
itself, and for our own sociology of knowledge. Recent sociological analyses have rightly stressed the local, situated character of
knowledge and its production. The wider grip of different knowl-
edges is then accounted as liaisons between these locales, the
multiplication of the contexts in which specific techniques work
and are compelling. Hence our interest in lectures and advertisements, textbooks and travellers, and our concern with the sociology of credit. Credit demanded appropriate public performances.

In 1713 a contemporary judged that 'many good men' went bankrupt by 'living up to support a credit and shoar up a reputation
(no mean mystery in this world)'. Credit was judged the basis of,
and yet the threat to, social order. 'Tis a strange thing to think
how absolute this Lady is', stated Defoe in 1706, 'how despotickly
she governs all her Actions.' Defoe famously analysed all social
relations, and especially English ones, as vulnerable to others'
judgments and hence inherently unstable. Terms of trade were
explicitly assimilated to languages of trust and honour and then
judged to be moveable. 'A sort of Lunacy attends all its Circumstances, and no Man can give a rational Account of it.' Yet, he
insisted, the invulnerability of credit to the dictates of state tyr-
anny provided the basis of a free and enlightened public sphere.[26]
These paradoxes of trust, interest, and reliance on other's judgments
inform both Stewart's picture of Newtonian life on the Exchange
and Golinski's account of the construction of the public culture of
chemical knowledge. More generally, they also characterise analyses of the way knowledge is made reliable. Richard Sennett, for
example, has argued that the new social conditions of the great
eighteenth century cities, especially London, faced citizens with
'the question of living with or being a stranger'. As conventional
hierarchies were challenged, stable resources for mutual judgment
were destabilised. 'Because hierarchy became an uncertain measure when dealing with a stranger, the problem of audience arose.'
This has material and cultural implications. Elias describes good
society in early eighteenth century England as 'a market of opinions',
in which reputation was valued, won and lost. He links this with
the increasingly subtle and rigorous conventions of bodily self-
control when out in public. Bodily gestures and relations of honour
were changed.[27]

These changes were especially important for the making of
conditions for plausible knowledge. In a society of orders, conventions of gentlemanliness might allow a judgment of the credit of a
witness independently of the content of the witness's report. Within
the experimental community, efforts were made to displace the
difficulties of credit with the material technologies of instrumental
performance and the theoretical technologies of mathematical
calculation. Eighteenth century communities of natural philosophers shared conventions which were sceptical of the capacity of
hirelings, women, children, the sick or the mad to give evidence of

their own experiences.[28] New institutions helped sustain new relations of authority. This may be compared with contemporary
changes in physicians' attitudes to the medical histories of their
clients. The empowerment of genteel patients meant that physicians varied their medical theories as part of a process of product
differentiation at the wealthy bedside. For the poor, institutionalisation of hospital medicine was accompanied by a devaluation of
patients' own accounts of their sufferings and the authorisation of
a range of diagnostic techniques which were to displace the patient's own power over the disease.[29] Increasingly, instrumentation
and calculation were designed to provide evidence which it was
reckoned the vulgar could not give. In 1753 the London electri-
cian John Canton was told of a story about a lightning strike at
Wells Cathedral which impressed the congregation with figures of
the cross. 'I could wish the Bishop's attention had not been so
much absorbed in the Wonderful, and that we had more accurate
note of the form of the cross, the nature of the impression,
&c . . . this story may lead you to some Experiments that may
strike a farther light into these curious but difficult matters.'[30]
Marvellous lighting strikes were still plausible events. The means
for investigating them had changed, and a good living earnt by
showing their effects to the public.

Many contemporaries saw a link between fashions for public
calculation and the diseases of credit which infected social judgment. In 1743 Henry Fielding used the recent learned interest in
Abraham Trembley's story about the regeneration of the polyp to
announce a newly discovered beast, the 'terrestrial chrysipus or
golden guinea', which was even more lively and self-generative.
The joke was on the rationalists who so energetically touted the
possibility of managing credit through sums. In 1727 William
Hogarth drew a 'Lecherometer' on the walls of a crowded masquerade, and in 1739 depicted a thermometer plunged into an
enthusiast's brain at a fanatics' prayer meeting. Sites of public
trade, demonstration and deceit were also places where measurement and calculation paraded their ludicrous claims. Even God
lost his credit, noted Bernard de Mandeville, medic and satiric
moralist, in the wake of the bursting of the South Sea Bubble in
the 1720s. The public were now governed by 'the uncertainty of
things, and the vicissitudes of human Affairs. The Mathematicks
become the only valuable Study, and are made use of in every

thing even where it is ridiculous, and Men seem to repose no greater Trust in providence than they would in a Broken Merchant'.[31]

Regimes of calculation

Mathematisation has often been seen as an inevitable accompaniment of the increasing grasp of the sciences over nature. Numbering makes claims plausible. Eighteenth century natural philosophy looks like a case history in the triumph of precision measurement over qualitative experience.[32] This story assumes that a search for precision needs no further justification, that the measurable stands for the real, and that natural philosophers adopted a general programme of quantification, heedless of which systems of values they endorsed in so doing. All of these assumptions need qualification. The basis of eighteenth century measurement can only be displayed through a local analysis of contemporary natural philosophers' practices of measurement. It demands a social history. At the start of the century, a small number of quantitative principles had been established, principally in the realms of mixed mathematics, such as optics, mechanics, music and astronomy. The relationship between air's spring and its volume, for example, was not understood in quantitative terms. Evelyn Fox Keller has argued that 'the fact that Boyle's Law is not wrong must not be forgotten', but that 'the success of Boyle's law must be recognized as circumscribed and hence limited by the context in which it arises'. Boyle's original context was a fight with a Jesuit anti-mechanist, against whom he wished to urge the power of the air's spring. Boyle did not express his work on air in any precise, quantitative form. 'I shall not venture to determine whether or no the intimated theory will hold universally and precisely.' As Steven Shapin shows, Boyle's moral values ruled precise values out of experimental natural philosophy.[33] 'Success' needs to be accounted as an exercise of power. Different measurement schemes are different social practices. Each scheme needs defending against rivals. These practices give meaning to different systems of values, and make those values legitimate. Measurement and calculation defend and propagate a value system at the expense of others. This is why different regimes of plausibility were credited in eighteenth century society.

During 1758, London newspapers carried many reports and discussions of an approaching comet, that supposedly predicted by Edmond Halley in the first decades of the century. The astronomer and journalist John Bevis quoted Halley's view that

it may justly be reckoned one of the principal uses of the Mathematical Sciences, that they are in many cases able to prevent or correct the superstition of the unskilful vulgar; and by shewing them the genuine causes of rare appearances, to deliver them from the vain apprehensions they are apt to entertain of what they call *Prodigies*, which sometimes by the artifices of designing men (as of late with regard to the expected Comet) have been made use of to very ill purposes.

The thought that calculation could quell public error was not shared by all. Such mathematical 'positiveness' was 'an evil arising from too great an opinion a man conceives of his own abilities', according to one critic of the cometary writings of the foremost London instrument maker Benjamin Martin.[34] For Augustan writers, the power of regimes of calculation and measurement to render claims plausible was neither self-evident nor unchallenged. The Scriblerian wit and physician John Arbuthnot mounted violent attacks on mathematicians such as William Whiston or Edmond Halley, who used calculations for what he deemed the wrong purposes. In the Scriblerians' remarkable *Memoirs* (1714) the achievements of natural philosophy, including those associated with Newton's disciples, were fiercely satirised. But Arbuthnot also penned a celebrated *Essay on the Usefulness of Mathematical Learning* (1700) and a paper on the argument for divine design from the relative numbers of male and female births (1711). He reckoned that calculation 'is the true political knowledge'.[35]

Scriblerian satire against the immoral dogmatism and irrationality of the purveyors of mathematical reason was just one aspect of this critique. Assurance schemes grew because of, and foundered despite, a very widespread optimism in the power of calculation. What was plausible was defined as what a highly idealised 'reasonable man' would reckon.[36] Controversies on the values of mathematical reason exploded in the 1730s following the work of the Scriblerians' colleague, George Berkeley, whose *Analyst* (1734) aimed to twit the Whig mathematicians opposed to the High Church with their own irrational faith in infinitesimals. The dispute in mathematics hinged on whether such entities, as Newton had supposed, had a plausible existence in nature. Disciples of fluxions answered that they were merely extending the 'geometry of the ancients' and that the minute quantities of which mathematicians spoke were naturally occurring objects.[37] If the precise became the real, then understanding the values sustained by different ways of measurement helps clarify what was given plausibility and represented through these different quantitative regimes. Standardisation, for example, works by stipulating the right places where calculation should be performed, such as the Mint and the Exchange, and disqualifying others, such as the field or the hearth. Metrology, which sets up local standards as universal values, was a crucial eighteenth century accomplishment in the social work which made a stable zone of operations for natural philosophers.[38]

In his brilliant studies of the history of metrology, Witold Kula has argued that conflicts about the imposition of measures 'have been an ever-present element in the struggle for power between interested representatives of the privileged class'. His examples are often drawn from fights over varying practices in the assessment of grain measures. Level measures and heaped measures were used to sustain very different local cultures in the *ancien régime*, especially in times of dearth, where accusations of corrupt trade were rife. The implication is that social historians should interpret different systems of measures as different institutions with contrasted purposes. John Brewer has pointed out the rapid institutionalisation of mathematical training and data production during the eighteenth century as a key aspect of the politics of information in the age of the fiscal-military state. The establishment of the Inspectorate-General of Imports and Exports (1696), the first state statistical bureau, was accompanied by an increase in provision of mathematics teaching in London and the provinces, at such sites as Christ's Hospital, the biggest school in London, and the Royal Mathematical School, founded in 1673 for maritime training.[39] The early eighteenth century boom in lectures on experimental philosophy and the mathematical sciences, of which Desaguliers and then Benjamin Martin were protagonists, has often been studied as an aspect of widespread modernisation. As Stewart and Jacob have both argued, these performances helped reinforce the connection between new models of 'public knowledge' and the rightful authority of mathematically competent practitioners.[40] Such widespread publications as the *Lady's Diary* (founded 1704) and its rival the *Gentleman's Diary* (1741) catered to a nationwide

network of 'philomaths' with pages on the calendar, interest tables, news, bibliography and a wealth of mathematical puzzles
and challenges to which readers were expected to respond. In
provincial centres such as Northampton, masters such as John
Ryland developed radical new pedagogies which turned domestic
experience to the ends of calculation. Chambermaids' mops were
pressed into service to illustrate planetary motion; farmers' accounts were used to try out formal mathematical sums.[41] The
celebrated entrepreneur and bookseller John Newbery peddled a
range of texts on popular science and children's education, including the dialogues featuring 'Tom Telescope' which, as Jim Secord
argues, were designed to teach the offspring of professionals and
merchants that natural knowledge was linked to the landed gentry. The information which such magazines and lecturers peddled
was often proffered as self-evidently 'useful'. As John Brewer urges,
however, their utility at least partly lay in their capacity to record
knowledge of the world and to display the public sphere as a
linked network of commercial and entrepreneurial relationships.[42]

Moral economy and the new husbandry

The chief site of calculation in eighteenth century culture was the
market. The system of distribution and exchange is a good place
to see valuation moralised and the delimitation of the plausible
contents of the world. The existence of what E.P. Thompson has
described as 'the moral economy' reminds us that rationality cannot be seen as the prerogative of the friends of the capitalist market.
The conflicts between rival accounts of this economy hinged on
the values invested in metrology, in the reckoning of standards for
price, quantity and production. At the start of the century, the
agricultural market was widely agreed to be governed by a moral
code, sanctioned by custom and Scripture. Agricultural labour
transferred the divine product of God's earth from soil to table.
The ultimate producer was God's action in earth. Divinity acted
as fertility. Whoever intervened in this process, by forestalling or
regrating, by trading in the sacred territory between the fields and
the home, was guilty of blasphemy. A writer of 1718 condemned
such traders as 'a vagabond sort of people' who 'have the mark
of Cain, and like him wander from place to place, driving an
interloping trade between the fair dealer and the honest consumer'.[43]

Political economists sought to place this language in the context of superstition and vulgarity. Smith famously observed that 'the laws concerning corn may everywhere be compared to the laws concerning religion', and that the 'popular fear of engrossing and forestalling may be compared to the popular terrors and suspicions of witchcraft'. So to repeal the corn laws would be comparable with the act banning witchcraft persecutions. God's action in the soil and the existence of demons were equally implausible.[44] The capitalisation of agricultural production, enclosure of common lands and the disruption of traditional use rights were all contests over the plausible contents of nature and of nature's bounty. Fiscal provisions, excise calculations and penal legislation of the 1730s and after were directed against those who defended traditional rights and plausibilities.[45]

Different models of the real economy also relied on different natural philosophies. The moral economy prompted the search for a divinely sustained active principle in earth which guaranteed its fertility. A traditional chemical discourse, represented after the Restoration by writers such as John Beale, John Evelyn and John Worlidge, endorsed by the Royal Society's Georgical Committee and its leaders such as Robert Boyle, sustained this view that in earth natural philosophy would locate some active power which, if left to act freely, would generate agricultural surpluses.[46] The name of this power was variously the *spiritus mundi*, the *terra pinguis*, or some form of 'niter'. Evelyn wrote a 'Philosophical Discourse of Earth' which celebrated 'that intestine fermentation . . . which derives life and growth and motion to all that [the Earth] produces'. Worlidge pushed an attack on 'the vast numbers of vagrants and idle persons that are spread throughout the great part of England' by appealing to 'the highest fertility and improvements' to be expected from 'due Preservation, Reception and right disposing and ordering of that Spiritus Mundi every where found and to be attained without Cost as well by the Poor as the Rich'.[47] These substances defined the plausibly divine contents of the earth. They also found their place in a contemporary 'sacred history of the Earth', a genre rife in the 1690s, which helped link the theological philosophy of the soil to Scriptural history. Sacred histories such as those of Thomas Burnet, John Ray or John Woodward used events in the divinely planned history of the world, especially the Fall and the Deluge to position the origin of labour, the catastrophic decline in earthly fertility and the continued warrant of God's grace, within a philosophical constructed narrative of chemistry and mechanics.[48] To attack this set of moral philosophies was to undermine the claim that the surplus depended on an agent derived from God's activity in the soil. A change in natural philosophical strategies and authority, a switch to the plausible effects of labour power rather than that of God's agents, was to be a crucial change in the social relations of agriculture.

An excellent case of the new social values embodied in this process, especially those of measurement and control, is provided by the work of Jethro Tull, a Whig lawyer and farmer whose estate, 'Prosperous' in Berkshire, was a proving ground for new techniques of exploitation in the first three decades of the century. In his *New Horse-Houghing Husbandry* (1731), sponsored by Robert Walpole and influential Whig lords, Tull announced the principles of his new scheme. The text took its place in a new public sphere of coffeehouse projects and social change. Tull's projects included improved seed drilling and techniques of deep tillage.[49] Tull also denied the possibility of legitimation of agricultural surplus through Scriptural history and the chemistry of divinely sustained active principles. He accepted the relatively novel possibility of acting as a spokesman for an explicitly antagonistic social group – the landowner. By swiftly abandoning any account of 'specifick qualities' in earth, Tull shifted attention to labour.[50] He rejected sacred histories of the Earth, such as those of Woodward. Fertility was deprived of its connection with God's action before and after the Deluge. 'Swine had practised the art of turning the soil, and so had men long before the fictitious deity of Ceres was invented.' He used the term 'mathematics' precisely to distinguish his work from the moral economists: 'why they did not improve the plough so that it might also till as well as the spade seems owing to the Primitive Theory, which gave no Mathematical Reason to shew wherein the true method of Tillage did consist'. This 'reason' was designed to make new economic relations more plausible.[51]

Tull did not speak of a patriarchal family-based husbandman, but an exploitative proprietor. Using terms which matched those of public talk about insubordinate servants and persistently rebellious plebs, he recalled his development of seed-drilling 'about the time when plough servants first began to exalt their dominion over their masters, so that a gentleman farmer was alow'd to make but a little profit of his arable lands'. Just before Tull's book, Defoe had complained of similar problems in his *Great Law of Subordination Consider'd*, a text which registered the increase in contractual, rather than paternal, labour relations. Compare Desaguliers' contemporary argument that an innumerate master would be incapable of managing his workmen, because 'a light Sketch of a design and general proportions are often called a *Theory*, which being *incompleat* will fail in the Practice . . . and the Knave will disappoint his master's Design by performing ill what he can declare *was not his own Scheme or Project*'. Similarly, knavish artisans 'look upon him as a false Brother who lets Gentlemen into their Manner of Working, and the Knowledge of the Price of all the Materials'. The solution was to forge a new role: the philosophically competent mechanic who could simultaneously break 'the Combination among most Workmen to make a Mystery of their Arts' and master the philosophical principles which governed machines. Tull agreed: quantitative trials of new seeds were frustrated by labourers who were 'jealous that if a great quantity of land should be taken from the plough, it might prove a diminution of their power . . . I was forc'd to dismiss my labourers, resolving to quit my scheme unless I could contrive an engine to plant more faithfully than such hands could do.'[52]

The precise assessment of trials' success and the exact execution of farming schemes hinged on this new mechanical system. And this new system demanded a new account of the plausible source of agricultural surplus. Bruno Latour has depicted the success of Louis Pasteur in transforming his French field station from farm to rural laboratory, and then using this site to guarantee his power over anthrax bacilli, already proved in the laboratory, as it moved to the field. Tull's aims were similar. He reckoned he could gain power over indisciplined men and thus proclaim the simultaneous end of superstition and resistance. The 'mathematical rules' which he derived were directed at disciplining treacherous employees and his philosophy of earth was a break with the mandate of heaven, not a consequence of its will. He explained that 'the Ancients' had absurdly told us that 'without all these Accidents meet . . . we must abstain from Ploughing. Our Ploughmen would be glad their Masters were as superstitious, for then the Plough might keep holidays enough.' The public sphere of Augustan handbooks of rational reckoning helped make this new authority: 'because there are no Mathematical Rules extant in any method a Man may practise the old random Husbandry all his life without attaining so much certainly in Agriculture as may be learn'd in a few Hours from such a Treatise'.[53] Tull's 'new husbandry' was often attacked, by organisations such as the significantly-named Society of Husbandmen and Planters. His machines were costly, and his methods hard to work on heavier soils. But his reputation as representative of a reformed field system was secured as an ally of calculation and control. Rebellious commoners began to look like irrational outlaws.[54]

A place *in rerum natura*

The countryside was treated here as an especially potent, and contested, source of authority. Raymond Williams' compelling account of this source has surely demonstrated its potency and its malleability.[55] It could be represented as a source of dangerous generation, as when, in 1726, a Godalming woman, Mary Toft, was reported to be giving birth to litters of rabbits. Her landlord was a friend of Walpole and Tull; her countryside was subjected to enclosure. London surgeons and savants debated the plausibility of her story. She was shifted from her rural home to a London brothel before being forced to confess deception. Metropolitan rivals used the episode to fight for their authority. Country tales, even this one, could always be used by the so-called 'country' opposition to portray Whig corruption.[56] As John Barrell observes of Alexander Pope's *Essay on Man* (1733), the position from which Pope and Bolingbroke, opposition voices, successfully divined 'this scene of Man' was that of the landed huntsman, who 'beat this ample field . . . eye Nature's Walks; shoot Folly as it flies'. This idyllic account of the genteel perspective may be compared with that of Pope's *Windsor Forest* (1704–13), which explicitly condemns 'sportive Tyrants', for whom 'the Subjects starv'd, the Beast was fed'. E.P. Thompson has noted the connection between Pope's family and the 'Blacks' who contested Walpole's campaign against traditional use rights within Windsor Forest in the early 1720s. This reading of Pope's verses remains conjectural and has been contested by other historians. But Thompson judges that this provides a clue to Pope's contrast between the perfected rural site from which an impartial gaze on nature was possible, and the corruption of the Whig laws which sought to disrupt it.[57]

Different representations of field pursuits did warrant different realities. For a fine picture of Whig engrossment of so 'gentle' a pursuit as fowling, turn to the frontispiece of the translation of Newton's *De methodis fluxionum et serierum infinitorum* so titled and prepared by his successor as Lucasian professor at Cambridge, John Colson, in 1736. Challenged by Pope's friend Berkeley to show that fluxions had a real existence, Colson aimed to make these differential elements 'the object of . . . the Imagination (which will only prove their possible existence) but even to Sense too, by making them actually to exist in a visible and sensible form'. His method was simple: he considered the case of a huntsman aiming to hit two ducks with one shot, and traced the locus of the fowler's eye as the result of a second order differential equation. Anything which could be represented like this 'must be allowed to have a place *in rerum natura*'. The scene is as rural as that evoked by Pope. Both contrast the authority of the ancients with current models of knowledge. Both treat genteel country pursuits as the site of plausibility. But Pope and Colson do so in the name of opposed systems of values, Cambridge mathematics and Twickenham pastoral.[58]

Life on the land might be treated as providing a privileged access to the nature of things. But this life had to be carefully reconstructed so that it could be judged reliable. Cottagers and huntsman might be represented as possessed of an authentic knowledge; they might be represented as obstacles to the achievement of that knowledge. The doyen of Georgian agricultural writers, Arthur Young, summed up the difficulties in making field trials along Tull's lines. He argued that the conditions such tests must meet to match those of experimental philosophy, of which metropolitan electrical trials provided the best model, would require the complete reorganisation of the management of the field. Agricultural experiments were slow and costly. 'Nor are time and money all that are wanting. The process is in the hands of clowns, and what is oftentimes much worse, of ill-educated, conceited, ignorant, pert bailiffs, who find either pleasure or profit in a miscarriage.' Young complained that open fields were 'liable to the plundering of thieves, to accidents from birds and reptiles, to the intrusion of another sort of vermin, sportsmen, whose object of a patridge or a fox will induce them to trample on pursuits they have no relish to enjoy, nor attention to understand'. Clear the field of extraneous obstacles and the truth would emerge. Scientific agriculture made itself plausible by reorganising the rural world. Critics spotted that 'the leading object of [Young's] pursuit was not agriculture but political oeconomy'. Young's society experienced a growth in the division of labour and an increased sense that the harmony of social order was threatened. But his cohort started to argue that such divisions might well aid social progress. As the political economists began to claim, individual pursuit of self-interest benefited the whole. The puzzle was that this benefit was invisible to almost all of society's members.[59]

The distanced, equable view of the propertied gentleman or the philosophical savant was claimed as the unique position from which the system of social order could be perceived. Local forms of knowledge were therefore disqualified and rendered implausible. A sociologically informed account may historicise this distanced overview, the 'view from nowhere', a utopia beloved of epistemologists of objective knowledge. The aim of this argument has been to connect interested conflicts about what the social order ought to contain with the process of establishing what the natural world might contain.

Notes

1   Manuel Schonhorn, ed., *Accounts of the Apparition of Mrs Veal* (Los Angeles: William Andrews Clark Library, 1985); Peter Broughton, 'The First Predicted Return of Comet Halley', *Journal for the History of Astronomy* 16 (1985), 123–33; S.A. Seligman, 'Mary Toft – the Rabbit Breeder', *Medical History* 5 (1961), 349–60; John Carswell, *The South Sea Bubble* (London: Cresset Press, 1961), p. 142; Henry Dircks, *Perpetuum Mobile*, 2 vols. (London: Spon, 1861 and 1870), 2: 94–116; Michael Hoskin, *Stellar Astronomy: Historical Studies* (Chalfont St Giles: Science History, 1982), pp. 13, 102; Stuart Piggott, *The Druids* (Harmondsworth: Penguin, 1974), pp. 131–5; Simon Schaffer, 'Newton's Comets and the Transformation of Astrology', in Patrick Curry, ed., *Astrology, Science, Society: Historical Studies* (Woodbridge: Boydell, 1987), 219–43, p. 241.

2   G.M. Trevelyan, *English Social History* (London: Longman, 1944), pp. 304, 339. For studies of rationalisation, from very different

perspectives, see Keith Thomas, *Religion and the Decline of Magic* (Harmondsworth: Penguin, 1972); Brian Easlea, *Witch-hunting, Magic and the New Philosophy* (Brighton: Harvester, 1980); Carolyn Merchant, *The Death of Nature* (London: Wildwood House, 1982).

3 For credit crises and projects, see Pat Rogers, 'Gulliver and the Engineers', in *Eighteenth Century Encounters* (Brighton: Harvester, 1985), 11–28; Larry Stewart and A.J.G. Cummings, 'The Case of the Eighteenth Century Projector', in Bruce Moran, ed., *Patronage and Institutions* (Woodbridge: Boydell, 1991), 235–61.

4 Ian Hacking, 'Michel Foucault's Immature Science', *Nous* 13 (1979), 39–51; Nicholas Jardine, *The Scenes of Inquiry* (Oxford University Press, 1991).

5 Lucien Febvre, *The Problem of Unbelief in the Sixteenth Century* (1942; Cambridge, MA.: Harvard University Press, 1982), pp. 150, 441; Febvre, 'Sensibility and History' (1941), reprinted in Peter Burke, ed., *A New Kind of History: from the writings of Febvre* (London: Routledge, 1973), 12–26, p. 26.

6 Jacques Revel, 'Forms of expertise: intellectuals and popular culture in France, 1650–1800', in Steven Kaplan, ed., *Understanding Popular Culture* (Paris and New York: Mouton, 1984), 255–73, p. 262. His source is J.M. Goulemot, 'Démons, merveilles et philosophie à l'âge classique', *Annales ESC* 35 (1980), 1223–50.

7 Mary Fissell, 'The Disappearance of the Patient's Narrative and the Invention of Hospital Medicine', in Roger French and Andrew Wear, eds., *British Medicine in an Age of Reform* (London: Routledge, 1991), 92–109, p. 103; Richard Bradley, *A General Treatise of Husbandry and Gardening*, 3 vols. (London, 1721–4), Vol. 2, p. 71, discussed in F.N. Egerton, 'Richard Bradley's Understanding of Biological Productivity', *Journal for the History of Biology* 2 (1969), 391–410.

8 For the discrediting of popular beliefs, see Peter Burke, *Popular Culture in Early Modern Europe* (London: Temple Smith, 1978), pp. 270–81; E.P. Thompson, *Customs in Common* (London: Merlin, 1991), pp. 49–58; T. Harris, ed., *Popular Culture in the Eighteenth Century* (London: Macmillan, 1991). For the historical relation between rationality, property and the state see Philip Corrigan and Derek Sayer, *The Great Arch: English State Formation as Cultural Revolution* (Oxford: Blackwell, 1985), pp. 93–9.

9 For the social use of these views, see Paul Wood, 'Methodology and Apologetics: Thomas Sprat's *History of the Royal Society*', *British Journal for the History of Science* 13 (1980), 1–26; Peter Dear, '*Totius in verba*: Rhetoric and Authority in the early Royal Society', *Isis* 76 (1985), 145–61; Steven Shapin, 'Pump and Circumstance: Robert Boyle's Literary Technology', *Social Studies of Science* 14 (1984),

481–520. For the proposed mottoes see Michael Hunter, *Establishing the New Science: the Experience of the early Royal Society* (Woodbridge: Boydell, 1989), p. 17.

10   An influential survey of scientific institutionalisation as the creation of intellectual autonomy was Joseph Ben-David, *The Scientist's Role in Society* (Englewood Cliffs: Prentice Hall, 1971). For sciences in the academies, see James E. McLellan, *Science Reorganized* (New York: Columbia, 1984).

11   Terry Eagleton, *The Function of Criticism* (London: Verso, 1984), p. 9; Peter Stallybrass and Allon White, *The Politics and Poetics of Transgression* (London: Methuen, 1986), pp. 82–4, 93–100. For urban change see Max Byrd, *London Transformed: Images of the City in the Eighteenth Century* (New Haven: Yale University Press, 1978), pp. 8–43.

12   Roy Porter, 'The Industrial Revolution and the Rise of the Science of Geology', in Mikulas Teich and Robert Young, eds., *Changing Perspectives in the History of Science* (London: Heinemann, 1973), 320–43, p. 342.

13   For sociology of science and of scientific knowledge see H.M. Collins, 'The Sociology of Scientific Knowledge', *American Review of Sociology* 9 (1983), 265–85. For the social history of boundaries in the sciences, see Steven Shapin, 'Discipline and Bounding: the History and Sociology of Science as seen through the Externalism-Internalism Debate', *History of Science* 30 (1992), 333–69.

14   Roy Porter, 'English Society in the Eighteenth Century Revisited', in Jeremy Black, ed., *British Politics and Society from Walpole to Pitt 1742–1789* (London: Macmillan, 1991), 29–52, p. 50. For birth rituals see Adrian Wilson, 'William Hunter and the Varieties of Man-Mid-wifery', in W.F. Bynum and Roy Porter, eds., *William Hunter and the Eighteenth Century World* (Cambridge University Press, 1985), pp. 343–69; on death see John McManners, *Death and the Enlightenment* (Oxford University Press, 1981).

15   David P. Miller, 'Into the Valley of Darkness: Reflections on the Royal Society in the Eighteenth Century', *History of Science* 27 (1989), 155–66, p. 164; compare G.N. Cantor, 'The Eighteenth Century Problem', *History of Science* 20 (1982), 44–68.

16   Eric Hobsbawm, 'Scottish Reformers of the Eighteenth Century and Capitalist Agriculture', in E.J. Hobsbawm *et al.*, eds., *Peasants in History* (Oxford University Press, 1980), 3–29 (also published as 'Capitalisme et agriculture: les réformateurs écossais au XVIIIe siècle', *Annales ESC* 33 (1978), 580–601); Michael Ignatieff, 'Primitive Accumulation Revisited', in Raphael Samuel, ed., *People's History and Socialist Theory* (London: Routledge, 1981), 130–5, pp. 132–3.

17   Istvan Hont and Michael Ignatieff, eds., *Wealth and Virtue*

(Cambridge University Press, 1983), p. 43; E.P. Thompson, *Customs in Common* (London: Merlin, 1991), pp. 200–3, 274–7 (which includes a republication of his 'The Moral Economy of the English Crowd in the Eighteenth Century', *Past and Present* 50 (1971), 76–136 and a response to Hont and Ignatieff).

18 Adam Smith, 'Early Draft of Part of *The Wealth of Nations*', in R.L. Meek, D.D. Raphael and P.G. Stein, eds., *Lectures on Jurisprudence* (Oxford: Clarendon Press, 1978), pp. 570–4. This draft of the chapter on division of labour is dated by its editors to spring 1763. For the final, published, version of this argument see Adam Smith, *An Inquiry into the Nature and Causes of the Wealth of Nations*, 2 vols. (London: Grant Richards, 1904), Vol. 1, pp. 12–19.

19 Thomas Reid to Richard Price (? 1772), in *Correspondence of Richard Price*, ed. W. Bernard Peach and D.O. Thomas (Durham: Duke University Press, 1983), pp. 153–4. For Desaguliers' role in the projectors' world see Larry Stewart, 'Public Lectures and Private Patronage in Newtonian England', *Isis* 77 (1986), 47–58.

20 Adam Smith, 'The Principles which Lead and Direct Philosophical Enquiries Illustrated by the History of Astronomy', in *Essays on Philosophical Subjects*, ed. W.P.D. Wightman, J.C. Bryce and I.S. Ross (Oxford: Clarendon Press, 1980), p. 66. The *Essays* were published posthumously under the editorship of Joseph Black and James Hutton in 1795.

21 Adam Smith, 'Early Draft of Part of *The Wealth of Nations*', p. 570.

22 Adam Ferguson, *An Essay on the History of Civil Society*, ed. Duncan Forbes (Edinburgh University Press, 1966), pp. 182–4.

23 Smith, 'History of Astronomy', pp. 104–5. For machines and systems see John R.R. Christie, 'Adam Smith's Metaphysics of Language', in A.E. Benjamin, G.N. Cantor and J.R.R. Christie, eds., *The Figural and the Literal* (Manchester University Press, 1987), 202–29, pp. 218–20.

24 Jan Golinski, *Science as Public Culture: Chemistry and Enlightenment in Britain, 1760–1820* (Cambridge University Press, 1992); Larry Stewart, *The Rise of Public Science: Rhetoric, Technology and Natural Philosophy in Newtonian Britain, 1660–1750* (Cambridge University Press, 1993).

25 Jürgen Habermas, *The Structural Transformation of the Public Sphere* (Cambridge: Polity Press, 1989); Norbert Elias, *The History of Manners* (New York: Pantheon Books, 1982), pp. 252–63; Reinhart Koselleck, *Critique and Crisis* (Oxford: Berg, 1988).

26 Thomas Goodinge, *The Law against Bankrupts* (1713), cited in Peter Earle, *The Making of the English Middle Class* (London: Methuen, 1989), p. 132; Defoe citations from J.G.A. Pocock, 'Early Modern Capitalism – the Augustan perception', in Eugene Kamenka and

R.S. Neale, eds., *Feudalism, Capitalism and Beyond* (London: Arnold, 1975), 62–83, pp. 78–80; compare Simon Schaffer, 'Defoe's Natural Philosophy and the Worlds of Credit', in John Christie and Sally Shuttleworth, eds., *Nature Transfigured* (Manchester University Press, 1989), 13–44.

27 Richard Sennett, *The Fall of Public Man* (London: Faber, 1986), p. 56; Norbert Elias, *The Court Society* (Oxford: Blackwell, 1983), p. 96.

28 For trust in experimental reports, see Steven Shapin, 'The Invisible Technician', *American Scientist* 77 (1989), 554–63; Simon Schaffer, 'Self Evidence', *Critical Inquiry* 18 (Winter 1992), 327–62.

29 Nicholas Jewson, 'The Disappearance of the Sick Man from Medical Cosmology 1770–1870', *Sociology* 10 (1976), 225–44; Malcolm Nicolson, 'The Metastatic Theory of Pathogenesis and the Professional Interests of the Eighteenth Century Physician', *Medical History* 32 (1988), 277–300; Fissell, 'The Disappearance of the Patient's Narrative'.

30 Thomas Harmer to John Canton, 11 December 1753, Royal Society Canton Papers 2, p. 28.

31 (Henry Fielding), *Some Papers . . . concerning the Terrestrial Chrysippus* (1743), described in Nellie B. Eales, 'A Satire on the Royal Society', *Notes and Records of the Royal Society* 23 (1968), 65–7; Bernard de Mandeville, *Fable of the Bees*, ed. Philip Harth (1723; Harmondsworth: Pelican, 1970), p. 323. William Hogarth, *Masquerade Ticket*, is discussed in Terry Castle, *Masquerade and Civilization: the Carnivalesque in Eighteenth Century English Culture and Fiction* (London: Methuen, 1986), p. 38; compare David Dabydeen, *Hogarth, Walpole and Commercial Britain* (London: Hansib, 1987).

32 Tore Frängsmyr, J.L. Heilbron and Robin E. Rider, eds., *The Quantifying Spirit in the Eighteenth Century* (Berkeley and Los Angeles: University of California Press, 1990).

33 Evelyn Fox Keller, *Reflections on Gender and Science* (New Haven: Yale University Press, 1945), p. 11; Robert Boyle, *Works*, ed. Thomas Birch, 6 vols, (London, 1772), Vol. 1, pp. 156, 159; Steven Shapin, 'Robert Boyle and Mathematics: Reality, Representation and Experimental Practice', *Science in Context* 2 (1988), 23–58, pp. 35–6.

34 Craig Waff, 'Comet Halley's First Expected Return: English Public Apprehensions 1755–58', *Journal for the History of Astronomy* 17 (1986), 1–37, pp. 26 (on Martin), 36 (on Bevis).

35 John Arbuthnot, *Life and Works*, ed. G.A. Aitken (London, 1892), pp. 409–35; *Memoirs of the Extraordinary, Life, Works and Discoveries of Martinus Scriblerus* (1742), ed. Charles Kerby-Miller (Oxford University Press, 1988), pp. 166–8. See Ian Hacking, *The Emergence*

of Probability (Cambridge University Press, 1975), pp. 166–9 for the design argument; G.S. Rousseau, ' "Wicked Whiston' and the Scriblerians', *Studies in Eighteenth Century Culture* 17 (1987), 17–44.

36 Peter Buck, 'People who Counted: Political Arithmetic in the Eighteenth Century', *Isis* 73 (1982), 28–45; Lorraine Daston, 'Mathematical Probability and the Reasonable Man of the Eighteenth Century', in J. Dauben and V. Sexton, eds., *History and Philosophy of Science: Selected Papers* (New York Academy of Sciences, 1983), 52–72.

37 Isaac Newton, *Opticks* (London, 1704), p. 165; Colin Maclaurin, *A Treatise of Fluxions* (Edinburgh, 1742), p. viii. See I. Grattan-Guinness, 'Berkeley's Criticisms of the Calculus', *Janus* 56 (1969), 213–27; G.N. Cantor, 'Berkeley's *The Analyst* Revisited', *Isis* 75 (1984), 666–83.

38 For metrology see Jean Lave, 'The Values of Quantification', in John Law, ed., *Power, action and belief* (London: Routledge, 1986), 88–111; Bruno Latour, 'Visualisation and Cognition', *Knowledge and Society* 6 (1986), 1–40, p. 30.

39 John Brewer, *The Sinews of Power* (London: Unwin Hyman, 1989), pp. 222–30; Earle, *Making of the English Middle Class*, pp. 66–8; Nicholas Hans, *New Trends in Education in the Eighteenth Century* (London: Routledge, 1951).

40 Larry Stewart, 'The Selling of Newton: Science and Technology in early Eighteenth Century England', *Journal of British Studies* 25 (1986), 78–92; M.C. Jacob, 'Scientific Culture in the Early English Enlightenment', in A.C. Kors and P.J. Korshin, eds., *Anticipations of the Enlightenment in England, France and Germany* (Philadelphia: University of Pennsylvania Press, 1987), 134–64.

41 Olaf Pedersen, 'The Philomaths of Eighteenth Century England', *Centaurus* 8 (1963), 238–62; P.J. Wallis, 'British Philomaths – mid-eighteenth century and earlier', *Centaurus* 17 (1973), 301–14; Diana Harding, 'Mathematics and Science Education in Eighteenth-Century Northamptonshire', *History of Education* 1 (1972), 139–59, pp. 144–6.

42 James A. Secord, 'Newton in the Nursery: Tom Telescope and the Philosophy of Tops and Balls 1761–1838', *History of Science* 23 (1985), 127–51, p. 137; Brewer, *Sinews of Power*, p. 228.

43 Thompson, *Customs in Common*, p. 208.

44 Smith, *Wealth of Nations*, Vol. 2, pp. 125, 132.

45 Joyce Appleby, *Economic Thought and Ideology in Seventeenth Century England* (Princeton University Press, 1978), chapter 9; E.P. Thompson, *Whigs and Hunters* (Harmondsworth: Penguin, 1977), chapter 9.

46 G.E. Fussell, *Crop Nutrition: Science and Practice before Liebig* (Lawrence: Kansas University Press, 1971), pp. 75–92; Mayling Stubbs, 'John Beale, Philosophical Gardener of Herefordshire: the Improvement of Agriculture and Trade in the Royal Society, 1663–1683', *Annals of Science* 46 (1989), 323–63. For the Georgical Committee see R.V. Lennard, 'English Agriculture under Charles II', *Economic History Review* 4 (1932–4), 23–45 and Hunter, *Establishing the New Science*, pp. 84–7, 105–14.

47 John Evelyn, *Sylva*, 3rd edn (London, 1679), p. 330; John Worlidge, *Systema agriculturae*, 3rd edn (London, 1681), pp. 6, 13. For the philosophy of husbandry see Keith Tribe, *Land, Labour and Economic Discourse* (London: Routledge, 1978), chapter 4.

48 See Roy Porter, 'Creation and Credence: the Career of Theories of the Earth in Britain, 1660–1820', in Barry Barnes and Steven Shapin, eds., *Natural Order* (Beverly Hills; Sage, 1979), 97–124.

49 T.H. Marshall, 'Jethro Tull and the New Husbandry', *Economic History Review* 2 (1929), 41–60; G.E. Fussell, *Jethro Tull: His Influence on Mechanized Practice* (Reading: Osprey, 1973).

50 Jethro Tull, *The New Horse-Houghing Husbandry* (London, 1731), p. 61.

51 Tull, *New Horse-Houghing Husbandry*, pp. 107–9.

52 Defoe, *The Great Law of Subordination Consider'd* (1724), is discussed in Thompson, *Customs in Common*, pp. 37–8. Citations from Tull, *New Horse-Houghing Husbandry*, pp. xii–xiii; John Theophilus Desaguliers, *A Course of Experimental Philosophy*, 2 vols, (London, 1734 and 1744), Vol. 2, p. 415.

53 Tull, *New Horse-Houghing Husbandry*, pp. 124n., 130; Bruno Latour, 'Give me a Laboratory and I will raise the World', in Karin Knorr-Cetina and Michael Mulkay, eds., *Science Observed* (Beverly Hills: Sage, 1983), 141–70.

54 G.E. Fussell, 'Science and Practice in Eighteenth Century British Agriculture', *Agricultural history* 43 (1969), 7–18.

55 Raymond Williams, *The Country and the City* (St Albans: Paladin, 1975).

56 The best treatment of the episode is Gill Hudson, 'The Politics of Credulity: the Mary Toft Case', M. Phil. dissertation, Wellcome Unit for the History of Medicine, Cambridge, 1987. I am grateful to Gill Hudson for a copy of this work.

57 John Barrell, *English Literature in History 1730–80* (London: Hutchinson, 1983), pp. 35–6; Thompson, *Whigs and Hunters*, pp. 278–94; Rogers, 'Blacks and Poetry and Pope', in *Eighteenth Century Encounters* 75–92.

58 John Colson, *The Method of Fluxions and Infinite Series* (London,

1736), pp. 271–4; Niccolò Guicciardini, 'Flowing Ducks and Vanishing Quantities', in Sergio Rossi, ed., *Science and Imagination in Eighteenth Century British Culture* (University of Milan, 1987), 231–5. For Pope and Newtonian natural philosophy, see M.H. Nicolson and G.S. Rousseau, *This Long Disease my Life: Alexander Pope and the Sciences* (Princeton University Press, 1968), pp. 138–45.

59 Arthur Young, *Annals of Agriculture* 5 (1786), 15–18; criticism in *Monthly Review* 10 (1793), 1–2. For Young, calculation and the experimental farm see Tribe, *Land, Labour and Economic Discourse*, pp. 66–79. The argument about the virtues of self-interest is discussed in Albert O. Hirschman, *The Passions and the Interests* (Princeton University Press, 1977), pp. 48–56. For the dilemmas of rational agriculture in Young see Williams, *The Country and the City*, pp. 84–6.

6 *Patrick Curry*

Towards a post-Marxist social history: Thompson, Clark and beyond

1991

The English Marxist Tradition

My concern here is the current condition and prospects for that school of social-history-writing, usually described as Marxist or socialist, that extends from the founding of the journal *Past and Present* in 1952 through the work of E.P. Thompson, Christopher Hill, Eric Hobsbawm and others to that of Raphael Samuel and the *History Workshop Journal*. I intend to approach the subject in relation to wider intellectual, social and political events and debates, emphasizing theory and historiography; and to introduce and prescribe a promising way forward from (I argue) the present impasse. Readers looking for a more detailed and/or internal analysis are therefore forewarned not to expect the work of a book in the space of a chapter.[1]

For the same reason, I also concentrate on the work of certain individuals as exemplars: Thompson, for English Marxist historians; J.C.D. Clark, for the younger historians who constitute their right-wing critics; and Ernesto Laclau and Chantal Mouffe, for current theorists sometimes described as post-Marxist. (I should add that given my choice of Thompson and Clark, it follows that there is a bias in favour of the early modern period.)

There is a reason for this asymmetry of subject-matter. I want to suggest not only that the historical discipline has yet to produce an adequate response to Clark and his colleagues, but that post-Marxism – properly understood – offers the theoretical resources needed to renew progressive English social-history-writing in the face of their challenge, and the larger challenge of the times generally. Intellectual disciplines have their own dynamics, of course, but as historians above all ought to recognize they are also the product of their own times and places. For historians who consider themselves to be more than antiquarian empiricists, then, these are extraordinary times indeed – and for none more so than Marxists and socialists.

The school of Marxist history-writing just referred to is very well-known, and has already been the object of study itself.[2] Nonetheless, it is worth recalling its provenance. It was initiated by the original members of the Historians Group of the Communist Party of Great Britain (CPGB), including Christopher Hill (writing on the English Revolution from the 1950s through *The World Turned Upside Down* (1972) and beyond), Eric Hobsbawm (on industrial capitalism and labour movements, culminating in *The Age of Capital* (1975) and *of Empire* (1987)), and E.P. Thompson (from *The Making of the English Working Class* (1963) through his later work on the eighteenth century). There is also the *History Workshop Journal* – which identifies itself as 'a journal of socialist and feminist historians' – and the History Workshop series of books from the 1970s and 1980s, both under the general editorship of Raphael Samuel (who was himself a young member of the CPGB Historians Group). While such a genealogy neglects many other historians, it is sufficient to locate this work as firmly on and of the Left – in the broadest sense, but nonetheless for that – and to remind us of its tremendous scope, quality and influence.

The Right fights back

For English historians on the Left, the change of political climate signified by Conservative electoral victories in 1979, 1983 and 1987, and their equivalents abroad in America and Europe, was deeply traumatic. Hill's *The Experience of Defeat* (1984) was apt in both title and substance. At the same time, accompanying this recrudescence of the Right, there was a corresponding new intellectual ascendency. Its epicentre lay in Peterhouse, Cambridge, with Roger Scruton's *Salisbury Review* and *The Spectator* its leading organs and the Murdoch-owned newspapers its chief popularizers. Under these auspices, political conservatism combined with economic liberalism made most if not all of the running in the last decade. Meanwhile, a number of movements and publications sprang up aiming to reverse this trend by in large part reforming the Left's own commitments and strategies from within: Charter 88, *Samizdat, Marxism Today* and some sections of the Socialist Society.

To add insult to injury, a largely younger generation of revisionist historians also appeared on the scene. It includes W.D. Rubinstein, Martin Weiner, J.C. Davis and arguably Alan Macfarlane.[3] Its most prominent representative, however, has been J.C.D. Clark. His ambitious and aggressive rewriting of 'the long eighteenth century', published in *English Society 1642–1832* (1985) and *Revolution and Rebellion* (1986), attracted widespread intellectual attention in a manner almost reminiscent of Thompson two decades ago.[4] In the words of a recent figure in film, however, Clark himself seems to have experienced 'the 1950s twice and then gone straight into the 70s'. His vision places the monarchy, aristocracy and established Church centre-stage – an *ancien régime* which survived the English Revolution largely intact, and was only undone to any serious extent by craven concessions in 1829–32.

Clark's work has received some telling criticism amid all the attention, and its limitations – beginning with the unfulfilled promise of his first title just mentioned – are now fairly clear. To attend to the matter purely on that level, however, is seriously to misjudge it. It is touching the way many historians still seem to think that either substantive or technical refutation results in virtual de-struction. Nowhere in human endeavour is that true, however, no matter how purely intellectual it may appear to be. What really counts – what has effects – is the extent and ways in which Clark, in this instance, is *perceived* to be correct; or in other words, who is widely read, winning the arguments in people's minds, and therefore forms the basis, rather than the object, of continuing discussion. (This point is not idealist; in fact, only a materialist outlook can recognize that 'purely' intellectual analysis, while an important part of determining wider convictions, is not identical with it.) That is why Clark must be taken seriously; his books sell, his views have now been widely disseminated, and a reasonably typical conclusion among his commentators is that while far from vanquished, liberal and/or Marxist historians of the period 'had better raise their game before the next encounter'.[5]

Let me remind the reader that Clark seeks to overturn the ways in which Whiggishly liberal ('Old Hat') and Marxist ('Old Guard') historians have portrayed 1660–1832, and replace them with the picture of an overwhelmingly rural, deferential and patriarchal society, permeated as well as dominated by the values of its royal, aristocratic and ecclesiastical leaders. Religion, which he argues has been egregiously neglected, plays a major role in Clark's England – both as sustainer of the *ancien régime* (through popular as well as elite Anglicanism) and as its eventual undoing (through Dissent).

Driving this view lies an ambitious historiographical programme. Negatively, Clark is keen to root out advocates of 'the spurious notions of a bourgeois revolution, of a constitutionalist teleology and an issueless political stability . . . of a proletariat without belief or dignity, exploited to finance a bleak new world of possessive individualism'. Positively, his aim is 'to relate eighteenth-century England to its seventeenth-century origins rather than to its nineteenth-century outcome', using for this purpose 'a non-positivist, anti-reductionist methodology' rather than 'an unreal dynamic and an illusory teleology'.[6]

In order to grasp the theoretical essence of these charges, a brief discussion of their keywords is in order. 'Anachronism' means of course the explanation of historical phenomena in terms of their outcomes or subsequent meanings, rather than prior and contemporary events and meanings. The implication is that history has a necessary goal(s) and therefore direction, which its subjects (whether they know it or not) are struggling to realize. 'Reductionism' involves explaining actions or beliefs that are not apparently related to the realization of such goals in terms of ones which are (whether or not such terms would reasonably be recognized by the historical actors themselves). 'Teleology' is the closely related belief that an end or outcome can act as a cause, even for those for whom it is not a conscious goal. In intellectual practice, all three terms have an epistemological component without which they would be useless: someone, whether an individual or a group, must be in a privileged position in order to *know* what are the real meta-historical goals that are allowed to determine what events are important and what are not, or what behaviour is historically congruent and what is not.[7]

What is the justice of Clark's charges? There are many problems with his historical picture: its neglect of towns, and the north of England generally; a tendency to portray the Church (never mind the Christian 'mental universe') as monolithic; the marginalizing of commerce and of popular political dissent; the reinstatement of politics as purely of the 'high' sort. There is also the question of his abrasively polemical treatment of other historians – not necessarily a problem in itself (and Thompson for one is in a poor position to complain), but it does overlap with a tendency to caricature their positions. Finally, it could plausibly be maintained that Clark's programme, along with the wider political one that has sustained him, is now approaching exhaustion; a certain thinness and sense of anticlimax are already perceptible.

Nevertheless, that does not amount to a refutation, let alone replacement. And I think it should be possible to admit – without decrying the insights and accomplishments of Hill, Thompson, Hobsbawm *et al.*, which only a fool or a knave would wholly deny – that Clark is not entirely wide of the mark. Even Joanna Innes, writing in (and arguably for) *Past and Present*, says that he 'grossly overplays what need not have been a bad hand'.[8] To assert, as Lawrence Stone did in 1980, that the English Revolution 'was unsuccessful because it was premature' is a luxury we can no longer afford. Similarly, statements such as that it 'embodied aspirations that clearly prefigured the liberal society still far off in the future' (Zagorin), or that its result was significant chiefly because the administrative organs that most impeded capitalist development had been removed' (Hill), are elaborations of a model whose basis is now indefensible. That model also accounts for the way religious belief has been consistently underestimated and/or explained away by early modern historians of the same persuasion.[9]

It is highly ironic that Clark's direction (if not his intended destination) bring him into close agreement on a number of points with one of his *bêtes noires*, E.P. Thompson. The list is impressive: the polarity of patrician and plebeian;[10] the 'tardy' development of mature classes;[11] the closing of patrician ranks after 1760;[12] the distancing of Anglican clergy from their parishioners;[13] and the importance of gentry hegemony as well as the timing of its decline, including its first fracturing in the 1790s and more seriously in 1828–32, which is viewed by both men as the sign of a newly powerful and independent middle class.[14] Last but certainly not least, there is their shared rejection of economistic teleology, and emphasis instead on taking people's beliefs seriously in the contingent circumstances of their precise historical circumstances.

Clark's declaration that he is seeking 'to rescue past people from the imputation of stupidity in failing to perceive the answers' (that is, the 'correct' answers) chimes unmistakably with Thompson's famous earlier vow to rescue his historical subjects from 'the enormous condescension of posterity'.[15]

Given this degree of apparent accord – which has been admitted (under pressure) but left unexplored by Clark himself – why is it that in the words of one reviewer, his 'choicest venom is reserved for E.P. Thompson'?[16] Of course, this betrays Clark's resort to caricature: probably the foremost critic of Marxist teleology and reductionism, since at least 1963 and consistently (not to say extravagantly) ever since, is . . . a Marxist.[17] But the answer is more significant than that; it can only be that Clark objects not to Thompson's methodology, nor even many of his historical conclusions, but to his values. Here the resemblance breaks down completely, to be replaced by a highly polarized symmetry. Clark wants to celebrate precisely what to Thompson is the power of the enemy, which the latter has laid bare in order to decry.

In other words, nothing could better demonstrate that the conclusions Clark infers from the material using his anti-teleological methodological premises, and associates with them, are by no means the only possible ones. *There is nothing necessarily conservative or reactionary about those premises*; far from it. They don't, for example, downplay social structure. Clark suggests, rather, that structures are mediated (in highly complex ways) by experience, adding indeed that '*all* elements in society' – including social and economic structures – 'are subject to continual change, decay and renovation'.[18] While he may not himself have realized the radical implications of this point, it is one that might also find some Marxists anxious to enter reservations. At any rate, it seems undeniable that many social historians, among others, had grown complacent about the possibility of reaction (whether state or civil), and the fragility and indeed reversibility of progressive gains. I would even cautiously endorse Clark's point that the historiographical landscape 'has changed radically since *c.*1980: an orthodoxy has disintegrated'.[19] For it is just my point that the tradition of which Thompson has been arguably the leading exemplar stands in urgent need of renewal; that its accumulation of reductionist residues (economist, statist and classist), despite his strictures, provided much of the opening for

Clark's and others' reactionary work; but that Clark's own premises, anti-teleological and therefore potentially radically anti-elitist, can be taken in the direction of greater democratic pluralism in historical practice. (Although I cannot discuss it here, the potential of such a starting-point has already been clearly demonstrated in an adjacent discipline: namely the history of science, where a burgeoning body of vigorously critical work has broken the highly conservative and teleological consensus of scientific triumphalism.[20])

Before exploring that potential further, however, I would like to take a closer look at Thompson's work. After all, if it has all of Clark's virtues without the latter's political ethos, why worry? To anticipate, answering that will lead us to the problem of 'hegemony' – a crucial one, since it is where ultimately both Clark and Thompson take their stand, but equally one which they have both neglected to develop.

E.P. Thompson

I have already remarked on the significance of Thompson's work, which I have no intention of demeaning. But we need to be aware of its limitations too. For both purposes, in my view, his most important writings are *Whigs and Hunters* (1975) and his two papers of the 1970s, 'Patrician Society, Plebeian Culture' and 'Eighteenth-Century English Society: Class Struggle Without Class?'[21] The key idea therein is the cultural hegemony of the gentry, which is seen as the principal weapon for maintaining contemporary ruling-class control – more effective than direct military or even economic means, although not of course unsupplemented by them. Thompson portrayed plebeian culture as 'constrained within [these] parameters' until the 1790s. Nonetheless, it was not simply the passive victim of imposition, but exacted concessions itself. Furthermore, 'while such cultural hegemony may define the limits of what is possible . . . there is nothing determined or automatic about this process. Such hegemony can be sustained by the rulers only by the constant exercise of skill, of theatre and of concession.'[22]

The last point is important. There is a particular Marxist view that since class relations are expressed through the apparatus of the law (which Thompson accepts), the latter is no more than an expression of ruling-class interests (which he denies). In *Whigs and Hunters*, he maintained that

immense efforts were made . . . to project the image of a ruling-class which was itself subject to the rule of law, and whose legitimacy rested upon the equity and universality of those legal forms. And the rulers were, in a serious sense, whether willingly or unwillingly, the prisoners of their own rhetoric; they played games of power according to rules which suited them, but they could not break those rules or the whole game would be thrown away. And, finally, so far from the ruled shrugging off this rhetoric as a hypocrisy, some part of it at least was taken over as part of the rhetoric of the plebeian crowd, of the 'free-born Englishman'.[23]

For his pains, Thompson was severely taken to task by some of his younger comrades who were unimpressed by the acuity of this kind of analysis: in particular Perry Anderson, for 'a definition of class that is far too voluntarist and subjective', and Richard Johnson, for 'culturalism'.[24] In this context, such terms are strongly-charged and connect to others, including 'idealism', 'moralism' and 'humanism', which together express the Marxist fear that subjective or cultural considerations are being overvalued at the expense of objective or structural ones. Provoked by Thompson's unbuttoned attack on Althusserian structural Marxism in 1978, a fractious debate on the subject ensued among historians and social theorists of the Left.[25] Perhaps its most unfortunate consequence – and one to which Thompson himself, it must be said, contributed to some extent – was this polarization of culture and structure.

Such a choice is ultimately sterile and misleading, because both components are equally indispensable. However, as Tony Bennett has pointed out, this debate became in turn a stimulus for the widespread 'turn to Gramsci' of the 1980s. As he explains, 'In Gramsci's prospectus, popular culture is viewed neither as the site of the people's cultural deformation nor . . . in any simple Thompsonian sense, of their own self-making; rather it is viewed as a force-field of relationships shaped, precisely, by these contradictory pressures and tendencies.'[26]

It could be argued that Thompson had already anticipated this approach in its essentials: for example, 'classes do not exist as separate entities, look around, find an enemy class, and then start to struggle'. Furthermore, 'Class and class-consciousness are always the last, not the first stage in the real historical process . . . [Therefore] No actual class formation in history is any truer or more real than any other, and class defines itself as, in fact, it eventuates.' For that reason, the 'mature' class of nineteenth-century industrial societies 'has in fact no claim to universality'.[27]

Since this formulation offers several propositions that I go on to advance and defend in other respects, what is the problem? The answer is that Thompson's concept of hegemony is still basically intuitive and undeveloped – an excellent start, but properly followed up and worked out by neither himself nor others. For example, he sometimes conflates hegemony proper – that is, as Gramsci defined it, 'moral and philosophical leadership' which wins consent through strategic concessions – with simple ideological domination, which limits but offers little reciprocal purchase.[28] In either case, hegemony is still closely tied, one-to-one, to social class. Even before the 1790s, this fails adequately to recognize the cross-class character of the eighteenth-century patrician bloc, with its unstable melding of gentry and middle-class interests.[29] *A fortiori*, the same objection applies to the complexities that resulted from patrician accommodations and therefore alterations in the face of both growing middle-class independence and working-class demands in the early nineteenth century. As Gramsci perceived, the crucial entity of modern times is not class (nor the mode of production that supposedly produces it) so much as the historical bloc.

But Thompson does not, or cannot, move things on. Ideologies and mentalities remain tied to classes, and classes (despite his strictures on universality) remain the fundamental social concern. His deep commitment to the peace movement in the 1980s, of course, effectively ended Thompson's own historical work.[30] More worryingly (if more contentiously), I see few signs of the historians who might be counted as his successors developing his work in a way that genuinely extends and deepens it – as distinct from elaborations and piecemeal corrections.[31] There are a few possible exceptions. One is of course feminist history, although it could well be seen as more of a new departure than a renewal. Where class does come into the picture here, however, progress is sometimes hampered by a tendency simply to add gender arithmetical-ly, as it were, rather than focus on the critically important question of inter-relations between the two – relations which change the nature of both.[32]

The other exception, it could be said, is the work of Gareth

Stedman Jones.[33] There is no question that it was part, at least, of Stedman Jones's intention to advance the debate by following through on Thompson's dethroning of Marxist economistic and class reductionism. The operative term was 'discourse', flagging the putative independence and importance of social consciousness. Unfortunately, Stedman Jones used 'discourse' and 'language' as virtually synonymous terms. As a result, the gulf between material and cultural considerations which he hoped that political language would mediate and resolve remained unclosed; his overly linguistic model of the social assimilated it too closely to the cultural pole, thus failing to unify the two. (That such a programme was announced at a time when the limitations of linguistic structuralism had become increasingly clear only added to the confusion.) In addition to exercising their keen nose for heterodoxy, the majority of Marxist and socialist historians, perhaps understandably sensing only idealist backsliding, remained unconvinced, and Stedman Jones's contribution as a potential renewal of the tradition was effectively side-lined.[34]

As an overall appraisal of English Marxist social history, the above analysis may seem mean or ungrateful. Indeed, in better days, with a relatively enlightened government and declining social problems at home and abroad, we could doubtless honour the natural end of such a tradition and while perhaps looking for new ones, leave it at that. A moment's reflection will show how far we are from such comfort. One thing is sure: the resources for renewal will not come from Clark, Davis and Rubinstein *et al.* Their questions are pertinent but their answers are not; the relief from old sectarian burdens is only momentary, before the weight of new ones is felt. So it is not surprising that Clark's grasp of hegemony is even less developed – despite the implicit importance he accords it, and despite coming to it ten years later – than that of Thompson.

Hegemony and beyond: post-Marxism

I have suggested that hegemony offers a hopeful way forward. Without trying to conduct a thorough review of the subject, that is the thread I would now like to follow. As much as any other rich set of ideas, those of Gramsci have no timeless meaning regardless of context, no single 'correct' interpretation.[35] The context that concerns us here is English Marxist historiography, and the state of the latter points (I argue) to the recent post-Marxist interpretation of Ernesto Laclau and Chantal Mouffe.[36] By way of a general remark, however, it is worth noting that Gramsci's work has proved peculiarly unstable and contested in the Marxist tradition as a whole. The reason is that both theoretically and politically, it occupies an ambiguous space. Gramsci's critique of vulgar economism and Leninist state/party vanguardism, and his notion of historical blocs, took him to what many people, then and now, considered the very edge of Marxism. It's fair to say he stopped there, but not without having left the impression of having arbitrarily, or at least inconsistently, stopped short. While for some he is therefore already too unorthodox, others attempt to retain him as a good communist. Still others, however, have continued to develop his logic from its Marxist origins beyond the acceptable parameters of that tradition – hence, 'post-Marxism' (which is therefore by no means identical with non-, let alone anti-Marxism).

Chief among his virtues, Gramsci insisted on attending closely to what appears to be happening, in all its particularity; and equally, on resisting a facile reduction of 'superstructure' to 'base'. Especially in the case of modern Western societies with a robust civil society (as distinct from state), he argued that one must take ideas, politics and culture seriously in their own right. A socialist programme would not succeed simply by an imposition resulting from successful vanguardist manipulation; it must win the democratic support of people – not just one class or sector, note, but a broad progressive alliance constituting a 'historical bloc' or 'collective will' – achieved through genuine leadership. It follows that hegemony is constructed, not something already there waiting to be discovered or freed; therefore there is nothing automatic or guaranteed about its course and outcome. For that reason, 'false consciousness' is no longer a satisfactory explanatory or political option when the 'real' or 'necessary' fails to materialize, since the latter category has lost its primacy.

Actually, that conclusion points to the heart of Gramsci's own dilemma. As Michael Walzer has recently remarked, he was trapped by his reluctance finally to abandon Marxist teleology. 'He knows he can't lead them [i.e. the people] without their consent, but he also knows, and this time with a 'scientifically and coherently elaborated' knowledge, that they ought to consent, and in the course of 'real historical development' will consent, to his leadership.'[37]

This ambiguity is not confined to Gramsci; it runs throughout the Marxist tradition. On the one hand, there is a realist-rationalist emphasis on the mode of production and its corollary, class, and the resulting 'necessary' historical laws. On the other hand, such objectivism and universalism has had constantly to be supplemented by more contingent measures, in order (so to speak) to bring about the inevitable. For Marxists, these typically involve class struggle in the concrete and contingent circumstances of the moment.

Laclau and Mouffe go on to argue that (for whatever reasons) Gramsci did not develop the relativist and historicist implications of his own project. In particular, he continued to insist on only a single hegemonic centre at any one time, with its basis in one of the two 'fundamental economic classes' (bourgeoisie or proletariat). But by his own admission, hegemony is the ongoing outcome of hegemonic struggle. (This holds true, by the way, in a parallel but more comprehensive way to Thompson's assertion that class is whatever eventuates from class struggle, and for the same reason: it is a relation, not an essence.) Hegemony is therefore multiple, unstable and incomplete. Furthermore, no advance stipulations are possible concerning its nature or content; hegemonic ideas can (and usually do) cut across class, race, gender and so on. The importance of class therefore depends on the historical situation, not upon some *a priori* 'necessary' trans-historical role. In short, hegemony proceeds by what Laclau and Mouffe call 'a logic of articulation and contingency' – articulation in the sense of linkages of elements in ways that change (reinforce, redirect, etc.) their meaning; and contingency not as mere randomness, but as instability and unpredictability. And what is contingently articulated they term 'discourse'. That term has invited considerable misunderstanding; whatever its usage elsewhere, for Laclau and Mouffe discourse is *not* simply language, but includes both the linguistic and non-linguistic elements of any meaningful social behaviour and/or belief. It has no existence independent of material human life.[38]

In this view, the meanings of hegemonic ideas derive not from

their social (including class) origins – the old touchstone of the
Left – but from the ways in which they are connected up with and
embedded in other ideas and practices in the particular historical
situation concerned. Of course, there are limits to this process;
articulation cannot simply occur at will or arbitrarily. But the
limits themselves are contingent. As the French historian Paul Veyne
put it, 'In this world, we do not play chess with eternal figures like
the king and the pawn: the figures are what successive configurations
on the playing board make of them.'[39]

The implications are considerable. For example, if a worker is
no longer simply fundamentally that but embodies a number of
other potentially equal important identities, and if the relationship
between these roles is no longer underwritten by any 'laws of
history', then it cannot be guaranteed that his or her contribution
will assume a progressive form. Similarly, it is simply a myth of
the Left to assume that public or social ownership of the means
of production would also end other forms of oppression. There
are no necessary links between anti-capitalism and anti-sexism, for
example, or ecological concerns; such a unity can only result from
a hegemonic articulation. Laclau and Mouffe therefore identify
the goal of a Left or progressive politics as 'a radical and plural
democracy'. That *includes* tackling the oppressions caused by
uncontrolled capitalist relations of production; indeed, radical
democracy without this dimension would be impossible; but the
two can no longer be considered as identical. Socialism – defined,
as it should be, as the extension of democratic rights to the economy – is obviously one of the components of a radical democracy,
and not vice versa. By the same token, the working class emerges
as a social agent limited like any other. It no longer carries the
burden of being a 'universal class', the necessary agent of global
emancipation. Indeed, there no longer appears to be just one such
project, no one privileged struggle and its sole representatives.[40]

Notwithstanding some Marxist commentators, none of the above
constitutes a denial of the potential importance, let alone existence, of class.[41] It does mean that class exists on a *prima facie* equal
footing with other social identities and oppressions. By implication,
it is also time to let go of necessary 'stages' of history (and their
shortcuts), relative autonomy, 'determination in the last instance'
and all the other baggage of Marxist chiliasm and its scholastic
refinements. But there is more to Marx than that. I am not thinking

just of his moral stance. (And why is this something to be ashamed of, except as a crime against socialist scientism? Havel has shown, if it needed showing after Gandhi, that in the right circumstances morality can have material consequences.) Nor am I referring to his unmatched analyses of capital. I am thinking really, in the words of Pierre Vilar, of 'the historical critique of reason . . . Thinking everything historically is really the essence of Marxism.'[42] 'Everything' *includes* Marxism itself. Whatever the difficulties, the historicity of Marxist discourse too must be recognized. Indeed, Laclau argues that such a move is necessary in order for Marxism to retain its dignity and relevance: 'it will either be inscribed as a historical, partial and limited movement within a wider historical line, that of the radical tradition of the West, or it will be taken over by the boy scouts of the Trotskyist sects, who will continue to repeat a totally obsolete language – and thus nobody will remember Marxism in twenty years' time'.[43]

The overall implications of post-Marxism therefore reach beyond Leninism to Marxism itself. Not for nothing did the first anniversary of the Czech Revolution (well before his statues toppled in Russia) include a candle in the shape of Lenin's head, burning atop an overturned tank in Wenceslas Square. As Eric Hobsbawm bravely admitted early in 1990 – and as is now plain for all who will look to see – the whole tradition dominated and inspired by the October Revolution has now come to an end.[44] It is simply no longer morally, intellectually or politically acceptable to undertake projects in the name of the 'objective interests' of the people, attributed (without so much as asking them) by those who are supposedly in a position to know best. With each successive substitution masquerading as representation – the Proletariat for the People, the Party for the Proletariat, the leader for the Party – the potential for gross authoritarianism grows. The terminus of that practice was revealed (yet again) by Tienanmen Square.[45]

But such a revisioning extends to the fundamental categories of classical Marxism too. The latter, unrevised, are still underwritten by the assumption that the mode of production is a universal constant of history, and the working class therefore a privileged 'universal' class. The rejection of this dogma does not entail abandoning Marxist categories altogether; that would involve an unnecessarily wasteful and disruptive loss of tradition and resources. However, it does necessitate historicizing and relativizing them.

Hence Laclau and Mouffe's redefinition of the Left, in which traditional socialist concepts and demands share the stage with others – feminist, sexual, racial, ecological – as equals, without prior ideological guarantees. But that cannot occur 'without renouncing the discourse of the universal, and its implicit assumption of a privileged point of access to "the truth", which can only be reached by a limited number of subjects'.[46]

This is precisely the critique of teleology, reductionism and anachronism – summed up in Laclau and Mouffe's work as 'essentialism' – that we found at the heart of Thompsonian social history, and restated (for different purposes) by Clark. Before returning to English Marxist social history, however, I want to attend briefly to the critical reception of post-Marxism among leading English Marxists. That will provide an opportunity to judge the promise of the latter, and clear up some misunderstandings concerning the former.

The reaction of the old New Left

This is no place for a full review of the dreary abuse and denial that Laclau and Mouffe have elicited.[47] I only want to mention some examples, in order to point out the poverty of contemporary dogmatic Marxism to any readers who may still harbour the tender hope that the latter offers any resources for renewal. Ellen Meiksins Wood led off in 1986 with her *The Retreat from Class* (quickly awarded the Isaac Deutscher Prize for ideological soundness), which set out to vet the Left and weed out backsliders. Those smacked on the wrist include Stuart Hall, Gareth Stedman Jones, Gavin Kitching and especially Laclau and Mouffe. Eric Hobsbawm escapes lightly because despite some heterodoxy, 'He shows little interest in or sympathy for the "new social movements".' (It is revealing to find the 1960s as whipping-boy on both the socialist Left and New Right.) Nothing must compromise, and I quote, 'the constant light of class struggle'.[48]

Wood is an historian too. As such, she maintains that 'history does not proceed by means of clean breaks or in discontinuous pieces, but by transformations of inherited realities, changes within continuities'. Such sweet reason does not apply to her own faith, however – namely in 'the discontinuity, the radical break, between liberalism and socialism'. As a good materialist, this is no mere abstraction; but with the success of the latter, she foresees 'a qualitative leap to new forms of democracy with no successful precedent'. (Could these be the very 'new forms of power' which Thompson has warned us to 'watch . . . for a century or two before you cut your hedges down'?[49]) But *a priori* stagism rules unchallenged; liberalism is defined as eternally, everywhere and in all respects a primitive forebear of socialism. By the same token, 'To say that liberalism has a lesson for socialism . . . is, of course, to make a highly contentious assertion, namely that the state will persist as a problem in classless society.'[50]

In 1987, the *New Left Review* unleashed Norman Geras.[51] The result recalls Perry Anderson's attack on E.P. Thompson twenty years earlier, and sometimes with striking similar resonances.[52] In a paradigmatic example of sectarian venom, Geras opens and closes his account with *ad hominem* speculations about 'the ex-Marxist's conscience'. In between we find a stern reassertion of standard revolutionary Marxist dogmas, including the right and ability to attribute to a class its own 'objective interests', not to mention direct access to 'a pre-discursive reality and an extra-theoretical objectivity'. The only alternative, we are told, is 'utter arbitrariness and irrationalism'. His charge of relativism we will come to; meanwhile, Geras's stone-age epistemology reveals the true positivist's eagerness to say – for all of us – what 'actually is', as opposed to 'a superstition about it'. It's all rather like Desmond Oliver Dingle's summary of the message conveyed by the world's major religions: 'you are not here for why you think you are, you're here for another reason that we are not at liberty to tell you';[53] only more menacing.

Laclau and Mouffe, as putative defenders of liberalism, are also tainted with all 'the suffering, squalor and misery of actual, liberal, capitalisms'; whereas Marxism, whatever its historical record, 'has set its face . . . from the very beginning against all forms of oppression' – the same perverse logic of double-standards exhibited by Wood. It is little comfort that Geras takes it as 'axiomatic that socialism must be democratic'; being axiomatic, apparently no further discussion is needed.[54]

Along with Wood, Geras also contributed to the *Socialist Register 1990* and its excoriation of 'intellectuals in retreat'.[55] They were accompanied by Terry Eagleton, in a wonderful fit of radical pique.[56] Bryan D. Palmer's contribution, however, can detain us a

moment longer. It illustrates the truth of Pierre Vilar's observation
– as a very different sort of Marxist historian – that 'Any temptation a historian might feel to identify stabilities would be an
ideological one, stemming from his distress at change.'[57] For Palmer
is distressed by any number of changes: the effects of the recent
collapse of 'degenerate and deformed worker states' (which, being
simply unfortunate deformations, require taking no responsibility); the way Thompson and Williams weakened the authority of
the old base–superstructure model (although whether Williams
really deserves such credit may be questioned); the work of Stedman
Jones and François Furet; the impact of feminism and histories of
sexuality . . . There is no question of perceiving any ambiguities or
new opportunities, let alone gains, in these developments. Palmer
yearns to turn back the clock and retreat to (in Raymond Williams's
own words of comfort) 'forms of material production which
always and everywhere precede all other forms.'[58] The same note
was again recently sounded by Wood *qua* historian. In an essay on
Thompson, she engages in strenuous efforts to save the base–
superstructure metaphor – long ago rejected by Thompson himself
– while patronizing him as a slightly misguided practitioner of
'Marx's own account of historical materialism'.[59] Against this
background, I hope it is clear that unlike the real retreat I have
just been discussing – a nostalgic retreat to the dogmas and elitism
of teleology, reductionism and anachronism – Laclau and Mouffe's
work does indeed offer a potential renewal, no less in history-
writing than in other respects. The abiding after-image of the
intellectual hard-liners of the old New Left is Geras's own illustration of economic determinism: 'A length of chain secures me by
the ankle to a stout post. This limits what I can do but also leaves
me a certain freedom . . . it also compels me to certain actions.'[60]
Let us leave them there, guarding the portals of this Albania of the
mind, and salvage instead the truth of Gareth Stedman Jones's
recent observation that 'any attempt to insulate Marxism from the
end of communism is mistaken. It will ultimately do more harm
than good.'[61]

Real and pseudo-problems

It is not that there are no problems or dangers with post-Marxism.
One is that the emphasis on contingency and articulation (needed

to counter the essentialism of old) could lead to underestimat-
ing the durability of those discourses which are so widely-held
and deeply-felt as to be effectively, in those circumstances, non-
negotiable. For example, that could include overlooking the
effectiveness, in certain historical situations – although obviously
not all, as recent events have shown beyond any doubt – of
directly imposed physical or economic coercion. A corollary
would be to overestimate the ease with which discourses can be
rearticulated and redirected.

There is also a large question-mark hanging over the applicability of a post-Gramscian notion of hegemony in relation to historical period. This is not something that I can tackle in an essay
devoted primarily to theory and historiography, but as my remarks
about Thompson and Clark already indicate, I would maintain
that such a concept is highly germane to early modern English
social history, especially with the 'jumps' in socio-political complexity in the 1660s, 1790s and 1820s and 1830s. The coexistence
of hegemony with the heyday of mature class in the nineteenth
century is no paradox; indeed, the former permits us to see that
the latter was a unique product of contemporary contingencies,
rather than a universal archetype with mere forerunners and
subsequent elaborations. Laclau and Mouffe have specified the
conditions for hegemony as (broadly speaking) the uneven development and dislocations of contemporary capitalism. That may
be a precondition of the self-conscious definition, but it seems
clear to me that the phenomenon itself – albeit in a simpler and
more delimited way – was occurring as early as the late seventeenth
century.[62]

Thirdly, the contingent differences between different kinds of
social identity constitute an enormous challenge to historians trying to analyse their operation. The socio-historical origins and
therefore collective 'memories' of gender, race and class vary
enormously; in some situations one or more will dominate, but
mostly they will interact in complex and unpredictable ways. It is
liberating but daunting to start without *a priori* assumptions
concerning which is key.

At the moment, however, the list of theoretical non-problems
one has to contend with is considerably longer. Some have already
been mentioned: post-Marxism does not hold that class no longer
exists or matters, for example, or that discourse is synonymous

with language. Another charge much bandied about is 'relativism'. Laclau and Mouffe's position is very close in this respect – although not in their political theories – to that of Richard Rorty or Paul Feyerabend.[63] Some elementary points here need to be cleared up. None of these authors are relativists in the caricatured sense of holding every belief to be as good as any other (let alone that one can believe anything one wants). No serious 'postmodernist' has ever argued that because reality is socially constructed and truth is historical, those words have no meaning or use; their meaning is relative and contingent, but none the less indispensable for that. And none exempt their own statements from such constraints.[64] The issue is rather between people (like classical Marxists) who think beliefs can be backed up algorithmically or apodictically, and those who think that beliefs can only be supported, as Rorty says, 'conversationally'; in other words, by other beliefs. The point is not that (in the words of one newspaper article) there is now no such thing as truth in history; it is a very different one, namely that truth is itself historical.

Likewise, 'contingency' here is not equivalent to merely arbitrary randomness, but refers to the undecidability, following from the non-self-sufficient nature of identity, that denies full explicability or predictability. Nor does 'pluralism' follow either the American sociological term or the postmodernism of Baudrillard. It refers rather to the results of radical unevenness of development and dislocation in the world: neither the even diffusion of power nor ever-increasing flux and atomization, but new spaces for democratic projects and hegemonic alliances. These new demands and opportunities alike arise from such dislocations; and they include post-Marxism itself, which thus lays no claim to a covert universalism. It is an historically situated interpretation and therefore intervention, and not one masquerading as a perspectivelessly 'objective', 'exhaustive' or 'deep' analysis.

Politically, despite their sympathy with the spirit of '68, Laclau and Mouffe do not seek to replace the proletariat with the 'new social movements' or the Third World poor.[65] They question the very idea of such privileged and universal agents. Nor is a 'radical and plural democracy' identical with any particular set of institutions or structures, let alone the extant ones of liberal democracies. Although the latter are more sympathetic to its appearance than those dominated by a single state power (and therefore state

Truth), they are a precondition not an equivalent. That project arises only out of an articulation between various struggles that links and equates them; there are no single foundational moments or 'ruptures', and it is never finished and complete. In other words, one might say, it is not a 'system' – or rather, makes no pretence of being a system, whose spurious universalism therefore requires constant illicit intervention, which must itself continually be disguised or defended.[66]

In a variant of the relativism gambit, Laclau and Mouffe have also been accused of leaving us without any criteria for determining what is politically progressive. According to this view – held by, among others, Habermas – if ultimately hard and 'objective' criteria cannot be supplied, the only alternative is a slide into arbitrary irrationalism. Given the partial and contingent character of knowledge, however, human beings never find themselves in such God-like circumstances. When working in concrete historical situations, it is nonsense to suggest that these kinds of criteria can be sustained – or that in their absence, all alternatives have an arbitrary value for participants. But Laclau and Mouffe have gone further and suggested that the criterion for judging a struggle arises not from its social origins but its present links with other struggles. There is a world of difference, for example, between a green movement that invites repressive state action to preserve the environment, and one which sees its despoliation as of a piece with the unjust exploitation of human beings.

Finally, there is the matter of 'idealism' (as distinct from materialism). Suffice it to say that the real idealism is that of universalism, which permits certain discourses to live above, behind or even within the material world and direct its courses without, however, their identity (as distinct from mere 'forms') being thereby affected in return. It is materialist to hold rather that instead of existing transcendentally, 'the truth' comes to be decided by those participating in determining what it is; and that instead of operating independently, it can never make the slightest difference in or to the world except insofar as it is held by a sufficient number of real people (e.g. is hegemonically successful).

For Marxists, of course, the *deus ex machina* is the mode of production and its attendants; whereas for Laclau, 'history's ultimate unrepresentability is the condition for the recognition of our radical historicity'.[67] Far from an anti-historical idealism, then, post-Marxism sees everything with human meaning as an historical construction, and therefore as open to historical analysis. Nothing is permitted to hide behind 'guarantees' of 'necessity'; whatever is worth doing, asserting or defending must be pursued openly and fully.

We may seem to have wandered far from the main subject. I began by arguing that English Marxist social history is essentially exhausted; and that some of the recent criticism by the newer historians of the Right is apposite.[68] But my main purpose is to offer a prescription for renewal, centred on the post-Marxism of Laclau and Mouffe – theoretical sources with which readers are probably less familiar. I have tried to show the promise of the former, and the poverty of its opponents. Even though it originally nourished that extraordinary tradition of social history, Marxism will now be better served by rejoining the honourable ancestry of the larger radical tradition than by being maintained on a sectarian life-support system. Conversely, social history too needs new well-springs. Of course, Laclau and Mouffe are not the only ones to offer such resources. They may also be found in the work (to which I will return in a moment) of Walzer, Giddens, Rorty, Bauman and Gorz, among others; and in that of non-dogmatic socialists like Michael Rustin and Hilary Wainwright.[69]

Among social historians themselves, I also want to particularly mention Roger Chartier. The radical potential of such propositions of his as these has not yet been fully appreciated: 'There are no historical objects outside the ever-changing practices that constitute them'; 'The social sphere is no longer thought of as a fixed and hierarchical whole . . . but as a skein of complex relationships, all of which are constructed culturally, and in which the individual finds a place in multiple ways'; and what matters most is 'the different ways in which groups or individuals make use of, interpret and appropriate the intellectual motifs or cultural forms they share with others'.[70] *It is precisely Laclau and Mouffe's Marxist provenance*, however, that makes them uniquely suitable for a new generation wanting to take up and carry forward the best of Thompson, Hill *et al.* in the present. For truly democratic socialists to do so would be no betrayal, as is clearly shown by Thompson's own declaration that 'the project of Socialism is guaranteed BY NOTHING – certainly not by "Science", or by Marxism-Leninism – but can find its own guarantees only by *reason* and an open *choice of values*.'[71] To lose socialists who already subscribe to that view, with their moral courage and unique critical edge in questions of exploitation and economic injustice, would seriously diminish the project of a new social history. But they too would lose out; for Thompson's dictum is no longer enough to protect and re-connect the position it describes.

From Marxist to democratic social history

Taking Thompson's work (and the early modern period) as paradigmatic, its potential for a more democratic practice of social history should now be obvious enough; but so too are its natural limits, and the fact that it still remains mainly potential. I have already said that while there exists a body of subsequent additions and revisions, they do not seem to amount to a major extension or restatement. I would include in that category the quietly excellent work of Keith Wrightson, especially on social class; of Robert Gray, on hegemony in Victorian England; of Peter Burke, on the need for a more historicized view of cultural hegemony. Since Craig Calhoun's revisionist work on class struggle seems unjustly neglected, I would include his endorsement of Thompson's view that 'a "class" may not be identified outside of particular historical contexts', as well as his criticism of Thompson for too readily using the term ' "working class" for many different kinds of working people', and especially for assuming 'that these people had one struggle'. Note too Bill Schwartz's highly apposite observation (after citing Laclau) that 'The "free-born Englishman defending his home" is abstract until we know who he is defending it from – Nazi invasion and fascism, or Asians who have moved in next door.'[72] (This is a good example of the nature of contingency and articulation.) And I have mentioned Gareth Stedman Jones, while noting some of the reasons for his relative marginalization.[73]

Even counting this excellent work as a significant extension of the Thompsonian programme, however, it hardly amounts to a renewal. Apart from feminist history, which has opened up a whole new area and perspective far beyond my ability to tackle here, there are only a couple of possible exceptions. Firstly, a burgeoning body of work, based on anti-teleological premises, has appeared on the social history of marginalized 'fringe' beliefs and people.[74]

Its affiliation with Thompson's vow in 1963 to rescue from the enormous condescension of posterity 'even the deluded follower of Joanna Southcott' is plain.[75] (Although the word 'deluded' is not one that would be uncritically repeated today.) Secondly, there is Patrick Joyce's recent *Visions of the People*.[76] Appearing too late to be more than mentioned here, Joyce explores nineteenth-century class in a way that is non-dogmatic and sensitive to context and contingency. Whatever criticisms are possible – and Joyce's deflationary tone, in keeping with his strong sense of conducting work-in-progress, is not one – I think he has succeeded in producing the first substantive example, on the traditional terrain of English Marxist social history, of (in his words) 'a history that takes postmodernism and the Marxist legacy seriously'.[77]

I'm not sure, however, that even three swallows make a summer; and given the recent dominance of triumphalist right-wing history-writing, this is very worrying. I have argued that the critique of the old social history by Clark, among others, was not wholly unfounded. That part of his purpose is to celebrate past and by implication present inequalities does not cancel out the aptness of his negative point. Nor does it poison the progressive potential of his anti-teleological stance. But that stance has been embedded in a reactionary new synthesis, however debatable the latter may be. The sheen has now worn off, but that in itself will not prevent its progress as a damaging new orthodoxy – and just at a time when the price of inward- and backward-looking chauvinism amid the demands of a bewildering new congeries of 'others' (European and Muslim, in addition to the more familiar kinds) will prove higher than ever. Yet there is no hope whatsoever in trying to form a defensive laager around old truths. On the contrary, the only way to defend 'works whose credibility has collapsed', and to call Clark's bluff about a tradition that 'has finally hit the buffers', is to *develop that tradition anew* – to present a positive new alternative, rooted in the radical democratic potential we have identified at the heart of that tradition, but which has actually been lending a perverse life to reaction.[78] What are the signs that this sort of move is underway, particularly in what has been hitherto the arena of overtly Marxist or socialist history-writing?

Some portents were apparent at a conference, held on 9 July 1988, which was devoted to 'a day of discussion on the future of history.' Its credentials were impressive: sponsored by the

Communist Party Historians Group, History Workshop and the Society for the Study of Labour History, and organized by the publishers of Leslie Morton and (in English) Antonio Gramsci, Lawrence and Wishart.[79] The occasion was provided by the fiftieth anniversary of Morton's *A People's History of England*. His idea of 'the people' was subjected to some sharpish criticism by the succeeding generations of historians. A more marked contrast, however, was provided by an entertaining but depressingly sterile exchange between Ellen Meiksins Wood, as socialist Cerberus, and Paul Hirst, as leading apostate out to *épater les Marxists*.[80]

But the most striking contrast was between that kind of *pas de deux* and the aura of hope in the contributions of some of the younger historians present. Two in particular stood out. George Shire, speaking from his work on British black history, invited us to move beyond the concept of 'the people' to a newer and fuller 'recognition of difference'. Given 'the almost mystical status of race and nation', he pointed out that considerations of race and racism do not live at the periphery of English national identity but at its very core. Catherine Hall stressed that 'it is not just a question of including blacks and women in "the people" to make up for past neglect'. These inter-relations and their effects – the role of 'the other' in the construction of Englishness – will have to be rethought. Nothing less would do justice to people's richly multiple identities, interests and problems.[81] Such questions of identity – especially the conditions of identity, and including who or what it is constructed against – are at the heart of a post-Marxist programme.

The same kinds of concerns inform the latest History Workshop production: three volumes on *Patriotism*.[82] History Workshop proved a worthy successor to the Hill–Thompson–Hobsbawm impulse in the 1970s and 1980s. Its contributors have illuminated the lives of miners, fenwomen and socialist spiritualists, grappled with complex and at times explosive historiographical issues (such as those surrounding Thompson's *The Poverty of Theory*), and made invaluable space for those seeking to restore to the past and thereby present its invisible women and missing feminist dimension. (I am especially grateful to it for having thrown a lifeline to theory in those dark days.[83]) Not that there were no problems with History Workshop – usually the reverse side of its virtues. Too often the new women's history was simply added to the old

picture 'arithmetically' (as I said earlier) and without attempting
to rethink the whole picture, in just the manner criticized by
Catherine Hall. The originality of emphasizing labour history tended
to slip into a simple reversal of history 'from the top down',
generating its own sort of reverse elitism. The latter was sometimes reflected when Workshop historians turned their attention
to other 'non-socialist' identities, conveying a spurious air of derring-
do and slightly patronizing their wayward subjects.

Fortunately, it is not my purpose to attempt to evaluate History
Workshop as a whole. But I do want briefly to consider *Patriotism*.
From the very start, an unsettled, self-doubting, even divided
outlook is evident. As editor, Raphael Samuel prescribes 'a more
pluralistic understanding of the nation', correctly pointing out that
'We are all majorities or minorities, insiders or outsiders, aristo-
crats or peasants, depending on the optic under which we are
viewed.' In his view, the workshop sessions which gave rise to
Patriotism 'represented an attempt, albeit a theoretically unarticulated one, to escape from unity or essentialist notions of all
kinds ... If there is a single message of these volumes it is that
patriotism is never self-contained.' Writing about characters of
national fiction, Samuel notes that 'Ideologically these figures have
multiple significations, being subject to rival or contradictory interpretations.'[84] Now the choice of terms here – multiple identities
and readings, pluralism vs self-contained essentialism, and so on
– is highly significant, and resonates closely with the issues which
I have been discussing. In the context of History Workshop, it is
a genuinely daring programme.

Sadly, however, old habits die disappointingly hard in actual
historical practice. Samuel's construal of his particular *bête noir* –
the heritage outlook and its appropriation by English cultural
nationalism – sounds pretty single and self-contained to me: 'Con-
servation ... trades on regressive fantasies', its functions are
'consolatory' and 'inward-looking or backward-looking', and so
forth. Samuel not only communicates no sense that it can be
differently articulated for very different purposes – an insight available at least as long ago as Orwell – but his distinctly essentialist
approach even obliges him, bizarrely, to lump Tony Harrison in
with Kingsley Amis and Philip Larkin as purveyors of nostalgic
English patriotism.[85]

Another contributor, Stephen Howe, is left equally stranded

between worthy intention and its betrayal in practice. 'Hope,' he writes, 'lies in abandoning the totalising aspiration, in recognition of plural subjectivities, plural identities.' Some identities are still more equal than others, however, and apparently 'that of Englishness is irredeemably "bad" . . . something inherently antithetical to the aims of the left'.[86] Italics are hardly necessary to stress the contradiction.

In fact, of virtually all the contributors, only Anthony Barnett seems able to carry out the promise of surrendering essential identities and therefore single perspectives. Not coincidentally, he alone also escapes wallowing in defeat, and perceives enabling possibilities as well as complete write-offs. What must be avoided, he writes, is turning the past into 'a story that has a single message or one central, defining tradition' – *regardless* of how correct or desirable the putative content of that message or tradition. For the 'view that we have one true history is linked to a perspective that sees one true nation'. This view, of course, is exactly the positivist and teleological one – with all its elitist and authoritarian implications – taken by both New Right and old Left. 'The fact is,' he continues, 'that the victors – the topdogs – were and remain a defining part of our history.'[87]

Turning to nationalism (which seems to be a test), Barnett recognises that it 'strives to secure a unity. In itself, the very idea of a nation denies any possibility of a plural form'. But that doesn't lead him to suggest that the Left should either abandon it in despair to the Right *or* try to replace the latter as '*the* bearers of the nation's destiny'. 'Suppose that on the contrary, we [on the Left] insist upon the plurality of national allegiances . . . multiple loyalties . . . overlapping sovereignties.' Doing so, he suggests, might effectively dissolve the destructive monopoly claim of nationalism upon its subjects and their identities.[88] Such a proposal is no mere fantasy; it is at the heart of the Charter 88 campaign for constitutional reform and a citizen's charter, which Barnett also champions. (At the time of writing, this is something to which both the socialist and social democratic wings of the Labour Party are opposed, thus confirming that the instincts of English social democratic labourism are often as essentialist and anti-democratic as those of its sectarian socialist twin.) Neither is it a fantasy in the context of the European Community, nor the multiple ethnic and religious identities at home. For good or for ill, such issues will have enormous consequences. Why then is Barnett's paper the only one in this collection to address them both seriously and intelligently?

Perhaps it is because, as Samuel states in his first sentence, 'these volumes were born out of anger at the Falklands War', and carry its hallmark. Certainly that war, in addition to its amorality, pointed to the real problem of reactionary English nationalism and the enduring residues of Empire. But to remain mesmerised by it, and to treat the problem in a way that is itself inward-looking and backward-looking, leaves us without a past that offers any hope or guidance either in the present or for the future.

That the patriotism is not squarely faced, or is at least *mal posée*, was actually suggested from the start by the title. Samuel justifies the choice of 'British' rather than 'English' national identity by arguing that the former conveys 'a more pluralistic understanding of the nation, one which sees it as a citizenry rather than a folk'.[89] At a deeper level, however, this evades the central issue. 'Britain' is useful as a rubric to include the Scots, Welsh and arguably Northern Irish, but 'Britishness' has no substance whatsoever. It belies a specious pluralism with neither cultural nor real political content, whereas 'Englishness' is precisely the nub of the matter: the chief unexamined identity, the dominant resource and rallying-call – in short, the central problem and (in its transformation) opportunity. As Paul Gilroy put it, 'The idea of an authentic cultural content of our national life is . . . contructed through an appeal to Englishness rather than Britishness. It is around this concept that the difficult tasks of creating a more pluralistic sense of national identity and a new conception of national culture revolve.'[90] To reject that and start with Britishness is to shirk those tasks.

Another conference called to mark the publication of *Patriotism* – on 17 June 1989 – showcased Stuart Hall. Ironically, Hall, not a contributor to the books, urged that Englishness be taken seriously, and be tackled historically and relationally. He pointed out that insofar as national identity results from mobilising differences, the 'other(s)', although produced as outside the dominant national culture, must be viewed as integrally 'inside'. The question is, therefore: can the English become just another 'tribe', one among many? Or as Hall put it, 'Do they have to eat everybody else in order to be who they are? Or is there some other way they can decently be . . . an English ethnic group, with quite an interesting history and a rich language, in the twenty-first century?'[91]

Before concluding, I want to try spell out in more detail what difference to historical practice my prescription would actually make. (Note that I am not inviting herrings, red or otherwise, by asking 'Is post-Marxism true?' I am asking 'Would it help? Does it represent a potential advance?') There is no need to make grand claims about revolutionising social history; indeed, that would contradict the spirit of the theory itself. We only need to make a progressive difference – quite hard enough. Its heart, I think, is in Laclau and Mouffe's thesis that while power is constructed in a complex and pragmatic way – one that rules out our apprehending it in terms of simply a dominant class, sector or logic – neither is it so socially diffused (as Foucault implied) as to defy effective analysis.[92] Power exists and is undoubtedly exercised, but it is *constructed* and *relative*. As they go on to say,

This is the point at which many of the concepts of classical analysis – 'centre', 'power', 'autonomy', etc. – can be re-introduced, if their status is redefined: all of them are contingent *social logics* which, as such, acquire their meaning in precise conjunctural and relational contexts, where they will always be limited by other – frequently contradictory – logics; but none of them has absolute validity.[93]

Therein is the methodological key to the kind of renewal of progressive social history which this essay urges. As I see it, putting it into practice would have powerfully positive effects both 'internal' and 'external' to that tradition.

Internal in two respects: firstly, it would release such historians from the obligation necessarily to place economy and class before other considerations. (By the same token, and no less importantly, it would re-admit to the Left progressive historians who nonetheless, in defiance of this spurious demand, don't do so.) Exploitation then ceases to arrogate the exercise of power, and class ceases to be paradigmatic of the social. Instead, each becomes one of many kinds of social differentiation, relations and resulting identities, none of which has a privileged claim on our attention. Far from producing another wave of conservative and/or reactionary historians, such a move would free historians to give due weight to considerations of gender, race and other major but neglected aspects of human life. Nor would people so easily be seen as representatives (let alone 'bearers') of a single dimension such as class; attention would instead follow the recognition of the multiple identities, loyalties and roles which we all live, and in particular the ways these meld and clash. This approach is the best possible remedy for reductionist elitism whether apparently of the Left or Right, and for the alienation it generates.

Secondly, a radically democratic practice of history would undermine other and potentially equally limiting, even damaging essentialisms analogous to that surrounding the mode of production and class.[94] For just as the latter kind everywhere declines, hitherto 'repressed' other ones threaten to divert the positive energies thus released. (Nowhere is this more evident than in Eastern Europe and the USSR, where the decline has been the sharpest.) Although drastically less in scale and intensity in the historical disciplines, the lesson is nonetheless similar. Limitations of space and knowledge forbid even a superficial survey, but almost everywhere one looks there seems to be a struggle between essentialist and relativist-historicist approaches. I have already mentioned the largely untackled problem of unreconstructed Englishness; the counter-ethnic essentialism of much anti-racism – as distinct from a critical pluralism – will only play into its hands.[95]

Another contested area is the more literally battleground of Irish history, where essentialist intellectual practice[96] contributes to a racist national identity, erected on a pseudo-ethnic basis with a semi-mythological history, whose 'liberation' continues to inflict the obscenity of 'necessary deaths'. This species of romantic brutalism was well characterized by Louis MacNiece as one in which speech becomes 'cramped to Yea and Nay'. Fortunately, it has profoundly capable critics: politically, in the leadership of the Social Democratic and Labour Party, and historiographically in the 'revisionism' of Roy Foster and others.[97]

Yet another area of contention is feminist history-writing. As in feminism more generally, there is a strong strand of essentialism which seeks to turn attention away from the construction of 'woman' and 'the feminine' in favour of the liberation of a transcendental feminine essence, at once semi-mystical and quasi-biological, culminating in the defeatist withdrawal of separatism. Paradoxically, this is often accompanied by grandiose posturing about 'the present will to extirpate gender and sex hierarchy *altogether*, and with them *all* forms of domination'.[98] On the other hand there are more critical and historicist historians, who in the case of Elizabeth Fox-Genovese overlap with Marxists, arguing (in her words) that 'To the extent that male domination, like class domination, has obtained throughout history, there is no women's history, nor forms of female power, apart from it.'[99]

I haven't even mentioned the most ancient, powerful essentialism of all, with the most refined and popular brand of teleology, and its attendant historiography: that of religion. But all these dangers, these openings for 'bad histories', are simultaneously opportunities for good; and for that, a radically democratic intellectual practice, focused on historicity and contingency, is our best hope. (I should add that as a kind of side-benefit, such a practice might also make better sense of its own tradition than hitherto. The 'golden age' of socialist history that is now supposed to have disappeared certainly wasn't based in the dominant universities, which continued to reflect the mixed Tory and Whiggish influences of Namier and Plumb. Yet socialist history definitely possessed a kind of moral and intellectual ascendency, which has now been largely lost or replaced; in other words, and the choice of words is aptly unavoidable, both periods were phases in a continuing hegemonic struggle.[100])

I mentioned earlier that the kind of approach I am advocating also has a hopeful dimension *external* to the discipline of social history – external, but still affecting it. This too is true in two respects; firstly, it would connect our discipline to some of the most promising and exciting intellectual work today. The post-Marxism of Laclau and Mouffe is an integral part of this work, both cause and effect of the new-found freedom from scientistic and Marxist teleological realisms alike. Such a truncated list is hardly adequate, but I am thinking, for example, of Anthony Giddens and his 'theory of structuration';[101] Michael Walzer's 'critical pluralism';[102] Richard Rorty's 'liberal irony' and nominalist, historicist epistemology;[103] the 'democratic relativism' of Paul Feyerabend;[104] André Gortz, on socialism and ecology in a post-industrial society;[105] and Zygmunt Bauman, on the structure and nature of contemporary class.[106] Symbolic of the new convergence between left-liberals and post-Marxists, there is also the extraordinarily fresh relevance of Isaiah Berlin's work, with his advocacy of epistemological and political pluralism.[107] And I would like to mention June Jordan, whose activism and writing

both give the lie to any accusation that these ideas have no life
closer to street level:

Yes: race and class and gender remain as real as the weather. But what
they must mean about the contact between two individuals is less obvious
and, like the weather, not predictable. And these factors of race and class
and gender absolutely collapse whenever you try to use them as automatic
concepts of connection . . . *When we get the monsters off our backs all of
us may want to run in very different directions* . . . The ultimate connection must be the need that we find between us.[108]

The second kind of positive external connection that a post-
Marxist and radically democratic approach offers is to the larger
world, especially the dramatic changes in Eastern Europe and the
Soviet Union. For obvious reasons, those changes hold a special
piquancy both for Marxists and the old socialist social history,
and for the new democratic Left coming into being. There is no
need to belabour them, but at a time when ethnic nationalism and
an over-reliance on markets alone threaten to swamp their original impulse, I want to remind readers of just what that was and
remains: one of hope, human values and the real participation of
people (not class ciphers) in making their own historical destiny.

Closer to home, what was a gale of democracy in the East is still
only a breath of wind here, stirring the limp flags at Westminster.
Charter 88 has correctly identified democratic constitutional reform
of the sclerotic British state and its archaic institutions as the
Achilles heel of Tory England – whether the patriarchal and
paternalist old loyalists or the crass *nouveau* Thatcherite breed. But
closer integration with continental Europe, for which the traditional parochialism of both main parties alike leaves us utterly
unprepared, is probably the biggest challenge to English cultural
and national identity today. It goes hand-in-hand with the crisis
of identities and loyalties symbolised by the 'Rushdie affair'; for
Europeanisation has an outward-looking face, as well as inward.
So will it impoverish what it means to be English, or enrich it –
or both, in different ways? What are our historical resources, and
what strategies do they suggest, for a positive response?

No real alternative is yet apparent, however, to the smugly
triumphalist history underwritten by successive Conservative cab-
inet ministers (epitomised by Kenneth Baker) which is settling into
our educational syllabuses, reading lists and bookshops. Meanwhile
there is a new social reality already on the streets – but fragmented

and deracinated, untheorised, unrecognised. *The old Left holds out no hope here; nor does the New Right: only a truly new Left.* And in that work, a renewed social history has a vital place.

Notes

1 This essay assumed its final form in August 1991; only a few more recent references have been added. Earlier versions were read and discussed at meetings of the Society for the Study of Labour History (1987), the Department of Government at the University of Essex (1988) and the Postgraduate Seminar on Theory and Method at the Institute of Historical Research (1990). I am grateful for the invitations and to all those who participated. I would also like to thank Ernesto Laclau for patiently answering my queries; and Rohan McWilliams, Simon Schaffer, Jonathan Boswell, Clay Ramsay, Michael Winship and Adrian Wilson for their comments on various drafts.

2 For an overview see Harvey J. Kaye, *The British Marxist Historians*, Oxford, 1984; also Raphael Samuel, 'British Marxist Historians, 1880–1980', *New Left Review*, No. 120, 1980, pp. 42–55; and an excellent paper by Bill Schwarz, ' "The People" in History: The Communist Party Historians', in Richard Johnson, Gregor McLennan, Bill Schwarz and David Sutton, *Making Histories: Studies in History-Writing and Politics*, London, 1982, pp. 44–95.

3 W.D. Rubinstein, *Elites and the Wealthy in Modern Britain: Essays in Social and Economic History*, Brighton, 1987; Martin Weiner, *English Culture and the Decline of the Industrial Spirit*, Cambridge, 1981; J.C. Davis, *Fear, Myth and History: The Ranters and the Historians*, Cambridge, 1988; Alan Macfarlane, *The Origins of English Individualism*, Oxford, 1978. Note that the first explicitly identifies himself and Clark as part of the same revisionist school, aiming to reverse the direction of social history initiated by E.P. Thompson (p. 12). On the last, see K.D.M. Snell, 'English Historical Continuity and the Culture of Capitalism: The Work of Alan Macfarlane', *History Workshop Journal*, XXVII, 1989, pp. 154–63.

4 Reviews and responses to Clark include Joanna Innes, 'Jonathan Clark, Social History and England's "Ancien Regime" ', *Past and Present*, No. 115, 1987, pp. 165–200; Alan Ryan, 'Tory History', *London Review of Books*, 23 January 1986; John Kenyon, 'After the Revolution', *The Observer*, 26 January 1986; Linda Colley, 'Salvaging Lost Causes', *Times Literary Supplement*, 14 March 1986; Jeremy Black, 'Vicars of Bray?' *History Today*, XXXVI, February

1986; Mark Goldie, 'Levelling the Levellers', *Times Literary Supplement*, 23 January 1987; Leonard Tennenhouse, review in *History and Theory*, XXVII, 1988, pp. 312–21; and a feature article by Peter Watson, 'The Don Re-Writes History', *The Observer*, 31 January 1988.
5 Ryan, 'Tory History'.
6 J.C.D. Clark, 'On Hitting the Buffers: the Historiography of England's *Ancien Régime*', *Past and Present*, No. 127, 1987, pp. 195–207, p. 202; *Revolution and Rebellion: State and Society in England in the Seventeenth and Eighteenth Centuries*, Cambridge, 1986, p. 3; in *History Today*, XXXV, March 1985, pp. 43–4, p. 44; and 'Buffers', p. 202, n. 25.
7 For a good discussion of these issues, see Adrian Wilson and T.G. Ashplant, 'Whig History and Present-Centred History', *The Historical Journal*, XXXI, 1988, pp. 1–16, and T.G. Ashplant and Adrian Wilson, 'Present-Centred History and the Problem of Historical Knowledge', *The Historical Journal*, XXXI, 1988, pp. 253–74; also John Tosh, *The Pursuit of History: Aims, Methods and New Directions in the Study of Modern History*, London, 1984, pp. 127–51.
8 Innes, 'Jonathan Clark', p. 171.
9 Lawrence Stone, 'The Results of the English Revolution', pp. 23–108 in J.G.A. Pocock (ed.), *Three British Revolutions: 1641, 1688, 1776*, Princeton, 1980, p. 62; Perez Zagorin, *Provincial Rebellion: Revolutionary Civil Wars 1560–1660*, Cambridge, 1982, 2 vols., II, pp. 185–6; Christopher Hill, 'A Bourgeois Revolution?' pp. 109–39 in Pocock (ed.), *British Revolutions*, p. 134. (Compare the last with Hill's more full-blooded Marxist teleology, and reduction of religion, in his earlier *The English Revolution 1640*, London, 1955, third edn, p. 43.) *A fortiori* the same general point applies to Perry Anderson, *Lineages of the Absolutist State*, London, 1974. The Left's inattention to religion was somewhat remedied (not without soul-searching) by Lyndal Roper and Raphael Samuel (eds.), *Disciplines of Faith: Studies on Religion, Politics and Patriarchy*, London, 1987. For Clark's views on the subject, see his 'England's Ancien Régime as a Confessional State', *Albion*, XXI, 1989, pp. 450–74.
10 E.P. Thompson, 'Patrician Society, Plebeian Culture', *Journal of Social History*, VII, 1974, pp. 382–405, p. 393; 'Eighteenth-Century English Society: Class Struggle Without Class?', *Social History*, III, 1978, pp. 133–65, *passim*; Jonathan Clark, *English Society 1688–1832: Ideology, Social Structure and Political Practice During the Ancien Régime*, Cambridge, 1985, pp. 71, 90.
11 Thompson, 'Class Struggle', p. 150; Clark, 'Buffers', p. 198.

12 Thompson, 'Patrician Society', p. 403 and 'Class Struggle', p. 141; Clark, *English Society*, p. 68.
13 Thompson, 'Patrician Society', p. 391; Clark, *English Society*, p. 68.
14 Thompson, 'Patrician Society', p. 395 and 'Class Struggle', pp. 151, 163, 165; Clark, *English Society*, pp. 64, 88.
15 Clark, *Revolution*, p. 11; E.P. Thompson, *The Making of the English Working Class*, Harmondsworth, 1968, p. 12.
16 Clark, 'Buffers', p. 198, in response to Innes, 'Jonathan Clark', pp. 173–4; Goldie, 'Levelling'.
17 Although note that in an interview on 20 October 1985, Thompson described himself as 'less and less interested in Marxism as a theoretical system', adding that now 'I feel happier with the term historical materialism' ('Interview', *Radical History Review*, No. 36, 1986, pp. 37–42, pp. 39–40).
18 Clark, *Revolution*, p. 167.
19 Clark, 'Buffers', p. 196.
20 E.g., to select out of a large literature, Barry Barnes and Steven Shapin (eds.), *Natural Order; Historical Studies of Scientific Culture*, London, 1979; Steven Shapin, 'The Social Uses of Science', pp. 93–139 in G.S. Rousseau and Roy Porter (eds.), *The Ferment of Knowledge: Studies in the Historiography of Eighteenth-Century Science*, Cambridge, 1980; Steven Shapin and Simon Schaffer, *Leviathan and the Air-Pump: Hobbes, Boyle, and the Experimental Life*, Princeton, 1986; Simon Schaffer, 'Godly Men and Mechanical Philosophers: Souls and Spirits in Restoration Natural Philosophy', *Science in Context*, I, 1987, pp. 55–86; David Gooding, Trevor Pinch and Simon Schaffer (eds.), *The Uses of Experiment: Studies in Natural Science*, Cambridge, 1988; and Ludmilla Jordanova, *Sexual Visions: Images of Gender in Science and Medicine between the Eighteenth and Twentieth Centuries*, Hemel Hempstead, 1989. Some of the ground was first broken by Frances Yates, P.M. Rattansi and Charles Webster; see the latter's *From Paracelsus to Newton: Magic and the Making of Modern Science*, Cambridge, 1982. The work of Barry Barnes and David Bloor provides a link with closely related work in the sociology of science. For a recent anti-teleological analysis of science by a Marxist, see Stanley Aronowitz, *Science as Power: Discourse and Ideology in Modern Society*, London, 1989.
21 Thompson's eighteenth-century papers were recently (finally) published in a very welcome collection, *Customs in Common*, London, 1991. (I have however retained the page numbers to his journal articles here.)
22 Thompson, 'Class Struggle', pp. 158, 163–4.
23 E.P. Thompson, *Whigs and Hunters: The Origins of the Black Act*, Harmondsworth, 1977, pp. 263–4.

24   Perry Anderson, *Arguments Within English Marxism*, London, 1980,
     p. 40; Richard Johnson, 'Thompson, Genovese and Socialist
     Humanism' *History Workshop Journal*, VI, 1978, pp. 79–100.

25   See Gregor McLennan, 'E.P. Thompson and the Discipline of His-
     torical Context', pp. 96–130 in Richard Johnson *et al.* (eds.),
     Making Histories; pp. 375–408 in Raphael Samuel (ed.), *People's
     History and Socialist Theory*, London, 1981; and *History Work-
     shop Journal*, VIII–IX, 1979–80, *passim*.

26   Tony Bennett, 'Introduction: "The Turn to Gramsci"', in Tony
     Bennett, Colin Mercer and Janet Woollacott (eds.), *Popular Culture
     and Social Relations*, Milton Keynes, 1986, pp. xi–xix, p. xiii. In
     fairness to Thompson, the metaphor of a force-field was precisely
     the one he used in 'Class Struggle' – which shows, apart from the
     author's carelessness, how the mud of 'culturalism' stuck.

27   Thompson, 'Class Struggle', pp. 149–50, 151.

28   See the references given in note 35 below.

29   Succinctly analysed in Terry Eagleton, *The Function of Criticism*,
     London, 1984.

30   Thompson has recently resumed his historical work (see note 21
     above). For a good overview of his intellectual career, see the papers
     in Harvey J. Kaye and Keith McClelland (eds.), *E.P. Thompson:
     Critical Perspectives*, Cambridge, 1990. Also see interviews with
     Thompson in *Radical History Review*, No. 3, 1976, reproduced in
     Henry Abelove *et al.* (eds.), *Visions of History*, Manchester, 1983,
     pp. 5–25; and in *Radical History Review*, No. 36, 1986, pp. 37–
     42.

31   For example: Joanna Innes and John Styles, ' "The Crime Wave":
     Recent Writing on Crime and Criminal Justice in Eighteenth Cen-
     tury England', *Journal of British Studies*, XXV, 1986, pp. 380–435,
     and reprinted in this volume; Anthony Fletcher and John Stevenson
     (eds.), *Order and Disorder in Early Modern England*, Cambridge,
     1985, including the excellent Introduction (pp. 1–40) and John
     Stevenson, 'The "Moral Economy" of the Crowd: Myth and Reality',
     pp. 218–38; K.D.M. Snell, *Annals of the Labouring Poor: Social
     Change and Agrarian England, 1660–1900*, Cambridge, 1985; John
     Brewer and John Styles (eds.), *An Ungovernable People: The
     English and their Law in the Seventeenth and Eighteenth Centuries*,
     London, 1980; John Brewer, *Party Ideology and Popular Politics at
     the Accession of George III*, Cambridge, 1976. (John Brewer, *The
     Sinews of Power: War, Money and the English State, 1688–1783*,
     London, 1989, although important, is more an opening up of a
     previously neglected area.) For a later period, see Robert Gray, *The
     Labour Aristocracy in Victorian England*, Oxford, 1976. For an
     ambitious critical evaluation of Thompson's work, see Craig Calhoun,

The Question of Class Struggle: Social Foundations of Popular Radicalism During the Industrial Revolution, Oxford, 1982. For an excellent discussion of class, see Keith Wrightson, 'The Social Order of Early Modern England: Three Approaches', in Lloyd Bonfield, Richard M. Smith and Keith Wrightson (eds.), *The World We Have Gained: Histories of Population and Social Structure*, Oxford, 1986, pp. 177–202. For a good historiographical discussion, see Peter Burke, 'Revolution in Popular Culture', in Roy Porter and Mikulas Teich (eds.), *Revolution in History*, Cambridge, 1987, pp. 206–25. Is it significant that there are so few full-length (let alone major) studies that one can cite? For a recent exception, however, see my reference to Patrick Joyce (note 76 below).

32   For a solid contribution here, see Leonore Davidoff and Catherine Hall, *Family Fortunes: Men and Women of the English Middle-Class, 1780–1850*, London, 1987. See also the papers in Judith L. Newton, Mary P. Ryan and Judith R. Walkowitz (eds.), *Sex and Class in Women's History*, London, 1983; Barbara Taylor, *Eve and the New Jerusalem*, London, 1973; Sheila Rowbotham, *Hidden from History*, London, 1973; and Jordanova, *Sexual Visions*. For a good discussion of feminist historiography in relation to the kind of critique of essentialism that Laclau and Mouffe make, see Catherine Hall, 'Politics, Post-structuralism and Feminist History', *Gender and History* 3:2, 1991, pp. 204–10.

33   Gareth Stedman Jones, *Languages of Class: Studies in English Working Class History, 1832–1982*, Cambridge, 1983.

34   On the limitations of structuralism, see Anthony Giddens, *Central Problems in Social Theory*, London, 1979. For a fair-minded critique of Stedman Jones along the lines just mentioned, see John Foster, 'The Declassing of Language', *New Left Review*, No. 150, 1985, pp. 29–46. For a sectarian and polemical treatment (arguably more typical as a Marxist response), see Ellen Meiksins Wood, *The Retreat from Class: A New 'True' Socialism*, London, 1986.

35   There is a vast English-language literature on Antonio Gramsci's idea of hegemony, most of which is based on the *Selections from the Prison Notebooks of Antonio Gramsci*, ed. and transl. Quentin Hoare and G. Nowell Smith, London, 1971. (This is about to be superseded by a new and complete translation to be published by Columbia University Press.) See, for example, Roger Simon, *Gramsci's Political Thought: An Introduction*, London, 1982; Robert Bocock, *Hegemony*, London, 1986; and David Forgacs, 'Gramsci and Marxism in Britain', *New Left Review*, No. 176, 1989, pp. 70–88.

36   Ernesto Laclau and Chantal Mouffe, *Hegemony and Socialist Strategy: Towards a Radical Democratic Politics*, London, 1985; Ernesto Laclau, *New Reflections on the Revolution of our Time*,

London, 1991; Chantal Mouffe (ed.), *Dimensions of Radical Democracy*, London, 1992. See also Mouffe, 'Hegemony and Ideology in Gramsci', in Chantal Mouffe (ed.), *Gramsci and Marxist Theory*, pp. 168–204, London, 1979; Laclau, 'Class War and After', *Marxism Today*, April 1987, pp. 30–3; Mouffe, 'Hegemony and New Political Subjects: Towards a New Concept of Democracy', in Cary Nelson and Lawrence Grossberg (eds.), *Marxism and the Interpretation of Culture*, London, 1988, pp. 89–104; and Mouffe, 'Radical Democracy or Liberal Democracy?' *Socialist Register* 90:2, 1990, pp. 57–66. The work of Stuart Hall is fairly closely related: see references in note 44 below. (NB: There are some significant differences between Laclau and Mouffe and the American post-Marxists Samuel Bowles and Herbert Gintis in their *Democracy and Capitalism*, New York, 1986.)

37   Michael Walzer, *The Company of Critics: Social Criticism and Political Commitment in the Twentieth Century*, London, 1989, pp. 99–100.

38   Laclau and Mouffe, *Hegemony*, pp. 95, 105, 108–9.

39   Paul Veyne, *Comment On Ecrit L'Histoire, suivi de Foucault révolutionne L'Histoire*, Paris, 1987, p. 236 (translated from French).

40   Laclau and Mouffe, *Hegemony*, pp. 177, 36, 178; Laclau, 'Class War', p. 30.

41   Wood on post-Marxism, in *Retreat*, is almost entirely based on such a misunderstanding, but Frederic Jameson (p. 353 in Nelson and Grossberg, *Marxism*) surely knows better.

42   Pierre Vilar, 'Constructing Marxist History', in Jacques Le Goff and Pierre Nora (eds.), *Constructing the Past: Essays in Historical Methodology*, Cambridge, 1985, pp. 47–80, pp. 53, 79. For a recent example of Marxist history-writing vitiated by a determination to think everything *except* Marxist categories historically, see George C. Comninel, *Rethinking the French Revolution*, London, 1987. For an example of utterly reified and anti-historical Marxism – and thus, in my terms, thoroughly reactionary – see G.A. Cohen, *Karl Marx's Theory of History: A Defense*, Oxford, 1979.

43   Laclau, *New Reflections*, p. 179; cf. Oscar Negt, who makes the same point in 'What Is a Revival of Marxism and Why Do We Need One Today?': Centenary Lecture Commemorating the Death of Karl Marx', in Nelson and Grossberg, *Marxism*, pp. 211–34.

44   In his interview with Achille Occhetto in *Marxism Today*, February 1990, p. 15.

45   This practice was legitimized by, among others, Lenin's colleague Nikolai Bukharin in 1920: 'Proletarian coercion, in all its forms, from executions to forced labour, is, paradoxical as it may sound, the method of moulding communist humanity out of the human

material of the capitalist period.' (Bukharin himself was later executed
– sorry, moulded – by Stalin.) Cf. Parkin's sarcastic observation –
but based on Trotsky's sincere one – that 'To shoot down workers
in the defense of capitalism is a qualitatively different act from
shooting down workers in the name of socialism.' Frank Parkin,
Marxism and Class Theory: A Bourgeois Critique, London, 1979,
pp. 184–5.

46 Laclau and Mouffe, *Hegemony*, pp. 191–2, and Laclau, *New Reflections, passim*; cf. Paul Patton, 'Marxism and Beyond: Strategies
of Reterritorialization', pp. 123–39 in Nelson and Grossberg (eds.),
Marxism, on Marxist 'monoperspectivism'. Also see the writings
of Stuart Hall, including *The Hard Road to Renewal: Thatcherism
and the Crisis of the Left*, London, 1988; 'The Toad in the Garden',
pp. 35–73 in Nelson and Grossberg (eds.), *Marxism*; 'Notes on
Deconstructing "the Popular"', in Samuel, *People's History*, pp. 227–
40. For a recent and excellent re-definition of the Left as 'the democratic fight for more democracy', see John Keane, 'What's left of
what's Left', *Times Literary Supplement*, 21 June 1991, pp. 7–8.

47 In fairness, Laclau, *Reflections*, p. 130, nn. 1–6 lists some examples
of constructively critical engagement. For another example of a serious and fair-minded engagement, see 'Hegemony and Democracy:
A Post-Hegelian Perspective', in Fred Dallmayr, *Margins of Political
Discourse*, NY, 1989, pp. 116–36.

48 Wood, *Retreat*, pp. 3, 9, and chapters 4 and 5 *passim*.

49 Thompson, *Whigs*, p. 266.

50 Wood, Retreat, p. 154. (I love the 'of course'.) See also Ellen Meiksins
Wood, 'The Uses and Abuses of "Civil Society"', in Ralph Milliband
and Leo Panitch (eds.), *Socialist Register 1990: The Retreat of the
Intellectuals*, London, 1990, pp. 60–84.

51 Norman Geras, 'Post-Marxism?' *New Left Review*, No. 163, 1987,
pp. 40–82, pp. 47, 81, 43–4; also see his 'Ex-Marxism Without
Substance: Being a Real Reply to Laclau and Mouffe', *New Left
Review*, No. 169, 1988, pp. 34–62. Both have since appeared in his
*Discourses of Extremity: Radical Ethics and Post-Marxist Ex-
travagances*, London, 1990. Laclau and Mouffe's reply to the first
instalment is 'Post-Marxism Without Apologies', *New Left Review*,
No. 186, 1987, pp. 79–106; it is reprinted in Laclau, *New Reflections*, pp. 99–132.

52 In *Arguments Within English Marxism*, London, 1980, pp. 139–40,
Perry Anderson says of that attack (in 1966) that it was 'written
with a useless violence . . . to this day it remains an entirely isolated
episode within the annals of the *New Left Review*, which has never
published anything like it again'. It is a pity the current editor
should have since chosen to give the lie to this generous gesture. For

better discussions of Laclau and Mouffe in the same journal, however, see Nicos Mouzelis, 'Marxism or Post-Marxism? *New Left Review*, No. 167, 1988, pp. 107–23; and (especially) Andrew Gamble, 'Class Politics and Radical Democracy', *New Left Review*, No. 164, 1987, pp. 113–22.

53   Patrick Barlow, *All the World's A Globe*, London, 1987, p. 119.
54   Geras, 'Post-Marxism?' p. 67; 'Ex-Marxism', p. 59; 'Post-Marxism?', p. 66 (and cf. 'Ex-Marxism', pp. 56–7, 59–60); 'Post-Marxism?' pp. 79, 80, 82.
55   Norman Geras, 'Seven Types of Obloquy: Travesties of Marxism', pp. 1–34 in Milliband and Panitch, *Socialist Register*.
56   Terry Eagleton, 'Defending the Free World', pp. 85–94 in the same volume; e.g. p. 88: '[Marxists] don't believe that social class is a Bad Thing ... For Marxism, the working class is an excellent thing, since without it we [*sic*] would not be able to expropriate the bourgeoisie.' (Eagleton's recent book on ideology is disappointingly guarded by comparison; but then, in Max Beerbohm's words, to give an exhaustive and accurate account of the subject would need a far less brilliant pen than his.)
57   Vilar, 'Constructing', p. 61.
58   Bryan D. Palmer, 'The Eclipse of Materialism: Marxism and the Writing of Social History in the 1980s', in Milliband and Panitch (eds.), *Socialist Register*, pp. 111–46. He has subsequently published the luridly-titled *Descent into Discourse: The Reification of Language and the Writing of Social History* (Philadelphia, 1990). Williams is quoted by Palmer in 'Eclipse', p. 114. (Of course, Marxists are not the only ones to favour empty and discredited nostrums; and at least they have a theory. See e.g. Charles Tilly, on tying 'intellectual and cultural history down to the social, economic and political bedrock': 'The Old New Social History and the New Old Social History', VII, *Review* 1984, pp. 363–406, p. 395.)
59   Ellen Meiksins Wood, 'Falling Through the Cracks: E.P. Thompson and the Debate on Base and Superstructure', pp. 125–52 in Kaye and McClelland (eds.), *E.P. Thompson*, p. 141. (For an excellent essay in the same book, see Robert Gray, 'History, Marxism and Theory', pp. 153–82.)
60   Geras, 'Post-Marxism?' p. 49. For a more recent attack on Laclau and Mouffe from the same stable, see Peter Osborne, 'Radicalism Without Limit? Discourse, Democracy and the Politics of Identity', in Peter Osborne (ed.), *Socialism and the Limits of Liberalism*, London, 1990, pp. 201–25 – a disappointing piece for its defence of positivist epistemology and unargued assertion of 'the universalism of traditional socialist aspirations' (to say nothing of the book's remarkably untimely title).

61 Gareth Stedman Jones, 'Marx After Marxism', *Marxism Today*, February 1990, p. 3. (My metaphorical use of Albania may, of course, have been falsified by the time this gets read; I hope so. But I know I can count on the stalwarts of the *New Left Review* not to change their minds.)

62 See my *Prophecy and Power: Astrology in Early Modern England*, Cambridge, 1989.

63 Richard Rorty, *Consequences of Pragmatism*, Minneapolis, 1982, and *Contingency, Irony and Solidarity*, Cambridge, 1989; cf. an excellent discussion of relativism in Paul Feyerabend, *Farewell to Reason*, London, 1987, pp. 19–89. (I have already made the point when discussing J.C.D. Clark that the politics are not a necessary corollary of the epistemology; only an essentialist view of the latter sees them so.)

64 These elementary fallacies have recently been given a new lease of life by Richard Gott and James Wood in *The Guardian* and Ernst Gellner in his *Postmodernism, Reason and Religion*, London, 1992. The result is a vulgar postmodernism that suffices as an easy target in order to appear intellectually tough.

65 Like Andre Gorz and Jeremy Seabrook respectively.

66 Or as Fidel Castro ingeniously put it, 'we must correct the errors we made in correcting our errors'.

67 Laclau, *New Reflections*, p. 84; on relativism, see his 'Post-Marxism'. Cf. Gramsci on the obsession with base and superstructure: 'There is no doubt that all this is just an infantile derivation of the philosophy of praxis generated by the baroque conviction that the more one goes back to "material" objects, the more orthodox one must be' (*Prison Notebooks*, p. 205).

68 J.C.D. Clark has observed that Kaye's *British Marxist Historians* 'has about it the air of a group obituary' ('England's Ancien Régime', p. 450, n. 4). It is typical of Clark that the remark, however unfair, has enough truth to sting. Unfortunately it is also typical of Kaye, as one of that group's leading exponents, that his tepid respectfulness and reflex affiliation with the likes of Wood betokens no hope of ever proving Clark wrong ('E.P. Thompson, the British Marxist Tradition and the Contemporary Crisis', in Kaye and McClelland, *E.P. Thompson*, pp. 252–75; and see his letter in *New Statesman and Society*, 29 June 1990, to which I replied on 27 July).

69 E.g. Michael Rustin, *For a Pluralist Socialism*, London, 1985; Hilary Wainwright, *Labour: A Tale of Two Parties*, London, 1987.

70 E.g. Roger Chartier, *Cultural History: Between Practices and Representations*, Cambridge, 1988, pp. 60, 63, 102 (which I highly recommend).

71   E.P. Thompson, *The Poverty of Theory*, London, 1978, p. 363. See note 59 above.

72   See note 31 above; quotations are from Calhoun, *The Question of Class Struggle*, pp. 244, n. 42, and 19–20; and Schwarz, 'The People', p. 88.

73   See notes 32 and 33 above.

74   For example, Roger Cooter, *Cultural Meaning and Popular Science: Phrenology and the Organization of Consent in Nineteenth-Century Britain*, Cambridge, 1984, as well as his wonderful 'Deploying "Pseudo-science": Then and Now', in Marsha P. Hanen, Margaret J. Osler and Robert G. Weyant (eds.), *Science, Pseudo-Science and Society*, Waterloo Ontario, 1980, pp. 237–72, and his 'The History of Mesmerism in Britain: Poverty and Promise, in Heinz M. Schott (ed.), *Franz Anton Mesmer und die Geschicte des Mesmerismus*, Stuttgart, 1985, pp. 152–62; Logie Barrow's excellent *Independent Spirits: Spiritualism and English Plebeians, 1850–1910*, London, 1986; Alex Owen, *The Darkened Room: Women, Power and Spiritualism in Late Victorian England*, London, 1989. I have tried to contribute to this area with my *Prophecy and Power* (see note 62 above) and more recently *A Confusion of Prophets: Victorian and Edwardian Astrology*, London, 1992. For an historiographical discussion of the history of pseudo-science (in addition to Cooter, 'Deploying "Pseudo-science"'), see my 'Revisions of Science and Magic', *History of Science*, XXV, 1985, pp. 299–325. In connection with the message of this paper, note Barrow's brave call for 'a new democratic epistemology' (*Independent Spirits*, p. 279).

75   Thompson, *Making*, p. 12.

76   Patrick Joyce, *Visions of the People: Industrial England and the Question of Class, 1840–1914*, Cambridge, 1991.

77   Joyce quoted from his letter in the *Times Literary Supplement* of 13 September 1991. My own criticisms of *Visions* would be that its clarity suffers from theoretical undernourishment on both 'class' and 'populism', and from over-acceptance (in practice) of Stedman Jones's conflation of language with discourse. (It is perhaps unfair, for asking for what was not attempted, to note that it tends to neglect the crucial question of how class interacted with other kinds of social identity.)

78   Clark, 'Buffers', pp. 196, 207.

79   From the conference flyer. Press reports included Richard Gott, 'A History Lesson for the Left', *The Guardian*, 11 July 1988; and Bill Schwarz, 'Good History, Bad Politics', *New Statesman*, 15 July 1988.

80   Wood declared in passing that not only had post-Marxism not produced any good historical work – presumably since Laclau and

Mouffe's book appeared three years earlier – but that it *could not*: an interesting case of Marxist clairvoyance.

81 George Shire, 'Centring on Marginality: The Politics of Difference' in Joanna Coakley and Scott McCracken (eds.), *People's History and Popular Culture*, London, 1992. Cf. David Dabydeen, *Hogarth's Blacks: Images of Blacks in Eighteenth Century English Art*, Manchester, 1987. Catherine Hall in Coakley and McCracken (eds.), *People's History*; also Davidoff and Hall, *Family Fortunes*.

82 Raphael Samuel (ed.), *Patriotism: The Making and Unmaking of British National Identity*, London, 1989, 3 vols: I, *History and Politics*; II, *Minorities and Outsiders*; III, *National Fictions*.

83 Samuel, *People's History*; Raphael Samuel and Gareth Stedman Jones (eds.), *Culture, Ideology and Politics*, London, 1982.

84 Samuel, Patriotism, I, pp. xi, xiii, xvii, and III, p. xxxii. (One might well ask, though: *why* was it 'theoretically unarticulated'? Of all historians, History Workshop historians and Samuel in particular have surely had ready access to theoretical resources in history-writing.)

85 Samuel, I, pp. xviii–lxvii.

86 Stephen Howe, 'Labour Patriotism 1939–83', in Samuel, *Patriotism*, I, pp. 127–39, p. 137.

87 Anthony Barnett, 'After Nationalism', in Samuel, *Patriotism*, I, pp. 140–55, pp. 140–1.

88 Barnett, 'Nationalism', pp. 148–53.

89 Samuel, *Patriotism*, I, p. xi.

90 Paul Gilroy, 'The Island Race', *New Statesman and Society*, 2 February 1990, pp. 30–2, p. 31. This point is understood and fleshed out in Robert Colls and Philip Dodd (eds.), *Englishness: Politics and Culture 1880–1920*, Beckenham, 1986. Cf. also Bikhu Parekh's excellent 'British Citizenship and Cultural Difference', in Geoff Andrews, *Citizenship*, London, 1991, pp. 183–204.

91 Stuart Hall, in an interview on 'The Late Show', BBC2, 7 December 1989. See additional references in note 46 above.

92 See Hubert L. Dreyfus and Paul Rabinow, *Michel Foucault: Beyond Structuralism and Hermeneutics*, Brighton, 1982 (e.g. pp. 184–226). While there are significant overlaps between Foucault's 'programme' and that of Laclau and Mouffe, it is important to note this difference.

93 Laclau and Mouffe, *Hegemony*, p. 142.

94 Note that I am not advocating – as Laclau and Mouffe point out Thompson tends to, in *The Poverty of Theory* – a humanistic counter-essentialism around the pole 'Man': *Hegemony*, p. 147, n. 28.

95 See Gilroy, 'Island Race', p. 31.

96 Including that of Terry Eagleton – a good example of someone

schooled in scholastic Marxist essentialism who merely transfers the same mode to nationalism. For the basis of an alternative, see Hugh Kearney's excellent *The British Isles: A History of Four Nations*, Cambridge, 1989.

97 Roy Foster, *Modern Ireland*, London, 1988.

98 Joan Kelly, 'The Doubled Vision of Feminist Theory', in Judith L. Newton, *et al.* (eds.), *Sex and Class*, pp. 259–70, p. 266; my italics, Cf. Marilyn French, *Beyond Power: On Women, Men and Morals*, London, 1986.

99 Elizabeth Fox-Genovese, 'Placing Women's History in History', *New Left Review*, No. 133, 1982, pp. 5–29. See the advice and work of Catherine Hall and Ludmilla Jordanova, already cited; also Sandra Harding, *The Science Question in Feminism*, Milton Keynes, 1986.

100 I owe this point, with thanks, to Simon Schaffer.

101 Anthony Giddens, *The Constitution of Society*, London, 1984, p. 245: 'All social life is contingent, all social change is conjunctural.'

102 Michael Walzer, 'The Good Life', *New Statesman and Society*, 6 October 1989, pp. 28–31, p. 31: hoping for a Left that is not 'represented in grandiose terms or underwritten with historical guarantees or achieved through a single unified struggle'. Also see his *Company of Critics*.

103 Rorty, *Contingency, Irony, Solidarity*.

104 Paul Feyerabend, *Farewell to Reason*, London, 1987 (his best book), p. 61: 'The attempt to enforce a universal truth (a universal way of finding truth) has led to disasters in the social domain and to empty formalisms combined with never-to-be-fulfilled promises in the natural sciences'.

105 E.g. Andre Gortz, *Critique of Economic Reason*, London, 1989, and see his 'Politics for the Twenty-First Century', *The Guardian*, 9–10 December 1989.

106 E.g. Zygmunt Bauman, *Memories of Class: the Prehistory and Afterlife of Class*, London, 1982, and see his 'New Kinds of Conflict', *Times Literary Supplement*, 12–18 January 1990.

107 E.g. Isaiah Berlin, *Four Essays on Liberty*, Oxford, 1969, especially 'Two Concepts of Liberty', pp. 118–72. For a recent discussion, see Ronald Dworkin, 'Two Concepts of Liberty', in Edna and Avishai Margalit (eds.), *Isaiah Berlin: A Celebration*, London, 1991, pp. 100–9; and a review by John Gray, 'The Unavoidable Conflict', *Times Literary Supplement*, 5 July 1991, p. 3. (Such a convergence is necessarily a 'retreat', by the way, only according to the tendentious teleology of unilinear historical 'stages', which there is no good reason – and now less so than ever – to accept.)

108 June Jordan, *Moving Towards Home: Political Essays*, London, 1989, p. 144.

The crime wave: recent writing on crime and criminal justice in eighteenth-century England[1]

Introduction

One of the most exciting and influential areas of research in eighteenth-century history over the last twenty years has been the study of crime and the criminal law. It is the purpose of this essay to map the subject for the interested non-specialist: to ask why historians have chosen to study it, to explain how they have come to approach it in particular ways, to describe something of what they have found, to evaluate those findings, and to suggest fruitful directions for further research. Like all maps, the one presented here is selective. The essay begins with a general analysis of the ways in which the field has developed and changed in its short life. It then proceeds to consider in more detail four areas of study: criminality, the criminal trial, punishment, and criminal legislation. This selection makes no pretence of providing an exhaustive coverage. A number of important areas have been omitted: for example, public order and policing.[2] However, the areas covered illustrate the range of approaches, problems and possibilities that lie within the field. We conclude with a discussion of the broader implications of the subject.

The development of the field

Before the 1960s, crime was not treated seriously by eighteenth-century historians. Accounts of crime and the criminal law rarely extended beyond a few brief remarks on lawlessness, the Bloody Code and the state of the prisons, often culled from Fielding, Hogarth and Howard. There were exceptions, but they fell outside the mainstream of eighteenth-century history. The multiple volumes of Leon Radzinowicz's monumental *History of the English Criminal Law* were published from 1948 onwards, but Radzinowicz worked in the Cambridge Law Faculty and Institute of Criminology and, as Derek Beales has pointed out, his findings were not quickly assimilated by historians.[3] The Webbs and the Hammonds had discussed various aspects of eighteenth-century disorder, crime and policing, but in this field at least they attracted few disciples.[4] Mainstream academic history of the 1950s and early 1960s characteristically focused on the sort of high politics associated with the work of Namier, or alternatively on the economic origins and characteristics of the Industrial Revolution, with a particular emphasis on the Rostowian problematic of take-off into sustained growth.

Since the late 1960s, by contrast, there has been an explosion of interest in eighteenth-century crime. In part this dramatic change must be understood in terms of wider academic developments. Both Britain and North America witnessed a boom in higher education in the 1960s. History shared in this general upsurge, and there was considerable expansion in the numbers both of professional historians and of history departments. Not surprisingly this expansion was associated with the exploration of new areas of research. The boom in the social sciences during the same period helped to nurture interest in social history in particular. The intellectual and academic success of the social science disciplines contributed to a demand for a 'new' social history that would transcend the antiquarian and anecdotal approach of much previous work.

To understand why crime and criminal justice in particular became a focus of interest, and why research on these subjects initially took the specific forms it did, it is necessary to refer to a number of the specific features which characterized the 'new' English social history as it developed in the 1960s. Three tendencies within the 'new' social history have been especially influential.

First, and most important, history from below. By this we understand an approach which emphasizes the need to explore and imaginatively to reconstruct the experiences of the dispossessed and inarticulate. In the 1960s and 1970s the study of crime and the criminal law came to be seen as a useful means to this end, especially for periods before the emergence of an independent working class politics. Edward Thompson's work was seminal in this regard. Although all his work has been concerned with the culture of the dispossessed, with the transforming impact of capitalism, and with the nature of class relationships, during these years its emphasis shifted. It underwent a chronological shift from the early nineteenth to the early eighteenth century and at the same time reoriented its focus away from popular politics first to popular disorder and then to certain types of criminality. Thompson's *The Making of the English Working Class*, first published in 1963, charted the emergence of a working class politics in the late eighteenth and early nineteenth centuries. Following this, his 1971 article 'The moral economy of the English crowd in the eighteenth century' explored the 'pre-political' ideas and crowd actions associated with eighteenth-century popular resistance to the imposition of a free market in foodstuffs. Finally, in 1975, *Whigs and Hunters* concerned itself with the resistance, by means of a variety of activities defined as 'crimes', of the early eighteenth-century forest communities of south-east England to the elimination of their customary rights, and with the bloody legislation that the Hanoverian state enacted to crush these initiatives.[5] As he changed course, Thompson drew a number of his research students in his wake. He and they collaborated in the collection *Albion's Fatal Tree*, also published in 1975. For all the contributors it was axiomatic that the study of crime and the criminal law 'were central to unlocking the meanings of eighteenth-century social history'.[6]

The second important tendency within the 'new' social history was that which drew on the methods of positivist social science. The social scientific approach emphasized the discovery and explanation of significant patterns, particularly statistical patterns, in social behaviour. This entailed treating crime as a 'social fact' and using aggregate crime statistics to identify and measure continuities and changes. Those who adopted this approach sought explanations for the patterns they found not in the meanings of actions for individual or collective social actors (as in history from below), but instead in correlative (and arguably causal) relationships between a variety of social facts, for example crime and dearth, or crime and political tension, or crime and the Industrial Revolution. Some of John Beattie's early work best illustrates this approach. Thus his 1975 article on the criminality of women in eighteenth-century England set out 'to uncover the patterns of offences charged against women and to suggest what they reveal about the place of women and the nature of crime'.[7]

The third tendency within the 'new' social history which bears on our concerns was one that will be termed here the 'reform perspective'. The reform perspective was to a great extent an inheritance from an older historiographical tradition, but during the 1960s and 1970s it gained a new lease of life from its ready compatibility with other preoccupations of the day. Adopting a reform perspective has traditionally entailed accepting at least a substantial part of the account of eighteenth-century society and its institutions propounded by late-eighteenth- and early-nineteenth-century reformers. It has meant accepting their view that early-eighteenth-century government was grossly corrupt and inefficient, and hailing as a major watershed in English social and political development a set of changes in society, in ideas and in policy thought to have taken place in the late eighteenth and early nineteenth centuries. Both the Webbs' and Radzinowicz's accounts of, for example, policing and punishment are substantially written from a reform perspective.

Historians of the 1960s and 1970s have very frequently taken a more jaundiced view of the content of 'reform' than their predecessors. At the same time, it is striking how commonly they have reproduced a traditional view of the chronology of change, and of the relative significance of institutional developments at different periods. Developments late in the century have remained central to their concerns. The continuing appeal of this view of the basic shape of history in the period is probably partly to be explained in terms of its neat fit with a notion of a late-eighteenth-century industrial revolution effecting a general social transformation. Whether in its Weberian or Marxist variants, the notion of industrialization has often been elevated to a position of central causal significance in the recent history of crime and the law, as in the 'new' social history more generally. Michael Ignatieff is certainly inclined to assign it a major causal role in his study of prison reform, *A Just Measure of Pain* – a study which exemplifies the reform perspective at its most sophisticated.[8]

The distinction between these various tendencies is helpful in as much as it serves to clarify the development of the field. But it must be emphasized that the tendencies do not represent three opposed schools. In particular, it must be stressed that the distinction between history from below and statistical approaches has not corresponded – at least in the history of crime and the criminal law – to a distinction between Marxists and non-Marxists. Thus Douglas Hay has been a student of both John Beattie and Edward Thompson, and his work, though broadly Marxian in emphasis, has involved (amongst other things) both statistical analysis and the study of crime as resistance.[9] In general, scholars working on the history of crime over the last twenty years have been markedly disposed to cooperate with each other, to learn from and adopt each other's ideas and approaches, and to welcome insights from other periods and disciplines. But it is also noteworthy that, for some, the field has not fulfilled its early promise. Eric Hobsbawm, in particular, has not followed up his early contribution on social protest and social crime.[10]

If the field has lost its attraction for some, this may be because the concerns of research have shifted. The first two tendencies outlined above, whatever the differences between them, did at least share a concern with the actions of those who offended against the criminal laws. Both histories from below and positivist histories represented the study of those actions as a key to understanding the wider society. However, during the last decade there has been a shift from the study of offences towards the study of the institutions and more particularly the processes associated with the administration of the criminal law. Indeed much of the work currently being undertaken in the field might justly be called administrative history, despite the fact that few of its practitioners would want to describe themselves as administrative historians. Unlike much traditional administrative history, this new work on the administration of the criminal law is strongly contextual. Its proponents have sought to understand the advantages and shortcomings of eighteenth-century arrangements as these were understood by those who lived with, sustained, or contemporaneously sought to change them. As a result of applying this approach to the earlier eighteenth century, at least some historians have now begun to question the reform perspective. They are beginning to uncover a dense and complex pattern of early-eighteenth-century legal and institutional change.

Why has this shift in emphasis in favour of the study of legal institutions and processes come about? A number of influences seem to have been in play. First, historians of crime have developed an increasingly sophisticated awareness of the limitations, as well as the possibilities, of their sources. This has been a general trend in early modern social history, but has been particularly important in the study of criminality. Early studies that focused on the behaviour of offenders relied heavily on an analysis of court records. It was assumed that those records could be made to tell us about crime and criminal offenders in general. But to use court records to study criminal behaviour in the world at large demands at the very least an understanding of the highly selective ways in which the machinery of criminal justice responded to offences and offenders. Historians were of course quick to recognize the need to study both why and how this machinery was set into motion, but were nonetheless initially oversanguine as to how easy it would be to control for consequent 'distortions'.[11] Subsequently, many have come to doubt that the records can properly be used in the ways they at first envisaged. However, in the meantime institutional studies originally undertaken as a means to an end have come to win acceptance as worthwhile exercises in their own right. As interest in the character and operations of institutions has grown, historians have increasingly come to accept that in the machinery of criminal justice we are dealing with an instrument of state power, but, nonetheless, disputes continue as to how important an instrument this was, and as to which groups or interests participated in its exercise and benefited from it.

Another factor which has encouraged a shift in emphasis towards the study of the administration of criminal justice has been interaction between historians of eighteenth-century crime and British sociologists. Two concerns in recent British sociology have been particularly influential: labelling theory and theories of the state. Labelling theory is associated with the British 'new' criminology of the late 1960s (though the theory's origins are in fact American). Labelling theorists argue that 'deviance is *not* a quality of the act the person commits, but rather a consequence of the application by others of rules and sanctions to an "offender" '.[12] In this view, the records of the courts or the police merely chronicle the activities of the controllers. The controllers' activities have their own momentum and the records they generate bear no relationship to the incidence of 'real' crime.[13] The influence of labelling theory has served to reinforce historians' own scepticism about the court records as a source for the history of crime – and, indeed, about the very possibility of such a history.

An interest in theories of the state, particularly Marxist theories of the state, was one of the most striking developments in British sociology from the late 1960s. It was part of a wider revival of Marxist ideas in British intellectual circles and grew specifically out of a dissatisfaction on the left with pluralist political science. Hence questions about how, why, and whether the state was the tool of a particular class predominated, although the answers offered were extremely diverse. The influence of these developments on historians has been important but diffuse, a matter of sensitizing them to and encouraging their interest in conceptual issues regarding class, ideology, and state power. It should be noted, however, that the flow of ideas has not been only, or even predominantly, from sociology to history. Two powerful interpretations of the character of state power were presented by Edward Thompson in *Whigs and Hunters* and Douglas Hay in *Albion's Fatal Tree*. Both have influenced sociologists.[14]

Finally, a third factor that has prompted a shift towards the study of the administration of criminal justice has been the influence of legal history. Before the mid 1970s there was little work by legal historians on the eighteenth century (Radzinowicz apart). The new work on eighteenth-century crime and the criminal law has been greeted with some suspicion by legal historians, but also with much interest.[15] Legal historians are now coming increasingly to work in the field. Legal history has a long tradition of internalist explanation of legal change: of explaining changes in the law in terms of developments internal to the law and the legal system. The long dominance of this approach to the subject means that all legal historians share an awareness of its importance, although some have recently been moved to challenge it.[16] As legal historians have come to work on eighteenth-century criminal law, social historians have been made increasingly aware of the need to pay serious attention to the legal complexities of the machinery of criminal justice.

The shift of emphasis towards institutions and processes has been regretted by some.[17] It is argued that it involves an undesirable shift away from big historical questions about the relationship between crime and capitalism, or crime and industrialization, questions which give the subject significance in the eyes of non-specialists and undergraduates. It is true that the newer approaches demand much more careful attention to the workings of the criminal justice system, to the meanings of the sources and to the ways in which concepts like capitalism or industrialization are deployed as explanations. However, very often criticisms of the newer approaches amount to little more than an attempt to reinstate a version of the reform perspective, with its glib assumptions about the all-transforming character of an 'industrial revolution' which, it is increasingly clear, is incapable of bearing the explanatory demands placed on it.[18] The newer approaches still seek to address general questions about the relationship between crime, the criminal law, and the broader society and economy, but general questions that are better specified theoretically, better articulated archivally and better grounded in an understanding of the complexities and ambiguities of the administrative process. It is possible to make these accessible to a non-specialist audience.

That is not to say it is easy. The pattern of publication in the field testifies to this. Most work has appeared in the form of articles or essays, despite the existence of a number of long-completed and important doctoral dissertations, in particular Douglas Hay's magnificent 1975 dissertation, a model and inspiration for all students in the field.[19] It was only with the publication in 1986 of John Beattie's *Crime and the Courts in England 1660–1800*, that monographs began to appear.[20] The delay is a measure of the difficulty of opening up a subject that hardly existed twenty years ago. Although a number of provocative interpretations were generated quite rapidly, the process of testing and refining those ideas has been an arduous one. It is that process that is discussed in the rest of this essay, by means of an examination of four areas of study that are particularly important to the past and the future development of the subject.

Crime and criminality

As remarked above, 'criminality', as distinctive social phenomenon, though originally central to the concerns of those who pioneered the new history of crime, has recently ceased to be the focus of the most innovative work in the field. Work has continued to appear, witness the chapters devoted to crime and criminality in John Beattie's largely Surrey-based study *Crime and the Courts in England 1660–1800* and in several recent theses.[21] Nonetheless, neither in terms of sources exploited, nor in terms of categories and analytical techniques employed does this new work mark much of an advance beyond Beattie's own 1974 article 'The pattern of crime in England' and the essays in *Albion's Fatal Tree*. Instead, we see the application of established techniques to new data, or critical reflection on established techniques and categories, or their defence against criticism. Douglas Hay's 1982 article 'War, dearth and theft', an enquiry into the merits and limitations of aggregate statistics – one of the most impressive of these studies – is characteristic in being primarily defensive in purpose.

There are, it will be argued, good reasons why research in this field should have stalled, for there are very real and intractable difficulties associated with both of the main approaches historians have so far adopted to the study of crime: the positivist, statistics-based approach, and the quest for the meanings of criminal behaviour. A number of the problems that have become apparent are outlined in the next few pages. Although it is argued that some lines of enquiry have proved to be dead ends, it is also suggested that there may yet be a way forward.

It is easy to understand what first attracted historians of crime to the study of statistical time series. Criminal indictments – the documents from which time series have most commonly been constructed – are highly standardized in form, and survive in larger numbers than have the other records of the criminal courts. Their terse and formulaic character, which renders them almost useless to historians bent on reconstructing the character of criminal activity, suits them admirably for quantification. Time series founded on indictments hold out the promise of chronological precision, unobtainable by other means. They can readily be correlated with time series measuring other economic and social phenomena. Furthermore, exercises of this kind have a long, albeit controversial, pedigree among criminologists.

Eighteenth-century historians who have adopted a statistical approach have increasingly limited their attention to the study of short-term fluctuations in property crime, fluctuations over say five or ten years. Neither sixteenth- and seventeenth- nor nineteenth- and twentieth-century historians have confined themselves so narrowly: they have dealt with both short- and long-term fluctuations, with offences against the person as well as those against property.[22] Eighteenth-century historians have been well aware that they might address this wider range of topics. If they have held back it is because they have justifiably doubted the value of most of these exercises – at least as a source of insights into the changing character of criminal behaviour.

Long-term changes in the volume of any sort of indictments are formidably difficult to interpret. The influences possibly at work changing the relationship between 'real' levels of crime and levels of crime prosecuted are so numerous, and so resistant to measurement, that it seems impossible to pronounce with any confidence on the meanings of the patterns observed. Where indictments for interpersonal violence are concerned, the significance of both long- and short-term fluctuations has been sharply questioned. Such supplementary evidence as survives to illuminate the nature of the encounters which gave rise to indictments for assault (the principal prosecuted offence in this area) suggests that both the circumstances of assaults and the degree of violence involved varied enormously. In other words, it is not at all clear that the events at issue had enough in common to justify their aggregation. Furthermore, it appears that a strikingly high proportion of indictments for assault arose out of quarrels between men of the 'middling sort' (farmers, tradesmen, artisans).[23] If indictments for assault were, as this suggests, no more than a means by which the middling sort pursued their differences, there is no reason to believe that changes in their number will shed much light on general levels of violence in the society. Finally, even if we accept such changes as an index of changes in the propensity to violence in society at large, it is questionable whether we stand to learn much from correlating them with time series charting, say, the changing cost of living, or levels of political tension. Although there are a number of sociological and psychological theories linking violence to social tension, it seems unlikely that the very crude social and economic indicators available for the eighteenth century could ever serve adequately as even approximate indicators of such tension.[24]

Acts of illegal appropriation, like acts of interpersonal violence, were undoubtedly more various in character than the indictments reveal. However, a much more powerful case can be made for correlating short-term changes in the former with movements in other time series, particularly time series which attempt to chart changing levels of material deprivation. Between one-half and three-quarters of those prosecuted for property crimes were drawn from the 'labouring poor'. Their offences characteristically involved the theft of items of small value in an opportunistic fashion. We know that many of the eighteenth-century 'poorer sort' were recurrently un- or underemployed, that they were vulnerable to short-term increases in the cost of living, and that even at the best of times they might have difficulty obtaining adequate supplies of food and fuel. It is a reasonable hypothesis that fluctuations in the level of indictments for property offences may have been causally related to fluctuations in the cost of living and in the earning capacity of the working population.

Recent studies have identified as points of especial interest two characteristic features of short-term fluctuations in indictments for property offences. First and most strikingly, periods of peace contrast with periods of war, peace being attended with relatively high indictment levels, war with low ones. The transition from war to peace was usually marked by a very steep rise in the number of indictments. Second, in wartime (but not in peacetime) there was a strong positive correlation between annual changes in the numbers of indictments and annual changes in the cost of living.

Historians have tended to interpret these findings in broadly similar ways. Douglas Hay marshals the argument most convincingly.[25] Crucial to his interpretation is a distinction between two kinds of theft: minor thefts, undertaken by the normally law-abiding under pressure of destitution, and more serious and more skilled capital thefts, undertaken by people who stole with some regularity and not merely under pressure of immediate need.

During wars, Hay suggests, the level of indictments was low because the often forced recruitment of tens of thousands of young men removed from the country a large proportion of adult males from among the labouring poor. Those recruited were from the class and age group most likely to face unemployment. Young men suspected by their neighbours of being habitual thieves were especially likely to be recruited. Men engaged in crime both sporadically and habitually must have been among those extracted. Their removal explains the fall in indictments, and, in particular, the observed disproportionate fall in the more skilled and serious forms of offence. In their absence, it was the minor thefts, committed under pressure of immediate need, that pre-dominated, hence the strong positive correlation during wars be-tween fluctuations in the indictments for property offences and fluctuations in the cost of living.

Peace and rapid demobilization not only released on the country men previously suspected or even convicted of offences, but also glutted labour markets. Both habitual offenders and the chronical-ly unemployed might turn to theft, particularly to such serious offences as highway robbery and burglary. Indictments for prop-erty offences in general, but especially for serious theft, accordingly registered massive increases with the end of each war, remaining at high levels as long as peace continued. With the reappearance of such offenders, the wartime correlation between property crime and dearth disappeared.

In his 1974 article, John Beattie summed up his reading of the evidence thus: 'The evidence of the indictments seems to point clearly to this conclusion: that crimes against property in the eighteenth century arose primarily from problems of employment, wages and prices.'[26] Although Hay's argument allows some role to habitual offenders, who were not necessarily responding to eco-nomic pressures, clearly his interpretation too attaches great weight to material circumstance.

However, there remains a major difficulty here, a difficulty associated with all attempts to interpret criminal statistics. Hay's argument turns on the assumption that the relationship between numbers of indictments and numbers of offences remained fairly constant, such that changes in numbers of indictments can be taken to reflect real changes in the criminal behaviour of the poor. Yet this is a highly questionable assumption.

Hay, once again, has marshalled the most persuasive arguments in its favour. Although his analysis is too rich to summarize here in its entirety, two of its more ingenious features are worth exam-ining in detail. Criminologists have argued that modern crime statistics are distorted by the activities of those who enforce the law, whose own priorities may be idiosyncratic and may change over time. Hay suggests that the absence from eighteenth-century England of any professional police force or prosecution service eliminates this problem. Eighteenth-century prosecutors were usu-ally the victims of the crimes concerned, individually making their thousands of independent decisions.

Hay acknowledges that the propensity of victims to prosecute may have varied collectively as a result of widely-shared prejudices or pressures, which are virtually impossible to measure. He suggests that the same variations should, however, be observable in the well-documented decisions of juries, because they were composed of men from a similar social position. Juries, it emerges, were more likely to be lenient in years of high prices. If prosecutors were moved by similar instincts, then high indictment levels in high price years are more likely to under- than to overstate 'real' levels of crime. The suggested relationship between times of need and crime still holds good.

Despite the elegance and apparent force of Hay's argument, it remains vulnerable, we believe, to certain damning objections. The key difficulty has been well-expressed by Peter King. So long as the ratio of prosecuted crime to all crime was low (and eighteenth-century commentators and modern historians share the belief that it was) even small changes in the behaviour of prosecutors would have had far greater effects on fluctuations in the movement of indictments than quite large changes in the behaviour of offenders.[27] Furthermore, it seems likely that changes in the behaviour of prosecutors were more common and also more difficult to measure than Hay would have us believe.

Consider, for example, the low incidence of indictments for serious offences during wartime. The pressures on local officials to encourage recruitment were intense. It is therefore not surprising that diaries and the newspapers mention (although not in any systematic way) prosecutors giving apprehended offenders the option of enlistment as an alternative to prosecution, often at the behest of the examining magistrate. Thus at Leeds in 1762 an apprehended burglar was taken before a magistrate 'who gave him his choice, whether he would inlist into his Majesty's service, or be committed to York Castle, the former of which he accepted'.[28] Such a procedure had its attractions for magistrate, prosecutor and offender alike. The magistrate secured a recruit; the prosecutor, the removal of the offender from the locality without the trouble or expense of a trial; the offender, relief from a period of pre-trial imprisonment, and perhaps from the threat of a capital sentence. Yet it was a procedure not available on any scale during peacetime. Documentation of this kind of informal arrangement is too unsystematic to allow us to calculate precisely how many were extracted from the criminal process in this way, but they need have constituted no more than a small fraction of the tens of thousands who were recruited to explain a large part of the fall-off in property crimes during wartime.[29] Even a large county like Staffordshire saw no more than forty to fifty fewer indictments a year in war than in peace.[30] The case for interpreting the evidence of the indictments as an index of a fall in 'real' crime consequently seems a shaky one.

Similarly there are difficulties with Hay's interpretation of the effect of high prices on prosecutors. While prosecutors may have shared broadly similar backgrounds and therefore attitudes with jurymen (though even this is debatable), high-price years did not necessarily have the same practical consequences for their behaviour towards criminal offenders. Even if, like jurymen, prosecutors were disposed to be more merciful in years of dearth, at the same time they were more likely to face offenders unable, because of financial hardship, to buy off prosecution. Buying off prosecutors was believed to be very common, and the vast majority of references to it mention cash payments. If the propensity to mercy tilted the balance one way, therefore, a decline in the ability of offenders to buy forgiveness may have tilted it the other – and there is no way of knowing which carried the more weight. In these circumstances once again it is difficult to put much faith in movements in indictment levels as indicators of movements in 'real' crime.

It is doubtful, in sum, whether time series based on indictments can be used as indices of the behaviour of property offenders. But even if those time series were an accurate guide to changes in the level of 'real' crime, doubts would remain concerning the manner in which correlative techniques have been applied in analysing them, and the conclusions that have been drawn from the use of those techniques. Doubts about the way the techniques have been used centre on the questionable consistency of the relationship between fluctuations in prices and in indictments during wartime. If that relationship was very strong in years of exceptionally high prices and very weak in years of moderate or low prices it would be misleading to use, as Hay does, time series compiled without reference to this distinction as the basis for price–indictment correlations. At least one of the county studies, the study of Essex by Peter King, suggests that the relation did vary in this fashion.

King points out that, if the exceptional years of high prices –
1740–1, 1772, and 1800–1 – are removed from the Essex data,
the wartime correlation between fluctuations in indictments and
fluctuations in the cost of living is reduced to a level that is
statistically meaningless. In Hay's Staffordshire it is reduced to a
level of significance verging on the marginal.[31] Even if it could be
assumed that the indictment series did accurately measure changes
in the level of crime, these findings would indicate that it was only
in years of exceptional hardship that necessity obliged the poor to
turn on any scale to theft.

Also important to bear in mind is a fact that is often overlooked
in the excitement when the computer finally declares that the
relationship between two time series wrung from intractable historical sources is characterized by a strongly positive coefficient of
correlation. These statistical techniques measure the extent to which
changes in one variable reflect changes in another. They do not
demonstrate that the relationship was one of cause and effect.
Even if there are firm grounds for believing that a causal relationship was involved, it extends only to the changes in the two
variables. Thus if a strong positive correlation could be established
with confidence between changes in annual totals of offences (as
opposed to indictments) and changes in prices, it would still not
necessarily follow, to paraphrase Beattie, that all crime against
property arose primarily from problems of prices. It would merely
suggest that changes in the numbers of such crimes were related
to such problems, and that, given the precariousness of the bud-
gets of the poor, the relationship was probably a causal one.

This section of the discussion has been developed at some length.
The shortcomings of studies based on time series derived from
indictments deserve careful attention because, given a longstanding
academic and popular obsession with rises and falls in crime, the
approach they embody has proved extremely seductive. However,
while the valiant efforts of historians to render the statistics intelligible have undoubtedly deepened our knowledge of the processes
of prosecution and trial, it has yet to be demonstrated that such
studies can contribute very significantly to our understanding of
criminal behaviour.

The same complaint might be levelled against the other principal approach thus far adopted to the study of eighteenth-century
criminality: that which has attempted to distinguish between

different forms of behaviour defined as criminal in terms of popular attitudes towards them and in terms of their implications for broader economic and social conflicts. The approach in question is that which has emphasized distinctions between 'social criminality' and other types of criminality.

Social criminality is not a concept that has been specified very tightly. Thus for Eric Hobsbawm, who first defined the concept for historians, it 'occurs when there is a conflict of laws, e.g. between an official and an unofficial system, or when acts of law-breaking have a distinct element of social protest in them, or when they are closely linked with the development of social and political unrest.'[32] At its weakest, therefore, the notion of 'social crime' amounts to little more than an acknowledgement that in the eighteenth century, as before and since, a large number of activities defined by the law as criminal were not recognized as such by large sections of the population. At its strongest, it implies that at least some of these activities were, either explicitly or implicitly, proto-political forms of protest or resistance by the poor: a form of opposition, perhaps the only possible form of opposition, to their exploitation and subordination by the rich.

It is their fascination with this second, stronger version of 'social crime' that has attracted eighteenth-century social historians to the study of activities like smuggling, poaching, wrecking, and certain types of gleaning, wood gathering, and pilfering in the workplace.[33] Their concern has been to explore the ideas – the legitimizing notions – through which popular sympathy for these activities was expressed, and to relate those ideas to the material conflicts involved. The key point of departure here has been Edward Thompson's study of the moral economy of the English crowd in the eighteenth century. Thompson argued that 'it is possible to detect in almost every eighteenth-century crowd action some legitimizing notion. By the notion of legitimation I mean that the men and women in the crowd were informed by the belief that they were defending traditional rights or customs; and, in general, that they were supported by the wider consensus of the community.'[34] The traditional rights and customs defended in the food riots that were the subject of Thompson's 1972 article were those pre-eighteenth-century regulations concerning the distribution of grain that required that the needs of the poor consumer should have priority in times of scarcity. The enemy against which this moral economy of provision had to be defended was the profit-orientated, unregulated market economy.

For Thompson, this analysis of the food riot was a key which unlocked the meaning of whole areas of eighteenth-century popular culture: a culture which 'resists, in the name of "custom", those economic innovations and rationalizations . . . which the rulers or employers seek to impose. [These are] most often experienced by the plebs in the form of exploitation, or the expropriation of customary use rights, or the violent disruption of valued patterns of work and leisure.' Thus most forms of crowd action, and many of the other kinds of illegal activity which enjoyed widespread popular support, emerge as forms of popular resistance to a specifically eighteenth-century 'innovation of capitalist process'.[35]

The merits of this approach with regard to the study of crowd action need not detain us.[36] Whatever its shortcomings in that context, there can be no doubt that it has immensely enriched our understanding of the eighteenth-century crowd. Its success in illuminating the character of eighteenth-century criminality has been much more qualified. The most obvious difficulty here is the relegation of offences which lack the historiographically attractive, proto-political associations of the 'social crimes' to the status of unintelligible counterpoint. While historians working with this approach have spawned studies of several armies of 'social criminals', we have no detailed studies of the petty larcenists, burglars, horse stealers, and highway robbers who made up the bulk of the business of the courts of Quarter Sessions and Assizes.[37]

Given that within this framework it is the proto-political implications of the 'social crimes' that make them historically interesting, one way to render 'normal' crime intelligible in the same terms has been to downplay the validity of the social crime/normal crime distinction altogether. Instead it is asserted that much property crime, irrespective of whether it involved explicit, collective opposition to capitalist innovation, was a result of such innovation and a challenge to it. Thus, for Peter Linebaugh, the creation of 'a "free" mobile labour force, ready to submit to the discipline of working for hire', required on the one hand the destruction of old, customary forms of work and income, often by transforming customary practices into crimes, and on the other the removal of 'the possibilities of living without "visible means of support" or "living by one's wits" ', by enhancing and enforcing the whole range of laws against theft.[38] In this perspective, most of the crimes of the labouring poor become, implicitly if not explicitly, forms of resistance to the development of capitalism – a development Linebaugh suggests to have been taking place at a particularly marked pace in the eighteenth century.

This approach fails to convince on several counts. It has marked shortcomings conceptually, chronologically, and empirically. It is not at all clear that working for hire was something that had to be forced on people: waged labour was often embraced with enthusiasm. Nor is it evident that the reason people turned to theft was to avoid submitting to the discipline of the wage. Even if it had been necessary to discipline people into waged labour by means of the repression of theft and the use of the law to attack customary work practices, neither these activities nor attempts to suppress them were peculiar to the eighteenth century. It is true that some of the offenders who came before the eighteenth-century courts of Quarter Sessions and Assizes were charged with offences newly created in the eighteenth century to defend new forms of commercial property, but these were a small minority. The bulk of property offenders continued to be charged with offences that could have occasioned similar proceedings in the same courts two hundred years earlier.

Some of these points also bear on the more conventional uses of the notion of social criminality by historians of the eighteenth century. The idea that offences which enjoyed widespread popular support necessarily involved resistance to a capitalist economic order is highly problematic. It is difficult to see smuggling, the greatest illegal business of all, as a form of resistance to commercial capitalism, whatever difficulties it posed for the eighteenth-century fiscal state. Poaching was an attack on one of the landed gentry's most prized marks of status, not on their capacity to profit from a commercialized agriculture. It supplied the commercial trade in game to which it was the gentry that offered resistance.[39] Even in the case of those illegal activities enjoying popular support which can most plausibly be represented as having created difficulties for 'capitalists', it is doubtful whether that support was characteristically a product of resistance to capitalist initiatives peculiar to the eighteenth century. Take pilfering in the outwork industries, for example. It is far from clear that manufacturers in general were more concerned to redefine and restrict the property rights of the labouring poor in the eighteenth century than they had been in the seventeenth.[40]

The fundamental problem here is that we are presented with an oversimplified and overly determinist view of the nature of social and economic change, and of the relationship to it of the criminal law on the one hand and of the poorer section of the population on the other. The development of capitalist relations of production and consumption is presented as a unilinear evolution in which the eighteenth century comprised a distinct stage, with a particular emphasis on the redefinition of property rights,[41] whereas, in fact, such development, insofar as it can be traced, was extremely protracted, remarkably uneven, and remained incomplete. It is assumed that from some logic of capitalist development can be read off discernible 'tasks' or 'needs' which are necessary for its successful realization. The law is one of a number of tools used by the capitalist ruling class to achieve these requirements, as, for example, in the elimination of customary property rights. However, it is highly questionable whether capitalism can be usefully portrayed as having specific 'needs'.[42] On the contrary, it can flourish under a remarkably wide range of social and institutional arrangements. Finally, it is assumed that the attitudes of the poor to capitalist innovation tended to be hostile. In fact, attitudes were ambivalent and contingent, hostile to certain forms of expropriation and impoverishment, but enthusiastic towards some opportunities for new forms of work and consumption.

The argument so far has been that both the main approaches to the study of eighteenth-century crime adopted by historians over the last twenty years – the use of statistical time series and the use of the notion of 'social crime' – are unsatisfactory. In particular, it has been argued that what makes them unsatisfactory are the ways in which they try to provide an understanding of criminality in terms of the social relationships, understandings, and changes which characterized the wider society. Such an understanding certainly remains an admirable goal; the problem, however, is how to achieve it.

Despite the problems that beset existing approaches, it is possible to indicate ways in which they might be further refined. Statistical work has remained largely confined to the study of indictments. This is in contrast to work on modern crime statistics, where an intensive effort has been made to probe behind the official statistics by interviewing both the public at large and offenders about numbers of offences. Interviews are obviously an option that is closed to the eighteenth-century historian, but it is surprising that those pre-prosecution records of crime that do survive, particularly newspaper advertisements and diaries, have not been brought systematically to bear on the debates about fluctuations in the level of crime. More comparative work might be done on the indictments themselves, involving more counties, larger samples, and a move into the late seventeenth and early eighteenth centuries, which remain remarkably underexplored. Even if studies of time series will not reveal for us the pattern of 'real' crime, the compilation of indictment statistics remains a necessary starting point for students wishing to explore other records (such as depositions), or other stages in the machinery of criminal justice (such as trial or sentencing).[43]

Similarly, within a loosely 'social crime' perspective, a great deal of important work remains to be done on the precise constellations of support that characterized the different offences enjoying extensive public sympathy. Not all such offences attracted support from the same social groups, nor, for that matter, were they all justified in terms of custom.[44] Rather than represent such activities as part of a general defence of popular custom and of an undifferentiated popular culture of resistance, we need to explain how it was that different activities, different people, and different legitimizing notions could all be associated with collective opposition to the law.

At the same time it must be recognized that these refinements will not by themselves substantially enhance our understanding of the bulk of the offences against property that came before the criminal courts. At this stage in the development of the subject it is these forms of criminality that cry out for investigation, but it is precisely these forms of criminality that neither the statistical time series approach, nor the 'social crime' approach can adequately illuminate, given the difficulty of rendering the statistics intelligible and the way the analytical purchase of the 'social crime' approach is confined to those offences enjoying wide collective support. In our opinion what is required here is an approach that considers these activities from three points of view.

First, much more attention needs to be paid to the ways different forms of illegal appropriation were undertaken and organized:

what was stolen, how it was stolen, what was done with the stolen property. In other words we need systematically to investigate different forms of illegal appropriation as economic activities with their own histories. Sources for such studies are available not only in the depositions which survive in huge numbers for many Quarter Sessions and Assizes, but also in newspaper reports, diaries, and criminal life histories. Ironically, some of this work is already being done, not by historians of crime, but by historians interested in the economic history of particular commodities, such as Peter Edwards in his work on horse stealing in the seventeenth century.[45] The need for systematic investigation must be stressed. One of the attractions of counting crimes is the precision and the possibility of comparison across time and space that it appears to offer. A systematic qualitative analysis can offer some of the same advantages.[46]

Second, although it must not be assumed that crime is an automatic or even an obvious response to poverty, or that the relationship between the law and the poor was necessarily a hostile one, we need to locate the various forms of illegal appropriation that enjoyed the attention of the courts in relation to the various solidarities, attitudes, and material cultures which characterized the enormous range of people whom the rulers of eighteenth-century society labelled the 'poorer sort' or the 'labouring poor'.[47] Given the difficulty of securing evidence about the behaviour and attitudes of the poor, work like that by Peter King on the age of prosecuted offenders and that by Peter Linebaugh on the life histories of offenders is important here.[48] Useful too would be attempts systematically to analyse depositions and newspapers to establish the willingness or otherwise of different kinds of people to apprehend and provide evidence against different kinds of offenders.[49]

Third, it must be recognized that, in practice, there can be no history of criminality separate from the history of law enforcement. In one sense, this statement amounts simply to a reiteration of the problem of the representativeness of prosecuted offences that was raised in the discussion of the use of time series. To some extent the approaches we have outlined here can get round that problem. Qualitative analyses do not require the sort of statistical precision quantitative analyses demand. Furthermore, in a systematic qualitative analysis, law enforcement will not appear mainly as a distorting factor: a consideration of the risks of apprehension and prosecution will be an integral part of any such analysis. Finally, sources like newspapers and life histories make it possible to penetrate, to some extent, beyond that fraction of offences that was prosecuted.[50]

Problems of evidence may determine that the history of criminality cannot be separated from that of the law and its enforcement, but there are other considerations which suggest that any attempt to separate them would be misdirected. The history of property crime is, to a considerable extent, the history of the control of large sections of the poor. Then, as now, it was their infractions that were legislated against more harshly and their infractions that were prosecuted more rigourously. To understand how and why the poor were selected for these attentions, it is necessary to look beyond the condition of the poor themselves to the preoccupations of those who shaped the law and set it in motion. At the same time, due consideration must be given to those aspects of the life of the poor which attracted such attentions. It is possible to shift the emphasis of analysis either towards the activities of the poor as law breakers, or towards the activities of the law enforcers and law makers, but the two can never be separated. In this respect Douglas Hay is certainly correct. Although certain aspects of his work on crime have been singled out for criticism in this section, it must be acknowledged that in his unpublished work, he has gone further than most other historians of crime in applying those qualitative techniques which we consider potentially the most fruitful approach to future research on eighteenth-century criminality.[51]

The criminal trial

The history of the eighteenth-century criminal trial is a field which has only recently been opened up by research. This development is symptomatic of the shift in favour of the study of institutions and processes which we have noted as characteristic of the last decade. Douglas Hay's 1975 essay 'Property, authority and the criminal law' must be given a large part of the credit for stimulating interest in trials, but important new lines of investigation have also been initiated by legal historians.[52] Indeed it is undoubtedly in this field that legal historians have made their most important contributions to date.

Hay's essay deals with much more than simply the conduct of trials and some other aspects of his discussion are touched on in subsequent sections. Among the many topics his essay has laid open to enquiry, however, are two that can be conveniently discussed in this connection. First, the essay has provoked research and debate as to the social status of those who participated in criminal trials. Second, it has stimulated interest in the character of the decision-making process which produced verdicts and sentences.

Hay's essay highlights what he himself identifies as a curious paradox at the heart of the eighteenth-century system of criminal justice. At a period when parliament created huge numbers of new capital offences against property and resisted calls for reform of the capital code, the proportion of death sentences actually carried out was small and declining. To explain this apparent discrepancy, Hay points to the enormous discretion available at almost all levels of the judicial process and particularly to prosecutors, juries, and judges. He argues that this discretion was subject to the control of a small eighteenth-century ruling class, who used it to sustain their authority over the common people and to protect their own interests. The combination of capital punishment and extensive discretion enabled them to secure acquiescence of their rule by means of both coercion (the occasional exemplary hanging) and benevolence (the calculated act of mercy in forgoing a prosecution, acquitting on a technicality, or securing a pardon). The criminal law achieved an ideological hegemony over the common people by means of public spectacle, the selective application of the prerogative of mercy, and the reaffirmation of the ideal of justice through the occasional punishment of the mighty on the gallows.

Peter King and (in part on the basis of King's work) John Langbein have both taken issue with several parts of Hay's account and interpretation.[53] Further criticisms have come more recently from Thomas Green.[54] None of Hay's critics has disputed the importance of discretion in the administration of the eighteenth-century criminal law. However, King in particular has questioned whether this power was concentrated in the hands of as narrow a social group as Hay implies and furthermore has argued that considerations other than those Hay details played a significant part in determining the outcome of trials.

On the question of the social distribution of power over the course of the trial and its outcome, King argues against Hay that it was 'possible for individuals or groups of widely differing social and economic status to modify or choose not to modify the severity of the law in line with their needs, beliefs and ideas of justice. These opportunities were not always equally distributed, but wide discretionary powers were available to middling men and in a more limited way to the labouring poor.'[55] By using recognizances and depositions from the court records, he shows that two-thirds of prosecutors in property cases tried at Quarter Sessions were farmers, tradesmen, or artisans. Both he and Langbein argue that petty jurors too were drawn from these middling groups in the population. King also points out that men of this sort formed the largest group among those who petitioned for pardons and enjoyed a success rate as high as that of the gentry.

These are very telling arguments against the Hay thesis because, although Hay is remarkably imprecise about who constituted his ruling class, on most occasions when the phrase is used in his essay it encompasses only the aristocracy, the gentry, and possibly the great merchants.[56] If the middling groups in English society participated in the exercise of discretion in the judicial process to the degree that King suggests, Hay's assertion that this discretion was subject to the control of the ruling class is rendered implausible, and Brewer and Styles's view that the law was 'a limited multiple-use right available to most Englishmen' is reinforced.[57]

Hay and King have worked out their differences most thoroughly in relation to the petty jury.[58] King has subjected evidence relating to Essex juries to detailed analysis while Hay has exploited Northamptonshire and Staffordshire sources. Both agree that, as a consequence of property qualifications established by statute, participation on juries was restricted to a good deal less than half the adult male population. Hay suggests that, at most, only the wealthiest quarter of adult males would have qualified. King is more reluctant to advance a precise percentage, but it is not clear that he would find this figure implausible. However, King's evidence allows him to be more precise than Hay about which elements of the population qualified. He establishes that the qualified minority did not simply represent a top slice from the wealth pyramid. The requirement that qualifying property be held in free-hold meant that tradesmen and farmers who were relatively small holders of land might be eligible for jury service, while substantial tenant farmers might be excluded.

This in itself is not incompatible with Hay's findings. The real difference between King and Hay lies in their assessment of the cohesiveness of the qualified group. Hay stresses the common interest of all the qualified that the criminal law should defend their property against propertyless thieves. King, by contrast, emphasizes the presence of fissures and tensions among those who qualified for jury service. The interests of the middling sort (who dominated petty juries) were not identical to those of the gentry (who avoided service); the middling sort were themselves hetero-geneous. As a consequence, King argues, the qualified did not always act in concert. His finding that jurors, though propertied, were not necessarily drawn from among the very wealthiest farm-ers and tradesmen in Essex parishes adds plausibility to this pic-ture of jury behaviour.

King's argument is not, however, based simply on a consider-ation of the kind of people that exercised discretionary power. He also challenges Hay's view that such discretion was based on 'class favouritism and games of influence' by asking on what principles discretionary decisions were made.[59] To answer this question, he analyses the criteria according to which pardons were granted to capital convicts, and the influence of age on sentencing.[60] His analysis reveals that the most important principles on which both sentencing and pardoning decisions were made consisted of ethical criteria for assessing culpability that were widely-recognized and long-established in English culture, such as the youth or infirmity of offenders, their good character and conduct, their prospects of employment or reform, and the desparateness of their destitution. In combination with King's scepticism about the importance of influential connections for securing a pardon, this evidence renders highly questionable Hay's contention that 'the claims of class saved far more men who had been left to hang . . . than did the claims of humanity'.[61]

Thomas Green's findings echo those of Peter King. Unlike King, Green focuses on only one level of discretionary influence within the machinery of criminal justice – the trial jury – but he is able to bring to bear on the discussion of eighteenth-century juries the fruits of his analysis of the institution across the medieval and early modern periods. Green contends that for many centuries participation by lay jurors in criminal trials had significantly constrained possible trial outcomes. Lay jurors typically shared with the populace at large, Green suggests, a reluctance to see the commission of any but a narrow and particularly abhorrent range of crimes result in the offender's death – except perhaps in cases where the offender's notorious bad character or the felt need for some monitory example removed the usual objections. Over the centuries, Green tells us, juries persistently showed themselves willing to twist or perversely misread the evidence in potentially capital cases in whatever way was necessary to secure what they judged to be a tolerable outcome. Both judges and legislators, unless they wished to attempt to dispense with juries altogether, had to resign themselves to accommodating jury prejudice.

Green's studies have persuaded him that juries were a force to be reckoned with. Hay, he suggests, is inclined to underrate them.[62] It is true that, although juries do figure in the argument of 'Property, authority and the criminal law', much more attention is paid to the role of judges and to the pardoning process. Green's criticisms raise the important issue of the balance of power between the different levels of discretionary influence within the machinery of criminal justice.

This question of balance must be numbered among the many topics thrown up by debate on Hay's essay which stand in need of further research. As has been noted, Hay and King have already carried forward the debate about the social composition of the jury and its implications for our understanding of the part played by that very loose and general category 'the middling sort' in the criminal justice system. Both in his book and in his contribution to the Cockburn and Green collection, John Beattie introduces a new consideration into the debate on the role of the jury.[63] Having demonstrated that most jurymen – in Surrey and the City of London at least – repeatedly served on trial juries, he argues that we must take their probable familiarity with the law and courtroom conventions into account in our speculations as to how much of an independent voice they may have had.

Further research may make Hay's suggestion that the nature of trial and sentencing procedures strengthened the hands of a relatively small ruling elite look more or less plausible. But it must be noted too that, at a certain rarefied level, Hay's original interpretation is scarcely open to falsification. Evidence that broad sectors of the population might participate in the criminal trial process, that jury prejudice constrained judicial (and legislative) options, or that humane criteria were applied in pardoning can in every case, with more or less effort, be incorporated into the original theory – every sign of weakness being read as a strategic concession whose ultimate effect was to strengthen ideological hegemony. Even evidence supplied by both Green and John Brewer that the conduct of criminal trials was frequently the subject of controversy and that critics of government repeatedly seized on issues raised by the conduct of trials to further their cause can carry little weight in the balance.[64] For after all, the ruling class continued to rule. However trials were conducted and however they were regarded, they cannot be assigned a part in its downfall.[65]

Debate stimulated by Hay's provocative essay has not generally been marked by a strong time dimension. Most contributors have been relatively little concerned with change over time, and even Thomas Green, who does take a long view, stresses continuity rather than change. By contrast, questions of change over time are central to the line of enquiry opened by a legal historian, John Langbein.

Langbein's interest in the history of the criminal trial derives essentially from modern controversy over the merits and limitations of Anglo-American trial procedures. He has been particularly concerned to trace the origins of that adversary procedure that he believes to have rendered criminal jury trial, in the United States at least, 'unworkable as a routine dispositive procedure'.[66] Langbein has used judges' notes and the detailed printed reports of the Old Bailey Sessions to argue that it was only from the 1730s that the judges allowed the accused to have the assistance of counsel and that this subsequently led to the silencing of the accused and the development for the first time of a substantial law of evidence.[67] His explanation for this change, though as yet not completely developed, is largely internalist. He points to the judges' concern about the admissibility of the evidence of accomplices and the misuse of the reward system. Unable, because of constitutional scruple, to deal with these problems by professionalizing policing and pre-trial procedure, they responded by importing into the criminal law, in an *ad hoc* manner, practices derived from the civil law, over which they also presided.[68]

These are important arguments in their own right. They also raise questions about the terms in which the debate around the Hay thesis has been conducted. For not only has that debate had relatively little to say about change over time, but also it has taken little account of the professional self-interest of lawyers, of the possibility of relatively autonomous developments in legal procedure, or of the impact either of these may have had on decision making, regardless of continuities in other aspects of the staging of trials.[69] Thus Langbein suggests that the balance of power between the trial judge and the jury was utterly transformed during the eighteenth century, from a situation in which the judge actively shaped the jury's adjudication to one in which he remained passive. Yet this transformation appears to have to have taken place without any significant change in the social composition of the jury.

Langbein has opened up an interesting line of enquiry and at the same time has highlighted some of the blind spots of an alternative approach. This is not to say that his own work is free of difficulties. Indeed several elements of his emerging explanation for the appearance of counsel and the development of the adversary system and the law of evidence fail to convince. It is not at all clear that, under eighteenth-century conditions, the professionalization of policing and pre-trial procedure would have removed the need for the evidence of accomplices of reward seekers.[70] Furthermore, Langbein has not yet been able to produce a chronology which plausibly links supposed cause and effect. Thus, he has made much of the blood money scandal of the 1750s, but has not demonstrated that the mid-century marked a watershed in courtroom procedure. This is not to say that a more plausible chronology, preserving important elements of his explanation, might not yet be worked out.[71] Finally, it has not yet been demonstrated that these procedural changes can adequately be explained in terms of developments entirely internal to the legal process. After all, the introduction of defence counsel in treason cases in 1696 was a political decision, and it appears that in the mid-eighteenth century legal decisions of an explicitly constitutional character, like the general warrants decision of 1763, could have a significant impact on the administration of the more mundane aspects of the criminal law.[72]

The eighteenth-century criminal trial is currently the area of most lively debate in the field of crime and criminal justice. It has also been characterized by particularly fruitful exchanges between scholars emerging from a number of different disciplines. In this section the frontiers of research and the directions in which established researchers are moving have both been indicated. In conclusion it should be noted that substantial parts of the subject still remain underexplored. More research is needed on the steps which led to offenders appearing in court. In particular, more needs to be known about the discretion exercised by prosecutors (touched on in the last section) and by law officers such as constables and magistrates. More needs to be known too about courts other than Quarter Sessions and Assizes. Summary hearings stand in urgent need of investigation – at the moment it is not even certain how they were conducted, let alone how much discretion was available to magistrate and prosecutor. It is far from clear that the image of unconstrained magisterial authority which the very adjective 'summary' so readily evokes is warranted.[73] Finally, there remains to be considered the role of the higher courts in London, particularly the court of King's Bench, which had a supervisory jurisdiction over the inferior courts.[74]

Punishment

In contrast to the history of trial, the history of punishment has long engaged the attention of historians. In this field too, however, it is noticeable how much the pace of research has recently quickened. Whereas for many decades historians contented themselves with building on foundations laid by a few classic early works, supplementing, perhaps in some respects refining their conclusions, more recently new research has gone off in a number of previously underexplored directions, and important features of the conventional wisdom have come under challenge.

Some of the new work on punishment has been undertaken by people more generally concerned to fashion a new history of crime and criminal justice. Thus Peter Linebaugh, Douglas Hay, and John Beattie, all of whom we have already mentioned in other connections, have all produced interesting work on punishment. Important contributions have also been made by scholars emerging from other disciplines, however, most notably from sociology or the social sciences. Scholars who are not historians by profession have been particularly active in reworking the history of prisons. It is easy to see why this subject should have aroused their especial interest, given the centrality of the prison in modern penology, and the by now well established notion that the late eighteenth and early nineteenth centuries constituted a crucial formative period in the shaping of the modern prison.[75]

This section begins with an account of the ways in which the history of eighteenth-century punishment has traditionally been approached. Some of the new directions recent research has taken and some of the new interpretations recent writers have offered are then indicated. Innovative features of recent works are noted, but it will also be remarked that, in certain important respects, recent writers have been inclined rather to echo than to question the habits and assumptions of their precursors. The account of punishment provided in John Beattie's 1986 study, *Crime and the courts in England 1660–1800*, has broken most decisively with older habits and assumptions, both in its approach and in its conclusions. For this reason, we devote most time and care to an exposition of Beattie's work.

The foundations of modern research in the history of eighteenth-century punishment were laid above all by two books which appeared in the first half of this century: Beatrice and Sidney Webb's study of *English Prisons under Local Government* – the first scholarly study to attempt to survey the development of English prisons – and the first volume of Leon Radzinowicz's *History of English Criminal Law and its Administration from 1750*, an account of the eighteenth- and early nineteenth-century history of capital punishment.[76] The Webbs' study has now been superseded, but Radzinowicz's *History* retains much value and significance, both because of the extraordinary amount of information it pulls together and because of the enduring influence of its interpretations.[77]

Two characteristics of these classic studies deserve special emphasis because of the part they appear to have played in shaping the course and character of subsequent work. First, both books adopt what we have termed a 'reform perspective' on their subject matter. Both, that is to say, effectively treat the early eighteenth century as a backdrop, against which they proceed to set a tale of late-eighteenth- and early-nineteenth-century humanitarian reforming endeavour. The end of the eighteenth and beginning of the nineteenth centuries are identified as critical periods of change, and the account of the disadvantages of the old and advantages of 'reformed' practice offered echoes of that which was provided by the reformers themselves.

Not only the basic shape that both the Webbs and Radzinowicz imposed upon their stories, but also their implicit definitions of the boundaries of their subject matter have influenced subsequent research. The Webbs' history of prisons is exclusively a history of prison management. To point to only one of the several topics they pass incuriously over, they show remarkably little interest in the grounds on which people were imprisoned, or in determining what was clearly the prison's changing role within the larger penal system. Radzinowicz's study ranges more widely. He not only surveys the history of capital statutes, and summarizes the substance of relevant parliamentary debates (chiefly those in which penal reformers inveighed against the incessant proliferation of capital statutes), but also investigates judicial interpretations of statutes, which of course affected their courtroom application, and even provides a lengthy account of the changing ways in which executions were actually carried out. However, Radzinowicz too has relatively little to say about sentencing patterns and the various influences bearing upon them, perhaps in part because this is a topic difficult to approach through the printed sources on which he mainly relies. Moreover, Radzinowicz too does relatively little to locate capital punishment in relation to other penal practices of the day.

Two impulses have powered recent work on the history of eighteenth-century punishment. First, the urge to probe more deeply into pre-reform practice, which older works illuminated only in a patchy and uneven fashion. Douglas Hay's essay, 'Property, authority and the criminal law', which has already figured in our discussion of trial, also merits attention in this connection. One of Hay's objects in this essay was to discover why some by no means illiberal or thoughtless eighteenth-century gentlemen (notably Archdeacon Paley), far from enlisting under the banner of penal reform, pronounced themselves substantially satisfied with the status quo. Hay's own account of the indirect contribution made by the drama of terror and mercy to the maintenance of the social order draws heavily on the writings of the Bloody Code's contemporary apologists. Another contributor to *Albion's Fatal Tree*, Peter

Linebaugh, explored some of the social tensions that hedged public execution in his ethnographically rich account of gallows riots against surgeons seeking bodies for their dissecting tables.[78] Roger Ekirch's study of transportation to the American colonies during its mid-century heyday is the first ever full-length study of this form of punishment – by far the most common fate visited upon men and women convicted of felony between the Hanoverian accession and the American war.[79]

Other writers have been happy to reproduce the traditional emphasis on the century's final decades, but have challenged traditional interpretations of reform. The motives and achievements of prison reformers have been subjected to especially searching scrutiny, notably by Rod Morgan in a brief article, and by Michael Ignatieff and Robin Evans in more substantial works.[80] The reformers' ostensible humanitarianism, we are now told, went hand in hand with a formidably severe disciplinary project. As a result of 'reforms', greater numbers of men and women than ever before were channelled into prisons (most of whom would previously not have been hanged, but transported, whipped or fined). Once inside, they were subjected to harsh and coercive systems of prison discipline. Michael Ignatieff, whose study is subtitled, *The Penitentiary in the Industrial Revolution*, argues that industrialization, rather than the rise of some socially inspecific humanitarian urge, provides the crucial context within which these developments must be set if they are to be understood.[81]

The best of these recent books and articles have certain characteristic merits. First, their authors display considerable sensitivity and imagination in their use of sources – especially when they are using these sources to shed light on the attitude and experiences of the punished. Second, by challenging conventional pieties, these writers have frequently been able to open up interesting new topics to enquiry. If reformed practice was not necessarily more humane, or even more effective, how can we explain why some came to champion it, and why their proposals were ultimately implemented, at least in part? If we find that the rhetoric and the reality of reform do not coincide, how should we interpret this discrepancy? Finally, it is a merit of much recent work that it has placed the question of the relationship between social and institutional change very firmly on the agenda. If some of the hypotheses offered as to the nature of that relationship have been overbold, at least they have helped to direct attention to the problem.

Novel features and novel emphases in recent work leap to the eye. Less immediately striking, but nonetheless worthy of note, are respects in which recent writers have tended to reproduce characteristics of older work. It is remarkable, for example, that traditional views of the basic chronology of change have not been more critically scrutinized. New work has more frequently challenged the substance of the older story than its general shape. If anything, 'revisionists' have been inclined to sharpen the traditional contrast between static pre- and dynamic post-reform eras. Thus, whereas older accounts commonly stressed the slow pace of ameliorative action, recently the accent has been placed instead on the speed and extent of change.[82] Similarly, the older notion that histories of punishment should concern themselves chiefly with the organization and application of punishments has persisted. Only rarely have attempts been made to link the history of punishment back into the wider history of crime and criminal justice, as that is now developing: to link punishment back to crime, to the management of prosecution and to the trial process.[83]

The great merit of John Beattie's study of punishment lies in its combination of those characteristics already commended in other recent works, with constructive innovations on several other fronts. Beattie shifts the time boundaries of our knowledge radically backwards. Beginning his study at the Restoration, he uncovers a rich and complex history of penal change and experimentation in the late seventeenth and early eighteenth centuries. He also grasps the nettle others have failed to grasp, and integrates his study of punishment into a broader study of crime and criminal justice. The brief exposition of Beattie's method and conclusions presented here is organized around an account of his approach to the subject and its implications. It will become clear as we proceed that it is in large part because of the approach he has adopted that he has been able so dramatically to expand our knowledge of the earlier years of the century.

Punishment is the subject of only the last third of Beattie's book, the first two-thirds being concerned with crime and trial respectively. Although the studies of crime and trial have their merits, the section which deals with punishment is undoubtedly the most impressive of the three. This is not to suggest that any of the sections could easily be disjoined from the others, however. The strengths of the section on punishment largely derive from the very fact that it is grounded on a careful study of the changing volume and composition of charges brought against offenders (at the Surrey and to a lesser extent Sussex courts of Assizes and Quarter Sessions), and of the ways in which these charges were handled in the courts.

The standard practice of historians of punishment before the publication of Beattie's book was to approach their subject from the other end, from punishment itself. Historians generally placed some instrument of punishment – the gallows, the prison – at the centre of their concerns and worked outwards from there. The shortcoming of this method is that it offers no ready way of relating different punishments to each other. In fact, one of the most striking features of the eighteenth-century English penal regime was what might be called its 'penal pluralism'. A wide variety of different forms of punishment were simultaneously in use: hanging, transportation, imprisonment, whipping, pillorying, and fining. Although the frequency with which different forms of punishment were employed changed over time, no one penal instrument was wholly abandoned in the course of the period, and even trends in use appear to have followed no very straightforward linear pattern. (In these circumstances, let it be noted that it behoves the historian of any single penal form to be modest in his or her claims as to quite how much light any monofocal study of punishment is likely to shed on eighteenth-century attitudes and social relations.)

Approaching the study of punishments, as he does, through a study of sentencing, Beattie, uniquely, encounters 'penal pluralism' not as a problem, but rather as a phenomenon which sets the terms of the problem. The analytical and interpretative task confronting the historian, as it presents itself from this angle, may be resolved into two main parts. First, it has to be established how judges, or others who had the opportunity to influence the outcome of the sentencing process, negotiated their way through the range of available options. What sorts of considerations led them to plump for one form of punishment rather than another? Second, one must clearly go on to ask what patterns of change over time emerge from a diachronic study of trial outcomes and sentencing patterns – and how the patterns of change thus revealed may best be explained.

It might be thought that this agenda is in at least one respect misconceived, that the punishments visited upon eighteenth-century offenders were determined, not by any courtroom or other decision-making process, but rather by the mechanical application of common law or the provisions of penal statutes, with the corollary that explaining change over time is chiefly a matter of explaining changes in the law. However, Beattie convincingly demonstrates (taking up a theme previously aired by Douglas Hay) how substantial were the opportunities for discretionary choice available in the interval between the first bringing of a complaint, and the final disposition of an offender. In some instances, common or statute law straightforwardly offered choices. When it did not, opportunities for the exercise of discretion could usually be manufactured, by manipulating the form of the charge, the precise character of the verdict, the rules determining eligibility for benefit of clergy, or, finally (the matter which particularly preoccupied Hay), the royal prerogative of mercy.

This is not to say the state of the law was irrelevant. Some laws constrained opportunities for the exercise of discretion more narrowly than others (for instance, by clauses disallowing benefit of clergy). The passage of a new law could make new penal options available for use in connection with particular categories of offender, or could make certain forms of punishment more readily available and thus open the way for their more extensive use. However, one of the interesting conclusions that Beattie's account nudges us towards is that it would be a mistake to conceive of eighteenth-century penal statutes as having emerged, in every instance, in an erratic and irrational fashion out of the deliberations of ill-informed legislators. Some statutes, at least, appear to have arisen out of, and very effectively to have addressed, problems encountered in the courtroom. In some instances the judiciary played a part in their drafting and promotion. In particular, the contribution of high court judges and the Attorney- and Solicitor-General to the shaping of eighteenth-century penal legislation merits further enquiry.[84]

Beattie is inclined to argue (with King and against Hay) that the choices made with regard to the disposition of particular offenders were chiefly influenced by such considerations as the offender's age and character. His most interesting findings relate not so much to the distribution of offenders between punishments at any moment, however, as to changes over time in the balance between punishments visited upon particular categories of offender. He is able to provide an elaborate chronology of, for example, the movement in and out of favour of execution, transportation, whipping, and imprisonment as punishments for particular forms of felony, and of fining and imprisonment as punishments for criminal assaults.

The most striking finding that emerges from this exercise undoubtedly concerns the late seventeenth and early eighteenth centuries, which now stand revealed as having witnessed several dramatic shifts in penal practice, as well as a number of interesting small-scale penal experiments – many of which have previously passed almost entirely unnoticed. Beattie has been able to reveal this interesting and generally unsuspected face of early-eighteenth-century penal history largely because of his chosen method of study. The ready availability in print of extensive pamphlet and parliamentary debate relating to possible modes of punishment long since alerted historians to the importance, in penal history, of the later decades of the century. In the absence of comparable earlier material, many scholars felt it safe to conclude that there were no comparable earlier doubts, projects, debates, or shifts in practice. It is clear now that this conclusion was unwarranted. What emerges as novel and distinctive about the later eighteenth century is not the fact of discontent with the penal status quo, or a willingness to experiment with new options, or even the character of the options experimented with (for example, there was also an early eighteenth-century experiment with the more extensive use of imprisonment), but rather the extent to which these questions were aired before and agitated among an extensive, concerned 'public'.

Beattie alerts us to a much longer and more complex history of penal innovation and experimentation than previous historians had led us to expect. What suggestions does he make as to how his revised version of the story should be explained? His treatment of this topic, and in particular his account of who participated, and in what ways, in the shaping of penal policy, is by no means exhaustive. Nonetheless he makes a large number of interesting, thoughtful, and well-documented suggestions.

He suggests first that the immediate stimulus for changes in penal practice was often provided by a surge in the number of cases (in general, or of some particular kind) coming before the courts. He is able to point to such apparent 'crime waves' as precipitants of change, of course, because he has grounded his study of punishments on a study of crime and trial.[85]

To identify a stimulus is not, of course, to explain a response. In order to pursue this question further it is necessary to distinguish between two possible kinds of response. 'Crime waves' sometimes triggered no more than a short-term, crisis response – usually an increase in the ratio of hangings to other lesser forms of corporal punishment. At other times, short-term shifts in favour of severity were accompanied by much more far-reaching attempts to rethink and reshape the conventional tariff of penalties. An innovative response was more likely to emerge in the face of a massive and prolonged 'crime wave', such as commonly occurred at the end of wars. Other features of the general political environment also might affect both the propensity to innovate, and the kinds of innovation discussed and adopted.

Beattie does carefully distinguish between the different character of the different considered responses mounted at different times. However, he also points to important continuities over time in the character of the options and strategies considered and favoured. From the very beginning of his period, he claims, policy makers were already inclined to believe that the most promising way forward lay in extending the range, and increasing the effectiveness of *secondary* punishments: punishments less final than death, more effectively deterrent than whipping or branding in the hand. The main contenders for the role of intermediate punishment were perennially two: transportation and imprisonment. The history of English penal policy from 1660 to 1800 is largely (though not exclusively) a story of the alternation of these two in favour, and of the changing (mainly growing) role assigned to such secondary punishments within the penal system at large. The arguments advanced in favour of intermediate punishments changed relatively little from one end of the period to the other. At all times reference was made to a venerable stock of ideas about the most effective ways to nip incipient delinquency in the bud, involving intervention at the earliest possible stage, and the removal (as far as possible) of all sources of moral contagion.

Finally, Beattie also suggests that lying behind and conditioning more particular and abrupt patterns of change was a long-term and gradual shift in sentiment against the use of physical violence, evident both in society at large and in the criminal justice system in particular. He suggests that the penal reform movement of the later eighteenth century should be seen in part as an outgrowth and expression of this more fundamental shift in attitudes, which (ironically but consistently) also found expression in a shift in favour of the more severe punishment of crimes of violence.

Beattie's work very substantially advances our understanding of the history of eighteenth-century punishment. The lesson other researchers should draw from his work is not that all studies should henceforth proceed along similar lines, however. There is room for *some* more work on similar lines: in particular, it would be interesting to know more about regional variations in penal practice. How typical were Surrey and Sussex? In general, one would expect a high degree of consistency between the sentencing practices of circuit courts in different parts of the country (which is very much what the Surrey/Sussex comparison suggests) but more variation at the level of Quarter Sessions. Beattie himself has now turned his attention to the City of London, a densely packed urban district with its own distinctive problems, where not only the Quarter Sessions, but also sessions of Gaol Delivery might be dominated by 'local' figures.[86] At the same time, other approaches remain not only legitimate, but necessary, to complement the work Beattie has already done. Thus, there is room for more work on the organization of punishment, on popular attitudes to punishment, and on the character of public and parliamentary debate.[87] Beattie has opened up to enquiry the subject of penal policy making (Who influenced the shaping of penal policy? What considerations bore most powerfully upon them?), but has himself only supplied a limited number of tentative answers to his own questions. There is clearly room for further interesting work in this area.

Those wishing to pursue these many alternative lines of enquiry are nonetheless likely to continue to find Beattie's work of great use – for in two, rather different senses, Beattie's study provides a map or a model, that should help future researchers to orient themselves and to direct their research intelligently. First, Beattie's work provides a rich and complex map of patterns of change over time; a map, moreover, which repeatedly highlights moments of crisis and change, of doubt and debate. Second, in the course of the three parts of his book Beattie painstakingly explores the interconnections between different parts of the machinery of criminal justice, suggesting how decisions made or developments set in motion in one sphere affected developments and decisions in other spheres. Armed with the knowledge and understanding of the larger context of their work (in these two senses) which Beattie's study provides, future researchers should be well placed both to home in quickly on topics worthy of study, and to reflect in an informed fashion on the plausibility and larger implications of their conclusions.

For all its merits, John Beattie's account of eighteenth-century punishment inevitably has certain limitations. We will conclude by noting two of these, in order to draw attention to certain topics we believe still to stand in need of investigation.

Beattie's book implicitly issues a major challenge to those who wish to insist on the peculiar and distinctive character of changes in penal practice in the final decades of the eighteenth century. The picture he paints of late-seventeenth- and early-eighteenth-century developments makes it difficult to maintain with as much confidence as once seemed appropriate that changes in the late eighteenth century were either extraordinary in extent or unprecedented in kind. But this is not to say that there was 'nothing new' about developments of the later eighteenth century, still less that the prison and more general penal reform movements had no features of special interest. Beattie himself identifies increasingly wide diffusion of humanitarian views as a distinctive feature of the later eighteenth century. But precisely what was new, in terms either of ideology or of tactics, about the classic penal reform movement needs more pertinacious and extended consideration in the light of Beattie's findings than he himself provides. Very probably this is a task not best approached, or not best approached solely, on the basis of one or two county studies. For while the local response to reform proposals certainly needs to find a place in the larger account (and there are reasons to think late-eighteenth-century local governors may well have taken up reform proposals more enthusiastically than their counterparts earlier in the century) at the same time it increasingly appears, as we have already remarked, that the manner in which the policy debate was carried on may have been one of the most distinctive features of late-eighteenth-century experience.[88]

A second limitation of Beattie's work is by no means peculiar to his study. Beattie's book, like most other recent accounts of eighteenth-century crime, concentrates on indictable offences – and consequently on the punishments attached to indictable crimes. Offences tried summarily in the eighteenth century were conventionally punished by some combination of whipping, fine, and imprisonment, the latter usually at hard labour in a house of correction. Summary offences, and administrative responses to them are not well documented. It is possible, however, to put together some picture of how houses of correction were employed, since calendars of prisoners admitted to them survive in some county record collections. Houses of correction have now begun to attract attention.[89] This attention seems well placed, for two reasons. First, the house of correction – in effect the first reformative prison – represented an interesting penal experiment, pioneered at lower levels within the penal system (from as early as the sixteenth century) before being adapted for more general use. Second, the study of house of correction records provides one of the few ways into the study, not only of punishments attached to summary crime, but also of summary crime itself. In this case it appears that punishment is a promising point of entry to the wider field.[90]

Criminal legislation

In the course of this essay we have expressed our belief that it is important for historians of crime and the law to treat eighteenth-century institutions seriously and to pay careful attention to developments during the first half of the eighteenth century. These considerations loom large in the ensuing discussion of criminal legislation. In this section we offer an assessment of existing work on the subject and a sketch of alternative approaches we ourselves are currently researching.[91]

One of the most striking features of existing accounts of eighteenth-century crime and the law is the amount of attention they have devoted to legislation. It has not been criminal legislation as a whole that has captured this attention, but rather the Bloody Code: the large number of statutes that attached the penalty of death by hanging to a wide variety of offences, both great and small. This body of statute had developed over several centuries and recent commentators have acknowledged that most of those who faced a capital charge during the eighteenth century were accused of offences that had been made capital by a small number of statutes in the sixteenth century. It is, however, the eighteenth-century proliferation of such statutes, irrespective of the extent to which they were applied in the courts, that has excited the interest of historians of crime and the law. The number of capital statutes grew from about fifty in 1689 to over two hundred by 1820. Most of the new statutes were concerned with offences against property. Douglas Hay's opinion that 'this flood of legislation is one of the great facts of the eighteenth century' is an eloquent statement of a widely-held view.[92]

In attempting to account for this 'great fact', historians have focused on the objectives which the capital statutes were designed to fulfil and the characteristics of the legislative system that produced them. The most influential interpretation is that provided by Radzinowicz, who draws heavily on the criticisms of the Bloody Code offered by late-eighteenth- and early-nineteenth-century law reformers.[93] He argues that eighteenth-century legislators were influenced by an exceptionally penal attitude towards property offences. Capital statutes were able to proliferate chiefly because almost any member of parliament, seized by the desire to make some offence capital, could obtain an act to such effect almost automatically. Eighteenth-century capital statutes imposed the death penalty for a wildly disparate range of offences, often taking little account of existing law regarding the offence in question. This, Radzinowicz argues, was because legislators lacked modern notions of 'scientific' legislation, with their general definitions of offences and general rules about the gradation of punishments. In the absence of such notions a particularistic and incoherent method of legislating resulted in a particularistic and incoherent body of capital statutes.

A more elaborate analysis of the objectives of the new laws is offered by Edward Thompson and Douglas Hay.[94] They argue that the new capital statutes were 'the legal instruments which enforced the division of property by terror', legal instruments which served both the personal interests of a handful of members of parliament and the broader needs of a developing capitalism.[95] They acknowledge, of course, that capital statutes were mitigated in practice – that not all those convicted were hanged. Nevertheless, they believe that this legislation retained enormous instrumental force. Thompson argues that the definition of crime was enlarged by means of the new capital statutes in order to crush various forms of appropriation by the poor that had previously been regarded, at most, as violations of trust or community obligation.[96] Hay points to the way the new capital statutes protected new forms of commercial property.[97] Both are agreed that the extent to which the legislation was concerned to defend property by means of the noose was both new and distinctive.

The picture that emerges has been best summarized by Douglas Hay himself in *Albion's Fatal Tree*:

What is certain is that Parliament did not often enact the new capital statutes as a matter of conscious public policy. Usually there was no debate, and most of the changes were related to specific, limited property interests, hitherto unprotected for one reason or another. Often they were the personal interest of a few members, and the Lords and Commons enacted them for the mere asking.[98]

At the heart of these accounts, then, are three linked propositions: that the numerical increase in capital offences in the eighteenth century was out of all proportion to what had gone before; that this increase was the work of a peculiarly ruthless ruling class, which, in its own interests, extended the scope of the death penalty to enforce radical redefinitions and restrictions on the property rights of the poor, as well as to defend new forms of commercial property; and that in a parliament that was the tool of this ruling class, the process by which new capital offences were created amounted simply to the uncritical rubber-stamping of any and every proposal. These are all highly questionable propositions and the next few paragraphs offer alternatives to each of them.

Consider first the way the proliferation of eighteenth-century capital statutes has been measured. We can approach this issue in two ways: in terms of the appropriate standard of measurement, and in terms of how the individual units to be counted have been defined. Century-by-century comparisons of legislative output have conventionally been handled by a straightforward juxtaposition of total numbers of statutes passed in the course of each century. But for many interpretative purposes such a comparison is much too simple-minded. If the question is whether there was an increase in the propensity of members of parliament to enact capital or other legislation from one century to the next (or between any two periods), surely what is needed is a standard of measurement that takes account of changes in the number, length, and regularity of parliamentary sessions, and hence of changes in opportunities to legislate. An unsophisticated but nevertheless effective way to achieve this would be to adjust century-by-century counts of capital statutes in such a way as to control for century-by-century changes in both the number of parliamentary sessions and the total number of statutes per parliamentary session. On this basis, the eighteenth century does not look as wildly out of step with earlier centuries as the conventional accounts imply, for a decisive change in the opportunities for legislating was brought about by the Glorious Revolution of 1688–9.

Before 1688, parliaments did not necessarily meet every year. When they met, it was often only for a few months at a time, and sessions were liable to be suddenly and unpredictably cut short by prorogations or dissolutions. In these circumstances, not only were opportunities to legislate intermittent, but even when they arose large numbers of bills met sudden death at the end of a session. After 1688, by contrast, parliaments invariably met annually and on a regular pattern, almost never for less than four months and sometimes for as many as six. One effect of this change was to create vast new openings for legislation. Obstacles like those faced by manufacturers promoting a bill against industrial embezzlement in 1621 were largely eliminated. That bill was 'well approved of by the whole House of Parliament, yet by reason of the sudden dissolution of the said session, nothing was done therein'.[99] Parliament met during only four of the subsequent eighteen years and provisions of the kind the manufacturers sought were not enacted until 1703.

However, the problems associated with measuring the expansion of eighteenth-century capital statutes are not simply a matter of the standard by which that expansion should be gauged. The successful employment of any standard of measurement depends on the consistency with which the units to be measured are defined. The way the units employed in measuring the eighteenth-century expansion of the capital sanction have usually been defined is in this respect deficient. The conventional accounts assume that the growth in the number of statutes entailed a meaningful expansion in the number of capital offences. Each statute, or sometimes each capital provision within a statute, is treated as a unit for the purpose of analysis. The growing number of those units is then taken as a reasonable indication of the extending scope of the capital sanction. On this basis, as we have seen, the eighteenth century does on the face of it look wildly out of step with both the seventeenth century and the nineteenth century in its propensity to provide for capital punishment. But did each eighteenth-century capital statute create one or more new capital offences in a sense that allows straightforward numerical comparisons with the proceeding and subsequent centuries? It is our contention that the apparent multiplication of individual capital provisions in the eighteenth century does not provide an unproblematic measure of the expansion in the numbers of capital offences. Studies which simply treat the multiplication of capital provisions as a 'great fact' should take account of the experience hard-won by students of eighteenth-century indictment statistics and pay more attention to how that fact was constituted.

In adopting this line of argument, we follow John Langbein, who has pointed out that to talk, as Radzinowicz does, of the number of capital offences being increased between 1689 and 1800 by perhaps two hundred is misleading. 'The English did not have 200 separate crimes in the modern sense that could be punished with death. Rather they lacked general definitions, especially for larceny and embezzlement, with the result that they were constantly having to add particularity in order to compensate for generality.'[100] Had modern notions of legislative consolidation been applied by eighteenth-century parliaments, the same range of activities could have been rendered subject to the death penalty by means of only a fraction of the number of statutes. There was an increase in the number of capital offences in the eighteenth century, but the conventional account of its size and significance, relative both to what came after and to what had gone before, needs to be reassessed.

Earlier capital legislation had not so commonly been particularistic. This goes a long way to explain why most of the new capital statutes of the period after 1688 were so little used. The capital statutes on which prosecutions were grounded most frequently in the eighteenth century continued to be that handful dating from the sixteenth century that dealt with broad categories of offences: for example, burglary (1547), horse stealing (1548), and pickpocketing (1565).[101] The majority of the new statutes (although by no means all of them) defined the offences concerned in such a narrow way that the number of potential prosecutions was inevitably tiny.[102] Each of the following, for example, was the occasion of a separate capital statute: forging an entry in a North Riding of Yorkshire land register (1735); destroying Fulham Bridge (1725); destroying Westminster Bridge (1736); embezzling notes by servants of the Bank of England (1742); embezzling the effects of the South Sea Company by its officers or servants (1751).[103]

Two conclusions, therefore, emerge from our assessment of the way the eighteenth-century capital statutes have been counted. If, as we have argued, a much larger proportion of the eighteenth-century statutes were particularistic than had been true earlier, then the proposition that eighteenth-century parliaments engineered an increase in the number of capital offences out of all proportion to that undertaken by previous parliaments is considerably weakened. Similarly, if the opportunities for legislating were much greater in the eighteenth century than had been the case before, doubt is also cast on the notion that eighteenth-century members of parliament had a greater propensity to enact capital legislation than had their predecessors.

The conventional accounts, however, propose not merely an expansion in the number of capital offences in the eighteenth century, but also (especially the work of Edward Thompson and Douglas Hay) a change in the sort of activities that were held to merit the death penalty. Even if the significance of the numerical expansion is, as we have argued, much more limited than the conventional accounts suggest, the change in character is not necessarily affected. Indeed it appears very likely that some of the new capital statutes did, as Edward Thompson argues in *Whigs and Hunters*, transform popular customs or their defence into capital crimes. It is important to note, however, that recent research suggests that the Black Act of 1723, which both Thompson and Radzinowicz present as a key index of the legislative sensibility that spawned other eighteenth-century capital statutes, does not easily fit into such a category. Thompson has argued that the act was a characteristically bloody response by the Hanoverian ruling class to episodes of deer killing and other outrages in the forests of Berkshire and Hampshire by the Blacks, who were foresters resisting the assault on their customary rights by 'improving' landlords and the forest authorities. New archival work suggests that the undoubtedly harsh terms of the act can best be explained not in terms of the need to sustain this rationalizing assault on forest custom, but by the fact that the act was first and foremost a political measure in the narrow sense, occasioned by the Blacks' Jacobite connections.[104]

Less open to contention is the claim that eighteenth-century parliaments extended the capital sanction to many new forms of commercial property (some of which may possibly have over-ridden customary rights). Examples are the forgery of a wide range of commercial paper and malicious damage to major capital in-vestments, such as the destruction of turnpikes (1735), or setting fire to coal mines (1737).[105] Yet we remain sceptical as to whether all this should be interpreted as a specifically eighteenth-century enlargement of basic principles regarding what sort of offences merited death. After all, coining and many serious thefts were already capital offences in the mid sixteenth century. In the eight-eenth century, the same basic principles which underlay the inflic-tion of the death penalty in these instances were often simply extended to equivalent forms of property that had subsequently come into existence, or become more prominent. Eighteenth-century England was a commercially and technologically more diverse society than had been the case in the sixteenth century. Many new forms of commercial paper and investment had emerged which could justify the protection of the death penalty on the basis of analogy with activities which had benefited from earlier capital legislation.[106]

Clearly this does not detract from the importance in practice of these extensions for the offenders concerned, nor can meaningful analogies be found in the sixteenth century for every new cap-ital offence created in the eighteenth. It is also true that late-seventeenth- and eighteenth-century parliaments did not much diminish the scope of capital punishment (although it is worth remembering that the capital statutes against the export smuggling of wool and against witchcraft were repealed in 1693 and 1736 respectively). Nevertheless, we remain unconvinced that they greatly extended the fundamental criteria determining the kind of offences that were believed to merit death.

A parliament which unevenly and often hesitatingly extended the capital sanction to offences analogous to those already liable to the death penalty, but which was decidedly reticent about extensions to the basic principles regarding which offences deserved death seems to be a parliament very different from the uncritical ruling class tool that emerges in the conventional accounts of the eighteenth-century legislature's enactment of capital statutes. Such accounts have also misrepresented the process by which parliament enacted capital and other criminal legislation. One of the most striking shortcomings of the picture they commonly offer is the way it wholly ignores the existence of the large numbers of legislative proposals which failed to reach the statute book. Excluding government-backed revenue or military measures (which were almost always enacted), over a third of bills failed in the eighteenth century. If, as the conventional accounts suggest, legislation was rarely the subject of debate, if parliament merely concerned itself with rubber-stamping private members' proposals, it is difficult to understand why so many bills (including many concerned with crime) should have failed. It is our belief that in order to explain the failure of so many proposals for legislation, it is necessary to acknowledge that legislation was often a matter of intense disagreement and debate in eighteenth-century parliaments.

Given the destruction of the manuscript records of the House of Commons and the sparseness, before the 1770s, of diary and newspaper accounts of debates other than those concerned with political or constitutional issues, it is difficult to establish the shape of debate. Insofar as we can reconstruct the parliamentary careers of criminal proposals (capital and non-capital), it appears that they were usually scrutinized with care and routinely subjected to debate, sometimes at great length.[107] A variety of outcomes was possible. A proposal might be introduced and debated in parliamentary session after session, but never enacted.[108] It might fail outright in one session and never reappear.[109] A bill might fail, but then be re-introduced and pass in a drastically modified form.[110] It might pass in the session it was first introduced, but nevertheless undergo significant changes in the course of its passage.[111]

It is only when we are fortunate enough to have copies of the bills and other evidence about their passage through parliament that the extent of the modifications and the reasons for them can be established. Such cases nonetheless alert us to the fact that even when a bill did pass unmolested in its first session, this was at least as likely to be a consequence of its inoffensiveness in terms of prevailing parliamentary criteria, as it was a result of its slipping through in a momentary lapse of parliamentary scrutiny (although this is not to deny that such lapses did occur). The need to avoid stirring up controversy was recognized by those who promoted legislation. The parliamentary manager of the 1749 industrial embezzlement act commented during its passage that 'care should be taken while endeavours are used to make it effectual, to make it so unexceptional as not to hazard the passing of it'.[112]

What forms did criticisms of such proposals take? This is not the place for a comprehensive account, but three sorts of issues were prominent. First, bills had to face practical criticisms as to their desirability, feasibility and scope. Thus William Hay MP spoke against a proposal to increase the penalties for assault with intent to rob in 1734 because he considered 'there was a sufficient punishment already, and a better than was proposed by the bill'.[113] Bills also had to confront competing views of the public interest. Thus the House of Lords' attempt to tack clauses dealing with deer stealing on to the transportation bill of 1717–18 was staunchly opposed in the Commons, with the argument that the offence was imprecisely defined, 'whereby innocent persons may be liable to prosecutions upon frivolous pretences'.[114] Finally, bills had to run the gauntlet of legalistic objections. Sir John Lowther MP, describing the debate in 1752 on a bill to make the unlawful taking of black lead (graphite) from mines a felony, bemoaned the fact that 'the lawyers make such distinctions between taking things before, or after the owner has sever'd them from the freehold, as if the injury was not equal'.[115]

This picture of lively and informed parliamentary debate is so much at odds with the conventional view of criminal legislation that one might well wonder how both can derive from the same set of sources. Part of the explanation lies in the superficial difficulties of the sources. Finding it hard to determine the character of parliamentary discussion, historians have been surprisingly willing to suggest that there was no discussion. When systematic reporting improves in the 1770s, historians begin talking of a new concern with the deficiencies of the criminal law, citing the reports of parliamentary debates as evidence. Interesting new developments were not lacking in the later eighteenth century, but the contrast between the periods before and after 1770 is easily exaggerated.

We have presented in this section some key elements in our reinterpretation of eighteenth-century capital legislation. Our thinking about each of the components of our argument is, as yet, far from complete, but a number of their implications for the broader study of eighteenth-century law and parliament are already clear. If, as we have argued, the significance attached in the existing accounts to the numerical increase in capital statutes has been exaggerated, then the failure of these accounts seriously to consider penal legislation which inflicted less severe punishments is highlighted. Not only was non-capital criminal legislation more important numerically than is commonly allowed, but also there is potentially a great deal to be learnt about the capital statutes themselves from an analysis that locates them alongside their non-capital counterparts. The more historians distance themselves from mere counting, the more possible it becomes to shift the emphasis of analysis towards qualitative distinctions between statutes: distinctions between, on the one hand, legislation of the importance of the transportation act of 1718, which (though not a capital statute) shaped the way all capital statutes were used during the rest of the century, and on the other, those numerous, but little-used capital statutes of the later eighteenth century which dealt with a multitude of narrowly defined acts of forgery.

This section has disputed Edward Thompson and Douglas Hay's proposition that eighteenth-century legislators were more prepared than their predecessors to extend the ways the capital sanction was used, in order to advance their own economic interests and those of other wealthy and powerful groups. Nevertheless, we remain sympathetic to their desire to understand criminal legislation in terms of the concerns of those with property and political influence in eighteenth-century society. What marks their accounts of criminal legislation is a repeated tendency to substitute the conspiratorial hand of an anthropomorphically self-conscious 'ruling class' for an analysis of the impact on criminal law making of those fractions of the adult male population which enjoyed at least some property and political influence. As we have indicated, criminal law making was often a contentious matter. Before we decide that the criminal law was the instrument of any single interest or class, we need to discover more about the individuals and groups who disputed it, the arguments to which they appealed and the legislative machinery available to them.

The picture we have provided of a parliament where debate over criminal legislation was both routine and important is in direct contradiction to that offered by existing accounts of the Bloody Code. But it is also at odds with the image of eighteenth-century parliaments as legislating bodies found in the mainstream political histories, an image which historians of crime and the law have simply reproduced. Even though eighteenth-century parliaments have been the commanding objects of political historians' attentions, their legislative concerns have been largely ignored. This is largely because Lewis Namier, the dominant figure in the study of eighteenth-century parliamentary history, had no interest in what parliament did (as opposed to its function as the crucible in which a ruling elite was fused). Political historians have subsequently been too busy debating the implications of Namier's views for the history of party and political ideas to contest the implications of those views for the study of legislation. Looking at parliament from the vantage point of the criminal law, however, what emerges most strikingly is how sustained and important a role it played in the domestic government of England by means of various kinds of legislation, including that concerned with crime. If work on criminal legislation can help generate new perspectives on the activities of eighteenth-century parliaments, then studies of crime and criminal justice will be contributing to an area that has as yet resisted their influence and, indeed, the influence of social history in general.

Conclusion

The second section of this essay quoted the statement made by the authors of *Albion's Fatal Tree* in 1975 to the effect that the issues addressed in the study of crime and the criminal law are 'central to unlocking the meanings of eighteenth-century social history'.[116] Despite the changes over the last fifteen years which we have outlined, this proposition still retains its force, both as a justification for working in the field and as a statement of the subject's potential. However, it is a proposition that should also alert us to the responsibility borne by historians of eighteenth-century crime and criminal justice to integrate their findings into a broader picture of eighteenth-century English society. Insofar as the field's potential has not yet been fully realized, this is because the ways in which historians have attempted that integration have been deficient.

This is not to suggest that historians in the field have been insensitive to the need to consider the broader implications of their work. The attraction for them of the three social historical approaches outlined in the second section was the distinctive way in which each approach made crime and criminal justice intelligible in terms of broader historical developments. For history from below such intelligibility lay in the transforming impact of capitalism upon the experience of the dispossessed; for social scientific positivism it was to be found in the relationship between crime and other social variables; and for more recent variants of the reform perspective it lay in the social tensions and administrative changes called forth by industrialization. As vehicles for integrating the history of crime and criminal justice into a broader picture of eighteenth-century English society, each of these approaches has had its strengths, but each has also had considerable shortcomings.

Thus although historians adopting a reform perspective have recognized the importance of the way the law was administered – of questions such as who staffed the machinery of criminal justice and how did it work – their emphasis on industrialization as the motor of change has left them incapable of addressing the earlier eighteenth century as anything other than a counterpoint against which the theme of reform is played. The positivist approach, because it involves no necessary assumptions about the trajectory of change, can avoid the teleology implicit in the reform perspective. But its narrow and mechanical comparisons between crime and other social facts cannot alone provide general explanations of the workings of the criminal law. Moreover, even these narrow comparisons have failed to fulfil their limited promise, as a result of the almost insuperable obstacle posed by the doubtful intelligibility of indictment-based time series.

The most fruitful of the attempts to integrate crime and criminal justice into a broader vision of eighteenth-century English society has undoubtedly come from the approach we termed history from below. The great strength of this approach, compared with the other approaches described, has lain in the ambitious efforts its practitioners have made to develop a coherent interpretation of what was distinctive about relationships of power and inequality in the eighteenth century. Armed with a set of ideas on this score, they have been able to provide a stimulating and broadly conceived account of how and why the criminal law was important in eighteenth-century society. In *Albion's Fatal Tree*, the conclusion they offer is that the criminal law was not merely important, but the essential cement which held a highly inegalitarian eighteenth-century social order together. Its preeminent role in this respect rested both on its capacity to discipline and change society, and on its potency as a system of ideas moulding people's understanding of that society.

Whereas historians working within the other two approaches have attempted to give the history of crime and the criminal law a broader significance simply by juxtaposing changes in crime or law enforcement to other historical changes that are considered significant (for example, changes in the cost of living, or the Industrial Revolution), those adopting a history-from-below approach have tried to provide some account of the processes that linked crime and criminal justice to the wider society. Their attention to process marks a considerable advance, but, nonetheless, the results of their work remain unsatisfactory. In particular the suggestion that the eighteenth-century criminal law held a position of overwhelming preeminence in sustaining the social order remains unconvincing. Proponents of this view have exaggerated both the extent to which the law replaced older instruments of control (whether institutionalized, like the poor law, or informal, like the authority exercised by landlords) and the extent to which it was an instrument of economic innovation and rationalization. They have also presented a much exaggerated estimate of the capacity of law to displace religion as the main source of legitimation for authority.[117] These exaggerations stem from a number of misconceptions about eighteenth-century society, misconceptions which touch on many of the issues already raised in this essay and which take us to the heart of the problem of how to integrate the study of crime and the criminal law into a broader picture of eighteenth-century England. These misconceptions are three.

First, a point we have previously noted and taken up, the idea that the eighteenth century witnessed a distinct stage or phase in capitalist innovation, during which the criminal law played a decisive role by enforcing new definitions of property. Insofar as the criminal law has played this role historically, it seems unlikely that it did so only during the eighteenth century. Here historians seem to have been mesmerized by the work of C.B. Macpherson and his account of the rise of the notion of absolute private property in the late seventeenth and early eighteenth centuries, an account that looks increasingly untenable in the light of subsequent work in the history of political thought.[118]

Second, an associated misconception is the notion that the eighteenth-century state was weak. The evidence offered for this proposition is the British state's failure to use force swiftly in episodes of public disorder, its display of ideological tenderness towards the liberties of the subject, and its lack of an effective bureaucracy.[119] As a result of this weakness, it is argued, it was the criminal law that became the principal terrain on which the eighteenth-century ruling class effected control of their social inferiors, a control which required the subtle manipulation of the law's coercive and ideological capacities. Not only is it inherently implausible to characterize as 'weak' a state which in recurrent international conflicts proved itself one of the most powerful in Europe, but also to do so is to overlook the proven capacity of the eighteenth-century state to pursue domestic policies in relation to, for example, taxation or the management of poverty with considerable success. In eighteenth-century terms, a state need not necessarily have been weak simply because it was obliged to affirm certain notions of individual liberty or because it lacked an administrative bureaucracy on the French model.[120]

Third and finally, historians adopting the history from below approach, in their concern to emphasize 'the great gulf between rich and poor', have been curiously blind to the size and importance of the large middling groups in English society and to their influence on the way the criminal law was used.[121] Edward Thompson in *Whigs and Hunters* has indeed argued that wide sections of the population could use the law defensively to hold off the rapacious exactions of the narrow eighteenth-century ruling class, but this fails to take sufficient account of the extent to which people from the middling groups in particular could put the law to use to pursue their own interests. Although the law did facilitate the exercise of authority by those at the apex of the eighteenth-century social hierarchy, it was principally employed by lesser men. Both as a practical instrument and as a system of ideas, 'the law was not the absolute property of patricians, but a limited multiple-use right available to most Englishmen'.[122]

These misconceptions all revolve around questions about the

character of the eighteenth-century British state. Who controlled it? To what ends was its power used? How great was that power? The answers to these questions provided in this essay are different from those offered by historians working with the approach we termed history from below. Nevertheless, like them, we believe the history of crime and the law can best be integrated into a broader picture of eighteenth-century English society by careful attention to its relationship with the history of the eighteenth-century state. We also believe the history of crime and the law can make an enormous contribution to providing better answers to these and other questions concerning the character of the state. The subject has, consequently, a great deal to offer that wider audience of historians and other scholars who are interested in coming to grips with questions of this kind. It is for this last reason in particular that the trend towards a greater emphasis on the study of process and institutions in work on eighteenth-century crime and the criminal law (often in reaction against work informed by the history from below approach, but at the same time stimulated by it) is so promising a development. It promises to enrich our knowledge of eighteenth-century governance by locating the criminal justice system alongside other policy areas like taxation or the poor law as part of the administrative repertoire of what is all too rarely recognized as a domestically active and, by contemporary standards, effective eighteenth-century state.

There is no doubt that much of this work involves a great stress on technicalities. This essay has included some discussion of these, if only because it is important that aspiring research students should be acquainted with some of the difficulties involved in research in the field. Nonetheless, we must remember that the study of such technicalities is a means to an end. That end is an understanding of the way eighteenth-century society was governed. Traditional political historians have offered a picture of eighteenth-century government which isolates a small group of men holding the reins of power and shows them exercising that power in a limited range of contexts (in particular, statesmanship and lining their own pockets). Those writing about eighteenth-century crime and the criminal law from a history from below standpoint have helped expand our view of what constituted the significant parts of the machinery of government and our sense of the problems with which government grappled. They have introduced into the picture the courts and the gallows, theft and public disorder, the use of brutal coercion, and the fostering of public consent.

Nevertheless, perhaps because this *is* history from below, for which the state represents a separate and antagonistic force, its practitioners (like the political historians) leave us with a vision of institutional power concentrated in the hands of an extremely limited group. They take insufficient account of the ways in which the substance of policies and the operation of institutions were shaped by the very extensive range of people who participated at one level or another (and to greater or lesser effect) in the machinery of government. In other words, the many faces and the many levels of institutional power – from parish to parliament – are not sufficiently explored. The history of crime and the criminal law can make a decisive contribution to their exploration. It is the most important task that faces students of eighteenth-century crime and criminal justice today.

Notes

1   This essay was first published in the *Journal of British Studies*, XXV, 1986, and has been updated to take account of subsequent publications. The authors would like to thank the *Journal of British Studies* and the University of Chicago Press for permission to re-publish it here. © 1986 by the North American Conference on British Studies. All rights reserved. 0021-9371/86/2504-0002$01.00.

2   For policing, see two important recent publications: D. Hay and F. Snyder, eds., *Policing and Prosecution in Britain, 1750–1850*, Oxford, 1989, and S.H. Palmer, *Police and Protest in England and Ireland, 1780–1850*, Cambridge, 1988.

3   Leon Radzinowicz, *A History of English Criminal Law and its Administration from 1750*, I, London, 1948, II, 1956, III, 1956, IV, 1968, V, with R. Hood, 1986; D. Beales, 'Peel, Russell and reform,' *Historical Journal*, XVII, 1974, p. 879.

4   S. and B. Webb, *English Local Government from the Revolution to the Municipal Corporations Act*, 9 vols., London, 1906–29; J.L. and B. Hammond, *The Village Labourer*, London, 1911, *The Town Labourer*, 1917, *The Skilled Labourer*, 1919. L.A. Knafla, 'Crime and criminal justice: a critical bibliography', in J.S. Cockburn, ed., *Crime in England*, London, 1977, offers an overview of work in the field at a time when the fruits of the new wave of research had scarcely begun to appear.

5   E.P. Thompson, *The Making of the English Working Class*, London, 1963; Thompson, 'The moral economy of the English crowd in the eighteenth century', *Past and Present*, L, 1971, pp. 76–136; Thompson, *Whigs and Hunters: The Origin of the Black Act*, London, 1975.

6   D. Hay, P. Linebaugh and E.P. Thompson, eds., *Albion's Fatal Tree*, London, 1975, p. 13.

7   J.M. Beattie, 'The criminality of women in eighteenth-century England,' *Journal of Social History*, VIII, 1975, p. 80. Also see J.M. Beattie, 'The pattern of crime in England, 1660–1800,' *Past and Present*, LXII, 1974, pp. 47–95.

8   M. Ignatieff, *A Just Measure of Pain: The Penitentiary in the Industrial Revolution, 1750–1850*, London, 1978. But see also his autocritique in 'State, civil society and total institutions: a critique of recent social histories of punishment', chapter 4 in S. Cohen and A. Scull, eds., *Social Control and the State*, Oxford, 1983.

9   D. Hay, 'War, dearth and theft in the eighteenth century: the record of the English courts', *Past and Present*, XCV, 1982, pp. 117–160, and 'Poaching and the game laws on Cannock Chase', chapter 5 in D. Hay, *et al.*, *Albion's Fatal Tree*.

10 E.J. Hobsbawm, 'Social Criminality', *Society for the Study of Labour History: Bulletin*, XXV, 1972, pp. 5–6.

11 For example, J.M. Beattie, 'Towards a study of crime in eighteenth-century England: a note on indictments', in P. Fritz and D. Williams, eds., *The Triumph of Culture: Eighteenth Century Perspectives*, Toronto, 1972, pp. 299–314.

12 H.S. Becker, *Outsiders: Studies in the Sociology of Deviance*, New York, 1973, p. 9.

13 For the most ambitious statement of this position, see J. Ditton, *Controlology: Beyond the New Criminology*, London, 1979. For the best discussion of its implications for the historian of crime and the criminal law, see V.A.C. Gatrell, 'The decline of theft and violence in Victorian and Edwardian England', chapter 9 in V.A.C. Gatrell, B. Lenman and G. Parker, eds., *Crime and the Law*, London, 1980.

14 See, for example, P. Corrigan and D. Sayer, *The Great Arch: English State Formation as Cultural Revolution*, Oxford, 1985. In turn, Hay's essay 'Property, authority and the criminal law', chapter 1 in Hay *et al.*, *Albion's Fatal Tree*, seems to draw heavily on Gramscian ideas.

15 J.H. Langbein, 'Albion's Fatal Flaws', *Past and Present*, XCVIII, pp. 96–120.

16 For example, D. Sugarman and G. Rubin, 'Introduction. Towards a new history of law and material society in England, 1750–1914', in

Rubin and Sugarman, eds., *Law, Economy and Society*, Abingdon, Oxon., 1984. For a historian's critical, though by no means unfriendly, assessment of legal historians' legal history, see D. Hay, 'The criminal prosecution in England and its historians', *Modern Law Review*, XLVII, 1984, pp. 1–29.

17 See the fears expressed by D. Philips, 'A just measure of crime, authority, hunters and blue locusts: the revisionist social history of crime and the law in Britain 1780–1950', chapter 3 in Cohen and Scull eds., *Social Control and the State*, pp. 67–8.

18 See M. Fores, 'The myth of a British industrial revolution', *History*, LXVI, 1981, pp. 181–98 and K. Tribe, *Genealogies of Capitalism*, London, 1981, chapter 3.

19 D. Hay, 'Crime, authority and the criminal law: Staffordshire, 1750–1800', University of Warwick Ph.D. dissertation, 1975.

20 J.M. Beattie, *Crime and the Courts in England 1660–1800*, Oxford, 1986.

21 See, in particular, P.J.R. King, 'Crime, law and society in Essex, 1740–1820', University of Cambridge Ph.D. dissertation, 1984, and S. Pole, 'Crime, society and law enforcement in Hanoverian Somerset', University of Cambridge Ph.D. dissertation, 1983. Some new directions have begun to be opened up by P. D'Sena, 'Perquisites and pilfering in the London docks, 1700–1800', Open University, M.Phil. dissertation, 1986, and R. Short, 'Female criminality, 1780–1830', Oxford University, M.Litt. dissertation, 1990.

22 The literature on these subjects is enormous. The following represent significant interventions in the debates and provide wide-ranging bibliographies. For interpersonal violence see T.R. Gurr, 'Historical trends in violent crimes: a critical review of the evidence', in M. Tonry and N. Morris, eds., *Crime and Justice*, III, Chicago, 1983, pp. 295–353; L. Stone, 'Interpersonal violence in English society', *Past and Present*, CI, 1983, pp. 22–33; J.A. Sharpe, 'The history of violence in England: some observations', *Past and Present*, CVIII, 1985, pp. 206–15, J.S. Cockburn, 'Patterns of violence in English society', *Past and Present*, CXXX, 1991, pp. 70–106. For offences against property, see J. Sharpe, *Crime in Early Modern England, 1550–1750*, London, 1984, chapter 3; Gatrell, 'The decline of theft and violence in Victorian and Edwardian England'.

23 Hay, 'Crime, authority and the criminal law: Staffordshire, 1750–1800', pp. 53–4; Pole, 'Crime, society and law enforcement in Hanoverian Somerset', pp. 180–1.

24 The relationship between violence and gender is another conceptual angle which is now attracting considerable interest. For contrasting approaches, see A. Clark, *Women's Silence, Men's Violence: Sexual Assault in England, 1770–1845*, London, 1987, R.

Porter, 'Rape: does it have a historical meaning?', is S. Tomaselli and R. Porter, eds., *Rape*, Oxford, 1987, and Short, 'Female criminality, 1780–1830'.

25 Hay, 'War, dearth and theft in the eighteenth century'.

26 Beattie, 'The pattern of crime in England', p. 95.

27 King, 'Crime, Law and Society in Essex, 1740–1820', p. 30.

28 *Leeds Intelligencer*, 9 February 1762.

29 S.R. Conway, 'The recruitment of criminals into the British army, 1775–1781', *Bulletin of the Institute of Historical Research*, LVIII, 1985, pp. 46–58, points out the many different channels through which offenders could find their way into the armed forces.

30 Hay, 'War, dearth and theft in the eighteenth century', p. 125.

31 King, 'Crime, law and society in Essex, 1740–1820', pp. 61–3.

32 E.J. Hobsbawm, 'Social criminality', p. 5.

33 See, for examples, 'Conference report: distinctions between socio-political and other forms of crime', *Society for the Study of Labour History: Bulletin*, XXV, 1972, pp. 5–21; Hay *et al.*, *Albion's Fatal Tree*; Thompson, *Whigs and Hunters*; J. Rule, 'Social crime in the rural south in the eighteenth and early nineteenth centuries', *Southern History*, I, 1979, pp. 135–53; B. Bushaway, *By Rite: Custom, Ceremony and Community in England, 1700–1880*, London, 1982, chapter 6.

34 Thompson, 'Moral economy', p. 78.

35 E.P. Thompson, 'Eighteenth-century English society: class struggle without class?', *Social History*, III, 1978, p. 154.

36 For a sympathetic but telling critique of Thompson's work on the crowd, see J. Bohstedt, *Riots and Community Politics in England and Wales 1790–1810*, Cambridge, Mass., 1983.

37 Though see D'Sena, 'Perquisites and pilfering in the London docks, 1700–1800', R.A.E. Wells, 'Sheep rustling in Yorkshire in the age of the industrial and agrarian revolutions', *Northern History*, XX, 1984, pp. 127–45, P. Edwards, *The Horse Trade of Tudor and Stuart England*, Cambridge, 1988, chapter 4.

38 P. Linebaugh, 'Eighteenth-century crime, popular movements and social control', *Society for the Study of Labour History: Bulation*, XXV, 1972, p. 12.

39 P.B. Munsche, *Gentlemen and Poachers*, Cambridge, 1981, chapter 3.

40 J. Styles, 'Embezzlement, industry and the law in England, 1500–1800', chapter 7 in M. Berg, P. Hudson and M. Sonenscher, eds., *Manufacture in Town and Country before the Factory*, Cambridge, 1983. For a similar argument in respect to gleaning, see P. King, 'Gleaners, farmers and the failure of legal sanctions in England, 1750–1850', *Past and Present*, CXXV, 1989, pp. 116–50.

41 The influence of C.B. Macpherson's *The Political Theory of Possessive Individualism*, Oxford, 1962 is crucial here.

42 For a critique of this mode of argument, see A. Giddens, *A Contemporary Critique of Historical Materialism*, London, 1981, pp. 18–19.

43 Beattie, *Crime and the Courts* illustrates the benefits of using the indictments as a starting point in this way. See our discussion of his work on pp. 230–40.

44 J. Styles, ' "Our traitorous money makers"; the Yorkshire coiners and the law, 1760–83', chapter 5 in J. Brewer and J. Styles, eds., *An Ungovernable People: The English and Their Law in the Seventeenth and Eighteenth Centuries*, London, 1980.

45 Edwards, *The Horse Trade of Tudor and Stuart England*, chapter 4. Also see B. Lemire, 'The theft of clothes and popular consumerism in early-modern England', *Journal of Social History*, XXIV, 1990, pp. 255–76, D'Sena, 'Perquisites and pilfering in the London docks, 1700–1800', and Wells, 'Sheep rustling in Yorkshire in the age of the industrial and agrarian revolutions'.

46 For a discussion by a modern criminologist of how such an analysis might be undertaken, see A.K. Cohen, 'The Concept of criminal organisation', *British Journal of Criminology*, XVII, 1977, pp. 97–111.

47 These and other eighteenth-century terms of social description require a great deal more investigation. Historians have made much play with the term 'labouring poor', but it is not clear that eighteenth-century usage warrants its by now almost standard employment as a supposedly non-anachronistic substitute for the modern term 'working class'.

48 P.J.R. King, 'Decision-makers and decision-making in the English criminal law, 1750–1800', *Historical Journal*, XXVII, 1984, pp. 25–58; P. Linebaugh, *The London Hanged*, London, 1991.

49 For an exploration of these issues in relation to horse theft, see J. Styles, 'Print and policing: crime advertising in eighteenth-century provincial England', in Hay and Snyder, eds., *Policing and Prosecution*, pp. 91 and 111.

50 See, for the use of such sources, P. King, 'Newspaper reporting prosecuting practice and perceptions of urban crime: the Colchester crime wave of 1765', *Continuity and Change*, II, 1987, pp. 423–54, and L.B. Faller, *Turned to Account: The Forms and Functions of Criminal Biography in Late Seventeenth- and Early Eighteenth-Century England*, Cambridge, 1987.

51 Hay, 'Crime, authority and the criminal law: Staffordshire, 1750–1800', chapters 2 and 3.

52 Hay, 'Property, authority and the criminal law'.

53   Langbein, 'Albion's Fatal Flaws'; King, 'Decision-makers and decision-making in the English criminal law'.
54   T.A. Green, *Verdict According to Conscience: Perspectives on the English Criminal Trial Jury, 1200–1800*, Chicago, 1985.
55   King, 'Decision-makers and decision-making in the English criminal law', p. 26.
56   For two rather different perspectives on who controlled the workings of the criminal law, compare Hay, 'Property, authority and the criminal law', pp. 38–9 and pp. 60–1.
57   Brewer and Styles, eds., *An Ungovernable People*, Introduction, p. 20.
58   P. King, ' "Illiterate plebians, easily misled": jury composition, experience and behaviour in Essex, 1735–1815', and D. Hay, 'The Class composition of the Palladium of Liberty: trial juries in the eighteenth century', in J. Cockburn and T.A. Green, eds., *Twelve Good Men and True: The Criminal Trial Jury in England, 1200–1800*, Princeton, 1988.
59   Hay, 'Property, authority and the criminal law', p. 46.
60   King, 'Decision-makers and decision-making in the English criminal law'.
61   Hay, 'Property, authority and the criminal law', p. 44.
62   Green, *Verdict according to conscience*, chapter 7, esp. footnote 156.
63   Beattie, *Crime and the courts*, chapter eight, and 'London juries in the 1690s', in Cockburn and Green (eds.), *Twelve Good men and True*.
64   Green, *Verdict according to conscience*, chapter 7; J. Brewer, 'The Wilkites and the law 1763–1774: a study of radical notions of governance', in Brewer and Styles, eds. *An Ungovernable People*, pp. 128–71.
65   For a characterisation of this self-confirming aspect of Hay's argument as a peculiarly Marxist shortcoming, see Langbein, 'Albion's Fatal Flaws', pp. 114–15. Note that here is little evidence that Hay himself wishes the argument to be carried on at this 'rarefied' level.
66   J.H. Langbein, 'Shaping the eighteenth-century criminal trial: a view from the Ryder sources', *The University of Chicago Law Review*, L, 1983, p. 134.
67   J.H. Langbein, 'The criminal trial before the lawyers', *The University of Chicago Law Review*, XLV, 1978, pp. 263–316, and Langbein, 'Shaping the eighteenth-century criminal trial'.
68   Langbein, 'Shaping the eighteenth-century criminal trial', p. 133.
69   For an account which stresses one lawyer's flamboyant self-promotion in the role of defence council, see J. Beattie, 'Garrow for the defence', *History Today*, XLI, February 1991, pp. 49–53.
70   It is necessary to ask what improvements in policing could, under

eighteenth-century conditions, have plausibly been made that would have achieved this goal. For a discussion of some of the possibilities an limitations of eighteenth-century police reform, see J. Styles, 'Sir John Fielding and the problem of criminal investigation in eighteenth-century England', *Transactions of the Royal Historical Society*, 5th series, XXXIII, 1983, pp. 127–49.

71 It may be, as John Beattie has tentatively suggested, that more extensive government involvement in criminal prosecutions was a stimulus to change.

72 Styles, 'Our traitorous money makers', p. 208 and footnote 177.

73 See Munsche, *Gentlemen and Poachers*, pp. 93–102 for what is perhaps an over-generous account of magisterial rectitude in these matters, and R.B. Shoemaker, *Prosecution and Punishment: Petty Crime and the Law in London and Rural Middlesex, c.1660–1725*, Cambridge, 1991, chapter 7 for a more sceptical view. For high court and parliamentary attempts to impose constraints on magistrates in the exercise of their summary powers, see N. Landau, *The Justices of the Peace 1679–1760*, Berkeley, 1984, pp. 348–52.

74 Landau, *Justices of the Peace*, pp. 343–59 tackles various aspects of this supervisory relationship. Douglas Hay and Ruth Paley are currently working on a calendar of references to Staffordshire cases in King's Bench archives which, when completed, will appear in the Staffordshire Record Series.

75 Michel Foucault's work – informed as it is by the notion that the prison is in some sense a representative modern institution – has undoubtedly played an especially important part in attracting social scientists to the history of prisons. See especially M. Foucault, *Surveillir et punir. Naissance de la prison*, Paris, 1975, translated into English by A. Sheridan as *Discipline and Punish*, New York, 1978, and also the comments of M. Ignatieff in 'State, civil society and total institutions'.

76 S. and B. Webb, *English Prisons under Local Government*, London, 1922; Radzinowicz, *History of English Criminal Law*, vol. I.

77 See, for example, Langbein, 'Albion's fatal flaws', pp. 115–19, and also pp. 240–50 below.

78 P. Linebaugh, 'The Tyburn riot against the surgeons', chapter 2 in Hay *et al.*, *Albion's Fatal Tree*.

79 R. Ekirch, *Bound for America: Convict Transportation, Crime and Society in the Eighteenth Century*, Oxford, 1987.

80 R. Morgan, 'Divine philanthropy: John Howard reconsidered', *History*, LXII, 1977, pp. 388–410; Ignatieff, *A Just Measure of Pain*; R. Evans, *The Fabrication of Virtue: English Prison Architecture, 1750–1840*, Cambridge, 1982.

81 Though see Ignatieff's second thoughts in his 'State, society and

total institutions'. Thomas Green's recent study of the criminal trial jury incidentally provides material for the reassessment of another set of 'reform' proposals. Green suggests that the campaign for reform of the capital statutes should be seen not primarily as an attempt to change the conventional tariff of penalties, but rather as an attempt to take the power to tailor a decision to fit their assessment of a particular case out of the hands of the jury, Green, *Verdict According to Conscience*, Chapter 7. Green naturally focuses on the jury, but in fact the argument can be given a more general reference. It is clear that many reformers were concerned to reduce the discretionary powers of judges also.

82 Though see Margaret DeLacy's critical comments in M.E. DeLacy, 'Grinding men good? Lancashire's prisons at mid-century', chapter 8 in V. Bailey, ed., *Policing and Punishment in Nineteenth Century Britain*, London, 1981, and also some questioning of the established chronology in her 1980 Princeton Ph.D. dissertation, 'County prison administration in Lancashire, 1690–1850', especially chapters 1 to 4. Michael Ignatieff, in 'State, civil society and total institutions', pp. 82–3, concedes in the face of DeLacy's criticisms that changes came more slowly and were implemented more unevenly than readers of his book may have been led to believe, but remains strikingly uninterested in the possibility that traditional views of the basic shape of change may be more fundamentally flawed.

83 Michael Ignatieff deserves credit for taking up the question of who was sentenced to imprisonment and on what grounds, and of the effect of changes of sentencing policy on penal administration in *A Just Measure of Pain*, especially chapters 2 and 4 – if only in a rather impressionistic fashion.

84 See J. Innes, 'Parliament and the shaping of eighteenth-century English social policy', *Transactions of the Royal Historical Society*, 5th series, XL, 1990 and J. Beattie, 'London crime and the making of the English criminal law, 1689–1718', in L. Davison, *et al.*, eds., *Reform and Regulation: The Debate over Social and Economic Problems in England, 1689–1750*, 1992.

85 We have previously expressed our own reservations about the usefulness of fluctuations in indictments as a guide to changes in the 'real' incidence of crime. However, it is clear that contemporaries did often respond to them on the assumption that they offered such a guide.

86 J. Beattie, 'London crime and the making of the English criminal law, 1689–1718', in L. Davison, *et al.* eds., *Reform and Regulation*.

87 For the most ambitious work in these areas to date, see R. McGowen, 'The body and punishment in eighteenth-century England', *Journal*

of Modern History, 59, 1987, pp. 651–79 and 'The changing face of God's justice: the debates over divine and human punishment in eighteenth-century England', *Criminal Justice History*, 9, 1988, pp. 63–98.

88 Landau, *Justices of the Peace*, chapter 11 and *passim*, supports the Webbs' view that justices of the peace tended to become more active and conscientious as the eighteenth century progressed, a change she describes in terms of a changing vision of the ideal justice. For the Webbs, see *The Parish and the County*, London, 1906, especially pp. 350–73.

89 J.M. Innes, 'Prisons for the poor: English Bridewells, 1555–1800', in F. Snyder and D. Hay eds., *Labour, Law and Crime* (London, 1987), pp. 42–122; R.B. Shoemaker, *Prosecution and Punishment: Petty Crime and the Law in London and Rural Middlesex, c.1660–1725*, Cambridge, 1991.

90 Justices' notebooks are the other indispensable source for the study of petty offences. The virtue of house of correction calendars as a source lies first in their wider chronological and geographical coverage, and second in the fact that they shed more light on the particulars of sentencing.

91 This section draws on our joint research in progress on eighteenth-century legislation in general and criminal legislation in particular, part of which has appeared in Innes, 'Parliament and the shaping of eighteenth-century English social policy'. We should like to express our gratitude to Sheila Lambert for her generosity in sharing with us her notes on failed bills, 1660–1792. Responsibility for the conclusions we have drawn from this material is entirely ours.

92 Hay, 'Property, authority and the criminal law', p. 18.

93 Radzinowicz, *History of the English Criminal Law*, vol. I, chapter 1.

94 Thompson, *Whigs and Hunters*; Hay, 'Property, authority and the criminal law'.

95 Hay, 'Property, authority and the criminal law', p. 21.

96 Thompson, *Whigs and Hunters*, p. 207.

97 Hay, 'Property, authority and the criminal law', pp. 20–1.

98 Hay, 'Property, authority and the criminal law', p. 20.

99 Public Record Office, SP 14/140, f. 82, State Papers James 1, 1622, petition of worsted makers in Norfolk, Suffolk and Essex, n.d. (1622–3).

100 Langbein, 'Albion's fatal flaws', p. 118.

101 1 Edw, VI, c.12; 2/3 Edw. VI, c.33; 8 Eliz., c.4.

102 One of the most important exceptions was 15 Geo. II, c.34, 1741, which made sheep stealing a capital offence. But capital statutes of

this kind, dealing in one statute with an offence that was very common, formed a much smaller proportion of capital statutes in the eighteenth century than they had in the sixteenth century.

103   8 Geo. II, c.6; 12 Geo. I, c.36; 9 Geo. II, c.29; 15 Geo. II, c.13; 24 Geo. II, c.11.

104   E. Cruikshanks and H. Erskine-Hill, 'The Waltham Black Act and Jacobitism', *Journal of British Studies*, XXIV, 1985, pp. 358–65; J. Styles, 'Criminal records', *Historical Journal*, XX, 1977, pp. 977–81.

105   8 Geo. II, c.20; 10 Geo. II, c.32.

106   For the statutes against forgery, see L. Davison, 'Public policy in an age of economic expansion: the search for commercial accountability in England, 1690–1750', Harvard University Ph.D. dissertation, 1990, chapter 8, and work in progress by Randall McGowen.

107   It is extremely difficult to establish precisely the kind of punishment intended in the case of failed bills, since even when the text of a draft bill survives, the specific punishments proposed were, as a matter of form, always left blank.

108   For example the succession of bills 'for the more effectual preventing, and punishing, the stealing, or unlawful killing of cattle', introduced in the sessions of 1714–15, 1715–16 and 1717–18; *Journals of the House of Commons*, XVIII, 1714–18.

109   For example the bill for 'better preventing the malicious burning and destroying houses, buildings, fences, corn, hay, grass and other improvements', introduced in 1698–9; *Journals of the House of Commons*, XII, 1697–9.

110   For example, 25 Geo. II, c.10, an act for the more effectual securing mines of black lead from theft and robbery.

111   For example, 22 Geo. II, c.27, an act for the more effectual preventing frauds and abuses committed by persons employed in various manufactures.

112   British Library, Additional Manuscripts 35590, folios 267–8, Horatio Walpole to the Earl of Hardwicke, 25 March 1749.

113   Northamptonshire Record Office, L(C) 1732, diary of William Hay, entry for 13 March 1733–4.

114   *Journals of the House of Commons*, XVIII, 1714–18, p. 768, 18 March 1717–18.

115   Cumbria Record Office, Carlisle, D/Lons/W/58, Lowther Manuscripts, Sir John Lowther to John Spedding, 11 February 1752.

116   Hay, *et al., Albion's Fatal Tree*, p. 13.

117   For an impassioned, if rather overwrought presentation of the ideological importance of religion in eighteenth-century England, see J.C.D. Clark, *English Society 1688–1832*, Cambridge, 1985, especially pp. 87–90.

118 Macpherson, *The Political Theory of Possessive Individualism*. For work that challenges Macpherson's account see A. Ryan, *Property and Political Theory*, Oxford, 1984, chapter 1, R. Tuck, *Natural Rights Theories*, Cambridge, 1979, especially pp. 2–3, and J. Tully, *A Discourse on Property*, Cambridge, 1980, especially p. 172.

119 E.P. Thompson, 'Patrician society, plebeian culture', *Journal of Social History*, VII, 1974, p. 403. A more nuanced analysis is Thompson, 'Eighteenth-century English society', especially p. 162. For a critique of Thompson's views, see p. Anderson, *Arguments within English Marxism*, London, 1980, pp. 87–94.

120 For a wide-ranging discussion of these issues, see J. Brewer, *The Sinews of Power: War Money and the English State, 1688–1783*, London, 1989.

121 Hay, 'Property, authority and the criminal law', p. 18. For a recent study which emphasises the significance of these groups, see P. Langford, *A Polite and Commercial People: England, 1727–1783*, Oxford, 1989.

122 Brewer and Styles, eds., *An Ungovernable People*, p. 20. It appears that even the labouring poor were able to share, to a greater extent than Brewer and Styles suggested, in this 'multiple-use right'.

Rough usage: prostitution, law and the social historian

Prostitution and the historian

It was almost twenty years ago, when the 'new' social history was in its infancy, that Carroll Smith-Rosenberg asserted that 'the most significant and intriguing historical questions relate to the events, the causal patterns, the psychodynamics of private places: the household, the family, the bed, the nursery, and kinship systems'.[1] Smith-Rosenberg develops a subtle interpretation of the relation between the public and the private, but subsequent studies have not always demonstrated so critical a discernment. The divide between the private – the favoured territory of much of the 'new' social history – and the well-worn grooves of the public has inevitably become problematised. For many feminist historians, acutely aware of the symbolic and actual ramifications of this dichotomy, the defining boundaries between these two spheres are neither simple nor static. The divide remains, for students of gender, a contested, paradoxical and constantly changing terrain.

Paradigmatic of this confusion, this blurring of seemingly simple divisions, is the phenomenon of prostitution, a topic which has received in recent years considerable historical attention.[2] Most British studies have concentrated on the notorious Contagious Diseases Acts of the mid nineteenth century.[3] Yet a broader historical consideration of prostitution has ramifications in a host of fields pertinent to social historians. Prostitution-related offences have always constituted a large proportion of female arrests. It has been a common means for women of earning a living, and insofar as it has represented a more lucrative option than other work generally available to them, it speaks of women's narrow economic and social options. The huge volume of nineteenth- and early-twentieth-century literature dealing with and detailing prostitution should alert us, too, to its historical centrality. Most of all, perhaps, prostitution encapsulates the paradox of the attempted naturalisation of socio-sexual roles in this period, through a codification of the private and the public.

My concern here is with how research in this area might pressure social history into a serious reconsideration of the limitations of such simple and uncontested dualities as the 'separate spheres'. A historical assessment of prostitution and responses to it will challenge overly simple thinking about the private and the public, and also prompt new approaches to topics which already boast an impressive historiographical heritage.

Prostitution renders public acts deemed appropriate only in private contexts. Though prostitution and sexuality are by no means coterminous, Judith Walkowitz's characterisation of sexuality in the Victorian age as a specially privileged 'core, private identity, yet also something publicly dangerous' offers a useful framework for considering prostitution historically.[4] In this trade, individuals defined as private by their sex (women) find a niche in the world of the public (the marketplace) – though the ugly sub-history of coercion modifies considerably the glories of their economic power. The Contagious Diseases Acts of the 1860s, the Criminal Law Amendment Acts of 1885 and 1912 and regulations promulgated between 1916 and 1918 under the wartime Defence of the Realm Act (DORA), demonstrate the responses of an increasingly interventionist state. The punitive impact of all of these measures was to deny women engaged in prostitution a separation between their private and their public lives, because they insisted on maintaining an inappropriate and public persona.[5]

Prostitution legislation has, in the modern period and arguably earlier as well, focused primarily on defining the public and the private, and on establishing the actions seemly within each. Regulations issued in 1162, governing London brothels, detail harsh punishment for women who attempted to prostitute in secret.[6] Public women were forced to relinquish their rights to privacy, without gaining any consonant rights in the public sphere.

Prostitution, despite legislative attempts in this arena, necessarily challenges how we read and understand the public and the private. It subverts how we read the world of work. And it complicates any simple dichotomy between resistance and exploitation. In all these ways, it offers historians new avenues for exploring old as well as newly-realised historical issues, necessitating a radical rethinking of hospital and health history, welfare history and legal history. A study of prostitution offers us an opportunity for a broader placement of the sex-power grid in our assessment of how discourses of power come to be, are resisted, and reformulated. It suggests, in short, a mechanism for finding points of continuity between political and social history.

It also raises allied questions about the nature and the legitimation of work, and the relation between the construction of identity and work. Though Luise White has argued a case for reading prostitution within a labour history framework – and there are good reasons for so doing – in the end, that approach will prove insufficient.[7] It will once more press our understanding into a mould already conditioned by existing definitions of public and private, consonant with our division of the political and the social. When we 'repoliticise' social history and conversely enter into a dialogue with the concerns of political history, when we draw together connecting strands that link these artificially separated camps of our scholarship, then can we hope to examine adequately a phenomenon as complex, as tenacious and as brutal as prostitution.

Social history is caught too often between microstudies of ever smaller 'communities' and the totalising tendencies of generalised theses. Prostitution deals with relatively small numbers of disparate and displaced persons, difficult to track and even more difficult to elucidate. At the same time, and not unconvincingly, prostitution has frequently been held up as a mirror of the female condition in any number of patriarchally-organised social settings. What social history must do is to reconcile the theory and the description, the general observations and the crucial case studies. Ellen Ross and Rayna Rapp have argued that community practices are termini for larger systems.[8] It is the challenge of social history to see and draw clearly that relationship.

Categorisation

Commentators on the 'social evil' abound in Victorian and Edwardian Britain. A significant characteristic of these writings

– in Europe and America as in Britain – is a view of prostitution as a fixed and categorisable phenomenon. This tendency, not wholly abandoned by modern historians, enacts very effectively some subtle and unstated moral codes which feed into broader cultural and moral practices. Categorising proved a superb mechanism for separating out and defining the oddity against the norm. A vast literature sought to identify the prostitute, to examine the causes of her (and it was always her) waywardness and assess the possibility of her reform, to castigate the class from which she was assumed to have been drawn and to ram home the evils of poverty, idleness, frivolity and alcohol.

This stress on the motives propelling women into prostitution is itself an important pathologising device. We do not ask what factors predispose some women to enter sweatshop textile work or trades as unpleasant as white lead production or match-making; we accept economic coercion in these cases as self-evident. Yet we continue to search for (and often find) special factors in the case of prostitution.[9] Are we, as were the investigators of the past, perpetuating a pathology of victimisation by so constantly harping on motive?

The prostitute, literally and metaphorically in this literature, becomes her body, that which Foucault would represent as one of the prime targets for the exercise of power in the modern world.[10] For women (a 'category' largely ignored in Foucault's otherwise important work) this was certainly the case. It was the body that was restrained and constrained by elaborate and exaggerated dress; it was the unclothed or inappropriately-clothed female body that was removed from the public sites of work as protective legislation closed doors on women's economic opportunities; and it was, in consequence but paradoxically, the prostitute body which theoretically served as women's final guarantee of supper and the 'security' of male attention. In the case of the prostitute, the thoroughness of this form of power was extraordinary, totally identifying woman and body. In late-medieval London, regulations named the prostitute 'as a woman who lives by her body', suggesting that Foucault's periodisation may not be wholly helpful for studying women.[11]

This sexualised identity while clearly paramount is yet endlessly contradictory. Women were represented as both in the grip of their natural and unrestrainable passions and at the same time victims of the cunning of others – of men, of foreigners and so on. Though both of these identities construe women as victims, they simultaneously suggest women's culpability. The assumption that uncoverable and explainable factors 'result' in the creation of a recognisable and bounded prostitute identity has produced a case history approach amongst both contemporary commentators and modern historians. Like Robert Padgug, I am dubious as to the value of this pathologically-oriented approach, and its encourage-ment of a psycho-pathology of discrete groups whose sexuality is fixed, individual and apparently unchanging.[12] The reality of life on the street and in the houses becomes a pawn in the hands of homogeneity. It opens the door to a denial of the different experi-ences that necessarily constitute an accurate picture, and offers a 'model' case history applicable across the board. Commentators speaking with one voice – that of a shamed or outraged moralism – assume one voice, the male, can lay bare the 'secrets' of this female trade.

In the absence of alternative direct testimony this approach has inevitably found favour amongst historians, and has contributed heavily to what Judith Walkowitz has termed the 'making of an outcast group', to the separate and external construction of a controllable identity. Indeed, anti-regulationist Yves Guyot pointed out in 1884 that registration encouraged 'people to look upon prostitutes as creatures different to themselves, having another sort of body, nerves, and brains than we have'.[13]

The commentaries of the nineteenth and early twentieth centuries form a remarkably coherent group. Empirical in emphasis, these studies were uniformly the work of men.[14] The same explanations, directives and homilies link their works;[15] doctors, police consta-bles, chaplains and journalists all draw similar profiles of the iden-tifiable prostitute (drawn from women working the streets) and of the causes of her 'fall'. All demonstrate the contradictions that arise out of this need for taxonomic identification, of labelling to construct simultaneously the deviant and the essential woman. On the one hand, we find constant allusion to a host of external reasons for prostitution – parental neglect, low wages, overcrowded housing, seduction – which allowed the new category of feminine, dependent, asexual, helpless 'Woman' to stand firm.[16] On the other hand, in the same works and alongside these empirically testable hypotheses, references to inherent female peccadilloes abound.

Women in prostitution demonstrated the 'worst' characteristics of their sex: 'bad' or 'loose' character, temperament, lust, laziness, inherent criminality.[17]

This essentialist doctrine is perhaps at its most revealing in the widely-remarked aggression and assertiveness which investigators found in their subject group. More than any other observation, it was this stress on female assertiveness which survived into the twentieth century. At the height of the nineteenth-century debate, commentators described how shameless women would flaunt themselves, plucking at the sleeves of strangers.

Have not our young men as they left office, counting house, or shop had the 'social evil' literally thrust upon them continually night after night? Is it not the fact that, whatever may be the original cause of their fall, women are too often the aggressors?[18]

The same voices were heard during the First World War. Military officials, journalists and politicians all railed against the inability of fighting men to rid themselves of persistent women hanging on their arms with seductive words. Earl Derby at the War Office described conditions to the Secretary of State for Home Affairs.

it is almost impossible for soldiers to escape the attentions of the women on the streets and those attentions almost take the form of highway robbery so violent in certain cases is the women's conduct in hanging onto soldiers in the streets.[19]

The confusion over which of these two creatures was 'natural woman' – the wronged or the incorrigible – left little space for the voices of actual women to be heard.

Little other than this pathology has survived. This generic profile reveals a deep, albeit contradictory, concern for maintaining consensual boundaries between public and private. Two distinct categories govern these explanations: public and external factors separate from the woman herself (though frequently grounded in domestic failure), and individual but feminine private failings of character or morals. That the two are kept separate as determinants, even if co-mingling within a given woman, is revealing of the need to maintain this ideological premise; that all the investigators called for action against prostitution, and that none were proponents of a *laissez-faire* approach, is similarly suggestive. Women, whether they chose to enter, or were catapulted into the public arena, were no longer private women; it was only public means that could succeed in returning them to their proper sphere.

These studies share, too, a conflation of prostitution with street-walking, the more visible and the most vulnerable sector of the trade. Traditionally the street trade has also been regarded as the least glamorous and most down-trodden sector, peopled by the poorest and least successful women. Yet this traditional scale of assessment may reflect assumption more than it does reality.[20] Street-walkers constitute, of course, the public face of prostitution. They have consistently, and increasingly, been the target of police and community action, a symbol of the defiant and deviant woman. Attention to and scorning of the public woman neatly feeds the maintenance of public and private.[21] Extensionist C.W. Shirley Deakin was comfortable in asserting that 'it is reasonable to treat as a common prostitute every woman who can be shown to be an habitual street walker ... or in the habit of hiring herself out to different men ... and whom no respectable man will acknowledge as either wife or mistress'.[22] Deakin here differentiates between an acceptable private prostitution aping the institutions of hetero-sexual monogamy, and the woman publicly flaunting this order. Moreover, his sentiments link prostitution back to men's choices. Deakin's definition, similar to that of other investigators, demon-strates where the power in naming the prostitute lay. The private 'private life' and individual subservience of mistresses clearly mitigated the irregularity of their affairs. Public women, on the other hand, in casting off the patronage of the individual male in favour of the monies of many, clearly crossed a crucial line be-tween public and private.

Criminalisation and resistance

It is this 'common prostitute', this 'public woman', who has con-sistently been the target of the criminal law. Today prostitution is heavily over-represented in the arrests of women; in the United States some 70% of incarcerated women were first arrested on charges of prostitution.[23] We have no comparable figures for the nineteenth century. Whilst not as massive as today, prostitution arrests figure largely in the annals of female crime. Barbara Hobson's work on nineteenth-century Boston indicates that 30% of female convictions in the period 1816–50 were for prostitution, and only drunkenness accounted for a larger percentage of female court appearances.[24] Women arraigned on unrelated charges frequently had (and have) experience in prostitution as well. Clive Emsley's observation of an increasing equivalence in popular thought between the prostitute and the woman criminal should come as no surprise: 'the description "hardened offender" and "abandoned prostitute" were almost synonymous'.[25]

Yet there is remarkably little British historical work specifically on women and crime in the modern period.[26] Emsley points out that women were regarded 'as appendages to thieves', a portrait often sustained by historians who show 'the women of the criminal class as, primarily, the aiders and abettors of their menfolk'.[27] Feminist criminologists argue that criminological thinking has neglected a consideration of an independent female criminality or of the meaning of female crime, marginalising women caught in the criminal justice net twice over.[28] Historians, it would seem, have followed suit.

In our period, soliciting was a criminal offence in England only when it caused annoyance to the person solicited. A series of acts nonetheless allowed for the apprehension of women for disorderly behaviour and loitering in a public place.[29] The legal issue at stake was what was being done in public. During the years of the Contagious Diseases Acts two sets of laws applied in different areas of the country. The trade of women working in the subjected districts was legalised on pain of regular examination for venereal disease, while in areas beyond the Acts' jurisdiction, women continued to be liable to arrest as vagrants or disorderly persons. The legal meaning of public and private had reached an experimental phase, though the ground rules remained in place. Prostitute women remained definitionally public, but now public control was stepped up in selected areas in ways which emphasised the ideological divide powerfully.

Brothels, though theoretically illegal, operated openly in areas scheduled under the Acts. Keepers' liability was effectively limited to prosecution for harbouring diseased prostitutes whom the Acts required to be examined or hospitalised, encouraging complicity between brothel-managers and police. Brothels became targets of judicial action only when they permitted refuge to individual suspects. In regulated Plymouth, the brothel was officially acknowledged. A local ordinance dictated that brothel keepers house

no more than one woman in each room.[30] The Minority Report
of the 1882 Commons Select Committee on the Acts, which called
for their repeal, attacked this public–private discrepancy in trenchant
terms: 'law designed for suppressing vice is used . . . as an instrument
for regulating vice in open co-operation with systematic law-
breakers . . . the system of toleration and co-operation thus established in reality amounts to a "licence" of brothel-keeping and of
prostitution'.[31]

While private non-street prostitution thus enjoyed some immunity, women in the trade – still dubbed public – were culpable at
every turn. The Acts legalised military prostitution but criminalised
its providers; refusal to submit to examination was criminally
punishable, and registration was achieved through police surveillance. These were public women and in 'choosing' what it meant
to be public and female were always liable to apprehension. In the
courtroom their testimonies were rarely entertained, and even where
magistrates dismissed cases against them on grounds of legal inadequacy, women in the dock could still expect a sermon on their
ill-doings before release.

During the latter months of the 1914–18 war, Defence of
the Realm Act Regulation 40D made it an offence for a woman
with a venereal disease to engage in or invite sexual relations
with a member of HM Armed Forces. No bar was placed on
the publication in the media of the names and addresses of
accused women, even though other forms of press censorship
were readily embraced under the Act. Protests led the government to request that the press desist from publication until after
disposition, but no obligatory procedure was ever laid down.
The identity of the accusing soldier was, as a matter of course,
withheld.

In both cases accused women, named as prostitutes, were objects of official and public suspicion. It was they who bore the
burden of proof, in a curious inversion of established judicial
protocol and principle. The contrast between the careful empirical
(if inaccurate) definition of the 'fallen' woman built up by investigators detailing age, occupation, literacy, religious beliefs, family
background and so on and the vagueness of the legal definition of
a 'common prostitute', or of the source of infection, is striking.[32]

The legal position of their clients further deepened the criminal
identity of the women. Though Cardwell's Army Order of 1873

docked the pay of soldiers contracting venereal disease, men were never targets of direct police and judicial scrutiny. Metropolitan Police employees seconded to Contagious Diseases Acts duty were concerned wholly with women as potential conduits of infection, and not with military personnel or civilian men. Half a century later, little had changed. The 1908 Royal Commission on the Metropolitan Police argued against legislation constraining men from soliciting women on the grounds that 'the community at large', supportive of more punitive responses to female unchastity, would find such laws unacceptable.[33] Figures reported to that Commission show that whilst in the years 1904–6, 7651 women were arrested for prostitution, and 7121 of them convicted, there were no male arrests for solicitation.[34]

'Prostitutes, like animals, had no legal personalities.'[35] Ironically, in the nineteenth century when women had few legal rights they could, nonetheless, still commit legal wrongs. The theme of the aggressive woman luring the unwary youth to his doom was a common one, as we have seen, and the law spoke specifically of the need to protect men. This protective position contrasts wildly, of course, with the state's insistence on non-interference in the labour context, where men's contractual rights appeared a sacrosanct and identity-giving power. Business contracts made for sexual purposes with prostitute women apparently fell under a separate category.[36] There can be little doubt that it was not the woman's right to contract her sexual services that was upheld by Britain's contract-based legal system.

This unevenness in the law's acknowledgement of women, alongside the constancy of its antipathy, is definitive of its treatment of what it rendered, with lingering medievalism, the female crime – prostitution.[37] The legal system, like other instruments of power, experimented with punitive and regulatory approaches to prostitution, sometimes separating and sometimes combining them. We see in these various legislative efforts an active process of naming and codification, a constant reworking of what constituted the natural and social role required of women and upheld by law. Marriage and prostitution, where sexuality forms a definitional base line, both demonstrate the law's part in legitimating normative patterns of behaviour and relations crucially and historically structured around gender.[38] Labour laws, where sexuality crucially determines suitability and access to employment, are similar. Both suggest that the law is 'a paradigm of maleness . . . a symbol and a vehicle of male authority'.[39]

Luise White contends that 'men and male control enter prostitution only *after* the state does'.[40] Whilst a case can be made for the encroachment of 'big crime' and thence male control of prostitution as a result of the state's success in driving prostitutes further and further into the underworld, this reading might also connote a genderless or gender-neutral state on whose mistakes men made good.[41] On the contrary, and as in the informal collusion of trade unionism and the state in the passing of protective labour legislation, it was a male state which made possible individual men's power-broking in a female world. An analysis of the law that ignored the input of its attendant institutions – the state and the police, in particular – would decontextualise the historical questions beyond use. Pinpointing timelessly precise relations or collusion between those who variously exercised power fixes an ahistorical gaze. A social history of the law will make little headway unless it can contextualise the law's doings as echoes of specific and unequal power relations which cast class, gender and race divisions as specifically natural barriers to change.

As we develop a better understanding of the complex relationships between state, law and work, a case may emerge for seeing large-scale prostitution (and its concomitant, a more attentive state) as the feminised auxiliary service industry to changing male work patterns, perhaps most particularly in 'frontier' contexts such as the opening of the American West, the Europeanising of South Africa or the development of Australia.[42] The impassioned statement of one woman befriended by Josephine Butler makes clear the nexus of domination which makes this possible.

It is *men*, only *men*, from the first to the last, that we have to do with! To please a man I did wrong at first, then I was flung about from man to man. Men police lay hand on us. By men we are examined, handled, doctored, and messed on with. In the hospital it is a man again who makes prayers and reads the Bible for us. We are up before magistrates who are men, and we never get out of the hands of men.[43]

Carol Smart has suggested that the law 'reproduces and perpetuates the most secure foundations of patriarchal relations, namely the family and gender divisions'.[44] To her list, we may add as a crucial element of defining and maintaining those gender divisions, the institution of female prostitution, and of prostitution as definitionally and essentially feminine. The making of a prostitute class of women, always available but always unacceptable, demonstrates the simultaneous consistency and contradiction of the public and the private as determining factors in the making of the modern legal system.

To see the law as a powerful vehicle for the construction of sexual identity does not necessarily suggest a monolithic reading of power which cannot account for subversion, resistance or change, though resistance seems to have led more frequently to modification rather than abandonment of controlling mechanisms. Control does not have to conjure up a vision of a monolithic and anonymous state, or indeed, of successful imposition by would-be controllers. In constructing an identity around the subject's failure to integrate – thereby creating the spectre of Otherness – these varying strategies could justify repression even while guaranteeing the continuity of the supply of women. We see, nonetheless, negligible variation in the sources of consternation, and little substantive change in where danger was located – in the publicly-displayed body of the self-motivated woman. When 'clandestine' prostitution surfaced as a concern at the end of the nineteenth century, reaching its height during the 1914–18 war (when 'giddy' young women rather than 'professional' prostitutes were perceived as a major source of military contagion), truly 'private' prostitution still remained untouched and undefined. The exercise of power is never successful and static. Shifts and relocations of targets demonstrate the historical, social and often experimental nature of power relations.

The very existence, however, of 'clandestine' women does suggest effective, though not necessarily organised, resistance which legislative and judicial action seemed unable wholly to dampen. Prostitute women found a host of (sometimes entertaining) ways to resist control, whether formal or informal. In the 1870s, the more mobile of those affected by the Contagious Diseases Acts moved their business out of the scheduled districts into areas where their liability and visibility would be reduced. Others found more dramatic means of demonstrating their dissatisfaction with the Acts. Reports from the detaining Lock Hospitals frequently discuss ways and means to dampen the actions of refractory women who were breaking windows, refusing orders and, not infrequently, running away.[45] Escape was not limited to women confined by law. Women in rescue homes and penitents' asylums often found

the conditions irksome and indulged in what the London Rescue Society deemed 'unauthorised leavetaking'. In the later nineteenth century, the figures released by the society suggest that
at least 12% of the inmates, and often more, annually left in this
manner.[46]

The growth of houses of prostitution disguised as massage
parlours in the later years of the century might also be read as a
quirky form of resistance, a means of duping the law by appearing
compliant while carrying on business regardless. The reports of
police assigned surveillance duty outside blocks of flats and massage establishments demonstrate considerable frustration.

We may also need to reframe our thinking about the meaning
and the timing of what we deem resistance to be. Early in the
twentieth century, on both sides of the Atlantic, prostitution was
increasingly represented as the province of the feeble-minded, a
group who contemporary practice might justifiably detain for their
own protection. Maude Royden defined the feeble-minded (with
little heed for grammatical elegance) as 'those with strong sexual
urges and little self-control and those non-resistant ones'.[47] Royden's
1916 investigation of women's 'downward path' listed 'wilful and
unmanageable' as among the causes of entry into prostitution. It
was the construction of what Steven Schlossman and Stephanie
Wallach call 'the crime of precocious sexuality'.[48] Their pioneering
analysis highlights a series of American court cases in which young
women's behaviour challenges the court's view of their proper
place and leads to their confinement in reformatories. Women's
potential for prostitution, demonstrated by non-conformity, was a
cause for alarm and, it would seem in retrospect, perhaps helped
to entrench the dependencies and labelling so often catalysing
women's move into prostitution. Jewish-American immigrant
Maimie Pinzer was arrested and confined for incorrigibility – and
found a living thereafter from sporadic prostitution – at the request
of her mother and uncle around 1898 or 1899.[49]

In such cases, the woman's identity as prostitute is constructed
through resistance. A prostitute woman was one who by definition
lived in defiance, in resistance – of the proper sphere of Woman,
of the male order, of respectability. It was all the more disturbing
for the opposition because this resistance exposed the threat of an
unordered female sexuality which had led to the need for these
new codifications of female sexuality; if prostitute women were

'real' women, then disorder must ensue. Thus resistance invited containment which prompted resistance – and new definitions were born.

This varied evidence of resistance also suggests that women were not hopelessly trapped in unchangeable situations. Nonetheless, and though it might not be currently fashionable to look askance at 'agency', we should be aware of the boundaries which established and limited these forms of resistance. For youngsters, after all, resistance ended in reformatory incarceration. In some respects, women working as prostitutes could claim more control over their lives than women tied to domestic or manufacturing jobs or to abusive husbands, but they experienced far more acute marginality, powerlessness, exploitation and social isolation. Forced into an outlaw status and subjected to medical, moral, legal and social investigation which produced a picture of a deviant world, they were removed from the mainstream and submerged, metaphorically if not always in practice, in misery, disease and degradation.

Medical policing

Attacks on the public world of prostitution were couched increasingly in the language and context of public health and sanitary policy. The need to combat venereal disease proved an effective rallying point both in peacetime and during war. The gradual shift from criminal proceeding to sanitary provision, though the two never really strayed far apart, ushered in new experiments in detention. One of the features of regulatory responses to health is the state's right to detain potential spreaders of infectious disease. In addition to hospitals functioning, and often harshly, as detention centres, the threat of criminal proceedings against intractable patients serves as a reminder of the punitive link at work here.

Disciplinary action against hospitalised women was common. The London Lock Hospital frequently reported clashes between patients from the subjected districts and staff, with women often discharging themselves unlawfully before their treatment was ended. Hospital Inspector Leonard recommended that the best course for responding to the 'noisy and troublesome' was to treat them 'like wayward children – put them to bed in a room by themselves and take their clothes from them.'[50] In short, the message was to reduce them to, and remind them of, proper Womanhood.

C.W.S. Deakin, a vocal supporter of the Acts, asked rhetorically, 'What right has a woman suffering from syphilis to continue her trade?'[51] Women working as prostitutes were, as we have seen, crossing boundaries; their rights in trade were, in any case, questionable. Justifying the suspension of their rights in a public health context was not difficult and acted in similar ways to literal criminalisation. It is not coincidental that when the strength of the repeal movement showed no signs of abating in the early 1870s, the Home Secretary's alternative proposal was an (unsuccessful) Detention in Hospitals Bill, the title of which makes explicit the hospital as surrogate prison. Contagious Diseases Acts repeal activist Mary Hume-Rothery colourfully referred to the Lock Hospitals as 'lazar jails'.[52]

During the First World War, the rights discourse emerged once more in the health field, though the context in which it was raised pushes us into the arena of medical ethics. In the summer of 1915, the London Lock Hospital had sought Home Office advice on its authority to confine a 'highly contagious' self-confessed 'camp follower' refusing treatment. The Home Office conceded that nothing could be done to detain her adding regretfully, in an internal memorandum on the subject, that 'if we set up a concentration camp for syphilitic prostitutes, it would be infinitely more useful than an aliens camp'.[53]

One can only speculate that Home Office officials would concur with the forthright opinions of General Childs expressed at a meeting of the conference on venereal disease and demobilisation some three years later. 'I am afraid we are suffering from too many rights in this country . . . under military government the question would be settled in a week.'[54]

Discussions of the state's role in the determination of health policy have rarely considered the impact of venereal disease, focusing more commonly on illnesses such as tuberculosis and cholera.[55] Yet throughout this period, medical and social commentators constantly invoked the depradations resultant upon rampant venereal infection, and consistently laid the blame for this at the feet of prostitution. US Army Medical Officer Edward Vedder was convinced that 'the root of the venereal disease problem lies in prostitution'.[56] Vedder's opinion was neither new nor original; the

Contagious Diseases Acts had been premised on just such a position. Venereal disease amongst Civil War forces did much to consolidate public health regulation in the US. Few health historians since have paid attention to what then aroused considerable fear.[57] Doctors and medical institutions often refused to treat venereal disease, on the grounds that it was brought about by the patient's own moral laxity.[58] Ignoring the venereal disease debate ironically echoes these physicians' attempts to ignore it by not treating it.

Publicity for this practice, beyond arousing public prurience, was a device for shaming the unworthy. The suspension of the confidential basis of the doctor–patient relationships reminded 'guilty' parties that their right to privacy was guaranteed only by their adherence to the boundaries of public and private. Descriptions of the public examinations of the 'private' parts of public women conducted under the Contagious Diseases Acts bear no resemblance to the decorous and discreet attentions of doctors treating a 'respectable' clientele. Hospitals and doctors found themselves in an enforcing more than a curative or preventive role in cases of this sort, and practitioners were, in the early twentieth century, increasingly called upon to testify in court as to a woman's medical condition. Justice of the Peace and social purity activist Charles Tarring pointed out that this constituted 'an abuse of a patient's confidence'.[59] The enthusiasm of the press for publishing the names of women accused of immorality or infection works similarly. The 'fallen' woman was subject to public scrutiny, a constant reminder of the price she paid. Men retained the privilege of moving between the two spheres, but for women the medical profession joined the law in drawing tightly-defined boundaries between the two spheres.

Medical parlance was thus captured by the moralists, just as judicial and penal themes found expression in health policy. Even when not suffering from an identifiable physical ailment, prostitute women were 'recovered' from their state of disgrace. Their rehabilitation was premised on supplanting their reliance on the sex trade with a commitment to respectable and status-appropriate work. Judith Walkowitz sees the laundering done by Lock Hospital inmates as a symbol of cleansing and purification by detention.[60] In keeping with the domestic tasks required of women in refuge homes and hospitals, attempts were made to find positions in service for them after rehabilitation. They were being returned in short to the private, proper sphere of Woman. Recovery and return, the movement from public to private, were synonymous.

Magdalen institutions were anxious to secure domestic positions which would distance women from urban and metropolitan temptation.[61] The city itself posed a significant threat as a symbol of autonomy, anonymity and independence; rural living was far easier to police. These anxieties also informed the siting of penitent homes.[62] In centrally-located institutions, bars, high walls and opaque windows closed off the threat of the outside world, sealing women off from the public world metaphorically and literally, reminding them of and returning them to their proper place.[63] The London Lock Hospital treated male patients on an out-patient basis and women almost always as in-patients. Venereal disease sufferers treated in workhouses experienced similarly segregated practices. An early twentieth century inquiry into public morality found that male venereal disease patients in the Leeds workhouse could take exercise but women were forbidden to do so because 'they might "escape" '.[64]

This removal and sealing-off of women suggests, too, some consonance with the metaphor of disorder through contagion. The literal transmission of disease was, and remains, a marvellously symbolic vehicle for imparting blame. In the early years of this century, writers were confidently asserting that 'it is scientifically accepted that, given no prostitutes, there would be no syphilis'.[65] Prostitutes were likened to malignant cancers, relishing – like vampires – any opportunity to bring another to degradation. William Bevan described the prostitute woman as 'a satanic malignity', Michael Ryan characterised her as 'malevolent, cruel, and revengeful'.[66] It was logical, thus, for writers to conclude that women were 'very zealous agents in the cause of evil'.[67] The dangers of contagion were so acute that even to speak of prostitution carried 'the danger of conveying a taint'.[68]

Those already tainted were, argued many, beyond reach. They were 'permanently brutalised'; 'an uncontrollable desire for repetition' was their ugly fate.[69] Uncontained the contagion would 'spread, wide and more wide', because woman once fallen 'becomes a moral pest, and a seducer of innocence'.[70] Contamination, infestation, invasion were all common descriptions which link prostitution to sanitation and health in a moralising discourse about the urgency of order and containment. Purgative and rehabilitative hopes for the 'infected' woman seem hopeless in this context. Many medical practitioners considered prostitutes vulnerable to venereal disease because they saw constant sexual contact as exciting women's infective propensity. Curing a woman of venereal disease was not, then, a 'solution', for it was the prostitute rather than her sexual actions who was the source of infestation. Defining prostitutes as a physically as well as a morally separate group made it simpler to argue that they were the very *fons et origo* of venereal contagion.[71] And if a woman once fallen was beyond the grasp of moral and medical treatments, then containment for the sake of both medical and moral order was the most fitting course of action.

In addition, and crucially, however, the existence of a female prostitution presented the reality of women at work, working in a sphere that had to remain – for moral and religious as much as political reasons – formally unacceptable. Thus, in the face of the reality of the business with its long hours and hard work, prostitution had to be portrayed not as a form of labour but as an expression of idleness, the pursuit of the will-not-works. It is this incredibly potent construction of the meaning of work that, in part, makes us ask even now why women become prostitutes, singling out these women as deviant among all women. As observed earlier, we may just as usefully wonder why they should become coal-drawers in the mines or factory hands in the mills.

This negation of the hard labour involved in prostitution ties into wider issues of moralism and poverty in nineteenth-century English thinking. Prostitutes, like paupers, lacked moral fibre. Not surprisingly, many venereal disease sufferers could find in-patient treatment only in workhouse infirmaries, and after 1867 paupers with venereal disease could be detained until cured.[72] This moralising of labour lent prostitute women the stigma of a double moral failure; stigmatised by their 'idleness' and poverty and simultaneously by their 'natural' propensity to venereal disease. The sickness was moral *and* physical; in the Sheffield workhouse, the venereal disease ward was labelled 'D.S.' for Dirty Sick.[73]

Beyond rough usages

The Contagious Diseases Acts have, not surprisingly, dominated considerations of prostitution in this period. The Acts were enormously controversial, and have also provided us with a mass of source materials unparalleled for the study of prostitution in modern England. We should not, however, take for granted that they represent a significant historical watershed. They are neither the beginning of a new mode of socio-sexual control nor, conversely, the dying gasp of one about to be discarded. After all, they continued to operate under various guises in Britain's colonies well into the twentieth century. The compulsory examination, regarded as the heart and soul of the Acts by repealers and extensionists alike, was in some colonies abandoned but brothel regulation and official funding for Lock Hospitals remained commonplace. Discussions of the Acts and their legislative cousins pepper the Parliamentary Returns and printed Correspondence from the colonies.

Moreover, scant attention has been paid to the punitive and one-sided regulations aimed at protecting soldiers in the First World War from venereal infection. The most controversial of these regulations – 40D – was only in force for a matter of months in 1918, which may explain why historians have largely ignored it.[74] At the time, though, it attracted considerable attention. Women's groups and churches, social purity organisations and reform institutions all bombarded government with protests, likening the regulation to the Contagious Diseases Acts. The legislative watershed may thus be not the Acts of the 1860s nor their suspension and subsequent repeal in the 1880s, but the near-simultaneous abandonment of 40D in late 1918 and passing of the Venereal Disease Act of 1917, which provided for free and confidential treatment for all sufferers.

The failure of the Contagious Diseases Acts did not lead to the abandonment of the principle of regulation, but to the adoption of different methods. On the contrary, the state's lack of success in this respect bolstered its determination to gain control over the recklessness and disorder of female independence, particularly in prostitution where, theoretically, sexual independence met financial autonomy. The Acts were followed by the massively conservative Criminal Law Amendment Acts of 1885 and 1912, by an increased policing of the streets and eventually by the criminalisation of solicitation in the post-war era.

Understanding prostitution, and the responses it engendered judicially and in other arenas, suggests that a wholly legalistic or juridical reading will miss many of the elements that served to construct the prostitute identity in this period. The law functioned as a powerful means of defining deviance and asserting control, but was enhanced by parallel assaults from its institutional kin, the medical profession, the church, social work – whom we might usefully see as 'filters' of the law. What they all shared was a perspective derived from implicit assumptions that prostitution, though deplorable when practised publicly, was 'inevitable' and thus an object requiring continual political governance. That the 'natural' propensities of woman to lust and frivolity and thence to prostitution should lead to a situation in which female sexuality was not controllable within an institutional heterosexuality only confounded an already paradoxical view of 'true Womanhood'. Controlling prostitution meant controlling women, because women, defined by their sexuality, threatened disorder and unruliness.

The dubious theoretical autonomy which prostitution offered women in a patriarchal society was and is deliberately and systematically undermined by the heightened vulnerability ensuing from legal, medical and social responses. The prostitute's relation to the law renders her vulnerable, if not to punishment and criminalisation then to requiring male protection and to isolation from the mainstream of women. She is vulnerable to abuse, infection and dishonesty from her clients, to social isolation from respectable society and to blame for the spread of disease. She is disenfranchised from citizenship and from contract, and rendered criminal through public action.

In asking 'how do we write about women whose working lives were documented only while they were being harassed?'[75] Luise White emphasises the created marginality of the prostitute woman. Yet our knowledge of women's – and men's – experience in legitimate areas of work is also often coloured by those junctures at which their protests rose to the articulate surface. The evidence of Royal Commissions on labouring conditions are not magically 'more' believable than those examining prostitution. Much of the testimony we have of the broader experience of poverty is also from the observations of outsiders. Why should we single out prostitution as an area in which to accept or remain with the comments of others rather than find innovative means of recovery?

Prostitute women have been a group consistently ill-used in every way. Upon their bodies were the contested arenas of public and private literally played out in their starkest form, with little ensuing benefit for the women. The determination to maintain homogeneous notions of prostitution as a category abandons their lives to a theory that explains and taxonomises them as subjects and targets of study. In *their* work, they have been subject to much rough usage: physical and verbal abuse, broken contracts along with broken bones, categorisation as criminals. They have been neglected and stereotyped by investigators who have privileged their own voices over those of the women walking the streets, staffing the houses and servicing the men. Time has seen remarkably little change in their situation, in the policing and legal tactics employed or in public opinion. In *our* work, we surely have a responsibility to point out and to examine – but surely not to perpetuate – that rough usage.

Notes

1   C. Smith-Rosenberg, 'The new woman and the new history', *Feminist Studies*, III, 1975, p. 185.
2   L. White details a 'miniature scholarly explosion' of books on the topic in her 'Prostitutes, reformers, and historians', *Criminal Justice History. An International Annual*, VI, 1985, p. 201.
3   R.L. Blanco, 'The attempted control of venereal disease in the army of mid-Victorian England', *Journal of the Society for Army Historical Research*, XLV, 1967, pp. 234–41; P. McHugh, *Prostitution and Victorian Social Reform*, London, 1980; J.B. Post, 'A Foreign Office survey of venereal disease and prostitution control, 1869–70', *Medical History* XXII, 1978, pp. 327–34; R. Davenport-Hines, *Sex, Death and Punishment. Attitudes to Sex and Sexuality in Britain since the Renaissance*, London, 1990; G. Petrie, *A Singular Iniquity. The Campaigns of Josephine Butler*, London, 1971; F.B. Smith, 'Ethics and disease in the later nineteenth century: the Contagious Diseases Acts', *Historical Studies (Melbourne)*, XV, 1971, pp. 118–35 and by the same author, 'The Contagious Diseases Acts reconsidered', *Social History of Medicine*, III, 1990, pp. 197–215; J.R. Walkowitz, *Prostitution and Victorian Society. Women, Class and the State*, Cambridge, 1980; N. Wood, 'Prostitution and feminism in nineteenth-century Britain', *m/f*, VII, 1982, pp. 61–77; and the wildly inaccurate J.G. Gamble, 'The origins, administration, and impact of the Contagious Diseases Acts from a military perspective', unpublished PhD thesis, University of Southern Mississippi, 1983. The exceptions

are F. Finnegan whose *Victorian Prostitution in York*, Cambridge, 1979, which profiles the trade in York, and L. Mahood, *The Magdalenes. Prostitution in the Nineteenth Century*, London, 1990, which takes Scotland as its focus.

4 J.R. Walkowitz (ed.) in Radical History Review Collective, 'Patrolling the borders: feminist historiography and the new historicism', *Radical History Review*, XLIII, 1989, p. 29. See also J. Weeks, *Sex, Politics and Society. The Regulation of Sexuality since 1800*, London, 1981.

5 Walkowitz, *Prostitution*, p. 202.

6 R.M. Karras, 'The regulation of brothels in later medieval England', *Signs*, XI, 1989, 21, p. 429.

7 White, 'Prostitutes', p. 206.

8 E. Ross and R. Rapp, 'Sex and society: a research note from social history and anthropology', in A. Snitow, C. Stansell and S. Thompson (eds.), *Powers of Desire. The Politics of Sexuality*, New York, 1983, p. 57.

9 My own work is not wholly free of this tendency: see my *Prostitution in Florida. A Report Presented to the Gender Bias Study Commission of the Supreme Court of Florida*, Tallahassee, 1988. This is not a problem confined only to historians: N. Erbe, 'Prostitutes; victims of men's exploitation and abuse', *Law and Inequality*, II, 1984, pp. 609–28; J. James and J. Meyerding, 'Early sexual experience and prostitution', *American Journal of Psychiatry*, CXXXIV, 1977, pp. 1381–5, and their 'Early sexual experience as a factor in prostitution', *Archives of Sexual Behavior*, VII, 1977, pp. 31–42; M.H. Silbert and A.M. Pines, 'Early sexual exploitation as an influence in prostitution', *Social Work*, XXVIII, 1983, pp. 285–90. L. Shrage's thoughtful work ('Should feminists oppose prostitution?', *Ethics*, XCIX, 1989, pp. 347–61) on the importance of focusing on other questions in the prostitution relationship is very useful. See too K. Barry, *Female Sexual Slavery*, New York, 1984.

10 B. Smart, 'On discipline and social regulation: a review of Foucault's genealogical analysis', in D. Garland and P. Young (eds.), *The Power To Punish. Contemporary Penality and Social Analysis*, London and New York, 1983, p. 64.

11 Karras, 'The regulation of brothels', p. 426.

12 R.A. Padgug, 'Sexual matters: on conceptualising sexuality in history', *Radical History Review*, XX, 1979, p. 8.

13 Y. Guyot, *A Study in Social Physiology. Prostitution under the Regulation System French and English*, London, 1884, p. 155.

14 Only early in the twentieth century did feminists begin exploring the topic in broader ways. See F.M. McNeill and F.J. Wakefield, *An Inquiry In Ten Towns in England and Wales into Subjects Connected*

with Public Morality, London, 1916, and A.M. Royden, *Downward Paths. An Inquiry into the Causes which Contribute to the Making of the Prostitute*, London, 1916.

15 Women writing at a slightly later date often, in fact, shared the assumptions of these authors, though in general, their solutions were less punitive.

16 W. Bevan, *Prostitution in the Borough Of Liverpool. A Lecture*, Liverpool, 1843; F.W. Lowndes, *Prostitution and Venereal Diseases in Liverpool*, London, 1886; J. Marchant, *The Master Problem*, London, 1917; G.P. Merrick, *Work Among the Fallen as Seen in the Prison Cells*, London, 1891; (J. Morley), 'A letter to some ladies', *Fortnightly Review*, VII, 1870, pp. 372–6; Royden, *Downward Paths*; M. Ryan, *Prostitution in London*, London, 1839; W. Tait, *Magdalenism. An Inquiry into the Extent, Causes and Consequences of Prostitution in Edinburgh*, Edinburgh, 1840; J.B. Talbot, *The Miseries of Prostitution*, London, 1844; and Public Record Office, London, HO45/9546/59343G.

17 Especially in Bevan, *Prostitution in Liverpool*; Lowndes, *Prostitution and Venereal Diseases*; Merrick, *Work among the Fallen*; Royden, *Downward Paths*; Ryan, *Prostitution in London*; Tait, *Magdalenism*; PRO, HO45/9546/59343G. See also the anonymous *The Social Evil with Suggestions for Its Suppression, and Revelations of the Working of the Contagious Diseases Acts by an Ex-Constable of the Devonport Division*, Bristol, 1883; R. Wardlaw, *Lectures on Female Prostitution. Its Nature, Extent, Effects, Guilt, Causes, and Remedy*, Glasgow, 1842; and PRO, HO45/10354/149817.

18 F.W. Lowndes, *Prostitution and Venereal Diseases*, p. 34.

19 Public Record Office, London. HO45/10802/307990/22A. Earl Derby, War Office to G. Cave, Home Office, 2 May 1917.

20 White, 'Prostitutes', pp. 213–14; 217. My own research on contemporary American prostitution upholds this too. Many police officers feel that women sent to a client in a hotel room by an escort agency face greater potential danger – and with less means of defence – than women on the street who have ample chance to assess a potential client themselves. These assessments of lesser and greater danger are, of course, relative to an absolute vulnerability which is the fate of any woman engaged in this trade, where violence against vendor is endemic and often serious in nature (*Prostitution in Florida*).

21 It is difficult not to be cynical, too, in seeing how her apparent lack of fortune might make the street-walker more attractive to the social historian whose *raison d'être* has so often been the recovery of the lost voices of the poor and 'insignificant'. Practically speaking, the relative proximity of this group to law enforcement and social workers

also means that data has been far easier to gather than for other less visible, ergo less public, groups.

22 C.W.S. Deakin, *The Contagious Diseases Acts. From A Sanitary and Economic Point of View*, London, 1872, p. 13.

23 D.L. Rhode, *Justice and Gender*, Cambridge, Massachusetts, 1989, p. 261; E.M. Miller, *Street Women*, Philadelphia, 1986. Prostitution in the US is a criminal offence except in rural counties in Nevada where there are legalised brothels but where street-walking remains illegal. In the nineteenth century, there was a less uniform approach to the issue and many places operated at least a *de facto* regulation with rotating fines and so on. With the exception of a four-year period in St Louis in the 1870s and a brief period in San Francisco in the early twentieth century, the industry remained largely criminalised. After the advent of the social purity movement of the early twentieth century and the alarms over the spread of venereal disease in the US military at the time of their entry into the 1914–18 war, crackdowns hardened the legal position. Thereafter, criminalisation became and remains the norm.

24 B.M. Hobson, *Uneasy Virtue. The Politics of Prostitution and the American Reform Tradition*, New York, 1987, p. 116.

25 C. Emsley, *Crime and Society in England 1750–1900*, London, 1987, pp. 67; 134.

26 See J.M. Beattie, 'The criminality of women in eighteenth-century England', *Journal of Social History*, VIII, 1975, pp. 80–116; D. Beddoe, *Welsh Convict Women. A Study of Women Transported form Wales to Australia, 1787–1852*, London, 1979; M.S. Hartman, *Victorian Murderesses. A True History of Thirteen Respectable French and English Women Accused of Unspeakable Crimes*, London, 1977.

27 Emsley, *Crime and Society*, pp. 67; 134.

28 M. Chesney-Lind, 'Women and crime: the female offender', *Signs*, XII, 1986, pp. 78–98; K. Daly and Chesney-Lind, 'Feminism and criminology', *Justice Quarterly*, V. 1988, pp. 497–538; C. Feinman, *Women in the Criminal Justice System*, New York, 1986; J. Gregory, 'Sex, class and crime: towards a non-sexist criminology', in R. Matthews and J. Young (eds.), *Confronting Crime*, London, 1986, pp. 53–71; A. Morris, *Women, Crime and Criminal Justice*, Oxford, 1987.

29 Amongst the relevant acts are the Vagrancy Act of 1824 (5 Geo IV. cap. 83), the Metropolitan Police Act of 1839 (2 & 3 Vic. cap. 47), the Town Police Clauses Act of 1847 (10 & 11 Vic. cap. 89), as well as various regional acts operable in urban centres such as Birmingham, Glasgow and Liverpool.

30 F.W. Lowndes, *The Working of the Contagious Diseases Acts at Aldershot, Chatham, Plymouth and Devonport*, London, 1876, p. 25.

31 *Minority Report of the Select Committee of the House of Commons on the Contagious Diseases Acts, 1882*, London, 1882 pp. 44; 45.
32 S.S.M. Edwards, 'Sex or gender: the prostitute in law', *British Journal of Sexual Medicine*, IX, 1982, p. 11.
33 Parliamentary Papers, House of Commons, 1908 (Cd. 4156) *Report of the Royal Commission upon the Duties of the Metropolitan Police* pp. 127; 120.
34 *ibid.*, pp. 94; 99.
35 Smith, 'Ethics and disease', p. 119.
36 See C. Pateman, *The Sexual Contract*, Oxford, 1988 for a thorough discussion of contract and gender. See also Z.R. Eisenstein, *The Female Body and the Law*, Berkeley, California, 1988 and R. Kezelson, *The Law as a System of Signs*, New York, 1988.
37 Karras, 'The regulation of brothels', p. 406.
38 C. Smart and J. Brophy, 'Locating law: a discussion of the place of law in feminist politics', in their *Women-in-Law. Explorations in Law, Family and Sexuality*, London, 1985 p. 1.
39 J. Rifkin, 'Toward a theory of law and patriarchy', *Harvard Women's Law Journal*, III, 1980, p. 84.
40 White, 'Prostitutes', p. 209.
41 See R. Rosen, *The Lost Sisterhood. Prostitution in America, 1900–1918*, Baltimore, 1982, in which she argues that increasing criminalisation and persecution by the state forced women to seek the 'protection' of pimps.
42 K. Ballhatchet, *Race, Sex and Class under the Raj. Imperial Attitudes and Policies and their Critics, 1793–1905*, London, 1980; A.M. Butler, *Daughters of Joy, Sisters of Misery. Prostitution in the American West*, Urbana, Illinois, 1985; M.S. Goldmann, *Gold Diggers and Silver Miners. Prostitution and Social Life on the Comstock Lode*, Ann Arbor, Michigan, 1981; C. van Onselen, *A Social and Economic History of the Witwatersrand, 1886–1914*, Johannesburg, 1982.
43 Quoted in Walkowitz, *Prostitution*, p. 128.
44 C. Smart, *The Ties That Bind. Law, Marriage and the Reproduction of Patriarchal Relations*, London, 1984, p. 4.
45 Walkowitz, *Prostitution*, pp. 78; 160; 184; 188; 214; 224–6; Royal College of Surgeons, London. Papers of the London Lock Hospital, *Reports*.
46 *Annual Reports of the Rescue Society*, London, 1870–1900.
47 Royden, *Downward Paths*, p. 125.
48 S. Schlossman and S. Wallach, 'The crime of precocious sexuality: female juvenile delinquency and the Progressive era', in D.K. Weisberg (ed.), *Women and the Law. A Social Historical Perspective. Vol 1. Women and the Criminal Law*, Cambridge, Massachusetts, 1982, pp. 45–84.

49 R. Rosen and S. Davidson (eds.), *The Maimie Papers*, London, 1974.
50 Royal College of Surgeons. London Lock Hospital. Manuscript Minute Books of Weekly Board. Vol. 27, f. 374. 24 October 1867.
51 Deakin, *The Contagious Diseases Acts*, p. 26
52 Quoted in Walkowitz, *Prostitution*, p. 130.
53 PRO, HO45/10724/251861/63. 11 May; 15 May 1915.
54 PRO, WO32/11404. Section VIII, p. 15.
55 L. Bryder, *Below The Magic Mountain. A Social History of Tuberculosis in Twentieth-Century Britain*, Oxford, 1988; F.B. Smith, *The Retreat of Tuberculosis 1850–1950*, London, 1988; M. Pelling, *Cholera, Fever and English Medicine 1825–65*, Oxford, 1978.
56 E.B. Vedder *Syphilis and Public Health*, Philadelphia, 1918, p. 212.
57 Though F.B. Smith devotes a few pages of his *The People's Health 1830–1910*, London, 1979, to the topic, there is no British equivalent of A.M. Brandt's full-scale study, *No Magic Bullet. A Social History of Venereal Disease in the United States Since 1880*, New York, 1985.
58 A celebrated example is physician Francis Champneys. His argument appears in a series of articles in *The Nineteenth Century and After* for 1917 and 1918.
59 Public Record Office, London. HO45/10893/359931. 1918.
60 Walkowitz, *Prostitution*, p. 221.
61 S.D. Nash, 'Social attitudes towards prostitution in London from 1725 to 1829', unpublished PhD thesis, New York University, 1980, p. 256.
62 H.F.B. Compston, *The Magdalen Hospital. The Story of A Great Charity*, London, 1917, pp. 89–90; 95; 102–3.
63 When the American city of St Louis introduced regulation briefly in the 1870s, its Social Evil Hospital was built on the outskirts of the city, in close proximity to the lunatic asylum and poorhouse. In addition to the need to contain women in a private space, political issues also affected the siting of such institutions. Even here, though, the metaphor of public and private was paramount since it was considered unseemly for indelicate institutions to be prominently placed.
64 McNeill and Wakefield, *An Inquiry*, p. 39.
65 Civis, 'The doctors and venereal disease', *English Review*, XV, 1913, p. 255n.
66 Bevan, *Prostitution in Liverpool*, p. 9; Ryan, *Prostitution in London*, p. 231.
67 Merrick, *Work Among the Fallen*, p. 59.
68 Wardlaw, *Lectures*, p. 2.
69 Morley, 'A Letter', p. 374; *The Social Evil*, p. 8. This contrasts strikingly, of course, with the work of William Acton whose work on

prostitution published in 1857 saw the trade as a fairly typical transitory experience of working-class women.

70 Wardlaw, pp. 64–5; Talbot, *Miseries*, p. 43.
71 See S.L. Gilman, *Sexuality. An Illustrated History. Representing the Sexual in Medicine and Culture from the Middle Ages to the Age of AIDS*, New York, 1989, pp. 240; 248.
72 Poor Law Amendment Act, 1867. 30 & 31 Vic. cap. 106, s. 22.
73 McNeill and Wakefield, *An Inquiry*, p. 37.
74 See E.H. Beardsley, 'Allied against sin: American and British responses to venereal disease in world war I', *Medical History*, XX, 1970, pp. 189–202; L. Bland, 'In the name of protection: the policing of women in the First World War', in Brophy and Smart (eds.), *Women-in-Law*, pp. 23–49; and S. Buckley, 'The failure to resolve the problem of venereal disease among the troops in Britain during world war I', in B. Bond and I. Roy (eds.), *War and Society. A Yearbook of Military History*, II, New York, 1977, pp. 65–85. There is a considerable volume of material on the American response to venereal disease during the 1914–18 war.
75 White, 'Prostitutes', p. 204.

[handwritten annotations:]

arbitrary: based on or derived from uninformed opinion or random choice; capricious

eclectic: deriving ideas, style etc from various sources; not exclusive

mutability - subject to change, fickle

arbitrary - ~~capricious, based on mere opinion or preference~~

eclectic diversity = that borrows or is borrowed from various sources; not exclusive

relativism the doctrine that knowledge is only of relations depending for meaning or significance on relationship between some things or persons

9 Adrian Wilson

Foundations of an integrated historiography

Preamble: the historian's dilemma

Can the discipline of history – whether social or otherwise – lay any claim to generating a reliable knowledge? Or do historians merely produce an unconstrained set of arbitrary, competing representations of the past? This perennial problem arises with renewed force in the 1990s; and it has a particular poignancy for social history. Its contemporary intensification is due to postmodernism, which insists on the variability and mutability of readings permitted by texts – which has seemed to some to imply the arbitrariness of any historical knowledge, based as it must be on interpretation of those texts. The eclectic diversity of modern historical scholarship seems to confirm this, producing as many 'pasts' as there are subdisciplines of history-writing, and thus implicitly suggesting a shared relativism. Social history's own form of the 'problem of historical knowledge' arises from the disparity between its questions and the available evidence. Such a disparity is apparent in each of the three forms of social history which were distinguished in Chapter 1. 'History from below', the modern successor to the earlier tradition of history-of-the-people, faces difficulties of coverage (is there any evidence at all?) and representativeness (whose voices are available?). The application of the social sciences (the approach which I have called the 'social history paradigm') requires that we cross-match different conceptual grids which may or may not be commensurable (and how can we discover whether they are?). And the 'history of society' raises the seemingly intractable problem that 'society', seen as a pattern of relationships, is never directly re-corded at all – in either the past or the present.[1]

Seen from the standpoint of the practising historian, this cluster of issues raises what could be called *the historian's dilemma.* On the one hand, practical experience brings the conviction that his-torical knowledge is possible, that the countless hours spent in the archives are not wasted, that the historian reconstructs (however incompletely and imperfectly) a past which actually happened, that his or her conclusions are based on real evidence. On the other hand, the foundations of this knowledge are elusive; the published reflections of individual historians yield no agreed canon of practice, and the relativist challenge has not been met by ex-isting textbooks of historical method. As we have seen in Chapter 1, this issue also bedevils historical sociology, which has not suc-ceeded in producing any methodology for empirical historical research.

the dilemma

The dilemma was addressed at length by Edward Thompson in his essay 'The poverty of theory', published in 1978. His argument – pitched against what he portrayed as the scepticism of philoso-phers, sociologists and anthropologists – was that the historical discipline possessed its own adequate methodological basis, a specific 'discourse of the proof' which he termed '*historical logic*'. Thompson defined this as 'a logical method of enquiry appropriate to historical materials, designed as far as possible to test hypothe-ses . . . and to eliminate self-confirming procedures'. The 'disciplined historical discourse of the proof', he continued, 'consists in a dia-logue between concept and evidence'. Yet Thompson deferred the task of explaining this 'dialogue', for 'to define this logic fully . . . would require writing a different, and more academic, essay'. Instead he shifted the focus from the historical discipline in general to his own particular approach to the study of the past, producing 'a defence of historical materialism' against 'the posi-tions of Althusser'. The eight propositions which made up that defence are not easily summarised, but perhaps their central point was that Marxist concepts are historical in a triple sense: devel-oped in a historical context; concerned with concrete human his-tory; and to be refined not by abstract theory, but by 'the test of historical logic'. Here and elsewhere in the essay, he elaborated particular aspects of the historian's methods – for instance, con-testing Popper's claim that historical knowledge was limited by *concept: a general notion, an abstract idea existing in thought rather than in matter*

the intentions of those who had written past records. But it was not Thompson's intention to produce a systematic account of 'historical logic', beyond his repeated assertion that it comprised a 'dialogue between concept and evidence'. In the end, then, Thompson had not resolved the 'historian's dilemma'.[2]

The persistence of the dilemma is evident in recent restatements by Penelope Corfield, Ludmilla Jordanova and Peter Burke. Corfield observes that 'Analytical rigour, definitional clarity, and fidelity to the sources remain cardinal principles for the study of history. But exemplary methods do not in themselves create knowledge. Nor do the sources alone reveal unproblematically to later generations history "as it really occurred".' Jordanova points out that 'history has the status of "knowledge", whilst primary sources have the status of "evidence" and . . . the transition from evidence to knowledge is highly problematic'. Similarly, Burke suggests that it is necessary to 'read the documents between the lines', points out that 'the principles underlying such reading are not always clear', and concludes that 'what is needed is a new "diplomatic" ' – that is, a new critical method appropriate to the concerns of social history.[3]

Now the difficulty of the problem is itself a clue to its nature. The foundations of historical inference are by their very nature hidden from view: they do not operate at the level of explicit interpretation; instead they work their effects from deep within those myriad private, mundane micro-activities which make up the practice of historical research. To put this another way, historical knowledge is founded upon a cluster of *tacit skills* which the historian deploys in mundane practice. These skills embody what might be called the 'invisibility paradox': on the one hand they are routinely practised and well-known, yet on the other hand they remain untheorised and indeed unnamed. This invisibility itself has important effects: not only has it obscured the foundational significance of these skills, but it has also restricted their application in the domain of practice. If we could render them explicit, we would not only demonstrate their epistemological importance; we would also increase their practical power.[4]

In what follows I attempt to characterise these skills, that is, to render explicit what Thompson called 'historical logic', the 'dialogue between concept and evidence'. Corresponding to the two terms of that dialogue, I delineate two practices in turn: first and

epistemology: the theory of knowledge, espec with regard to its methods & validation.

briefly what I shall call *concept-criticism*, then in more detail the *study of document-genesis*. Later we see that these are two aspects of a single process, and that once properly understood and deployed, these foundations of historical knowledge are not just useful defensive resources (arguments against postmodernist scepticism) or locally applicable techniques. On the contrary, they open the possibility of redressing the two structural problems of the history discipline which were outlined in Chapter 1: its internal division between State and social historiographies, and its external asymmetrical relationship with the social sciences.

? unbalanced

Concept-criticism

Wilson is attempting to show historical skills called by Thompson 'historical logic'.

From the time of Niebuhr and Ranke onwards, historians of the State have practised the 'criticism of sources'; and social historians have in their turn adopted this technique, as we shall later see. But historians have also developed another practice, pursued more hesitantly, practised perhaps more sporadically, and not (so far as I know) yet dignified with a name: a practice which is the very inverse of source-criticism, and which I therefore propose to call *concept-criticism*.[5]

By 'concept-criticism' I refer to a process of *modifying one's working concepts in the practical process of research*, through an active encounter with historical materials. The stimulus for this process is a perceived mismatch between concepts (or questions) and what is taken as evidence. Concept-criticism seeks to correct this perceived clash by modifying the array of concepts (questions) which the historian is deploying. Often the process is resisted – that is, a concept is treated as a loved one – sometimes for a long time, sometimes even for ever: there is nothing inevitable about it. Nevertheless its possibility is always present; the potential for concept-criticism is a structural feature of historical research.

I would venture that every historian has gone through this experience – though few have recorded it, since it seems to be regarded in hindsight with some embarrassment. But we can perhaps read what I am calling concept-criticism into Edward Thompson's 'dialogue between concept and evidence', and in his insistence that 'Historical evidence has determinate properties. While any number of questions may be put to it, only certain questions will be appropriate.' For if we discover that a question

(a) criticism of sources has been long practised
(b) criticism of concepts to be explained here!

is inappropriate, it follows that we should change the terms of the question – which is precisely to embark on concept-criticism. In my own view, this practice on the part of historians resembles the process of practical reasoning carried out by natural scientists when performing experimental research. In both scientific and historical research, the process can be described as one of *attuning*: of refining the fit between concepts and evidence. It is within the space of intersection between concepts and evidence that the object of knowledge is constructed. The thought-adjustments which take place in that space are therefore foundational. Yet they are also, inevitably, elusive to recovery.[6]

Concept-criticism has many varieties, differentiated in at least two dimensions. Here I set out a rough and provisional typology, in the belief that we will pursue the practice more effectively by clarifying what it involves. We can distinguish between what I shall term *adjustment, genealogy* and *self-examination* – though each of these can lead to the others. And there are different *degrees* of concept-criticism: the practice ranges from a personal process, concerned with local detail, to large-scale, disciplinary shifts in thinking.

Adjustment: If a piece of historical research is worth carrying out at all – that is, if it is seeking to discover something new – then there will probably be some mismatch between the questions we are asking and the documents we consult for evidence. Such a mismatch can take many different forms. It could consist in a clash of categories (say: we are interested in social class; our documents speak of ranks and degrees). It might be a problem of provenance (we are researching popular belief; the available records are not popular but official). Perhaps it comprises an absence (we are investigating sex; a diarist never mentions sex). Or an unsuspected presence (we are writing a book about A; a body of manuscripts keeps mentioning B, of whom we had never heard, in connection with A). And so on; the mismatch between our questions and past relics can pertain to content, to form, to provenance or to any admixture of these. Now if we notice this mismatch, and if we regard it as significant, and if we are prepared to do something about it – then the possibility has opened of *adjusting* our questions: that is, of modifying the concepts with which we began. From this point on, if we see and accept this possibility, there are many different forms and degrees of concept-criticism. The aim of this process is not on the whole to annihilate our concepts (though some may need to be jettisoned), but rather to refine and develop them. Part of this process is that half-conscious assumptions rise into our awareness and *become* concepts: and once articulated, they are open to criticism. Moreover, other concepts will be added: that is, we will forge new concepts through critical reflection upon the material with which we are wrestling. Gradually, to a greater or lesser degree, our initial array of concepts is transmuted into a new array, better attuned to the content, form and provenance of those documents we are appropriating as evidence.

Genealogy: Our own working concepts, whatever they are and however we derived them – for instance, through training, prejudice, reading, listening, assumption, guesswork, our own previous research or that of others – are themselves the products of historical processes. (One important aspect or variant of this is that they often result from historiographical processes, that is, from a tradition of history-writing, for instance within a subdiscipline.) The 'genealogical' form of concept-criticism consists in an *interrogation of the origins of our concepts*. This can and should extend to the present, into an analysis of the conditions that sustain our concepts. Now this interrogation need not necessarily be 'critical' in the sense of fault-finding; but it is likely to make us more cautious in the application of our concepts.[7]

Self-examination: As a working historian, I am responsible for my own concepts: whatever their genealogy, I have appropriated them for my own use in my own way. If I take this responsibility seriously, then any need for concept-criticism must entail some associated self-criticism, or to put it more generously, self-examination. How and why did I come to hold, to use, such-and-such a concept? Whence my attachment to it? Such critical interrogation of oneself is necessarily painful yet potentially liberating. Interestingly, it turns the historian her/himself into an object of study – that is, it entails treating oneself just as one treats those people in the past one is studying. To the extent that we succeed in this, we are achieving in our enquiries the delicate quality of reflexivity. And in embarking upon it, we open the way to recognising the political premises and significance of our activity as historians.

Degrees of concept-criticism: The small-scale forms of concept-criticism are difficult to illustrate, precisely because these are private and personal; I hope that those readers who are historians can all supply their own examples. On a larger scale, in public historiographical discourse, examples abound. Thus in the present volume, Innes and Styles depict a shift of attention away from '*crime*' and towards the *operation of law* in the tradition with which they are concerned – and they eloquently justify that shift as a conceptual refinement and improvement. In economic historiography there has been in recent years a critical questioning of the concept of '*Industrial Revolution*'; it is worth observing that this critique has involved both 'adjustment' (attempts to refine, replace or abandon the concept) and 'genealogy' (investigations of its origins and modes of deployment).[8] This is paralleled by a third example of large-scale concept-criticism, from the recent historiography of science, which it may be helpful to outline at slightly greater length. From the late 1940s onwards, the newly-flourishing subdiscipline of the history of science organised much of its output around the notion of the '*Scientific Revolution*'. The latter 'Revolution' was said to have comprised a shift in thought, worldview and practice, extending from Copernicus to Newton, centred above all in the seventeenth century, and giving rise by say 1700 to 'Modern Science'. But since the mid-1980s the consensus around this historiographic concept – or framework – has collapsed, for the concept has been subjected to systematic and devastating criticism on the grounds of anachronism. The results of this critique, and some of its grounds, have been elegantly summarised by Nicholas Jardine, who distinguishes two kinds of anachronism. 'Attributive anachronism' he defines as 'characterization of the actions and activities of past agents in ways that involve attribution to them of attitudes, beliefs, intentions, goals, etc., that they could not as a matter of historical possibility have had'. 'Evaluative anachronism' comprises 'the employment, tacit or explicit, of principles of selection, narration and estimation of past events that are informed by anachronistic views of their value and significance.' Both types of anachronism pervaded the traditional conception of a seventeenth-century 'Scientific Revolution':[9]

The disciplinary alliance that we call 'science' or 'natural science' is a creation of the early nineteenth century ... when we look at sixteenth- and early seventeenth-century classifications of the arts and sciences ... we find no category remotely corresponding to our science or natural science. Instead we find disciplines ancestral to components of our science dispersed over arts and sciences, operative and contemplative knowledge, *scientia* and *opinio*, arcane and mundane doctrine. Use of the terms 'science', 'scientist' and 'scientific' in describing practitioners of Early Modern arts and sciences and their activities involves gross attributive anachronism. So does the equation, tacit or explicit, of natural philosophy, mathematics or *scientia*, with science. Moreover, even where attributive anachronism is avoided, evaluative anachronism may be committed by undue concentration on disciplines ancestral to components of our science and on the authors, doctrines, works and practices that can in retrospect be seen as having contributed to or anticipated our scientific practice and beliefs.

Since concept-criticism has recently cast doubt on two very big 'Revolutions', it might be fruitful to extend this outwards and to interrogate the genealogy of 'Revolution' in general as a historiographic concept. This leads to the further observation that concept-criticism can and should be pursued without limits, as a continuous process. In this way we might do something to avoid the ossification so characteristic of subdisciplines. Concept-criticism, pursued in this spirit, offers the possibility of perpetual renewal and reinvigoration. Thus we should not aim to refine our concepts to some magical point of purity, appositeness, exactitude, upon which we could apply them mechanically. Not only is such a point unattainable, but also the aim of attaining it is damaging. For if we were to believe that we had refined our concepts in this way, we would confer on these concepts the quality of universals, which carries within it a profound reification, a denial of historicity.[10]

Now by pursuing concept-criticism without limit, we would eventually arrive at 'social history' itself as a concept available for criticism. This would be a thoroughly healthy development, leading in the direction of a reflexive practice. The application of concept-criticism to social history would have two very interesting aspects. First, it entails that we can and should problematise – not eliminate – the category 'society', not only in respect of its application to the past ('adjustment') but also with respect to its origins ('genealogy'). Such an enterprise would fit with the recent 'critique of "society"' which was discussed in Chapter 1, offering the possibility of historicising that critique. One inviting possibility in this domain is a consideration of what we might call the *imagined pasts* consistently created by the social sciences themselves. The concept of 'modern society', which is central to sociology, requires

3 distinct ways historians can apprehend documents, each
associated with a specific methodological practice.
Adrian Wilson calls these hermeneutic stances. (perhaps interpretative?)   301 stances?
they are practical attitudes

and constructs its imagined ancestor-opposite, 'traditional society', and necessitates some story explaining how the one turned
into the other: transition, modernisation, industrialisation, structural differentiation. The persistence of this theoretical need indicates its depth: such imagery extends from Durkheim through
Parsons to Habermas and Giddens. What are the meanings of this
ancestor-myth, so fragile and yet so potent?[11] Second, the exercise
would also involve taking seriously the 'history' term of our self-
definition. This would involve a critical and explanatory reconstruction of those processes of disciplinary formation, extending
for about a century from the 1860s to the 1960s, by which academic 'history' in Britain acquired its present shape, structure and
constellation of interests. I have offered a preliminary sketch of
this kind in Chapter 1, structured around that separation between
State and social historiographies which – so I have argued – needs
to be overcome. Perhaps that crude picture will stimulate others
to produce a more accurate, inclusive and contextualised account.
Coming to terms with our own history is the necessary starting-
point of a reflexive practice.

The study of document-genesis

The foundation of any historical knowledge resides in the way the
historian makes inferences about the past, using relics of the past
as sources of evidence. For the sake of brevity, let us use the
shorthand phrase '*the documents*' to refer to 'those relics of the
past from which the historian is making inferences' – always on
the understanding that this refers not only to manuscripts and
books but also to material artefacts and even to traces left on the
land and its vegetation. Now there seem to be three distinct ways
in which historians can apprehend the documents, each associated
with a specific methodological practice. I refer to these as three
'hermeneutic stances'. The following discussion begins with a brief
outline of these three stances, and of the practical method associated with each stance. Once these have been described we will
be in a position to compare and contrast their epistemological
rigour and practical implications. For the most part I consider
historical research in general; eventually the argument is applied
specifically to social history.[12]

But first, a caveat. In what follows, it will be convenient to draw on some of the theorisations – the more or less formal descriptions – which historians have given to these three 'stances'. But I must stress at the outset that each of these is in fact a *practical attitude*, an epistemological *stance* associated with a particular way of *doing*. I use theorisations for convenience, as they make these stances rather more explicit and thus permit a relatively compact discussion; but this move has its costs. One such cost is that we have to defer a discussion of the relationship between theory and practice. I make the provisional, working assumption that for the profession as a whole, the range of theorisations reflects the ensemble of actual practices; but we shall later see that this is in fact a simplification. And the relation between theorisation (or its absence!) and practice in the individual historian is a complex issue which I do not pursue at all. Another cost of resorting to theorisations is that this device compounds what would anyway be a further and serious difficulty, which must also be indicated here. In trying to articulate explicitly any 'practical attitude' (hermeneutic stance), we convey the impression of referring to a *conscious* attitude or conceptual framework; but the historian's hermeneutic stance towards the documents operates at a different level. At the level of conscious frameworks we encounter substantive interests, subdisciplinary affiliations, political allegiances, explicit techniques. In contrast, the historian's 'hermeneutic stance' pertains to the practical implementation of such frameworks, the ways they are made to engage with the documents; it resides not so much within consciousness as at its foundations. In fact, as emerges below, there is no simple relationship between conscious interpretative framework and hermeneutic stance. Thus it must be stressed that the following discussion concerns the *presuppositions* of practical research; that in articulating these explicitly we are translating the pre-conscious into the conscious; and that this translation is a problematic exercise. This difficulty attends any attempt to articulate the unspoken premises of practical reasoning. Knowing of no satisfactory solution, I can only draw attention to the problem and then proceed as best I can.[13]

(1) We can treat the documents as *authorities*; this leads to the method which R.G. Collingwood termed 'scissors-and-paste', the procedure of extracting the history from the authorities. Variant forms of this stance include treating the documents as *windows upon the past* – making what could be called the assumption of

transparency; as *voices of the past*; or as *records of the past*. This stance is seldom articulated explicitly, but it is implicit in any account of historical research as a process of 'selection' from pre-existent 'facts', as the assembling and analysis of 'data', or as the extraction of information.[14]

(2) We can see the documents as sources or as *witnesses* which offer evidence and can be interrogated; this stance is associated with the practice of 'source-criticism', also called 'critical history', 'historical criticism' or 'the critique of documents'. (One variant of this view is to regard the documents simply as *evidence*.) A classic theorisation of this stance was put forward by Marc Bloch, who saw the historian as an 'examining magistrate': not (he was at pains to note) a 'grumpy' magistrate, but a kindly one, who 'is primarily interested in making [his witnesses] speak so that he may understand them'. This second stance is much more sophisticated than the first, in regarding the documents not with awe but with scepticism; indeed Collingwood, writing in 1938, asserted that this stance produced 'scientific or Baconian history'. Yet, as Collingwood realised less than two years later, this approach also entails the assumption that the documents contain a direct record of the past, so that in the end the critical historian too has to resort to 'scissors-and-paste'. Bloch himself attested to this, describing the 'method of cross examination' as 'a magnet drawing findings out of the document' – a formulation in which historical method consists not of inference but of extraction. Thus, in a seeming paradox, the second stance converges with the first. Both stances require that the documents yield a direct record of the past, or in other words that there is an identity between the historian's object-of-knowledge and some body or item of evidence. The difference between them is that the first stance posits this identity as pre-existing, while the second stance sees it as something the historian has to create by active work. This is the purpose of source-criticism: to *turn* the documents, or portions thereof, *into* the form they are assigned within the first stance: into authorities (by winnowing out the false so as to leave a true residue), into windows (by cleaning the documents so as to create transparency), or into voices (for instance, by selective choice and attentive listening).[15]

(3) Finally, we may regard the documents as *effects,* that is, as reflecting some set of past processes which await discovery by the

historian; the consistent adoption of this attitude entails as a re-search method *the investigation of the genesis of the documents.* A variant form of this stance is to see the documents as *signs* whose meaning awaits investigation: this was Collingwood's final position, elaborated in an essay written in 1939 or 1940 and published posthumously as one section of his *The Idea of History.* It was from this new stance that Collingwood was able to distance himself from source-criticism; indeed, he now denounced it with lofty vehemence: 'Critical history is of interest to the student of historical method only as the final form taken by scissors-and-paste history on the eve of its dissolution.'[16] The method asso-ciated with the third stance – investigation of document-genesis – has been most closely adumbrated by G.R. Elton and E.P. Thompson. Both their formulations need some rewriting to fit with the third stance as I am defining it; I interpolate the necessary changes in parentheses. Elton has written that 'the first question' which historians 'must ask of all evidence' [documents] is: 'why and by whom was this material produced?' Thompson asserts: 'A his-torian is entitled in his practice to make a provisional assumption of an epistemological character: that the evidence [document] which he handles has a "real" (determinant) existence . . . that this evid-ence is witness to [document is the result of] a real historical process, and that this process (or some approximate understand-ing of it) is the object of historical knowledge.'[17]

  Now between these three stances there is a steep epistemological gradient, which has a twofold character. As we move from the first stance to the second, and from the second to the third, we move *away from our natural inclinations,* and *towards episte-mological rigour.* (1) It is natural to seek direct answers to our questions in the documents, that is, to treat them as authorities, windows, voices, records. Hence the fact that scissors-and-paste, the extraction of testimony from the documents, is the starting-point of all historiography. (2) It requires a struggle and an effort to recognise that our questions cannot in fact be answered so easily, that documents are not simple repositories of truth or fact, that they can and must be criticised and interrogated – in short, to treat them as witnesses, sources, evidence. Hence the celebra-tion of historical criticism by its enthusiasts. Bloch, for instance, described it as an 'immense advance' produced against massive resistance by more than 250 years of scholarship, starting from

epistemological (rigour) = theory of knowledge, espec with regard to its methods + validation

Mabillon's *De Re Diplomatica* in 1681, and as we have seen
Collingwood initially saw critical history as 'scientific'.[18] (3) It takes
a further struggle to recognise that source-criticism does not
transcend scissors-and-paste but merely perfects it, that the past is
not to be found in the documents but must be inferred from them
– in other words, to treat documents neither as authorities nor as
witnesses but as effects. Hence the fact that the move from source-
criticism to the study of document-genesis is only practised with
difficulty, has seldom been advocated explicitly, and has proved
deeply resistant to theorisation. This latter point – the difficulty of
developing a theoretical account of this stance – is aptly illustrated
by both the provenance and the fate of the first such account,
namely Collingwood's formulation. As to its provenance, it took
Collingwood – with his unique equipment of philosophical, historical and archaeological training – twenty years of work on the
philosophy of history to come to the view that source-criticism
could be transcended. As to the fate of this conception, historians
seem to have neglected it completely when discussing Collingwood's
views, and most philosophers of history have missed its epistemological significance.[19]

The gradient of difficulty is readily appreciated, So too is the
first step in the gradient of rigour: it is clearly more sophisticated
to interrogate the documents with scepticism than to treat them as
authorities, windows, voices or direct records. But the further step
in the 'gradient of rigour' – the move from the second stance to
the third – needs closer attention. One way to bring out the nature
and significance of this step is to notice that any such stance
necessarily *assigns to the documents a particular status*. The first
stance sees them as authorities (or other variants such as windows
on the past); the second stance construes them as witnesses (or for
instance as evidence); the third stance regards them as effects (or
as signs). There may well be other such epistemological stances, or
further variants of the three I have distinguished; but any such
stance would have to construe the documents in some way,
to fix them in some role, or as I am putting it, to assign them some
status.[20] Now what we must observe is that the status assigned to
the documents under the third stance is *different in kind* from that
assigned under either of the first two stances. For the third stance
assigns a status *without reference to the historian*; the documents
are seen as 'effects' or as 'signs' of antecedent historical processes.

In contrast, the first two stances assign a status *with reference to the historian's use* of the documents: the very names they assign to the documents attest to the presence of the historian. As we shall see by developing this theme, this has profound consequences for the entire way the documents are seen – and not seen.[21]

(1) It is readily apparent that the documents become 'authorities' *for the historian* and in relation to the historian's purposes; that in placing the documents in this role, the historian is assigning them a new function; and that this necessarily detaches them from their original functions. The same applies to the related apprehension of the documents as 'windows' or 'voices' or 'records'. (2) Similarly, the documents as 'sources' or 'witnesses' or 'evidence' are assigned this role *by the activity of the historian*; and once again this confers on the documents a new complex of functions, displacing their original ones. For example, the common locution 'evidence' as a term for the documents projects the historian's apprehension of the documents into the documents themselves. The practical consequences of this move are particularly interesting and subtle. Source-criticism approaches the document with caution, suspicion, scepticism, doubt, distrust. This positions the document within the interpretative space of the historian–document relationship, aptly described in Bloch's analogy of the courtroom. The animating questions are two: what can you tell me, document, which is pertinent to my investigation? and can I trust you, document, as a witness in my investigation? Each of these questions restricts and directs the domain of significance within which the document can 'speak'. Under the constraints of the first question, the document/witness is made to testify in the particular directions assigned by the historian/magistrate, excluding any meanings conceived to be irrelevant to the enquiry. From the second question there issue two typical concerns of classical source-criticism. One is the possibility of deceit: hence Acton's perpetual 'fascination' with 'the deliberate fabrication of false documents', Bloch's 'pursuit of fraud and error'. The other is the route by which the document came into the historian's witness-box: this is why, in Butterfield's words, 'Schlozer perpetually asks "Where does our knowledge come from and how has it reached us?" ', and why Bloch was so concerned with 'the transmission of evidence'.[22]

This complex of questions – arising entirely from the apprehension of the documents as witnesses – defines a horizon of interests which encloses the historian's inferences. For example, we cannot regard truth in witness-reports as relational, that is, as dependent on the position of the witness. On a relational view of truth, we would expect any such report to reflect *both* the phenomenon reported (a massacre, a riot, an interview . . .) *and* the stance from which the witness observed it (participant, victim, secretary . . .). We would then read the report as a multiple effect or signifier, reflecting the phenomenon, the observer's position, the relation between phenomenon and observer, the relation between observing and reporting; in principle it could shed light on all of these. But under the rubric of interrogation, these interpretative threads will only be pursued insofar as they illuminate the descriptive 'accuracy' of the report. In similar fashion, the concern with the transmission of documents works to exclude an interest in their original provenance. The source-critical historian, through a perpetual concern with the question 'How did you come *to me?*', closes off the question 'How did you come *to be?*' Hence, for instance, Bloch's almost complete indifference to the genesis of documents.[23] In short, the source-critical apprehension of documents is not a neutral instrument; in the very act of striving for detachment and objectivity it constrains interpretation and contracts the horizon of meaning.

I have been arguing that the move from the first stance through the second to the third entails a double 'gradient' of an epistemological kind. But it is beginning to emerge that this move entails another and different kind of 'gradient', namely *an expansion of the substantive horizon*. With respect to the shift from the first stance to the second, this was well attested by Bloch: one important aim of his 'interrogation' of source-witnesses was to extract from them testimony they would not otherwise have yielded, thereby enlarging the domain of the historian's investigation. Precisely the same point was made by Collingwood, in more philosophical language, during that long phase of his thought when he espoused the critical method as history's 'scientific' basis. What we are now beginning to see is that the shift from the second stance to the third entails a further opening of the historian's horizons.

We can appreciate this point by observing a further aspect of the relationship between the three stances, indeed yet another epistemological 'gradient' between them. Treating the second stance as 'higher' than the first, and the third as 'higher' again, we can enunciate the principle that *each stance includes within itself the possibility of adopting the stance or stances below it.*

(a) From the second stance we can, in a particular case and as a result of our enquiries, adopt the first stance. Indeed, this is precisely the point of taking up the second stance, that is, of practising the criticism of sources. Having critically scrutinised the credentials of the document with respect to the question being asked, we have placed ourselves in the position of being able to infer fact from evidence: we can trust the document (or some aspect of its contents) as a witness in our enquiry, because we have established its credentials.

(b) From the third stance we are in a position to adopt the second and the first. By investigating the genesis of the document, we place ourselves in a stronger position to establish its credentials than can be attained in any other way. This is far from being all that we do, or all that we seek to do, from this stance, but it is one of its effects. By logical extension, since the second stance contains the possibility of the first, the third achieves this as well.

My claim here is that the study of the genesis of documents stands to source-criticism in a relation of what Hegel called *Aufhebung* and Sartre termed *dépassement*, and which has been rendered in English by 'sublation' or 'transcendence': that is, that the study of document-genesis incorporates, negates and supersedes the criticism of sources. But historians have characterised the matter in a very different way: the study of document-genesis has been treated as a *means* towards the larger *end* of source-criticism. The effect of this view is that the investigation of the genesis of documents is seen as a merely technical device. Indeed, at the level of practice it was probably in just this way that document-genesis first came to be investigated: as an aspect of source-criticism, especially of what was known as 'external' source-criticism. I contend that the best historiographical practice has already moved beyond this; that is, that the study of the genesis of documents has begun to break the bounds of source-criticism, thereby moving from the second hermeneutic stance (the documents construed as sources) to the third (the documents construed as effects). But theorisations of practice have yet to capture this shift and its significance: at the level of theory, the study of document-genesis has been *enclosed within* the criticism of sources.[24]

This remains true even of the theorisations which most clearly advocate the practice of document-genetic research – those of Elton (in his *Political History*) and Thompson (in *The Poverty of Theory*). We saw earlier that in order to assimilate their accounts of such research to the 'third stance', some rewriting was necessary. The reason for this was precisely that in the brief versions quoted above, the investigation of the genesis of documents was encapsulated within the 'second stance'. A larger examination of their formulations will reveal that this was characteristic of both their accounts.

Elton referred to the documents (1) sometimes as records, (2) usually as evidence, (3) occasionally as relics or effects. Here all three stances were in play, with the second stance dominant. Again, his discussion of the interpretation of narrative sources was largely couched within the second stance, speaking of 'criticism or assessment' and of 'the criteria for judging them'. Although the practical method he was advocating consisted largely of the study of document-genesis, and although he argued very effectively for the power of that approach, this was all conceived within the framework of the second stance: the documents were construed as evidence, their study was described as criticism, and the aim of this process was to make a judgment of their accuracy. The second stance thus served as a discursive container which held the study of document-genesis within firmly-constructed boundaries.[25]

Thompson's most explicit characterisation of the historian – document relationship was as follows:

The historical evidence is there, in its primary form, not to disclose its own meaning, but to be interrogated by minds trained in a discipline of attentive disbelief. The discrete facts may be interrogated in at least six very different ways:

1) Before any other interrogation can be commenced, their credentials *as* historical facts must be scrutinised: how were they recorded? for what purpose? can they be confirmed from adjacent evidence? And so on. This is the bread-and-butter of the trade.

Here the investigation of the genesis of documents is described as a means to source-criticism, and the overall formulation is in characteristically source-critical form: evidence, credentials, interrogation, attentive disbelief. Thompson's five further forms of 'interrogation' included much that could be subsumed under the third hermeneutic stance, for instance:

5) As links in a lateral series of social/ideological/economic/political relations (as, for example – this contract is a special case of the general forms of contracts at the time: such contracts were governed by these forms of law; they enforced these forms of obligation and subordination), enabling us thereby to recover or infer, from many instances, at least a provisional 'section' of a given society in the past – its characteristic relations of power, domination, kinship, servitude, market relations, and the rest;

But in conceiving the documents as 'evidence' and the historian's enterprise as an 'interrogation', Thompson was enclosing this within the traditional framework of source-criticism, associated with the second stance.[26]

These accounts may be taken to represent the most sophisticated position that can be attained within the second stance. They have moved far beyond the limitations imposed by classical source-criticism, which as we saw pursued the *transmission* of 'evidence' to the systematic exclusion of its genesis. Indeed, so far have they advanced beyond, for instance, Marc Bloch's formulation that they must be regarded as embodying a distinct variety of the second stance – a variety which perhaps deserves some name of its own. At the point they delineate, the method associated with the second stance (source-criticism) has developed into a new practice (the study of document-genesis) whose further pursuit would undermine the stance itself. Hence, perhaps, the instability of terminology in both these accounts: their tendency to move between fact and evidence, record and relic as depictions of the documents, and to shift from interrogation to inference as descriptions of the historian's activity. Yet this point also defines their limit: their framework is defined by the second stance, enclosing the study of document-genesis firmly within the criticism of sources.[27]

This confirms, from a different angle, our earlier observation that the third stance has proved so resistant to theorisation. We saw the difficulty experienced by Collingwood, who approached the issue from a philosophical direction – that is, in pursuit of an *epistemological foundation* for 'scientific' history. Elton and Thompson have addressed our theme from a more practical angle, from a concern with what historians can and should *do*; and they, too, have come up against the conceptual wall imposed by the dominance of source-criticism and its underlying hermeneutic stance. This two-directional pattern helps us to illuminate the source of the difficulty: the foundations of historical knowledge reside precisely in the space of intersection between practice and epistemology, a space largely barred off by existing academic conventions and divisions.

I have made three central claims for the 'third hermeneutic stance': that it has foundational significance, that it tends to elude theorisation, and that it expands the substantive horizons of the historian. I now want to illustrate this triple claim through a little case-study in historiographic debate, pursued into a substantive illustration.

In 1980, *History Workshop Journal* published – much to its credit – an article by David Selborne which roundly attacked the practices of that journal and of the History Workshops from which the journal had sprung some five years earlier. In the pages immediately following Selborne's paper there appeared a detailed reply by Raphael Samuel. Selborne accused *History Workshop* of 'the hallucination of direct encounter with the past', based upon what he called 'resurrectionism', that is, 'the repeopling of the past by archival exhumation'. He argued that such 'resurrectionism' was 'prone to the illusion that it is an historian-free history; that it is history which speaks for itself'. In support of his argument he adduced Collingwood's observation that 'the facts are not empirically present to the historian's mind; they cannot be derived from perceptual experience; they are past events, to be apprehended not empirically, but by a process of inference . . . from data given or . . . discovered'. Seen from the standpoint I have been developing, Selborne's claim was that *History Workshop* historiography was trapped within the first hermeneutic stance: extracts from the documents were reproduced uncritically as if these were voices of the past. Thus Selborne's methodological critique addressed precisely the issues we have been considering here, invoking Collingwood in the process. There was much else in Selborne's essay, above all the argument that such historiography was un-Marxist. So too Samuel's reply went into a wide range of issues, such as the history and political orientation both of History Workshops and of the journal *History Workshop*, and their relation to the wider academic and political context. But it is his response to Selborne's methodological critique which is of particular interest in the present context. Taking up the challenge, Samuel

put forward his own account of the historian's practical procedures, making a rare and courageous attempt to articulate their
epistemological foundations.[28]

Samuel's discussion – summarised here with emphases added –
was literally haunted by the theme of document-genesis and by
the question as to whether document-genesis can be known or
studied: the account veered around these issues in a fascinating
way, finally dismissing them by a tactic of evasion. At an early
stage, document-genesis was depicted as a matter not of knowledge, but of 'speculation': 'The documents . . . can be stored in
files and indexed, but *their original context and relationships are
necessarily a matter for speculation.*' However, a little later it
emerged that '*it is possible to reveal something of the interstices
in which* [the documents] *existed*', suggesting that document-
genesis can be known – though perhaps significantly, only in part.
How, then, does the historian achieve this knowledge? All that the
account offered was a tantalising hint: '*often by juxtaposing them
against each other*'. This compact phrase was dense with significance: suppressing the historian's intellectual labour (by reducing
it to the act of 'juxtaposing'); assuming the corollary that the
sources contain the answer ('them against each other'); and destroying the possibility of a general formulation, so that ultimately
the historian's practice became a mystery (by means of the devastating little opening qualifier 'often'). Not surprisingly, it now
became necessary to produce some reassuring rhetoric: 'Nor is the
historian projecting fantasies onto the past. There is *a dialectical
play of subject and object*, and the terms of it will alter according
to the means to hand.'

Clearly everything hinged on the nature of this 'dialectical play'.
But so far from explaining such a dialectic, the discussion retreated
immediately into the assumption of transparency. Specifically, it
was argued by means of examples that different sources offer the
historian different degrees of access to the past. 'Some classes of
document do give a *more direct encounter with the past* than
others.' 'Here household inventories and diocesan court records
were instanced, for 'the level of material culture' and 'the occasions
of neighbourly quarrels' respectively. 'Again, there are certain
documents which *enable us to enter – or at any rate approach –
the mental landscape of the past.*' The examples given were In-
quisition records, the transcripts of the Putney debates, and the

poems of François Villon. Here the account of the historian's practical methods ended. Samuel had concluded that the historian's craft consists in finding the past in the sources and extracting it therefrom. The possibility of investigating document-genesis was half-seen and immediately shunned; the 'dialectical' nature of historical knowledge was invoked, but purely to rhetorical effect. In the end the account returned to the assumption of transparency, to the sources as voices of the past; translated into practice, this would entail neither more nor less than the method of scissors-and-paste. This was exactly what Selborne had criticised in the first place. In trying to defend *History Workshop Journal* against Selborne's charge of 'resurrectionism', Samuel had unwittingly fallen back on just that approach. Had his account spelt out a concrete meaning for the 'dialectical play of subject and object', that meaning would surely have been the study of document-genesis – the very possibility which danced and dissolved at the dangerous margins of the argument. But instead the account resorted to the assumption of transparency.

But perhaps the documents – or some of them, or parts of some of them – really are transparent. Indeed this is precisely what the historian wants to believe: that there exists some testimony from the past which directly and unambiguously records the intended object of knowledge. This deep-rooted desire continually propels us towards the primitive first hermeneutic stance, and the motley legion of documents from the past give us an ample body of material towards which we can take up that stance. Arguing against the effects of this desire, I have tried to show that the assumption of transparency is mistaken in principle. No individual instance can demonstrate this general claim, nor indeed can any number of such instances. Nevertheless it will be worth making the case for one specific example, taken from Samuel's shortlist of documents which 'do give a more direct encounter with the past'. This will also indicate in a concrete case the practical implications of each of the three interpretative stances distinguished above. The example I have chosen is 'cases in the diocesan courts', which as we saw 'testify to the occasions of neighbourly quarrels'. For simplicity, let us leave aside the complex and shifting variety of cases in such courts, and let us imagine that we are restricting our attention to some definable group of cases (perhaps defamation suits) which can be construed as reflections of 'neighbourly quarrels'.

Now in fact both the presence of such cases in the diocesan courts, and the process of their recording, resulted from *interactions* between 'neighbourly quarrels' on the one hand and the activities of ecclesiastical officers, churchwardens and ministers on the other. This follows in principle from the fact that these courts were instruments of the diocesan authorites (not of the neighbours), and that their records were produced by the ecclesiastical officers, for court use and following institutionally-determined procedures. The same is shown concretely by any study of church-court records which has attended to the conditions of their genesis.[29] Hence the records of the diocesan courts 'testify to the occasions of neighbourly quarrels' only *indirectly*. A neighbourly quarrel could only get into the court through some process of co-operation, or collusion, or coincidence between the quarrel itself and the activities and interests of the mediating authorities – ecclesiastical officers, minister and churchwardens. Thus, to begin with, the cases in the court 'testify' not to 'the occasions of neighbourly quarrel' in general, but rather to those cases of neighbourly quarrel which harmonised in some way with the activities and interests of the mediating authorities. Should we overlook this, and seek to use diocesan court records as transparent windows upon 'the occasions of neighbourly quarrel', our research procedure would consist simply of extracting the chosen cases from the documents. This would render our error invisible and its effects irrecoverable.

But this does not mean that the historian cannot recover 'the occasions of neighbourly quarrels' from these records. What it does mean is that, in order to do so with any reliability, the historian has to take account of the ways cases came into court and the procedures by which they were recorded. This necessarily entails a shift in the object of knowledge: the historian's gaze has widened, so that it now encompasses the interactions between 'the occasions of neighbourly quarrel' and the activities of those I have called the 'mediating authorities'. In moving beyond the naive assumption of transparency, we have enlarged the scope of our enquiries; this is necessary as a means to answering reliably the question with which we began.

At this point, however, we reach a cross-roads of interpretative strategy. Our hypothetical historian has reached the point of reconstructing certain 'interactions'. But she or he can pursue this task in either of two very different ways. In source-critical mode, the aim will be to *filter out* the contribution of the ecclesiastical and parochial officers, cleaning the documentary window so as to create transparency and thus render clearly visible the original object of study – 'the occasions of neighbourly quarrel'. Here the 'mediating authorities' are seen as imposing distortions on the record; correspondingly, the historian's task is to eliminate the distortions; and once this has been done, there is indeed a correspondence between record and object-of-study. Having begun with a dirty record, we end with a clean one: the nature of the record has been transformed by the historian's activity, the activity of source-criticism. The historian's questions, on the other hand, remain unchanged; after a temporary detour through document-genesis, for the purpose of source-criticism, we return to our original topic of the 'occasions of neighbourly quarrel'.

By contrast, under the rubric of document-genetic-investigation, the activities of the ecclesiastical and parochial officers would *become part of* the object of study. This would immediately widen that object, in a direction which extends into the very broad theme of the relations between Church and people. We would still be able to recover 'the occasions of neighbourly quarrel'; but we would also be investigating a far wider set of issues. Moreover, this could shed unexpected light on our original object of study: for instance, it might enable us to extend our brief from the occasions of neighbourly quarrel to the wider significance of those 'occasions', to their place in a set of structural and institutional relationships, their connection with the gender-order, their articulation with economic relationships . . . It is in just such ways as this that the third hermeneutic stance opens the domain of our enquiries, enlarges the scope of our inferences, extends the range of our subject-matter.

To this expansion of our horizons there is no limit. Under the third stance, any topic of research, no matter how restricted, can in principle open out onto the entire society. The fundamental reason for this – so simple that it has apparently escaped notice – is that the society we are studying generated the documents we are using. *In investigating the genesis of documents we are thus investigating that society.*

I have been arguing that the third hermeneutic stance supplies the necessary foundation of all historical knowledge. Applied to the particular concerns of social history, this argument yields two propositions:

(1) The methods of social history are to be sought not in exterior disciplines but from within the historical discipline itself. This is the very inversion of that importing of methods from the social sciences which comprises the 'social history paradigm'.

(2) The third hermeneutic stances enables us to resolve the specific epistemological dilemmas of social history.

Each of these claims requires some elaboration.

method validation

The limitations of the 'social history paradigm'

If the foundational significance of the third hermeneutic stance is accepted, then it follows that the 'social history paradigm' does not unproblematically enlarge the scope of historical understanding. (In this respect its significance parallels that of source-criticism: each has both enlarged and constrained historical understanding.) For that paradigm has worked in three linked ways to propel historians away from the third hermeneutic stance. In the first place, at the level of procedure, it has promoted a view of historical documents as bodies of 'data' ripe and ready for interrogation by social-scientific categories. The result has been a certain tendency for social history to resort to a scissors-and-paste method, sometimes enriched by source-criticism, sometimes not.[30] Second, as the other side of the same coin, the 'social history paradigm' has resulted in an asymmetrical treatment of – in E.P. Thompson's phrase – concept and evidence. Because the concepts have been treated as a set of fixed 'tools' with which to interpret 'the evidence', social historians have been relatively reluctant to use the 'evidence' to test the concepts, or indeed to see that this was a possibility.[31] Third, at the level of methodological reflection, this paradigm posited that the question of method resided entirely at the level of conscious category-frames and techniques, thus deflecting attention away from the historian's hermeneutic stance. As we have seen, the latter domain is inherently elusive to theorisation; the focus upon conscious category-frames has compounded this difficulty.

Now these considerations shed light on what must so far have seemed a paradox – the methodological convergence between

Geoffrey Elton and Edward Thompson; and it will be worth digressing from our proposition to consider this point. Earlier we saw that Elton and Thompson have been responsible for the clearest formulations of the need to study the genesis of documents. At first sight these two historians seem to be very strange bedfellows, profoundly opposed as they are in political allegiance, substantive interests, social location and historiographic roots: Thompson's approach was formed in the history-of-the-people tradition as refracted through the British Communist Party, Elton's in State historiography as taught by J.E. Neale. Indeed, all they appear to share is a certain combative seriousness which only sharpens their mutual opposition. Yet their concerns show some important points of intersection: the nature of political processes; the relationship between those processes and their 'structural' setting; the character, formation and activities of the British State; the active contribution of human agency to human history; the significance of *time* in human affairs. For each of them this latter point has been crucial. Characteristically, they have conceived it quite differently: for Thompson it raises the conceptual problem of the relation between process and structure, whereas for Elton it poses the literary challenge of a synthesis between narrative and analysis. Nevertheless this shared concern with time is a further indication of a certain kinship or affinity between their underlying conceptions of historical process.[32]

This centrality of time for Thompson and Elton is associated with a further convergence: each has consistently argued for the epistemological integrity of the historical discipline. For both of them, this has entailed contesting the 'social history paradigm'. Thompson developed this argument as early as 1963 with reference to functionalist sociology, extended it in 1972 to the historical application of anthropology and quantification, and in *The Poverty of Theory* (1978) applied it still more widely. Elton began to argue along these lines in 1967, refined his position in 1970, restated it in 1983, and was still contesting the issue in 1991. Strikingly, both of them took as a key early target Keith Thomas's 1966 essay entitled 'The tools and job', the clearest formulation of the social-history paradigm. It has been in the context of this argument that both Thompson and Elton have formulated the document-genetic approach to historical research.[33]

This resolves our paradox; the methodological convergence

between Elton and Thompson is intelligible as the result of a shared opposition to the 'social-history paradigm'. Their disquiet with that paradigm has driven both these historians to articulate in a new way the methodological foundations of the historical discipline – to push the concept of source-criticism to its outer limit as the study of the genesis of documents. This supports (albeit indirectly) the proposition from which we have been digressing, namely the present claim that the social-history paradigm tends to close off the third hermeneutic stance. Seen in this light, the formulation achieved by Thompson and Elton is an ironic and dialectical fruit of the social-history paradigm.

But our digression has touched on a further issue, which cannot be developed in detail here yet merits attention: namely the relationship between hermeneutic stance and conscious category-frames. Earlier I stressed that 'there is no simple relationship between conscious interpretative framework and hermeneutic stance'. The juxtaposition of Thompson and Elton confirms that the relationship is indeed far from 'simple', since their convergence over method coexists with a radical contrast of aims. Yet at the same time it appears that there is *some* relationship between the two domains, since their methodological convergence is linked to certain shared substantive concerns. This points to a fundamental ambiguity in the present account. On the one hand, I am concerned to argue that the third hermeneutic stance enlarges and enriches all historical research, whatever its starting-point and substantive theme. Moreover, I have claimed that it is possible from within this stance to take up the second stance and, by extension, the first. On these grounds it seems that the third stance always enlarges the scope of historical research, never contracts it; and this line of thought would suggest that substantive categories and hermeneutic stance are *mutually independent*. But on the other hand, any methodological proposal necessarily entails exclusion as well as inclusion, proscription as well as prescription; and along the way we have encountered various indications that the adoption of the third hermeneutic stance involves changes of practice. This might be taken to suggest that the adoption of the third hermeneutic stance would lead in particular interpretative directions; and the fact that Thompson and Elton share certain substantive concerns seems to support the latter reading. Following this line of thought, we might well infer that substantive categories and hermeneutic stance are

closely connected. Thus our two lines of thought produce dia-
metrically opposite conclusions. I can offer here no resolution of
this ambiguity; the issue will be clarified only through the concrete
practice of historical research.

*The resolution of social history's epistemological dilemmas
from the third hermeneutic stance*
Earlier we saw that each of the three dominant conceptions of
social history faced unresolved epistemological problems. The third
hermeneutic stance can resolve these as follows.

(a) The difficulties of coverage and representativeness faced by
'history from below' arise from the limitations of content and
provenance in the total ensemble of documents. Reconstructing the processes of genesis of the documents provides the
most inclusive means available for understanding and explaining those limitations, and hence of allowing for them.
(b) The main difficulty of the 'social history paradigm' lies in
assessing the commensurability of different conceptual grids,
which is ultimately a problem of meaning. Now meaning is
dependent upon the context of use, and it is precisely this
which is explored through the study of document-genesis.
(c) The 'history of society' is not directly inscribed in any records
at all, and is thus permanently elusive for the first and second
hermeneutic stances. But once we construe documents as
effects – that is, once we take up the third hermeneutic stance
– we see that society 'records itself' in the processes which
generate documents. From this viewpoint, *every* document is
a 'record' of the society! The key to such a reading is to shift
attention from the surface 'plane' (the content of documents)
to the underlying 'volume' (the processes which generated
those documents and their content).

To demonstrate this in detail, and to discuss all the modalities
of document-genetic research, would require a treatise in itself;
here I only offer a few observations.[34]
First, this way of reading documents is already widespread. We
encounter it, I suggest, as that loosely-formulated 'sense of
context', or 'discipline of historical context', which is widely held
to characterise the work of the trained historian. We see it too,
in very different guise, as an aspect of source-criticism – though

it needs to be liberated from the fetters of that method. It arises again in certain particular contexts where it just so happens that the historian's substantive interests lead in this direction – in administrative history; in studies of public conflicts, where printed tracts are seen as interventions; in the interpretation of specific genres, from imaginative literature (the 'new historicism') to folklore. Further, a move towards the third hermeneutic stance is precisely what is entailed in Quentin Skinner's approach to the history of ideas. For Skinner's shift of focus from the question *what did an author mean by X?* to the question *what did an author mean to do by saying X?* – that is, his insistence that the content of 'classic texts' must be located in a context of action – expands the historian's object of study from 'ideas' supposedly contained in 'texts' to the processes by which those 'texts' were generated. Moreover, the 'linguistic turn' has recently led some scholars to adopt the third hermeneutic stance, with highly fruitful results: Joan Scott on statistical representation, Dror Wahrman on Parliamentary reporting. Once its foundational significance and heuristic power are appreciated, this mode of historical research will come to be practised throughout the discipline.[35]

Second, research into document-genesis does not replace the substantive concerns of the historian: rather, it provides the very means for answering those questions. By accepting the document-genetic dimension of historical research, we are simply attuning our enquiry to the nature of its object. It is true that this will change the nature of our questions. But the changes this effects will be to improve those questions, to sharpen them, to align them with the social processes of the past we are studying. Of course we resist these alterations in our questions; there will always be a tension between present interrogative and the form and content of past relics. But this is a creative tension – provided we allow it to be.[36]

Third, such research embraces not only the genesis of particular documents, but also, more boldly, the origins of whole *genres* of documents. We have elsewhere in this book encountered two eighteenth-century genres which call for precisely this approach: the domestic novel and the literature of reform projects.[37] For nineteenth-century Britain the official publications of the State similarly need to be seen not just as convenient bodies of evidence but rather as reflections and instruments of a new kind of State. Thus Corrigan and Sayer have observed that

Those thousands of volumes of Blue Books (Parliamentary publications) which fill the rooms of what used to be called the State Paper Room of the British Museum (now the Official Publications room of the British Library) need to be reconceptualized as key instruments of the moral revolution of the nineteenth century. They are the English disciplines of State formation in this period.

The fruitfulness of exploring the genesis of such publications is amply illustrated by the separate studies of Goldman and Higgs on the activities of the General Register Office (GRO). Their initial results are highly consequential in substance (for instance, bearing on the invention of 'society' as an organism), in technical import (explaining the GRO's occupational categories as medically-inspired) and in breaking down modern disciplinary barriers (between social, political, medical and intellectual history). The reason that such research is so telling lies not in any particular quality of the GRO, but in the opening of horizons entailed in adopting the third hermeneutic stance.[38]

Finally, the study of document-genesis takes as its explanatory object not the mere existence of a given document or genre, but rather its very *content*. For example, this includes the origin of key items of vocabulary (thus incorporating a central lesson of the 'linguistic turn') and the influence of conventions of content (which connects the theme of content with that of genre). Moreover, a reconstruction of the genesis of content embraces the *boundaries* of that content: its outlines, its limits, the relation between what it includes and what it excludes. One might say that an adequate map of content is defined by non-content – by the silences, absences, gaps, emptinesses which by surrounding explicit content confer upon that content its peculiar shape and meaning. By attending to the genesis of content we can not only tackle but also exploit the uneven reflections of gender, class, age, power on the surface of the documents. This assumes critical importance with respect to the issue of gender. We are confronted in the first instance by a massive asymmetry: men predominate over women both as authors of documents and as agents mentioned within those documents. This asymmetry itself is of immense significance, not just as an obstacle to reconstructing the lives of women in the past, but rather as a phenomenon in its own right, with a particular texture and structure. For example, in eighteenth-century England, the gender-balance was very different in respect of the novel: the new genre was produced very largely *for* women, in important ways it was *about* women, and it was actually written at least as much *by* women as it was by men (a fact later obliterated by the conventional canon). This example, when contrasted with many other genres such as political pamphlets, reveals that the gender-balance of documents in this period was far from uniform. Taking this as a starting-point we could dissect the structure of this balance, characterise its profile, and seek to explain it in relational terms – an enterprise which would be posited upon the third hermeneutic stance. So too with individual documents, a shift of focus from their manifest content to the process of their genesis can reveal the agency of women in daily life, even starting from a document written very much from a male point of view.[39]

Conclusion

We began with the 'historian's dilemma', well captured in Jordanova's observation that 'history has the status of "knowledge", whilst primary sources have the status of "evidence" and . . . the transition from evidence to knowledge is highly problematic'. The source of that dilemma is that the very relationship between historian and 'evidence' is problematical. This can be formulated in various ways: as the problem of anachronism; as the conjoining of different discourses; as a disparity between language-games. Now it is this very issue which is addressed by each of the two practices we have been considering. Concept-criticism draws attention to the 'historian' side of the relationship; the study of document-genesis focuses upon the 'evidence' side. The two practices support and sustain each other; taken together, they comprise what Edward Thompson characterised as 'historical logic', which he described as a 'dialogue between concept and evidence'.[40]

Articulating Thompson's 'historical logic' has entailed changing two of its three terms. The seemingly-neutral term 'evidence' in fact contains the projected image of the historian; in its place I have used 'documents', as a convenient shorthand for the more accurate phrase *relics of the past*. The difficulty with 'dialogue' is of course its literal inaccuracy: in reality, the historian is engaged in a monologue, for the documents themselves cannot 'speak'. Thus the problem becomes: how is the historian to listen? That is: how is the historian to respond to the documents *as if* they could speak, to 'hear' in them any 'voice' of their own, apart from what the historian is projecting into them? The answer suggested here has been twofold. First, the practice of concept-criticism opens the historian's own categories to possible revision. Second, the adoption of the 'third hermeneutic stance' opens the historian's horizon of enquiry to the original context in which the documents were generated.

Seen in this light, concept-criticism and the study of document-genesis are indeed, as was hinted at the outset, 'two aspects of a single process'. We may also note in passing a further convergence between these two practices. The 'third hermeneutic stance' treats the relics of the past as products or effects. And concept-criticism, in its 'genealogical' form, treats our own concepts in exactly the same way. Thus 'historical logic' as adumbrated here is a reflexive method.

Just as concept-criticism should proceed without limits, so too with the study of document-genesis. Since the genesis of any document is ultimately the work of the whole society, the moment or point at which we close document-genetic enquiry is also, and very precisely, the moment of conceptual closure. The corollary is that the study of document-genesis can, and I suggest will, lead historians *back to the totality* – to that sense of the whole society which has proved so elusive for social history. The frustration of social history's totalising ambitions arises from two artefacts of its disciplinary structure: its internal fragmentation (ably described by Wrightson in Chapter 2), and its separation from other historical disciplines, particularly from State historiography (which I have stressed in Chapter 1). The study of document-genesis, leading as it does in open-ended directions, offers the possibility of transcending such disciplinary boundaries. What is most exciting about this prospect is that it does not matter where we start. There is no privileged vantage-point or starting-point: on the contrary, it will continue to enrich the subject if we begin from a plethora of *different* starting-points. Each such starting-point gives us a distinctive transection of the society we are studying; at the same time, these different transections can ultimately converge. Thus the study of document-genesis links together the activities of all historians, not only methodologically but also substantively. This opens the prospect of a reconciliation between State and social historiographies, of a healing of social history's internal divisions, and thus of a totalising historiography.

If, as I have argued, the epistemological foundations suggested here resolve the 'historian's dilemma', they also offer the possibility of a new, more reciprocal relationship between history and the social sciences. For those foundations, while derived from the discipline of history, are equally applicable to the objects of the social sciences. Historians will rightly continue to use conceptual resources from other disciplines; but in addition, those disciplines in their turn will look to historical scholarship for methodological resources. This gives a practical basis for that rapprochement between sociology and history of which Giddens and Abrams have laid the conceptual foundations.

A quarter of a century ago, the historical discipline in England began to open itself to the social sciences; Keith Wrightson has attested in this volume to the excitement this generated at the time. What is now opening up is a far more exciting prospect. Historians can, and will, transcend those disciplinary boundaries which both surround and divide their subject. And their reconstructions of the past will increasingly speak to the present.

Acknowledgments

For their advice and encouragement in the writing of this chapter and with the thinking behind it, I am grateful to Alessandra d'Acconti, Andrew Cunningham, Roger French, Peter Hennock, Sarah Irons, Nick Jardine, Ludmilla Jordanova, Maria Kiely and Simon Schaffer. I especially thank Peter Lipton, who has given much valuable help in the course of several discussions; and Timothy Ashplant, whose past and present collaboration and advice has contributed substantially to the framework developed here. The argument and its errors are nevertheless my own responsibility.

Notes

1   Maurice Mandelbaum, *The Problem of Historical Knowledge* (New York: Liveright, 1938). On post-modernism and history see Thomas

C. Patterson, 'Post-structuralism, post-modernism: implications for historians', *Social History* 14 (1989), pp. 83–8, at 87–8; F.R. Ankersmit, 'Historiography and postmodernism', *History and Theory* 28 (1989), pp. 137–53; Perez Zagorin, 'Historiography and postmodernism: reconsiderations', *History and Theory* 29 (1990), pp. 263–96; Keith Jenkins, *Rethinking History* (London: Routledge, 1991); Lawrence Stone, 'History and post-modernism', *Past and Present*, 131 (1991), pp. 217–18; and the subsequent debate in *ibid.*, 133 (1991), pp. 204–13 (Patrick Joyce, Catriona Kelly), and 135 (1992), pp. 189–208 (Stone again, Gabrielle M. Spiegel).

2 E.P. Thompson, *The Poverty of Theory* (London: Merlin, 1978), p. 231; for 'the test of historical logic', see p. 236; against Popper, p. 218. Robert Gray notes that Thompson elided the distinction between 'historical materialism' and the discipline of history: 'History, Marxism and theory', in Harvey J. Kaye and Keith McClelland eds., *E.P. Thompson: critical perspectives* (Cambridge: Polity 1990), pp. 153–182, at p. 166. Similarly, Thompson's account also conflated historical research as it is practised and as he believed it should be practised.

3 Penelope J. Corfield, 'Introduction', in Corfield ed., *Language, History and Class* (Oxford: Basil Blackwell, 1991), p. 12; Ludmilla Jordanova, 'The interpretation of nature', *Comparative Studies in Society and History* 29 (1987), pp. 195–200, at p. 198; Peter Burke, 'Overture: the new history, its past and its future', in Burke ed., *New Perspectives on Historical Writing* (Cambridge: Polity, 1991), pp. 12, 13, 15. For another recent statement of the unresolved theory/evidence problem, see Gray, 'History, Marxism and theory', pp. 169–70.

4 On tacit skills in the natural sciences, compare Harry Collins, *Changing Order: Replication and Induction in Scientific Practice* (London: Sage, 1985), Chapter 3, particularly pp. 56–8, 73.

5 Philip Abrams, *Historical Sociology* (Shepton Mellet: Open Books, 1982), p. 322, used the phrase 'the critique of categories' to refer to the cognate process by which organised empirical findings can make 'a contribution to criticism' in respect of 'analytical problems' (p. 320). Robert Gray argues that 'the discipline of the sources, and the possibility of challenge and refutation from a reading of sources is a central feature of history as a discipline, Marxist or otherwise' ('History, Marxism and theory', p. 177; see also p. 170). John Tosh writes in similar vein: *The Pursuit of History: aims, methods and new directions in the study of modern history*, (London: Longman, 1984), p. 124 (1992 edn, p. 150). Lawrence Stone has described 'that feedback process by which the historian normally thinks, thanks to which hunches are tested by data, and the data in turn generate new hunches', invoking this as an argument against the use of the computer: *The Past and the Present* (London: Routledge, 1981), p. 29.

6   For some examples of this process in the experimental sciences, see the essays in David Gooding, Trevor Pinch and Simon Schaffer eds., *The Uses of Experiment* (Cambridge University Press, 1989); and also David Gooding and Frank A.J.L. James eds., *Faraday Rediscovered: essays on the life and work of Michael Faraday, 1791–1867* (Basingstoke: Macmillan, 1985). It seems that the subsequent suppressing-forgetting-eliding, which confers retrospective invisibility upon an epistemologically crucial process, also occurs in experimental science, but that the associated psychic mechanisms are rather different there. See Collins, *Changing Order*, pp. 74–6.

7   As examples, see Simon Schaffer's historicisation of the concept of the scientific anomaly, 'Natural philosophy', in G.S. Rousseau and Roy Porter eds., *The Ferment of Knowledge* (Cambridge University Press, 1980), pp. 55–91; and Keith Tribe's treatment of economic categories in *Land, Labour and Economic Discourse* (London: Routledge, 1978).

8   See Tribe, *Land, Labour and Economic Discourse*; David Cannadine, 'The present and the past in the English industrial revolution 1880–1980', *Past and Present* 103 (1984), pp. 131–72; Corfield, 'Introduction', in Corfield ed., *Language, History and Class*, and references there cited.

9   Nicholas Jardine, 'Writing off the Scientific Revolution' (essay review of David C. Lindberg and Robert S. Westman eds., *Reappraisals of the Scientific Revolution*, Cambridge University Press, 1990), *Journal of the History of Astronomy* 22 (1991), pp. 311–18, quoted from pp. 312–13.

10 On 'revolution' see the essays in Roy Porter and Miklas Teich eds., *Revolution in History* (Cambridge University Press, 1986). On the reification of concepts see Derek Sayer, *The Violence of Abstraction: the analytic foundations of historical materialism* (Oxford: Blackwell, 1978), pp. 141–2 and *passim*, who suggests that this is exactly what happened to the method of Marx in the hands of Marxism: 'mutation from method to dogma' (p. 141). Compare Gray, 'History, Marxism and theory', p. 174. One currently fashionable concept which might benefit from criticism is that of *discourse*. Current usage seems to include some fundamental ambiguities. What is its referent: the sphere of language alone, or that of human activities? And in either case (more obviously so in the second) what is the relation between discourse and text?

11 I use the notion of 'imagined pasts' by analogy with Benedict Anderson, *Imagined Communities: reflections on the origins and spread of nationalism* (London: Verso, 1983). The issue of 'imagined pasts' is well-recognised on a smaller scale, in the context of community studies, as the problem of 'mythical pasts'. The latter concept was

apparently coined by Stephen Thernstrom in 1965, to describe a tendency for urban history to adopt as analytical categories the myths of the communities being studied. It is now being recognised that this problem extends more widely in contemporary sociology. See Stephen Kendrick, Pat Straw and David McCrone, 'Introduction: sociology and history, the past and the present', in Kendrick, Straw and McCrone eds., *Interpreting the Past, Understanding the Present* (London: Macmillan, 1990; British Sociological Association conference volume series, 'Explorations in Sociology', vol. 30), pp. 1–8, at 5–6, and Bob Hall, 'The historical reconstruction of rural localities: a New Zealand Case Study', in *ibid.*, pp. 100–21, at 101–2.

12 For the term 'hermeneutic stance' I am indebted to Peter Lipton.

13 What is described in Chapter 1 above as the historian's 'historical metaphysic' is perhaps intermediate between conscious category-frame and hermeneutic stance. The following discussion draws upon T.G. Ashplant and Adrian Wilson, 'Present-centred history and the problem of historical knowledge', *History Journal* 31 (1988), pp. 253–74, at 265–73 (for some practical examples see pp. 254–61, 271–2), and on the companion article, Adrian Wilson and T.G. Ashplant, 'Whig history and present-centred history', *ibid.*, pp. 1–16, at 12–13.

14 For facts and their selection see for instance Herbert Butterfield, *The Whig Interpretation of History* (London: Bell, 1931), and E.H. Carr, *What is History?* (London: Macmillan, 1961), especially Chapter 1 (but with an entirely contrary position obtruding on p. 13). Records of the past: J.H. Hexter, *The History Primer* (London: Allen Lane, 1971; first published New York: Basic Books, 1971), pp. 84–103. For 'data' see Lawrence Stone, 'History and the social sciences in the twentieth century', in *The Past and the Present, passim*, e.g. pp. 18, 20, 27, 29, 37. Historical research as extraction: Abrams, *Historical Sociology*, p. 318. For critiques of 'scissors-and-paste' see R.G. Collingwood, *The Idea of History* (Oxford University Press, 1961; first published Oxford: Clarendon Press, 1946), pp. 257–61; Ashplant and Wilson, 'Present-centred history', pp. 266–8. Another variant of the first hermeneutic stance can be seen in the apprehension of selected relics-of-the-past as 'texts' – an approach commonly deployed in the history of ideas, and associated with the concept of a tradition embodied in a canon of 'classic texts'. In this formulation, such relics are apprehended as the actual presence of the past: hence such locutions as 'Plato says' for *Plato wrote*, and 'Plato' for *the works of Plato*. The ceaseless reprinting of 'classic texts' makes this apprehension self-confirming, for it renders the past-as-texts literally present on our bookshelves.

15 Marc Bloch, *The Historian's Craft* (Manchester University Press, 1954; original edition in French, 1949), pp. 75 (magistrate), 54 (magnet),

and *passim*. In an earlier section (entitled 'General characteristics of historical observation', pp. 40–50), Bloch's terminology for the documents was both variable and, in relation to the three stances being distinguished here, ambiguous: for instance 'vestiges of the past' p. 44, 'residues' p. 45, 'tracks' p. 45, 'the mark[s] ... left behind' by phenomena p. 46. His characterisation became more precise as he turned to 'evidence' (pp. 50–7) and to 'the critical method' (pp. 66–75, 91–113). R.G. Collingwood, *An Autobiography* (1st edn, Oxford, Clarendon Press, 1939; 1970 edition, p. 133 (and see also p. 81); for the shift in Collingwood's views see below. Recent discussions of the source-critical method include Arthur Marwick, *The Nature of History* (London: Macmillan 1970), pp. 136–8, and Tosh, *The Pursuit of History*, Chapter 3, 'Using the sources'. Recent enthusiasts for Bloch's approach include Alan Macfarlane, *The Culture of Capitalism* (Oxford: Blackwell, 1987), 'Postscript', pp. 191–222; Burke, 'Overture'; Tosh, *The Pursuit of History*, 1984 edn, pp. 31, 51, 115 (1992 edn, pp. 34, 57, 138). For the concept of witnesses and testimony in the social sciences, see Agnes Heller, 'From hermeneutics in social science toward a hermeneutics of social science', *Theory and Society* 18 (1989), pp. 291–322, at pp. 306–8.

16 See Collingwood, *The Idea of History*, Part V, section 3, 'Historical Evidence', pp. 249–82, esp. 257–61. Unfortunately for the reader, in most other relevant passages of Part V (for instance, on p. 282), Collingwood continued to espouse 'critical history'. Thus the same book contains two very different positions; and moreover the section on 'The historical imagination' (pp. 231–49) may be regarded as transitional between these. To compound the difficulty, Collingwood used the very same language – 'Baconian', 'scientific' – first in praise of source-criticism (in *An Autobiography*, as we have seen, and also in the apparently transitional section of *The Idea of History*, p. 237) and then for the move *beyond* source-criticism (*The Idea of History*, p. 269). The reason for this confusing mixture of positions was that *The Idea of History* was posthumously compiled by Collingwood's editor (T.M. Knox) from manuscripts of complex provenance, composed over several years during which Collingwood was changing his ideas: see Knox's preface and W.J. Van der Dussen, *History as a Science: the philosophy of R.G. Collingwood* (The Hague: Nijhoff, 1981). Van der Dussen draws attention (pp. 286–7) to an earlier draft of 'The historical imagination', which would appear to include the first formulation of what I am calling the 'third stance'; remarkably enough, this draft seems to date from as early as 1935–6.

17 G.R. Elton, *Political History: principles and practice* (London: Allen Lane, 1970), 88; and see generally Chapter 3, pp. 73–111. Elton first formulated this approach in his *The Practice of History* (London:

Collins Fontana, 1969, first published Sydney University Press, 1967), Part II: see pp. 81–113, for instance at pp. 93, 100, 102, 103, 111. In *Political History*, published three years later, he considerably refined his account; and his recent *Return to Essentials* (Cambridge University Press, 1991), pp. 50–73, carries this still further. Thompson, *The Poverty of Theory*, p. 220. These statements of method have been largely neglected. Neither is cited in Tosh, *The Pursuit of History*, Chapter 3, 'Using the sources', though that chapter does quote *The Poverty of Theory* to different effect (1984 edn, p. 62; 1991 edn, p. 70). Gray, 'History, Marxism and theory', p. 166, discussing *The Poverty of Theory*, notes in an aside that Thompson 'has much of value to say' about 'the historian's way of working with sources' and there leaves the matter. Abrams, *Historical Sociology*, pp. 217–18, quoted Thompson's separate account of 'historical logic' (*The Poverty of Theory*, p. 231), but discussed this in the context of explanation and thus missed its epistemological significance. Ellen Kay Trimberger, 'E.P. Thompson: understanding the process of history', in Theda Skocpol ed., *Vision and Method in Historical Sociology* (Cambridge University Press, 1984), pp. 211–43, discussing *The Poverty of Theory* at pp. 228–9, omitted to mention Thompson's concept of 'historical logic', and assimilated his methodological arguments to the ideas of Gadamer, Giddens and Feyerabend – three highly improbable allies, none of whom he had in fact cited.

18   Bloch, *Historian's Craft*, pp. 110, 68–73. Again, the entire argument of Kitson Clark's *The Critical Historian* (London: Heinemann, 1967) is that critical history represents an important cultural advance.

19   For Collingwood's 20-year project see *Autobiography*, Chapters 9– 11. Historiographic citations of Collingwood include Carr, *What is History?*, pp. 15–23, the work which set the tone for most subsequent accounts; Elton, *The Practice of History*, p. 79; Elton, *Political History*, pp. 122, 133; Gordon Connell-Smith and Howell A. Lloyd, *The Relevance of History* (London: Heinemann, 1972), p. 38; Marwick, *The Nature of History*, pp. 81–2; Thompson, *Poverty of Theory*, pp. 212, 223 note 32; Tosh, *The Pursuit of History*, pp. 110, 116, 121, 199; Corfield, 'Introduction' to Corfield ed., *Language and Class*, p. 19. The best-informed such account is Michael Stanford, *The Nature of Historical Knowledge* (Oxford: Blackwell, 1986), pp. 53–4, 76–8. Discussions of Collingwood by philosophers of history can only be cited selectively here. Van der Dussen, *History as a Science* surveys in detail the content, development and reception of Collingwood's philosophy of history, criticises the usual readings (e.g. p. 312), draws attention to the neglect of Collingwood's methodological thinking (p. 295), and gives an extensive bibliography down to 1980. Two recent articles are G.S. Couse, 'Collingwood's

detective image of the historian and the study of Hadrian's Wall', *History and Theory* **29** (1990), *Beiheft* **29**, 'Reassessing Collingwood', pp. 57–77, and Leon J. Goldstein, 'Historical Being', *The Monist* **74** (2) (1991), issue on 'The Ontology of History', pp. 206–16; these cite the post-1980 literature, as do other papers in the same issues of the respective journals. Goldstein's earlier *Historical Knowing* (Austin, Texas University of Texas Press, 1976) used resources supplied by Collingwood to arrive at an account of historical research compatible with what is described here as the third hermeneutic stance. For another theorisation, again drawing on Collingwood, see Ashplant and Wilson, 'Present-centred history'.

20 This might perhaps be described in the language of Heidegger, as I understand it from the English renditions by Macquarrie and Robinson and by Dreyfus, as follows. A mere relic of the past (let us call it *R*) is simply 'present-at-hand' or 'occurrent' (*vorhanden*): that is, it exists in our presence but has no use or significance for us. In putting *R* to use, we render *R* 'ready-to-hand' or 'available' (*zuhanden*), that is, we appropriate *R* in some way: *R* is now tied to us. But we do not apprehend it as *R*, for in the same act, we necessarily assign it a name: for instance, *source*, which we can here render by *S*. This name, *S*, itself embodies the use to which we are putting *R*, and as I have put it, 'assigns a particular status' to *R*. Thereupon, what we both use and contemplate is not *R* but *S*; *R* has become covered-over by *S*. It now requires a mental effort of uncovering (*Entdeckend*) to return from *S* to *R*, that is, from apprehension of the given relic as ready-to-hand, an object for our use, to its apprehension as merely present-at-hand, a thing in itself. Hence the extreme difficulty of developing a suitable terminology for *R*: here I am using 'document', but this is not entirely satisfactory. This interlocking process of naming, perceiving and using helps to explain the theoretical elusiveness of what is here called the third hermeneutic stance. See Martin Heidegger, *Being and Time* (trans. John Macquarrie and Edward Robinson, Oxford: Blackwell, 1962; German original 1927), pp. 102–7 (present-at-hand, ready-to-hand), 57, 261, 408–15 (uncovering), glossary, and index; Hubert L. Dreyfus, *Being-in-the-World: a commentary on Heidegger's* Being and Time, *Division I* (MIT Press, 1991), p. xi (for 'occurrent' and 'available' as alternative renderings of *vorhanden* and *zuhanden*). Although *Being and Time* included very perceptive comments on the meanings of 'history', the significance of 'past', and the interpretation of material relics (pp. 430–2), that work did not address the issue of practical epistemology. Hence the fact that Heidegger did not delineate the third hermeneutic stance, even though some of his formulations were compatible with that stance (see for instance p. 449). This epistemological silence on Heidegger's part is

ably discussed by David Couzens Hoy, 'History, Historicity, and Historiography in *Being and Time*', in Michael Murray ed., *Heidegger and Modern Philosophy: critical essays* (New Haven and London: Yale University Press, 1978), pp. 329–53, at 346–53, particularly p. 347 n13. On the complex relationship between Heidegger's *Being and Time* and his subsequent Nazism, see Jurgen Habermas, *The Philosophical Discourse of Modernity: twelve lectures* (trans. Frederick Lawrence; Cambridge: Polity, 1987), pp. 131–60, especially 144f., 154f. (where it emerges that truth-questions are implicated in this issue), 157 and note 41.

21 A complementary way of bringing out the same point is to observe that what the third stance *investigates* – the genesis of documents – the first two stances *assume*; for these two stances posit that the documents arose, from the matter the historian is studying (for instance events, ideas), through some such process as deposit (deliberate or accidental) or recording (accurate or inaccurate).

22 For August Ludwig Schlozer (1735–1809, a precocious member of the German school) and Lord Acton, see Herbert Butterfield, *Man on His Past* (Cambridge University Press, 1959), pp. 58, 75–6. For Bloch's interest in these themes, *The Historian's Craft*, pp. 75–91 ('In pursuit of fraud and error'), 57–65 ('The transmission of evidence'). Precisely the same set of themes ran through Charles Oman, *On the Writing of History* (New York: Barnes and Noble, and London: Methuen, 1939), Chapters 2–4, and Clark, *The Critical Historian*. For more recent discussions see Jerzy Topolski, *Methodology of History* (transl. Olgierd Wojtasiewicz, Dordrecht: Reidel, 1976; Polish original 1973), pp. 439–40; Tosh, *The Pursuit of History*, pp. 51–3.

23 See Bloch, *The Historian's Craft, passim*; p. 77 is a rare moment of interest in this theme. The same asymmetry permeates Clark, *The Critical Historian* and Oman, *On the Writing of History*, Chapters 2–4.

24 For 'sublation' see *OED*; for 'transcendence', Jean-Paul Sartre, *Critique of Dialectical Reason: I. Theory of practical ensembles*, trans. Alan Sheridan-Smith (London: NLB, 1976; French original Paris: Gallimard 1960), pp. 11, 830, and R.D. Laing and D.G. Cooper, *Reason and Violence: a decade of Sartre's philosophy 1950–1960* (London: Tavistock 1964), p. 13. For the distinction between 'internal' and 'external' source-criticism, and for elaborations of document-genetic study as an aspect of the latter, see Tosh, *The Pursuit of History*, pp. 51–3; Topolski, *Methodology of History*, pp. 433–52; and Marwick, *The Nature of History*, p. 137.

25 See Elton, *Political History*, Chapter 3, 'Evidence', as follows. Characterisations of the documents: (1) records, pp. 83–94; (2) evidence (the chapter-title), *passim*, and also sources e.g. p. 83; (3) relics pp. 133, 160, and 'the materials produced by the political process'

p. 80. Interpretation of narrative sources: pp. 77–82, quoted from pp. 77, 82. It should be noted here that the discussion in Elton's recent *Return to Essentials*, pp. 50–73, extends the scope of this argument, and clarifies the respective uses of 'relic' and 'evidence'. For other uses of the term 'relics of the past' see Collingwood, *The Idea of History*, p. 282; Wilson and Ashplant, 'Whig history and present-centred history', p. 12.

26 Thompson, *The Poverty of Theory*, pp. 220–3, quoting 220f. It is Thompson's formulation that 'the evidence' must be 'interrogated by minds trained in a discipline of attentive disbelief' which is quoted by Tosh, *The Pursuit of History*, Chapter 3, 'Using the sources' (1984 edn, p. 62; 1991 edn, p. 70).

27 In Robert William Fogel and G.R. Elton, *Which Road to the Past? Two views of history* (New Haven and London: Yale University Press, 1983), pp. 91–5, Elton has explicitly criticised the model of witness-interrogation; yet (like Thompson) he appears to understate the originality of his own conception.

28 David Selborne, 'On the methods of History Workshop', *History Workshop Journal* 9 (1980), pp. 150–61, at pp. 151, 156, 152, quoting Collingwood, *The Idea of History*, p. 176; Raphael Samuel, 'On the methods of History Workshop: a reply', *History Workshop Journal* 9 (1980), pp. 162–76, at pp. 171–2. For the record, Samuel did not refer to Collingwood, and neither Selborne nor Samuel discussed Thompson's 'The poverty of theory'. The debate was considered by Abrams, *Historical Sociology*, pp. 326, 322–3.

29 Ronald A. Marchant, *The Church Under the Law* (Cambridge University Press, 1969); Rosemary O'Day and Felicity Heal eds., *Continuity and Change: personnel and administration of the church in England 1500–1642* (Leicester University Press, 1976); R.A. Houlbrooke, *Church Courts and the People during the English Reformation* (Oxford University Press, 1979); Martin Ingram, *Church Courts, Sex and Marriage in England, 1570–1640* (Cambridge University Press, 1987).

30 For some examples see the critical analyses in Geoffrey Holmes, 'Gregory King and the social structure of preindustrial England', *Transactions of the Royal Historical Society* 5th series, 27 (1977), pp. 41–68; Jordanova, 'The interpretation of nature'; Ashplant and Wilson, 'Present-centred history', pp. 254–60, 271–2.

31 Abrams, *Historical Sociology*, pp. 318–26, implicitly criticised this approach, but was unable to resolve the problem (cf. p. 333). His inability to develop a solution may reflect his ahistorical concept of research technique and his extractive model of historical research (p. 318), both of which close off the possibility of taking up the third hermeneutic stance.

32 Compare the social theory of Anthony Giddens, which resembles
    Elton and Thompson in linking time, structure and agency, but differs
    in considering these themes and their connections abstractly – which
    in the eyes of Elton and Thompson would presumably be to miss the
    point. See *A Contemporary Critique of Historical Materialism: Vol.
    I Power, property and the state* (London: Macmillan, 1981),
    Chapters 1 and 6; *The Constitution of Society: outline of the theory
    of structuration* (Cambridge: Polity 1984), pp. 34–7, 110–61, 355–
    63; *Social Theory and Modern Sociology* (Cambridge: Polity 1987),
    Chapter 6. The latter book elsewhere, in Chapter 9, discusses
    Thompson's work with reference to the structure/agency issue, but
    does not deal with Thompson's conception of time. For critiques of
    Giddens's 'structuration' theory as insufficiently concrete and historical,
    see Richard Kilminster, 'Structuration theory as a world-view', in
    Christopher A. Bryant and David Jary eds., *Giddens' Theory of
    Structuration : a critical appreciation* (London: Routledge 1991),
    pp. 74–115, and Derek Sayer, 'Reinventing the wheel: Anthony
    Giddens, Karl Marx and social change', in Jon Clark, Celia Modgil
    and Sohan Modgil eds., *Anthony Giddens: consensus and contro-
    versy* (Basingstoke: Falmer Press, 1990), pp. 235–50. It may be noted
    that Sayer here praises the work of both Thompson and Elton (see
    pp. 245–250).

33 For Thompson, see *The Making of the English Working Class* (1963),
    pp. 9–12 and *passim*; 'Anthropology and the discipline of historical
    context', *Midland History* 1 (1972), pp. 41–55 (references to Thomas's
    essay pp. 41, 45, 46, 48, 49, 55); *The Poverty of Theory*, esp. pp.
    220-1 (linked at note 26 with *The Making of the English Working
    Class*), 237–9, 267–81, 298–302, 342–4, 360. For Elton, see *The
    Practice of History*, esp. pp. 17–20, 36–56 (Thomas's essay was
    discussed on pp. 18, 39, 42, 48, 51); *Political History*, pp. 48–9, 57–
    72, 158–9, 172–6 (here notice a favourable mention of Thompson's
    Making of the English Working Class on p. 173); Fogel and Elton,
    Which Road to the Past?, pp. 89–103; *Return to Essentials*, pp.
    50–73.

34 It might be thought that these considerations can be set aside in
    studies based on record-linkage, since the latter method infers 'facts'
    not from a single record whose transparency is at issue, but rather
    from the interconnection of multiple records which could perhaps be
    taken to be mutually confirming. However, document-genesis is as
    relevant to record-linkage as it is to other kinds of historical research.
    This is clear from the following three points in the standard litera-
    ture. First, the documents on which record-linkage is based pose the
    usual problems of ambiguity and representativeness. Second, the
    methods used in linkage have to deal with these issues. Third, an

understanding of the genesis of the documents is entailed in the very use of those documents at all, is implicit in the philosophy of record-linkage, and is called upon both in resolving ambiguities and in assessing the methods of linkage. See Alan Macfarlane, Sarah Harrison and Charles Jardine, *Reconstructing Historical Communities* (Cambridge University Press, 1977), pp. 114–15, 123; and the essays in E.A. Wrigley ed., *Identifying People in the Past* (London: Edward Arnold, 1973), pp. 15–16 (Wrigley), 19, 21, 27, 28 (Winchester), 47–50 (Herlihy), 67, 74, 96–7 (Wrigley and Schofield), 107–8 (Skolnick), 143–4, 149 (Winchester).

35 For 'the discipline of historical context' see Thompson, 'Anthropology and the discipline of historical context'; Tosh, *The Pursuit of History*, 1984 edn, p. 124, 1992 edn, p. 150. It is notable that the source-critical approach of Tosh's Chapter 3 ('Using the sources') eventually has to be supplemented by something more: here 'the discipline of historical context', elsewhere an 'imagined picture' or 'flair and judgment' (1984 edn, pp. 116, 147; 1992 edn, pp. 140, 176). On document-genesis in administrative history, see *ibid.*, 1984 edn, p. 56; 1992 edn, p. 63; on folklore, Ruth B. Bottigheimer, 'Fairy tales, folk narrative research and history', *Social History* 14 (1989), pp. 343–57. For Skinner's approach see James Tully ed., *Meaning and Context: Quentin Skinner and his critics* (Cambridge: Polity, 1988), especially Skinner's 'A reply to my critics', pp. 231–88. It should be observed that Skinner's move towards the third hermeneutic stance, admirable so far as it goes, is restricted by his using the traditional vocabulary of 'texts' (compare note 14 above); this may help to explain the limited impact of his methodology, on which see Richard Tuck, 'History of political thought', in Burke ed., *New Perspectives on Historical Writing*, pp. 194, 203–4. Joan Scott, 'A statistical representation of work: La Statistique de 1'industrie à Paris, 1847–1848', in *Gender and the Politics of History*, Chapter 6; Dror Wahrman, 'Virtual representation: Parliamentary reporting and languages of class in the 1790s', *Past and Present* 136 (1992), pp. 83–113, particularly pp. 108–9.

36 So too in the natural sciences, the operations and forces of Nature are not directly legible in the phenomena: rather, those operations and forces have to be inferred from their effects. The knowledge-making power of science derives in part from its *acceptance* of the fact that Nature does not provide explicit testimony, and from its adjustment of its methods to this problem of legibility.

37 See respectively Chapter 1 above, and my remarks in the Introduction on the essay by Innes and Styles.

38 Philip Corrigan and Derek Sayer, *The Great Arch: English state formation as cultural revolution* (Oxford: Blackwell, 1985), p. 124;

Lawrence Goldman, 'Statistics and the science of society in early Victorian Britain: an intellectual context for the General Register Office', *Social History of Medicine* 4 (3) (1991), pp. 415–34; Edward Higgs, 'Disease, febrile poisons, and statistics: the Census as a medical survey, 1841–1911', *ibid.*, pp. 465–78.

39 For an example concerning vocabulary, see Wahrman, 'National society, communal culture', pp. 65–7, who argues that the idiom of 'middle class' in England was specifically generated not just in the 1790s (a point noted in 1974 by Asa Briggs), but specifically by 'the anti-war liberals and the Friends of Peace'. On the eighteenth-century novel, see the literature cited in Chapter 1, especially Armstrong, *Desire and Domestic Fiction;* Spencer, *The Rise of the Woman Novelist;* Spender, *Mothers of the Novel;* Watt, *Rise of the Novel.* For an example of women's agency inferred from male documentation, see my 'The ceremony of childbirth and its interpretation', in Valerie Fildes ed., *Women as mothers in pre-industrial England: essays in memory of Dorothy McLaren* (London: Routledge, 1989), pp. 68–107.

40 Jordanova, 'The interpretation of nature', p. 198. For a formulation in terms of anachronism, see Wilson and Ashplant, 'Whig history and present-centred history', and Ashplant and Wilson, 'Present-centred history and the problem of historical knowledge'. On the conjoining of different discourses see Paul Ricoeur, *Hermeneutics and the human sciences: essays on language, action and interpretation* (trans. and ed. John Thompson; Cambridge University Press, 1981) p. 158: 'To read is, on any hypothesis, to conjoin a new discourse to the discourse of the text.' Wittgenstein's concept of language-games lends itself to a similar formulation, once it is recognised that the historian is engaged in a different language-game from that which produced the documents she or he is using as evidence.

Index of personal names

Abrams, Philip, 32, 40, 41, 43, 69, 324
Acton, Lord, 11, 306
Althusser, Louis, 165, 294
Amis, Kingsley, 182
Amussen, Susan, 79
Anderson, Perry, 165, 173
Arbuthnot, John, 142
Ariès, Philippe, 79
Ashley, Maurice P., 12
Aylmer, G.E., 82

Bacon, Francis, 131, 303
Bailyn, Bernard, 68
Baker, Kenneth, 188
Baldwin, Thomas, 86
Barlow, Patrick, *see* Dingle, Desmond Oliver
Barnett, Anthony, 183–4
Barrell, John, 148
Barrington, Sir Thomas, 85
Baudrillard, Jean, 176
Bauman, Zygmunt, 178, 187
Beale, John, 145
Beales, Derek, 202
Beattie, John, 6, 203, 205, 208–9, 212, 215, 216, 229, 230, 233–40
Beddoes, Thomas, 138
Bennett, Tony, 165
Berkeley, George, 142, 149

Berlin, Isaiah, 187
Bevan, William, 282
Bevis, John, 142
Black, Joseph, 138
Bloch, Marc, 16, 20, 43, 303, 304–5, 306–7, 310
Bloor, David, 39, 40
Bolingbroke, Lord, 148
Bourne, Anthony, 89
Bourne, Elizabeth, 89
Boyle, Robert, 30, 141, 145
Braithwaite, Richard, 85
Braudel, Fernand, 16
Braverman, Harry, 44
Brewer, John, 28, 143, 144, 224, 227
Briggs, Asa, 20
Brooks, C.W., 70
Bryce, James, 10, 11
Buer, Margaret, 101
Burghley, Lord, 85, 87
Burke, Peter, 179, 295
Burnet, Thomas, 145
Bury, J.B., 11
Butler, Josephine, 276
Butterfield, Herbert, 13, 306

Cain, 144
Calhoun, Craig, 179
Cannadine, David, 21, 73
Canton, John, 140